# Changing Inequalities in Rich Countries

# Changing Inequalities in Rich Countries

## Analytical and Comparative Perspectives

*Edited by*
Wiemer Salverda, Brian Nolan, Daniele Checchi,
Ive Marx, Abigail McKnight, István György Tóth,
and Herman van de Werfhorst

OXFORD
UNIVERSITY PRESS

# OXFORD
UNIVERSITY PRESS

Great Clarendon Street, Oxford, OX2 6DP,
United Kingdom

Oxford University Press is a department of the University of Oxford.
It furthers the University's objective of excellence in research, scholarship,
and education by publishing worldwide. Oxford is a registered trade mark of
Oxford University Press in the UK and in certain other countries

© Oxford University Press 2014

The moral rights of the authors have been asserted

First Edition published in 2014

Published in the United States of America by Oxford University Press
198 Madison Avenue, New York, NY 10016, United States of America

British Library Cataloguing in Publication Data
Data available

Library of Congress Control Number: 2013955767

ISBN 978–0–19–968743–5

# Preface

This volume is the product of an extensive and fruitful scientific collaboration across countries and disciplines, focused on issues of central importance to modern societies. It is a core output of the *Growing Inequalities' Impacts—GINI*—research project, funded by the European Commission under the Socio-Economic Sciences and Humanities theme of the Seventh Framework programme. This project has addressed pressing questions about the evolution of inequalities in income, wealth, and educational outcomes and opportunities, the social, political, and cultural impacts these may have, and the policy context and implications. In doing so, it has drawn on the expertise and commitment of over 150 social scientists, drawn from the disciplines of economics, sociology, political science, and public health, and covering a total of thirty countries—twenty-five of the twenty-seven European Union member states (the exceptions being Cyprus and Malta), Australia, Canada, Japan, Korea, and the USA. This exceptionally wide span is an essential component and strength of the scientific endeavour. The project combined comparative analysis and in-depth country studies of inequality trends, the drivers of those trends, their social and political/cultural impacts, and the policies that affect them. The present volume brings together the key findings from the research project as a whole, highlighting the results of comparative analysis while incorporating lessons from individual countries. The findings of the country case studies, where their individual experiences are examined through a common analytical framework, are discussed country by country in a companion volume also being published by Oxford University Press under the title *Changing Inequalities and Societal Impacts in Rich Countries: Thirty Countries' Experiences*.

The GINI research project has been structured around six core research partners with their teams in the *Amsterdam Institute for Advanced Labour Studies* (AIAS) and the *Amsterdam Centre for Inequality Studies* (AMCIS), both at the University of Amsterdam, the *College of Human Sciences* and *Geary Institute* at University College Dublin, the *Herman Deleeck Centre for Social Policy* at the University of Antwerp, the *Work, Training and Welfare interdisciplinary research centre* (WTW) at the University of Milan, the *Centre for Analysis of Social Exclusion* (CASE) at the London School of Economics and Political

Science, and *TÁRKI Social Research Institute*, Budapest. These coordinated the work of another twenty country teams that were joined later by the Korean team, which volunteered to participate in the project with the support of the National Research Foundation of Korea in December 2011. The work has generated substantial country reports that provide the background to the chapters of the companion volume. In addition, twenty-three individual research associates committed themselves to the project from the start, while in the course of the project many other experts accepted our invitations to contribute in their fields. As a result, more than eighty GINI discussion papers have been produced, and these, mostly comparative in nature, are at the core of the present book. The full listing of contributors (country team members and individual experts), their reports and the discussion papers can be found at the website of the project: gini-research.org. As project co-ordinators and as editors of this volume, we are extremely grateful to all these participants for their intensive engagement throughout the project.

The project has also benefited greatly from the input and advice of its advisory board comprising Professors Tony Atkinson (Nuffield College Oxford), Gøsta Esping-Andersen (Pompeu Fabra University, Barcelona), John Hills (CASE at the LSE), Jonas Pontusson (University of Geneva) Haya Stier (Tel Aviv University), Jane Waldfogel (Columbia University and LSE), Richard Wilkinson (University of Nottingham), and Marco Mira d'Ercole (OECD). We are very grateful to them for their thoughtful advice and their involvement in guiding what has been a particularly complex project, both in terms of structure and range of challenging topics to be investigated, and the contribution of their own views at the meetings that we have organized.

The substantial funding provided by the European Commission's programmes for international scientific collaboration was an essential underpinning to a multi-year, multi-country study of this type.[1] We have received extremely helpful guidance and support from Ronan O'Brien and Marie Ramot of the Commission's Directorate General for Research and Innovation, and also very helpful input from Georg Fisher, Director for Analysis, Evaluation, and External Relations in the Directorate General for Employment, Social Affairs, and Inclusion.

Finally, we have been in good hands throughout with Oxford University Press, and wish to express our deep appreciation of the support received from its commissioning editor Adam Swallow from the outset, which has been

[1] The 7th Framework Programme in the field of Socio-Economic Sciences and Humanities awarded grant No 244592 to the GINI proposal, submitted in January 2009 and very favourably reviewed by the Commission's independent and anonymous referees, whom we thank for their support. The GINI project started in February 2010 and concluded in July 2013.

critically important, as well as to Aimee Wright and colleagues in shepherding the volume through the production process.

The research project on which this book is based has been challenging but highly rewarding, and we trust that the broad-ranging findings will deepen understanding, act as a springboard for further research, and inform policy in relation to inequality and its impacts, which is crucially important for the development of our societies.

*Wiemer Salverda (Amsterdam), Brian Nolan (Dublin), Daniele Checchi (Milan), Ive Marx (Antwerp), Abigail McKnight (London), István György Tóth (Budapest), and Herman van de Werfhorst (Amsterdam)*

# Contents

## Contents

# List of Figures

# List of Tables

# Notes on Contributors

**Robert Andersen** is Professor of Sociology and Political Science at the University of Toronto. His teaching and research interests are in political sociology (especially the social bases of attitudes and political actions), social stratification, applied statistics, and survey methods. Most recently, he has been exploring the contextual factors associated with national differences in social and political attitudes and civic participation.

**Gabriele Ballarino** is Professor of Economic Sociology at the University of Milan. His research focuses on the relations between educational systems, labour markets, and social stratification.

**Francesco Bogliacino** was a postdoctoral researcher at the Amsterdam Institute for Advanced Labour Studies for the GINI project. He is currently a professor at the Konrad Lorenz University, Bogotá. Francesco graduated from the University of Pavia with a thesis on wage inequality. He was a Professor at Universidad EAFIT in Medellin (Colombia) and a scientific grant-holder at the European Commission Joint Research Center IPTS in Seville (Spain). His research interests are behavioural economics, labour economics, development economics, and economics of innovation.

**Michela Braga** is a postdoctoral fellow at the Department of Economics of the University of Milan and a researcher at the Fondazione Rodolfo DeBenedetti. Her main research interests are in labour economics, education, and development economics.

**Massimiliano Bratti** (PhD, University of Warwick) is Associate Professor of Economics at the University of Milan (Italy), where he teaches Labour and Education Economics. His main research topics are female labour force participation and fertility decisions, pecuniary and non-pecuniary (mainly health) returns to education, the effect of parental health on children's outcomes, and the determinants of firms' innovation performance.

**Brian Burgoon** (PhD, Massachusetts Institute of Technology) is Professor of International Relations in the Department of Political Science at the University of Amsterdam. His main research focus is on the politics of economic globalization, particularly on policy and political responses to the distributional consequences of trade and investment openness—ranging from welfare compensation, to trade protectionism, to right- and left-wing political extremism. He also researches topics in comparative political economy.

**Daniele Checchi** is Professor of Labour Economics at the University of Milan (Italy). He co-coordinated the drivers of inequalities work package of the GINI project. He has published on the role of labour market institutions, on intergenerational mobility, and more recently on educational reforms.

**Frank Cowell** is Professor of Economics in the Department of Economics and Director of the Distributional Analysis Research Programme (DARP) within the Suntory and Toyota International Centres for Economics and Related Disciplines (STICERD) at the London School of Economics. His research interests are inequality and poverty, income and wealth distribution, and taxation. He is author of several books and numerous articles on the subject of inequality, including *Measuring Inequality* (2009).

**Antonio Filippin** studied economics at Bocconi University and received a PhD degree at the European University Institute. He is assistant professor at the University of Milan, where he teaches Behavioural Economics, as well as a research fellow at IZA. His research interests encompass educational choices and inequality, and concentrate mainly on the experimental methodology as far as the empirical analysis is concerned.

**Carlo Fiorio** is Associate Professor of Public Finance at the University of Milan. His research interests focus on inequality measurement, tax and benefit simulation, empirical public economics, and labour economics.

**Christina Haas** was a Research Masters student of sociology and a junior researcher at the Amsterdam Institute for Advanced Labour Studies for the GINI project, and is currently a research associate at the Integrative Research Unit on Social and Individual Development (INSIDE) of the University of Luxembourg. Her research interests concern inequality, educational inequality, and school-to-work-transitions.

**Dániel Horn** is a joint research fellow at the Institute of Economics, Center for Economic and Regional Studies, Hungarian Academy of Sciences and at the Department of Economics, ELTE, Budapest. His research interests concern economics, social research methods and methodology, education (social policy), and educational policy.

**Marco Leonardi** is Associate Professor of Economics at the University of Milan. He studied economics at Bocconi University in Milan, and took his PhD at the London School of Economics. He was a visiting scholar at the MIT Department of Economics, UC Berkeley, and Georgetown University, and he worked at IZA, Bonn. His research interests are in labour economics with particular reference to wage inequality, earnings mobility, and unemployment.

**Abigail McKnight**, a senior research fellow at the Centre for Analysis of Social Exclusion (CASE), is an economist specializing in labour economics. She co-coordinated the social impacts work package of the GINI project. Her research interests include low-wage employment, earnings inequality and mobility, wealth inequality and asset-based welfare, evaluation of active labour market programmes, and the economics of education.

**Virginia Maestri** was a postdoctoral researcher at the Amsterdam Institute for Advanced Labour Studies for the GINI project. She currently works for the European Commission, DG Employment, Social Affairs and Exclusion. She is an economist with an interest in inequality, taxation, housing, labour markets, and education.

**Ive Marx** is Associate Professor at the University of Antwerp and Chair of the Department of Sociology. He coordinates research on poverty and income distribution, labour, and migration at the Centre for Social Policy at the University of Antwerp, Belgium. He coordinated the policy work package of the GINI project. He is a political and social scientist and an economist. The main focus of his research is poverty and minimum income protection, especially in relation to labour-market change and migration.

**Márton Medgyesi** has been a researcher at TÁRKI Social Research Institute since 1997 and regularly lectures on social policy at the Corvinus University. He holds an MSc in Applied Economics from IEP Paris and a PhD in Sociology from Corvinus University in Budapest. His main research interests are income distribution, private and public intergenerational transfers, and redistribution.

**Elena Meschi** is Assistant Professor at Ca' Foscari University of Venice, Department of Economics. Her main research interests are in labour economics, education, trade, and applied microeconometrics. In particular, her recent research has focused on the trade- and technology-related determinants of income inequality and on several aspects of educational inequality.

**Brian Nolan** is Professor of Public Policy and Principal of the College of Human Sciences, University College Dublin. He acted as research coordinator of the GINI project and co-coordinated its social impacts work package together with Abigail McKnight. He is an economist, with a PhD from the London School of Economics. He has published widely on income inequality, poverty, public economics, social policy, and health economics.

**Wiemer Salverda** is Emeritus Director of the Amsterdam Institute for Advanced Labour Studies (AIAS) at the University of Amsterdam. He coordinated the activities of the GINI project and co-coordinated its drivers of inequalities work package. He is a labour economist and his research focuses on the low-wage labour market and earnings inequality from an international comparative perspective. His work also targets comparative employment performance, top incomes, ageing, and the youth labour market.

**Francesco Scervini** is a postdoctoral researcher at the University of Milan. He studied at Bocconi University and took his MSc and PhD from the University of Turin. His research interests focus on inequality and its relationships with public choice on redistribution and with educational frameworks. He received the Aldi Hagenaars award from the Luxembourg Income Study in 2012.

**István György Tóth** is a sociologist and Director of TÁRKI Social Research Institute, and Docent, Department of Sociology, Corvinus University, Budapest. He co-coordinated the political and cultural impacts work package of the GINI project. He was project director of the Hungarian Household Panel Study and projects on income distribution and social policies, authoring reports for the European Observatory on the Social Situation and editing the TÁRKI Social Reports. He is also an advisory board member of the Luxembourg Income Study.

**Herman van de Werfhorst** is Professor of Sociology and Director of the Amsterdam Centre for Inequality Studies (AMCIS) at the University of Amsterdam. He co-coordinated the political and cultural impacts work package of the GINI project. Together with Robert Erikson and Magnus Nermo of Stockholm University, he coordinates the Network of Excellence EQUALSOC. He works on the role of education in issues of inequality, in terms of social stratification and political outcomes.

**Tim Van Rie** is a sociologist and was a junior researcher at the Herman Deleeck Centre for Social Policy, Antwerp, during the GINI project.

**Gerlinde Verbist** is senior researcher and research coordinator for education, migration, and simulation models at the Herman Deleeck Centre for Social Policy, Antwerp. She is an economist and her main research interests concern micro-simulation modelling, the measurement of income inequality, the effects of taxation policy, and the interactions between migration and the welfare state. She worked part-time at the *Social Policy Division* of the OECD and contributed to the *Growing Unequal* report.

**Christopher T. Whelan** is currently an Emeritus Professor in the School of Sociology, University College Dublin, a Senior Fellow at the Geary Institute, and also a professor in sociology at the School of Sociology, Social Policy and Social Work Queen's University Belfast. His research interests include the causes and consequences of poverty and inequality, quality of life and social mobility, and inequality of opportunity. He has published extensively on these topics and also on economic and social change in Ireland.

# 1

# Introduction

*Wiemer Salverda, Brian Nolan, Daniele Checchi, Ive Marx, Abigail McKnight, István György Tóth, and Herman van de Werfhorst*

Inequality and its impacts now loom large in public debate and policy discussion in the richer countries of the world, and are the focus of research from a variety of disciplinary perspectives and of intense debate among those carrying it out. This is reflected in the titles of two recent influential OECD studies, *Growing Unequal: Income Distribution and Poverty in OECD Countries* (2008) and *Divided We Stand: Why Inequality Keeps Rising* (2011). There has been a particularly striking rise in income inequality over the past thirty years or so in countries such as the USA and the UK, and the economic crisis from 2007/08 has strongly reinforced the widespread sense that increasing inequality represents a fundamental challenge to the cohesion of advanced societies and the wellbeing of their citizens, as well as to the smooth functioning of their economies. Against that background, even the resumption of broad-based economic growth, however welcome, might not be adequate if an increasing proportion of the income and wealth generated goes towards the top, potentially exacerbating social problems, fuelling alienation, and undermining political processes and social cohesion.

This book is the product of a major international research project aimed at discovering what has been happening to economic inequality in the richer countries, understanding why, and teasing out its impact on social, political, and cultural behaviours and outcomes. The project, entitled *Growing Inequalities' Impacts* or GINI for short, was funded by the European Union's Framework Programme for internationally cooperative scientific research. It covers twenty-five of the twenty-seven countries of the European Union (the exceptions being Cyprus and Malta), together with Australia, Canada, Japan, Korea,[1] and the

[1] FP7 Contract No 244592 (2010–2013). The Korean team joined the international project with the support of National Research Foundation of Korea Grant NFR-2011-330-B00052.

United States.[2] The project combined comparative analysis and in-depth country studies of inequality trends, the drivers of those trends, their social and political/ cultural impacts, and the policies that affect them. The findings of the country case studies, where their individual experiences are examined through a common analytical framework, are discussed country by country in a companion volume, also published by Oxford University Press, entitled *Changing Inequalities and Societal Impacts in Rich Countries: Thirty Countries' Experiences* (Nolan et al., 2014). The present volume, by contrast, concentrates on the key findings from the research as a whole, much of it comparative in nature, while incorporating lessons from specific country experiences. It builds on those country foundations by drawing on the contributions of GINI discussion papers on a wide range of topics and the wider literature, and presenting results of further comparative research.

In this introductory chapter we discuss the point of departure and context for the book, the key challenges it faces in seeking to address complex questions about inequality and its impacts, and the approach and analytical framework adopted. We then highlight some key patterns in the evolution of income inequality over time revealed by data from the country case studies, which serve as a central point of reference throughout the rest of the book. Finally, the structure of the book and the thread of the argument running through it are set out.

## 1.1 Point of Departure, Context, and Key Challenges

The resurgence in academic interest in economic inequality in recent years is a product of inequality trends themselves, the changing policy environment in which research is carried out, and improved data and methods for research. The dramatic widening in earnings dispersion and in overall income inequality in the UK and the USA in the 1980s prompted a sustained stream of research by economists and sociologists on the returns to different levels of education and skill, occupational earnings differentials, and the implications for broader inequalities in income across households (see, for example, Gottschalk and Smeeding, 1997; Blau and Kahn, 2009). While this research is largely based on data from household surveys and earnings surveys, analysis of data collected by tax authorities has more recently revealed a substantial increase in the share of household income going to the very top of the distribution in many rich countries (e.g. Atkinson and

---

[2] Of the thirty countries covered, all are members of the OECD except Bulgaria, Latvia, Lithuania, and Romania, so that twenty-six of the thirty-four OECD members are included.

Piketty, 2007), underpinning widespread comment and debate about the '1%' versus the '99%'. A complex set of potential 'drivers' of these trends in inequality, including technological change and globalization, has been put forward, examined, and debated in the academic literature (see, for example, Atkinson et al., 2011). At the same time, educational attainment continues to play a central role in influencing the socioeconomic fortunes of individuals over their lifetimes, but faith in the transformative power of education as an equalizing force, within and across generations, has been waning.

As inequality and the forces driving it have been investigated, research and public debate more broadly have also focused on the potential consequences of growing inequality for major social and political outcomes. Wilkinson and Pickett's (2009a) *The Spirit Level* has been particularly effective in generating a wide-ranging debate about the potentially harmful impact of inequality. It argues that income inequality is harmful to society by virtue of its relationship to many different undesirable outcomes, that societies with higher income inequality have lower levels of social cohesion, exemplified in outcomes such as more social problems, higher crime rates, higher mortality rates, worse health, higher dropout rates from schools, lower social trust, and lower political involvement. Such potentially negative social outcomes have long been a subject of study, with the interaction between health and socioeconomic inequalities in particular being a core focus for public health specialists and other social scientists for many years. What is new in this debate is the extent to which income inequality per se, rather than the myriad of factors associated with or underpinning it in the literature in terms of social stratification more generally, is put forward as driving worse social outcomes—as we shall see, a claim that is hotly contested. In the political sphere, the notion that concentration of income and wealth impacts on democratic processes and outcomes has a long lineage, but recent concerns about waning trust in politicians and declining voter turnout, exacerbated by the economic crisis, have been combined with a renewed focus on the linkages between the economic power of the elite—the '1%'—and their political influence.

Inequalities in income, wealth, and education reflect the broad nature of the economic system but are not simply determined by it: the particular institutions and policies in place in an individual country at a particular point in time have a profound impact on the extent and nature of those inequalities and their societal significance. The development of modern welfare states has brought with it the capacity to influence distributional outcomes in a fundamental way, even if that capacity varies noticeably between countries and is constrained by market forces. The dynamics of the evolution of those welfare states over time and the policy choices they have made over the last

3

thirty years are central to understanding changing patterns of inequality and their impacts, however important the role of global economic forces may be. Nation-states remain the key site for political decision-making, and it is national or indeed local concerns, about the welfare of families and communities, that fuel the broad debates about inequality and its impacts towards which this book is directed.

In addressing these questions many thorny analytical challenges must be faced, and it is important to be clear about these, and their implications, from the outset. In seeking to capture what has actually been happening to inequality in the first place, one has to deal with intricate issues of definition, measurement, data, and interpretation. The scholarly literature has intensively investigated how best to think about and measure income inequality for forty years or more, and enormous strides have been made in the availability of data to which these methods can be applied. Nonetheless, the general picture of income inequality underpinning current debates is often based on generalization from the experience of particular countries or sets of countries—notably the USA and UK—or on comparative data that is not truly comparable or relates only to specific years or periods, which may pose problems of comparability. Comparison of levels and trends in wealth inequality is even more difficult as data are much more limited, as their sensitivity hampers provision by respondents and their complexity (wealth can take many forms, relates to debt, and crosses boundaries more easily) encumbers collection by surveys, though there have been some recent improvements. The analysis of educational systems, attainment, and access has a long history, including in a comparative context, but linking concepts and measures with appropriate, internationally comparable data remains difficult, particularly when looking across generations.

Having done one's best to capture levels and trends in such inequalities, the even more complex but essential task is to try to identify the causal forces at work and assess their relative importance. While the availability of suitable data and measures is key, this enterprise cannot be divorced from the theoretical frameworks of analysis which are brought to bear from a variety of disciplinary perspectives. To take income inequality as an example, much of the relevant research has been based in an economic framework that sees the labour-market returns to education and skills as central, supplemented by analysis of the ownership of and returns to capital. This framework has generated valuable hypotheses about the impact of factors such as technological change and globalization—the opening up of labour and capital markets—towards which much valuable research has been directed. However, it has proved difficult to establish robust conclusions about the factors driving the dispersion in earnings across individuals, and the picture becomes significantly more complicated when one shifts the focus to households rather than individuals. The income of the household generally plays the major role in the living standards attained by its members, so the way earners and non-earners are grouped together in households, and how that varies across countries and changes over time, has to be incorporated into the analysis and understood. Income coming into the household from sources other than earnings also has to be included in the analysis, not only income from capital but also private pensions and cash transfers from the state, as do the direct taxes which also impact on household disposable income. Encompassing all these drivers within a unified analytical framework is enormously challenging, even if one did not seek to go beyond the economic perspective to incorporate social and political factors that may play a key role—for example, in attitudes to and treatment of welfare recipients or, at the other end of the income scale, top executives and the super-rich.

Turning to the potential impacts of increasing inequalities on social and political behaviours and outcomes, the first challenge to be faced is that these cover a very broad range of social and political behaviours and outcomes, so the investigation has to be equally broad-ranging. Seeking to encompass in a single study such very different dimensions of life as the family, crime, health, social attitudes, and political behaviour, each of which has very specific characteristics and is the subject of quite distinct scholarly literatures, is clearly extremely ambitious in itself. The more fundamental analytical challenge, though, arises because of the tremendously complex nature of the potential channels of influence running from inequalities to social and political outcomes—and indeed in the opposite direction—and the methodological difficulties in establishing with any degree of certainty the causal relationships involved. For example, a common starting point has been to line up indicators of various social outcomes for different countries against a summary measure of income inequality, such as the Gini coefficient, and see whether they appear to be related. Wilkinson and Pickett (2009a), for example, have plotted a variety of such bivariate relationships across countries, and a good deal of (at times acrimonious) debate among researchers and more broadly has focused on whether the particular countries or specific social and political indicators selected make a major difference to the observed degree of correlation or association (Saunders, 2010; Snowdon, 2010; Wilkinson and Pickett, 2010).

However, even when such a relationship is observed consistently and robustly, its causal interpretation presents formidable difficulties. Observing, for example, that average life expectancy is longer in societies where income inequality is relatively low would not mean the two are necessarily connected; they could in fact be entirely independent, or could both be reflections of some more fundamental feature(s) of the societies in question. Sophisticated statistical techniques, including for example multi-level models, can assist in controlling for a range of societal characteristics that may be correlated with income inequality. Fundamentally, though, as Van de Werfhorst and Salverda (2012) emphasize, arriving at a causal interpretation of the consequences of inequality also requires deductive theory-building and hypothesis formulation and testing. This is an example of what Goldthorpe (2001) labels 'causation as a generative process', aiming to explain empirical regularities by specifying hypotheses that are derived from a 'causal narrative' at the level of individual actions, which can then be put to empirical test. For an association between inequality and outcomes to be pursued scientifically, there need to be clearly articulated theoretical arguments about why inequality could be related to such outcomes, and the hypotheses this produces have to be tested with empirical evidence.

The difficulties in doing so may be illustrated by the example of a specific much-debated hypothesis advanced by Wilkinson and Pickett. They place considerable emphasis on the 'psychosocial' implications of status differences in more unequal societies, arguing that low social status and perceptions of inferiority produce negative emotions such as shame that directly damage individual health through stress reactions,[3] as well as undermining supportive community and social relations. Other researchers into health inequalities adopt what has been termed the neo-materialist perspective, emphasizing the role of different levels and distribution of resources available within societies related to differential levels of investment in social and institutional infrastructure (Davey Smith and Egger, 1996; Lynch et al., 1998, 2000). It has proved very difficult to conclusively distinguish between these hypotheses empirically, and indeed their perspectives are increasingly being seen as complementary rather than competing (Elgar and Aitken, 2011; Layte, 2012).

Another key point to be emphasized in this context is that income inequality is only one manifestation of broader socioeconomic inequalities, and that the causal 'stories' advanced in relation to social and political impacts may often relate more to inequalities in terms of social status or social class, for example, than to income inequality per se. In that context Goldthorpe (2010) makes the important point that social stratification cannot be seen as one-dimensional. One cannot, for example, treat 'class' and 'status' as essentially synonymous (see also Chan and Goldthorpe, 2007), and the relationships between economic inequality and other forms of stratification are contingent rather than fixed. The ways in which objective social inequalities come to be subjectively experienced are also highly complex and contingent. This means that in trying to tease out the impact of income inequality

---

[3] On this, see also Marmot (2004), Marmot and Wilkinson (2006, 2009).

or educational inequalities, one has to take into account the complexities of their relationships with social status and social class, since these may be implicated in the processes and mechanisms through which negative social or political outcomes are thought to arise. Adding to the complexity, distinct dimensions of stratification relating to income, education, social class, and status may operate rather differently in different countries, and indeed for different groups within countries (Erikson and Torsander, 2008; Torsander and Erikson, 2009; Ultee, 1986). On top of this, the state of the (inter)national economy, cross-country or cross-time, adds further complexity to objective as well as subjective effects. The sudden broad awareness of the 1% versus the 99% under the influence of the current crisis is a case in point.

All these complexities mean that establishing strict causality in a scientific sense is too ambitious an aim, but that should not be taken as a counsel of despair. A variety of methodological approaches can usefully be applied to a range of countries, data, and time-periods, drawing on various disciplinary perspectives, and these can indeed enhance our understanding of inequality and its impacts and of the influence of policy. We go on in the next section to describe the approach adopted in this book and where it seeks to make its contribution to this task.

## 1.2 Approach and Framework

Against this backdrop, this book addresses the complex and multifaceted questions outlined above about inequality and its impacts using a variety of analytical approaches and methods, drawn primarily from the disciplinary perspectives of economics, sociology, political science, and (social) policy analysis. Crucially, the core of the research design has been to apply these methods to as broad a set of data as possible by incorporating most of the advanced countries into the analysis, and by covering a period of up to thirty years where possible. Including such a wide range of countries both increases the number of observations on which analysis can rest and provides a way of avoiding the risk that patterns and relationships observed in a given country or small set of countries arise for idiosyncratic reasons specific to those countries. Combining the cross-country with an over-time perspective also increases the number of observations available very substantially, but also, crucially, allows a dynamic perspective to be adopted in looking at the impacts of inequalities. Rather than asking only whether specific social problems are more severe in countries where inequality is high than where it is low, this allows us to assess whether those social problems are seen to become more severe when inequality increases. Those are different questions, since observing a robust cross-sectional association would not necessarily lead to the expectation of a similarly strong relationship over time, for a variety of reasons—something that is not always reflected in debates about inequality and its impacts. Arriving at even preliminary, tentative answers to both questions would significantly advance our understanding and inform policy.

As well as combining the comparative and dynamic perspectives, the research project on which this book is based was designed from the outset as comprising parallel streams of analysis by topic and by country that complement one another. The topic-focused stream produced over ninety discussion papers, which adopted a variety of analytical methods, depending on the nature of the question being addressed and the evidence available. Some papers focus in an over-time single-country perspective on unearthing specific mechanisms at work. Many other papers draw on large datasets to explore patterns of association, either in a purely cross-sectional context or pooling multiple observations for a set of countries over time, and applying more or less sophisticated statistical methods. One of the significant challenges for such comparative analyses is not to lose sight of the contextual factors and specific experiences of individual countries, which may be crucial in understanding the patterns observed and teasing out their implications. In order to address this the project also incorporated a parallel analytical stream whereby the experiences of each country were examined by expert teams familiar with the local context, institutions, data, and research, but applying a common framework and approach to addressing the same set of topics and questions from one country to the next. The individual country 'stories' that these reveal are of very significant interest in themselves, and are summarized in the companion volume mentioned earlier. Bringing these streams together—the ambitious goal of the present volume—then provides a unique set of insights into what has actually been happening to economic inequality across most of the richer countries and also provides evidence about whether the negative social, political, and cultural impacts that have been debated are to be seen at this stage.

The approach adopted throughout views the bringing together of appropriate data—in as harmonized a fashion as possible—as requiring significant attention in itself, in relation to both trends in inequality and the areas in which impacts might be seen. As far as inequality trends are concerned, it is also taken to be important to go beyond what a single measure such as the Gini coefficient can offer, distinguishing where possible what has been happening towards the bottom, middle, top, and very top of the distribution. In tracing potential impacts on social and political outcomes/indicators, it has also been seen as important to go beyond averages to look also at gradients across individuals and households in terms of income, social class, and also education.

8

We have emphasized from the outset the difficulties faced in trying to understand the complex phenomena being studied here, and in particular in seeking to establish causal relationships in a rigorous manner. Nonetheless, capturing and analysing patterns across countries and over time in inequality and in a wide range of social and political indicators, with due consideration for national specificities and the role of policies and institutions, and applying sophisticated statistical techniques where feasible, but not relying solely on them, offers the best hope of advancing knowledge. We now turn to an overview of the trends in inequality revealed by the country studies brought together and described in detail in the companion volume from the project, to provide an important part of the context for the rest of this volume.

## 1.3 An Overview of Income Inequality

Drivers and impacts of growing inequalities are at the heart of this book and the research on which it draws, and differences between and within countries in inequality levels and trends, as well as being of central interest in themselves, provide crucial analytical leverage in seeking to identify those drivers and impacts and tease out the implications for policy. The country reports completed for the thirty countries in the project presented and examined data on key variables following a pre-agreed template, over as much of the thirty-year time span from 1980 to 2010 as possible. When brought together into a common database, the summary income inequality and income poverty measures included provide a valuable window onto levels and trends, with about 600 observations of Gini coefficients for equivalized disposable income and over 550 of relative poverty levels, as described and analysed by Tóth (2013) in the companion volume. Despite all efforts of the GINI team to achieve a fully comparable poverty and inequality dataset, there remain some differences across countries in the precise measure of income employed (including the exact adjustments for household size), and there are also some breaks in series for particular countries over time. Nonetheless, the GINI database has the significant advantage for present purposes of offering a more complete picture of inequality from year to year than comparative datasets such as the Luxembourg Income Study and the OECD, which to date have data only at approximately five-year intervals. While an in-depth discussion of income inequality trends and drivers will be the subject of Chapter 2, it is useful to flag up at this introductory stage some key findings from these country data in relation to trends in income inequality, to set the context for what follows.

Studies based on the data collected by the OECD and the Luxembourg Study point to a general though not uniform increase in income inequality over the past three decades, as captured in a chapter sub-heading in OECD (2011): *The Big Picture: Inequality on the Rise in Most OECD Countries* (see also OECD, 2008; Brandolini and Smeeding, 2009). Inequality is noted to have followed different patterns across the OECD countries over time, with the increase in income inequality starting in the late 1970s and early 1980s in the UK and USA, but becoming more widespread from the late 1980s. Against this background, examination of the (mostly) year-by-year data from the GINI project country studies brings out the degree of heterogeneity across countries in the evolution of income inequality, highlights that inequality increases have often occurred in discrete spells rather than steadily and consistently over a longer period of time, and also reveals some interesting spells of inequality decline. Importantly, the findings challenge the common view that changes in inequality over time do not disturb long-standing rankings of high-, medium-, or low-inequality countries.

The evolution of inequality in the thirty countries can usefully be seen in terms of six groupings, albeit with significant mutual differences:

- five Continental European welfare states (Austria, Belgium, France, Germany, and Luxembourg)
- four Nordic countries and the Netherlands (Denmark, Finland, Sweden, and the Netherlands)
- five English-speaking liberal countries (Australia, Canada, Ireland, UK, and USA)
- four Mediterranean countries (Greece, Italy, Portugal, and Spain)
- two Asian countries (Japan and Korea), and
- ten Central and Eastern European countries (Baltic states, Bulgaria, Czech Republic, Hungary, Poland, Romania, Slovakia, Slovenia).

The data show, first and foremost, that inequality has indeed increased on average across the countries included in the analysis, with the range of Gini coefficients at a higher level at the end of the period (from 0.228 to 0.373) than it was at the beginning (from 0.201 to 0.331). Secondly, the growth in inequality was far from uniform. In certain countries (such as Austria, Belgium, France, Italy, Ireland, and Slovenia) the level of inequality remained largely unchanged or fluctuated around the same level, while in others it increased substantially. The most dramatic increase in inequality was experienced by some transition countries (Bulgaria, Estonia, Lithuania, Latvia, Romania, and Hungary) and, to a lesser but still significant extent, some Nordic countries, notably Sweden and Finland. In some of these countries the increase was sudden and large (as in the Baltics, Bulgaria, and Romania); in others it accumulated more gradually but not necessarily fully evenly over time (the Nordic group, Netherlands).

Third, the pattern of change in inequality does not always point upwards. There are countries where inequality declined for shorter or for longer periods. Such spells of decline were also observed in Estonia, Bulgaria, and Hungary, for example, sometimes after sharp increases. Fourth, over time countries can in fact shift between inequality regimes, belonging to a different segment of the international league at the end versus the beginning of the period. The Nordic countries have long been seen as having the lowest levels of inequality in Europe, but now no longer belong to the lowest division of the inequality 'league table'. Some of the transition countries such as the Baltics, Romania, and Bulgaria also witnessed very large changes that have put their inequality levels in a different range.

The picture these figures provide of inequality levels and trends is summarized in Table 1.1, which groups countries in terms of their inequality levels during three different parts of the thirty-year period scrutinized here: 1980–1984, 1996–2000, and 2006–2010. To smooth out measurement uncertainties and cyclical trends, values for the Gini coefficient are averaged

**Table 1.1.** Change in inequality levels (Gini coefficient values) during three periods

| Gini coefficients | 1980–1984 | 1996–2000 | 2006–2010 |
|---|---|---|---|
| above 0.350 | | Estonia, Portugal, Romania, United States | Latvia, Lithuania, Portugal, Romania, United Kingdom, United States |
| 0.301 to 0.350 | Greece, Spain, United States | Australia, Bulgaria, Canada, Greece, Hungary, Ireland, Italy, Korea, Latvia, Lithuania, Romania, Spain, UK | Australia, Bulgaria, Canada, Estonia, Greece, Ireland, Italy, Korea, Poland, Spain |
| 0.251 to 0.300 | Australia, Canada, Denmark, France, Germany (West), Italy, Japan, United Kingdom | Austria, Belgium, Denmark, France, Germany and Germany (West), Japan, Luxembourg, Poland, Netherlands, Sweden | Austria, Belgium, Denmark, Finland, France, Germany and Germany (West), Hungary, Korea, Luxembourg, Netherlands, Sweden |
| up to 0.250 | Austria, Bulgaria, Czech Republic, Estonia, Finland, Hungary, Latvia, Netherlands, Lithuania, Slovakia, Sweden | Czech Republic, Finland, Germany (East), Slovakia, Slovenia | Czech Republic, Germany (East), Slovakia, Slovenia |
| no data | Belgium, Germany (East), Ireland, Korea, Luxembourg, Portugal, Romania, Slovenia | | Japan |

*Source:* See Tóth (2013).

for these periods. The table shows a clear upward trend in general. No country had a Gini above 0.35 in the first period, whereas six countries had reached this level of inequality in the latest period, three of them belonging to the post-communist bloc. There were eleven countries in the first half of the 1980s with a Gini value below 0.25, but the number of countries with this low level of inequality then declined considerably, so only the Czech Republic, Slovakia, and Slovenia (and Eastern Germany) were at that level in the latest period. The Nordic countries by that point cluster together with the Continental European welfare states in the 0.251–0.300 range of Gini coefficients.

Understanding the causal factors underpinning this variation in income inequality across countries and over time is a major challenge, as discussed in some detail in the next chapter. What is worth flagging at this point is the diverging paths seen in various countries, including ones with similar starting points and/or histories, which suggest that inequality is not simply driven in a more or less uniform fashion by exogenous forces: political processes, societal institutions, and policies matter, as will be brought out in what follows. This is most obvious from the fact that one sees cases where the transition from dictatorship to democracy was associated with or followed by large or small, positive or negative changes in inequality. As well as seeking to understand common underlying forces at work, incorporating this variety of country experiences is key to a rounded analysis of inequality and its impacts.

## 1.4 Structure of the Book

Having described the focus and aim of the volume and how the task at hand is to be approached, it is now helpful to set out the way in which the content of the book is structured. Chapters 2 to 5 focus on the evolution of inequality and its understanding, Chapters 6 to 9 elaborate on the impacts of inequalities, Chapters 10 to 12 address the role of policies, and Chapter 13 concludes.

First, Chapters 2 to 5 range from dissections of the trends in income inequality just described, serving as points of departure and looking at the drivers behind them, to detailed examinations of the contribution made to income inequality by employee earnings, the role of the distribution of wealth, and the evolution of inequalities in the rapidly changing field of education.

The drivers of income inequality are assessed, discussing the role played by various sources of income, demographic factors, and state intervention, with a particular emphasis on the interaction between economic and political change. The possible role of increasing inequality in the recent financial crisis, and the broader relationship between inequality, macroeconomic performance, and instability, are also discussed. Chapter 3 then concentrates on labour earnings—by far the most important component of income in the richer countries—and their role in household income inequality, highlighting the effects of household joint labour supply and the concomitant distribution of jobs and working hours, and examining the diverging patterns of household formation across twenty-five European countries. Income is a key element in household resources and a key influence on living standards, but next to this wealth and debt are an essential dimension of household resources, and these are the topic of Chapter 4. The distribution of wealth and its relationship with income inequality are examined in a comparative perspective, bringing together as much information as the available data allow and accounting for the complex nature of wealth. Factors contributing to cross-country differences and trends are discussed, notably demographic structures, institutional factors, the labour market, debt holdings, asset prices and composition, and tax policies. Educational inequalities are the focus of Chapter 5, documenting the spectacular trends in the general level of educational attainment, in the evolution of equality of opportunities (measured by the gradient of parental education on children's schooling), and in measures of educational inequality. The role of institutional design factors (such as the age at which compulsory education begins and ends, tracking, cost) and of cohort effects on patterns of educational attainments are also examined. Special attention is paid to the international variation in access to and attainment in tertiary education.

Turning from different aspects of inequality to its potential impacts, Chapters 6 and 7 deal with social impacts while Chapters 8 and 9 focus on political and cultural impacts. First, poverty and disadvantage, the family, social order, and social inclusion are examined in Chapter 6 and related to levels and trends in inequality, drawing on both comparative analyses and the country case studies. Chapter 7 deals with the potential impacts of inequality in the areas of health, wealth, housing, and intergenerational mobility, discussing social gradients and other measures of inequality and the channels through which inequality may have an impact.

Chapter 8 then deals with inequality perceptions, redistributive claims, and political participation, presenting in-depth comparisons across countries and over time and analysing the determinants of attitudes towards redistribution and the role of inequality perceptions in shaping redistributive claims and political participation (including voting). The complementary topic of Chapter 9 is inequality, legitimacy, and the political system, studying the relationship between income inequality and the functioning of democracy in terms of legitimacy, public opinion, and the orientations of political parties.

The role of policy is the subject of Chapters 10, 11, and 12. Chapter 10 deals with policies relating to income redistribution, especially the impact of taxes and transfers, how that has evolved over recent decades, and how one might think about reframing it for the future. Chapter 11 directs its attention towards employment policies and in-kind provisions, impacting on redistribution and inequality indirectly but still of fundamental importance. The links between individual employment outcomes, household work intensity, and poverty are examined, and the redistributive impact of education, health, childcare, and other social services assessed. Chapter 12 deals with education policies, its analysis suggesting that inclusive policies such as the expansion of pre-primary and compulsory education are more effective in achieving an overall increase in educational attainment in the population than simply expanding tertiary education, though structures within secondary education with respect to, for example, 'tracking' may also be significant.

Finally, the concluding Chapter 13 brings together and summarizes the evidence presented about how inequalities in income and education have been changing across the rich countries and the robustness (or otherwise) of conclusions, theoretical and empirical, as to their social, political, and cultural effects on these societies. It also highlights the central implications of the patterns, trends, and causal processes discussed for policies and for the future of the societies being studied. Inequality and its impacts are a core concern for these societies, and the principal aim of the book, and the research underpinning it, is to contribute to an informed and wide-ranging debate.

# 2

# Increasing Economic Inequalities?

*Francesco Bogliacino and Virginia Maestri[1]*

## 2.1 Introduction: Mapping Economic Inequality in the Last Thirty Years

Since the onset of the Great Recession, the topic of inequality has attracted unprecedented attention. The growth of disposable income inequality over the 1980s–2000s has been widely documented (OECD, 2008, 2011), although the extent and timing of changes vary across countries. Nevertheless, these trends require careful teasing out, because measurement or aggregation issues may hide the variation of inequality. We first present the evidence for disposable income (Section 2.1.1); secondly, we discuss the role of the tails, which are less visible in the Gini coefficient (Section 2.1.2); thirdly, we discuss trends in various sources of income (Section 2.1.3); we then move to the regional dimension of inequality (Section 2.1.4), and close with the most recent evidence on the post-crisis evolution of inequality.

### 2.1.1 The Story: Trends in Disposable Income Inequality

Disposable income inequality increased in most OECD countries, more specifically:

- In Baltic and the other Eastern European countries the end of the communist period translated into a considerable increase in disposable

[1] We thank all the participants at a workshop in Rome and at the GINI Conference in Budapest. Special thanks are due to Daniele Checchi, Ive Marx, Brian Nolan, Wiemer Salverda, István Tóth, and Gerlinde Verbist for specific comments on this chapter and to Giacomo Corneo for comments on the GINI WP3 Report on which it is partly based.

income inequality: the pattern of transition was very diversified.[2] Some countries, such as Estonia and Lithuania among the Baltics, experienced an abrupt increase and others a more gradual and persistent rise (e.g. Latvia);

- In Nordic countries (in particular in Sweden and Finland), the increase occurred throughout the 1990s and 2000s;

- In some English-speaking countries (excluding Ireland) the increase was persistent over the last decades, while in the United Kingdom it was concentrated in the 1980s;

- In Japan the increase was concentrated in the 1980s, but in Korea it was concentrated after the 1997 financial crisis.

Continental European countries experienced more modest changes in disposable income inequality. In Austria, Belgium, and Luxembourg, disposable income inequality increased only slightly. In France, the decrease in disposable income inequality experienced during the 1980s was reversed by the increase of the late 1990s. In Germany, the rise in income inequality followed the reunification of the country, although strong welfare provisions helped to contain the increase in disposable income inequality.

The end of dictatorships in Mediterranean countries led to a considerable reduction in the high levels of disposable income inequality that had characterized Greece, Spain, and Portugal.[3] However, during the 1990s–2000s the patterns differ. In Greece and Spain, disposable income inequality continued to decrease, whereas in Portugal it increased. In Italy, the increase in disposable income inequality was pronounced and very concentrated in the years following the recession of the early 1990s.

Besides the difference in timing and dynamics, it should be remarked that inequality increases almost everywhere, thus contradicting once more the thesis that being in advanced stages of development growth is equality-enhancing (the Kuznets hypothesis). A summary of the evidence is provided in Figure 2.1 below (using data from the OECD), where we report the trend for available OECD countries which are included also in the GINI project.

---

[2] For a more detailed analysis of the trends in disposable income inequality in transition countries see Tóth (2013) in the companion volume of this book.
[3] Based on OECD inequality data and relative to the change from mid-1970s to mid-1990s for Greece, from mid-1970s to around 1990s for Portugal, and from mid-1980s to around 1990s for Spain.

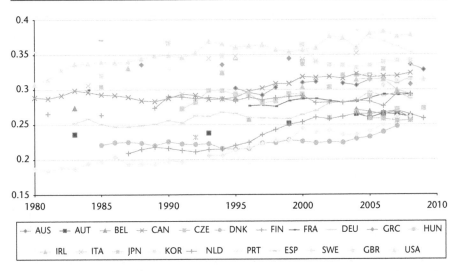

**Figure 2.1.** Trends in net equivalized household disposable income for OECD countries

*Source*: OECD income distribution and poverty database.

### 2.1.2 Gini Does Not Capture It All: The Central Part and the Right Tail of the Distribution

The shape of the income distribution varies by country. In Mediterranean countries, like Italy or Spain, and in Sweden the income gap between the richest decile and the middle-income group is larger than the gap between the middle and poorest households, while in Anglo-Saxon countries and Germany the distance between the poor and the middle class is larger (Bogliacino and Maestri, 2012a).

Different summary measures of inequality (e.g. Gini, variance of logarithms, mean log deviation) are generally correlated: according to OECD (2008) the cross-sectional correlation of Gini with mean log deviation is 0.99, with the standard coefficient of variation it is 0.8, and with P90/P10 and P50/P10 it is respectively 0.96 and 0.88 (data for mid-2000s). In most cases, the trend of inequality measured by other indices such as the variance of logarithm parallels the trend of inequality measured with the Gini coefficient, as seen in Figure 2.2 (based on data from Krueger et al., 2010)—Italy is one example. However, in the short run different measures of inequality may show some inconsistencies (e.g. Canada). Absolute measures of inequality such as the P-ratio can offer a useful insight into the changes occurring in different parts of the distribution. For instance, in the UK the increasing difference between the middle and bottom deciles seems to dominate, with a slower increasing trend in the divergence between the top and middle deciles.

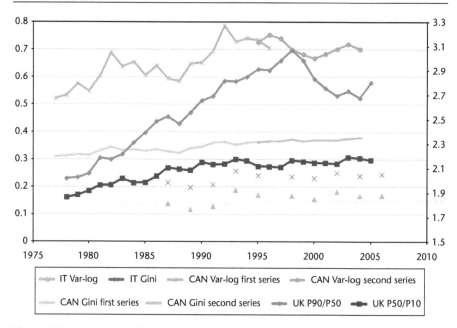

**Figure 2.2.** Var-log and Gini of earnings, Canada, Italy, and UK

*Source*: RED. RED data refer to the special issue of Review of Economic Dynamics that presented comparable data related to inequality for a selection of countries. For details see Krueger et al. (2010).

In some cases, the analysis of the tails of the income distribution highlights significant features of the way overall inequality has evolved. Among Baltic countries the transition from communism led to a considerable increase in income inequality. However, the patterns of this increase differ among the three countries. Estonia had a sharp increase at the beginning of the transition period and, after its peak in the early 1990s, a gradual decline. Lithuania also witnessed a large jump in income inequality after the transition, which gradually increased afterwards. Latvia had a more gradual, though considerable, increase in income inequality (Tóth, 2013). Figure 2.3 shows the ratio of the (net) income share of the top and bottom deciles. The analysis of the tails of the income distribution confirms that the largest shock in inequality was registered in Estonia. However, after a considerable decline in the ratio up to the mid-1990s the decile ratio started to increase again and converge towards the other two Baltic countries.

The analysis of top incomes shows a rather striking pattern of change in income inequality. Top income shares, in particular the top 1 per cent, increased in most countries over the period between the 1980s and the 2000s, with remarkable variations in Anglo-Saxon countries. However, some

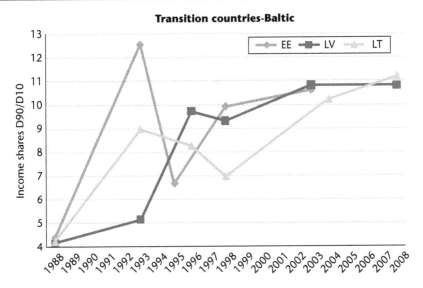

**Figure 2.3.** D90/D10 for Baltic countries

*Source*: Authors' own elaboration based on GINI country report for Baltic countries. Original source: World Bank database.

countries did not show a parallel increase in income inequality as measured by the Gini coefficient. For instance, Tóth (2013) reports a stable trend of disposable income inequality in Ireland, Italy, France, and Japan (among others),[4] a 'fluctuating' trend after the increase of the Thatcher years in the UK, and a declining trend during the second half of the 2000s for Portugal (as happens in Spain according to OECD, 2008). Top income data reported in Figure 2.4 show that the income share of the top 1% was increasing considerably in all these countries; these are derived from tax returns, which may capture trends at the top more accurately than the household surveys on which measures of overall inequality are generally based.

Although these measures of top incomes refer to gross income, we show below that top income marginal taxes declined over the same period—so net top income shares should also have risen.

[4] Although in the case of Japan it seems to depend on data sources used, since according to the GINI country report for Japan there has been an increase. The discussion of alternative data sources is beyond the scope of this chapter, but should be taken into account in assessing trends. For most of the OECD countries the trends are clear-cut, although Eurostat data tend to overestimate disposable income inequality for Luxembourg and Netherlands and underestimate it for Germany and Italy (Bogliacino and Maestri, 2012). However, for less developed or transition countries, the lack of data forces one to use imputed data such as SWIID (Solt, 2009). Comparing SWIID and EU-SILC for Lithuania in the second half of the 2000s, according to the former there is an increasing trend, while for the latter the pattern is U-shaped.

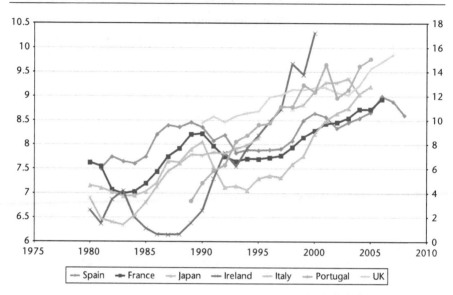

**Figure 2.4.** Top 1% share of total income, various countries (UK is on right axis)
*Source*: Paris School of Economics Top Incomes Database, see Atkinson et al. (2011).

### 2.1.3 Beyond Disposable Income: Other Sources of Economic Inequality

Disposable income is composed of labour and capital income, cash transfers, and pensions, all net of taxes, and decomposing by the different sources of income provides insights into the drivers of increasing income inequality. The largest component of income is labour income, which in turn is the product of hours worked and hourly wages. While the distribution of hours worked seems more stable across countries and over time, the increase in inequality appears to be concentrated in hourly wages and earnings (Bell and Freeman, 2001; RED). While unemployment (hours worked) plays an important role in explaining cyclical variations in inequality (Maestri and Roventini, 2012), the long-term increase in income inequality seems rather explained by an increase in inequality of hourly wages, given that employment increased in most of the countries. Beyond labour, capital income can contribute substantially to the increase in income inequality (García-Peñalosa and Olgiazzi, 2011). Figure 2.5 shows that inequality in hourly wages increased more than inequality in hours of work, apart from Italy.

Inequality in hours of work was rather stable in the last decades and, for example, in Germany it decreased. The steeper trend of earnings inequality observable for all countries reported in the same figure is due to two factors. First, there is a positive correlation between hourly wages and hours of work. Second, the measure of earnings inequality reported in the figure is

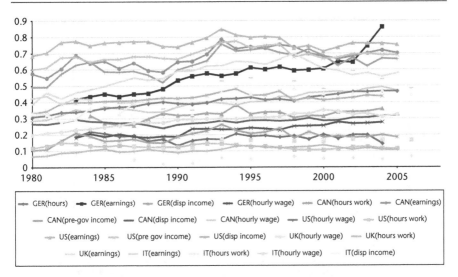

**Figure 2.5.** Var-log of various sources of income, various countries
*Source*: RED.

calculated at the household level. Therefore, the increase in earnings inequality is also explained by the combination of labour supply and household composition. The dynamics between individual and household measures of income and earnings inequality are explored in Chapter 3 of this volume.

Another important trend to discuss is the pattern of consumption inequality. From the 1990s onwards there is evidence of an increasing gap between disposable income inequality and consumption inequality, although this is not uniform across countries. Figure 2.6 reports the evolution of the gap between these two sources of inequality. The UK, USA, and Italy show a considerable diverging trend over the last decades. In Canada and Spain the gap was amplified throughout the 1990s, although in Canada it returned to its original level in the mid-2000s. Sweden, surprisingly, has a level of consumption inequality higher than that of disposable income, but the two series tend to converge, with disposable income inequality increasing faster than consumption inequality.

The divergence between levels and trends of consumption and disposable income inequality is not easy to explain. With regards to the Italian experience, Jappelli and Pistaferri (2010) suggest that this may be explained by transitory income shocks. Consumption smoothing explains the lower level of consumption inequality with respect to income inequality. In a business cycle framework, expansions are associated with lower income inequality but with higher consumption inequality (Maestri and Roventini, 2012).[5]

---

[5] Evidence for the USA and the UK; long and continuous series for consumption inequality were not available for the other countries considered in Maestri and Roventini (2012).

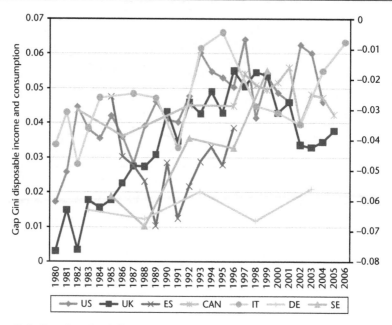

**Figure 2.6.** Trend in the difference between (non-durable) consumption and disposable income inequality

*Source*: Authors' own elaboration based on RED database. Notes: SE series is reported on the right axis.

However, long-run diverging trends of income and consumption inequality can hardly be explained by a life-cycle motive. A plausible explanation of this evolution is the increasing role of debt, as suggested by Fitoussi and Saraceno (2010). The effect of this increasing access to debt will be discussed in Section 2.3.

### 2.1.4 National or Regional Inequality?

Individual European countries are generally less unequal than the USA, but if income inequality is calculated among all European citizens it is higher than in the USA (Galbraith, 2012). The ranking of regions according to their level of income inequality shows some surprising results compared with the national picture. For instance, the Italian North-East has a relatively low level of disposable income inequality and the Brussels Capital Region a relatively high one,[6] while Belgium and Italy rank respectively low and high in income inequality. In Italy, the levels of within-region income inequality are similar across regions and lower than the national level of inequality, which is

---

[6] The data refer to 2006 and are calculated in Frattini (2012) based on EU-SILC data.

high due to the absolute differences in average income levels across regions. Conversely, Belgium has rather different levels of inequality across regions, with Flanders and Wallonia having a relatively low level of inequality and the Brussels Capital Region a very high level.

The trends of inequality at the national level and within regions may also show very different patterns, as seen in Figure 2.7. For instance, Belgium has a stable overall level of disposable income inequality, but within regions there is a different pattern between the Capital Region and the others.

The choice of the reference population for the estimation of inequality is particularly important for the study of its social and political impacts, since people's behaviour may respond to changes in income inequality in their reference group, but that may not coincide with the national population. (It is worth noting, though, that regional indicators based on survey data may be 'noisy' due to small sample size.)

### 2.1.5 Disposable Income Inequality and the Crisis

The early phases of the Great Recession have seen a decrease in disposable income inequality in many countries (Tóth, 2013; Jenkins et al., 2012). However, there is some evidence of countercyclical behaviour in income inequality (Maestri and Roventini, 2012), and this immediate impact may not persist.

Figure 2.8 shows the change in the period 2007–10 against the following year. There is a large group of countries for which, immediately after the recession, disposable income inequality fell (together with a considerable decline in median income), probably due to the fall in capital income; for these countries inequality started to increase again in 2010. This is clearly visible in countries subject to austerity measures (e.g. the Mediterranean countries and Ireland). Another group of countries has exactly the opposite dynamics. Nordic countries tend to witness an increase across the overall period. The only two countries which experienced a fall in disposable income inequality in both phases are Romania and Germany. Jenkins et al. (2013) also stress that standard measures of disposable income inequality do not take into account the effect that reducing in-kind benefits and increasing indirect taxes, central to austerity programmes, will have on living standards more broadly.

To summarize, the analysis of the trends of economic inequality over the 1980s–2000s shows that:

- Inequality increased in most countries regardless of the rate of growth in GDP per capita;

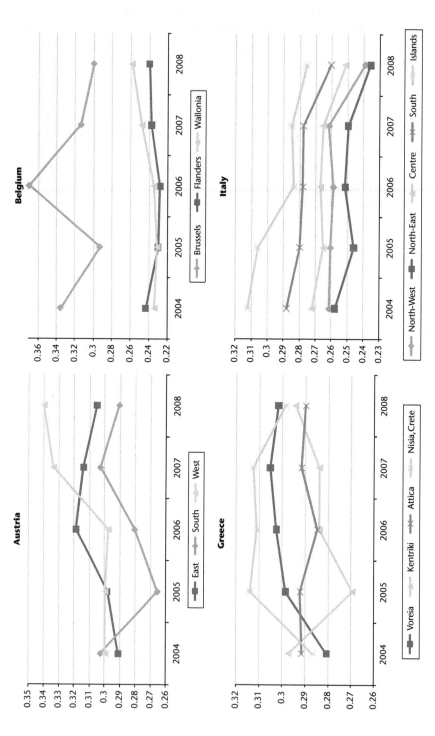

**Figure 2.7.** Evolution of inequality at regional level for Austria, Belgium, Italy, and Greece

*Note:* Gini coefficients are calculated on the native population for NUTS1 regions.

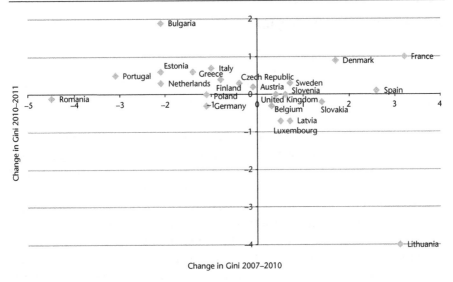

**Figure 2.8.** Inequality and the Great Recession (2007–10 and 2010–11)
*Source*: Eurostat indicators of disposable income inequality based on EU-SILC data.

- Different groups of countries experienced different patterns, with episodic or gradual changes in inequality and, in some cases, periods of falling inequality, especially after peaks;
- Top incomes tend to increase everywhere, even where overall inequality is seen to be stable;
- Hourly wages and earnings inequality generally increased more than disposable income inequality or inequality in hours of work;
- Consumption inequality and income inequality may have different trends, and need to be reconciled;
- Regional inequality may be increasing despite a stable trend at the national level;
- Different data sources should be handled with care;
- The medium- and long-term effects of the Crisis on inequality may be very different from its immediate impact.

This chapter proceeds as follows: Section 2.2 discusses the drivers of increasing inequality, distinguishing between proximate determinants and underlying causes; Section 2.3 analyses the potential negative effects of inequality on the economic system; finally, Section 2.4 concludes.

## 2.2 Drivers of Increasing Inequality

### 2.2.1 A General Approach

The concept that is generally used to calculate summary indicators of income inequality is net equivalized household disposable income, which has three main components.

The first building block is market flows of income received as remuneration for productive factors (capital and labour) or as a return to managerial etc. activity in productive units. The main determinants behind the formation of market incomes are: (i) the endowments of individuals; (ii) decisions allocating the factors to production; (iii) the demand for the factors by the producers; and (iv) the institutional settings that determine how labour demand and supply are matched. For example, under the first category we consider both the role of the existing stocks of wealth and of educational attainment, under the second both the propensity to save and the labour supply in the job market, under the third category the technology employed by the firm, which determines the use of the factors and their productivity, and finally, of course, in the last category we can include all the possible variables that affect the bargaining power of individuals, their involuntary unemployment, or the ease in finding a counterpart with which to trade.

The second block of relevant factors is related to the role of demographic variables. Fertility, mating, and longevity tend to affect the distribution at the household level.

Finally, state intervention through taxes and benefits redistributes income flows across households and within the family, altering the level of inequality emerging from market flows.

The development of income inequality depends on the evolution and combination of all three building blocks. Some elements are not captured by standard measures of disposable income inequality such as those provided by national statistical offices, in particular in-kind income[7] and benefits and consumption taxes. Table 2.1 distinguishes between gross income, disposable income (on which standard measures of income inequality are based), and extended disposable income and summarizes their main components.

A specific dimension of inequality that has recently received significant attention is the share of income that accrues to the very top, with important new estimates based on tax-records data now available for a significant number of countries (Atkinson et al., 2011). This is of interest because the

---

[7] A few countries include imputed rent in the definition of income for their national indicator of income inequality (e.g. the Netherlands).

**Table 2.1.** Extended concepts of income and their determinants

| Gross income | Disposable income | Extended disposable income |
|---|---|---|
| Gross earnings | – Personal income tax (PIT)<br>– Social security contributions (SSC)<br>+ Tax reliefs | |
| Gross self-employment | – Self-employment taxes | |
| Other capital income | – Capital income taxes | |
| | + Cash benefits (e.g. pensions and unemployment benefits) | + In-kind benefits (e.g. health, education, and social housing)<br>+ In-kind income (e.g. imputed rents)<br>– Consumption taxes |

widely used Gini summary measure gives more weight to changes occurring around the middle of the distribution than the tails, but more substantively because it is argued that increasing shares for the top may have a variety of damaging social, political, and indeed economic consequences (Stiglitz, 2012).

The income of those at the top is distinctive in terms of relative importance of different components: the share of capital in income is relatively larger, while the importance of income received through the welfare state is of course less important.

Most of these factors are, however, 'proximate causes' in the sense that they tend to evolve together with other variables in the system, while an assessment of the determinants should seek to isolate the drivers underlying those co-movements. In the following paragraphs we will try to describe the patterns of the former (the proximate causes) before moving to a discussion of the potential underlying causes proposed by the literature and of the empirical evidence available for assessing them.

### 2.2.2 Proximate Causes

An individual's income is the sum of the various flows, including both market flows and redistributive intervention by the state. When we move from the individual income to the aggregate measures, the Gini can be shown to depend upon the concentration of individual sources of income and the weight of the latter in total income.[8]

---

[8] See Cornia (2012) and the discussion in OECD (2011).

CAPITAL INCOME

The first proximate factor that has played a decisive role in the growth of inequality has been the increasing importance of capital and self-employment income. As discussed by OECD (2011), in the decade from 1995 to 2005 the change in Gini has been increasingly explained by the role of capital income (together with a reduced role of redistribution by the state, obtained through a reduction of benefits). A similar role has been played by self-employment income in a subset of countries, especially in Southern Europe. An increase in the role of capital and self-employment income is confirmed also by García-Peñalosa and Olgiazzi (2011), using LIS data for Canada, Germany, Norway, Sweden, the UK, and the USA.

Behind this inequality-increasing role of capital at the microeconomic level there is a macroeconomic phenomenon: as discussed by OECD (2012a), the labour share of income has declined in favour of the capital share. In OECD countries, the median labour share has declined from 66.1% to 61.7% between the early 1990s and the late 2000s, but for some of the countries the tendency started in the 1980s. This is probably underestimated in the statistics for some countries; because of the remuneration policies in US companies some of what is paid as wages is actually a part of profits. In Figure 2.9,

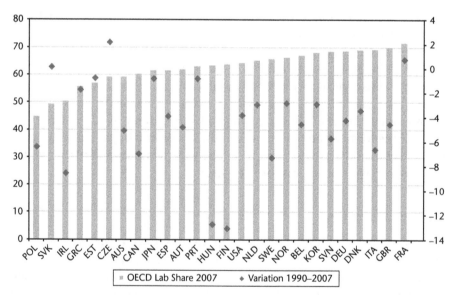

**Figure 2.9.** Level of business-sector labour share in 2007 (left axis) and change 1990–2007 (right axis)

*Note:* (For the initial year) Germany and Hungary: 1992; Czech Republic, Estonia, Greece, Poland, Slovakia, and Slovenia: 1995; (for the final year) Canada: 2004; Korea and Portugal: 2005; Japan, Poland, and Slovenia: 2006; for all the other countries the years are 1990 and 2007.

*Source:* OECD calculations based on OECD STAN and EUKLEMS.

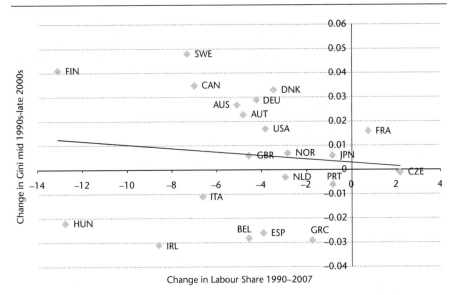

**Figure 2.10.** Change in labour share and change in Gini of net household disposable income

*Note*: (For the initial year) Germany and Hungary: 1992; Czech Republic, Estonia, Greece, Poland, Slovakia, and Slovenia: 1995; (for the final year) Canada: 2004; Korea and Portugal: 2005; Japan, Poland, and Slovenia: 2006; for all the other countries the years are 1990 and 2007.

*Source*: OECD income distribution and poverty database for Gini; OECD STAN and EUKLEMS for labour share.

from OECD (2012a), one can see the change in the business-sector labour share between 1990 and 2007.

The inequality-enhancing effect of capital and self-employment income is due to the combination of a greater concentration across the distribution and an increasing weight in the overall income: the combined result of the two trends is an increase of overall income concentration. As can be seen from Figure 2.10, even at aggregate level there is a negative correlation between the change in labour share and the change in the Gini for net household disposable income, although countries appear clearly clustered.

On the other hand, a particular form of (in-kind) return to capital contributed to reducing income inequality. The income advantage of home ownership (imputed rent) reduces income inequality in most countries, as it represents a considerable source of income for the bottom deciles[9] (Eurostat, 2010; Frick et al., 2010). However, the inclusion of imputed rent in the income concept and its limited taxation reduce the redistributive power of taxation

---

[9] The concept of imputed rent considers also the income advantage of paying a rent below market prices.

and considerably re-rank households along the income distribution (Maestri, 2012a). Although data on imputed rent are available only for recent years, the increasing share of home ownership (in particular at the bottom of the income distribution) experienced by most countries suggests a negative contribution to (an extended concept of) income inequality and a diminished redistributive power of taxation. Nonetheless, in very recent years the equalizing effect of imputed rent weakened in some countries (Eurostat, 2012).

It is very likely that the effect of the change in capital share in terms of top earners is much larger than in the case of the overall Gini. In fact, capital represents a relatively larger source of income of these households. At the same time, (profit) performance-based wages are an important part of the income of CEOs, significant among top earners.

## WAGE DISTRIBUTION, PARTICIPATION IN THE LABOUR MARKET, AND FAMILY FORMATION

The second proximate cause of increasing inequality is the change in the distribution of wages. The wage component is by far the largest in individual income and represents the primary income for most of the individuals across the distribution. Thus, an increase in inequality in its distribution has a first-order effect in the overall Gini. In Table 2.2 we summarize the main stylized facts on the labour market, drawn from the GINI project country reports.

This increase in wage inequality requires some qualifications. As explained by OECD (2011), the contribution of wage inequality to explaining the change in income inequality has been unchanged or declining in the 1990s and 2000s. Across all countries there is a clear gradient of access to employment and of wage differentials according to educational attainment. However, as shown in Table 2.2, the steepness of the educational gradient in the employment rate and the *skill premium* have increased in some but not all the countries. Even among the Anglo-Saxon countries, where this stylized fact has generated a sizeable literature, we can find the example of Canada where the educational premium decreased, but across different areas we can find similar cases, e.g. Italy and Greece among the Mediterranean countries, France, some central European countries, and Denmark. Most of the increase of earnings inequality is not related to observable variables: estimating Mincerian regressions on LIS data,[10] Bogliacino and Maestri (2012a) show that both the level and the increase in variability are mainly explained by the residual.

---

[10] The equation is obtained from a human-capital model where the main regressors are educational attainment and experience (usually proxied by age and with a quadratic term). A set of further controls captures the possibility of segmentation: sex, married (interacted with the female dummy), immigration, NUTS regions, industry classification, and occupational groups. The sample includes people 15–65 years old, excluding zero incomes, the income variable is *labour income per person* from LIS, which comprises regular paid employment income (basic

**Table 2.2.** A summary of the labour market stylised facts, GINI project countries, 1980s–2000s

| | Wage inequality | Educational gradient in access to employment | Return to education | Flexibilization of the labour market and/or increase in part-time jobs | Female participation rate and/or employment rate |
|---|---|---|---|---|---|
| Increasing | Australia, Austria, Bulgaria, Canada, Denmark, France, Hungary, Italy, Korea, Luxembourg, Netherlands, Poland, Portugal, Czech Republic and Slovakia, Romania, Slovenia, Sweden, United Kingdom, USA | Austria, Bulgaria, Canada, Finland, Hungary, Japan, Korea, Luxembourg, Netherlands, Portugal, Czech Republic and Slovakia (slight increase), Romania, Slovenia | Baltic states, Finland, Hungary, Korea, Luxembourg, Poland, Romania, Czech Republic and Slovakia, USA | Australia, Austria, Belgium, Canada, Finland, Germany, Ireland, Italy, Japan, Korea, Luxembourg, Netherlands, Slovenia, Spain, Sweden | Australia, Belgium, Baltic states, Canada, Germany, Greece, Ireland, Italy, Luxembourg, Spain, United Kingdom |
| Stable and/or unclear trend | Belgium, Baltic states, Germany | Belgium, Baltic states, Denmark, France, Germany, Greece, Ireland, Italy, Portugal, Spain, USA | Belgium, Canada, Japan, Ireland, Netherlands | Greece | |
| Decreasing | Greece, Ireland, Spain | | Austria, Denmark, Italy, Portugal, Spain | | Romania |

*Source*: GINI country reports.

Not all tendencies at work in the labour market went in the direction of increasing inequality. As stressed by OECD (2011), increasing female labour market participation and educational levels have contributed to reducing inequality in most of the countries, at least at the individual level (but not necessarily at the household level in cases of assortative mating). Indeed, female participation has increased virtually everywhere (see the last column in Table 2.2), and the increase in educational attainment has been quite

wages and salaries; wage supplements; director wages), casual paid employment income, farm self-employment income, and non-farm self-employment income. Of course, results of these regressions are not deemed to identify the causal impact, since, for example, ISCO classification dummies may partly capture the return to education (access to better tasks in the labour market).

substantial across all developed countries (as shown by Ballarino et al. in Chapter 5 of this volume). At the same time, the considerable use of part-time employment (e.g. Germany, Ireland, Luxembourg), particularly widespread among women, may have served as a counteracting force, further increasing inequality at the personal level.

The labour market also has a strong impact on top income shares because of increasing remuneration to superstars (the working rich, in the words of Atkinson et al. 2011). However, the debate over the nature of this remuneration is still open (Stiglitz, 2012): the inclusion of stock options and other stock market performance-related mechanisms partly hides the profit nature of these payments.

A proximate cause can be identified in demographic factors. They have been discussed by Burtless (2011) and OECD (2008). One candidate explanation is assortative mating, where high-income or high-education individuals tend to form families together. Some empirical evidence is in OECD (2011) for income correlation among families, and for households compared to individuals in Chapter 3 of this book. Immigration does not seem to have a causal effect on income dispersion (Frattini, 2012). In some countries, notably Japan and Korea, according the GINI country reports, population ageing played a role in the change of inequality.

REDISTRIBUTION

Finally, we should discuss efforts at redistribution by the state. In this section we will focus on taxes, as OECD (2011), Marx and Van Rie (Chapter 11 of this volume), and Marx and Verbist (Chapter 12 of this volume) have an in-depth discussion on benefits. Considering the effect of taxes is complicated. Besides the direct 'static' effect, the economic literature points to the existence of behavioural effects, affecting incentives to provide effort and to supply factors of production. However, the relationship between growth and inequality is far from obvious.[11]

Keeping this in mind, there appears to be some consensus on the static effects of taxation along the following lines:

1. Progressive personal income taxes and cash benefits are an efficient tool for the redistribution of incomes. The redistributive effect of PIT depends on the weight and progressivity of PIT. Together with cash

---

[11] The debate on the role of inequality in the development process is inconclusive: after the East Asian miracle there seemed to be a consensus that egalitarian policies (educational policies and land reform) were preconditions of development, but an alternative position emerged where concentration was considered to be a precondition for physical capital accumulation (Galor, 2011; Galor and Tsiddon, 1997). For some debate and empirical estimates see Aghion et al. (1999), Forbes (2000), Galbraith (2007).

benefits, they reduce market income inequality by around 25% to 33%, on average, across OECD countries (OECD, 2008).

2. Employee social security contributions are generally not progressive because the tax base on which they are paid is usually capped.[12]

3. The amount of deductions may alter the distributional effect of other taxes. Mortgage interest tax reliefs are often important, since home ownership is common, and are generally regressive, as higher-income taxpayers benefit more. Replacing existing forms of housing-related policies by a universal housing transfer could lower disposable income inequality by a minimum of 0.1% in Greece and up to 4.1% in the Netherlands (Matsaganis and Flevotomou, 2007). The regressive impact of mortgage interest relief depends on its design (tax credit versus tax deduction, full or partial deductibility, cap on interest repayments to which the relief is applicable) and on the mortgage take-up rate in the population (e.g. Italy and Greece have a low take-up rate, Finland medium, Sweden and Netherlands high).

4. Taxes on capital incomes are expected to be redistributive due to the high concentration of capital incomes (excluding in-kind income derived from home ownership) towards the top. However, the redistributive effect depends on whether capital income is taxed as a separate tax base.

5. Indirect taxes are generally independent of the income capacity of consumers but are differentiated according to the type of good. Lower income groups spend a larger share of their budget on consumption.[13] The inclusion of VAT payments in the income concept, for instance, increases inequality from 2.6% in Belgium up to 10% in Greece (Figari and Paulus, 2012). However, this effect will not be captured by standard measures of disposable income inequality.

6. Tax evasion can be inequality-enhancing or -reducing, depending on the propensity to evade across the deciles of the distributions. For behavioural reasons the individual position in the income distribution seems to affect the probability of tax evasion. The Cox Paradox portrays a situation in which the highest and lowest income taxpayers have greater opportunities to evade, whereas middle-income taxpayers find this harder (Bloomquist, 2003). The consequences of the Cox Paradox for inequality depend on the relative extent of tax evasion of the top and bottom income groups. Among high-featuring tax evasion

---

[12] Most of the evidence is for the USA: Coronado et al. (2000); Liebman (2002).

[13] However, poorer individuals pay a smaller proportion of their total expenditure in VAT and excise duties than richer individuals. The reason is that VAT-exempted or reduced-rate goods are overrepresented in the expenditure of poorer individuals (Figari, 2012).

countries, tax evasion increases income inequality with respect to a situation of full tax compliance by 3.5% in Greece up to 6.8% in Hungary (Matsaganis et al., 2010). Moreover, tax evasion seems to increase with income inequality (Christie and Holzner, 2006; Bloomquist, 2003). A further phenomenon that affects inequality is represented by tax off-shoring. Considerable assets are moved abroad and, consequently, the taxes on their returns are lost.

7. In-kind benefits (education, health, housing) have an equalizing effect on disposable income. However, this will not be captured by standard measures of disposable income and needs to be appropriately estimated. They reduce income inequality by around 12.5–15% (OECD, 2008). Moving from cash to extended income (i.e. income that includes the value of the total of services), Marx and Verbist (Chapter 11 of this volume) calculate a reduction of Gini by 20% through expenditure in services (including all services).

Looking at the trends of the last decades, we observe that:

1. Income tax rates were lowered, on the one hand, and, on the other, the degree of progressivity increased (OECD, 2008). This had a counterbalancing effect and did not help to reduce income inequality. Since the mid-1990s, the reduced capacity of the redistributive tax and benefits system was one of the main sources of increased inequality. Between 1995 and 2005 changes in tax burdens and benefit entitlements were mostly regressive, especially for single people and childless families. In general, taxes and benefits were more effective in reducing income inequality at the bottom than at the top. However in the last decades, most countries experienced an increase in top income shares (OECD, 2008). Since the 1980s, the number of personal income tax brackets was often drastically reduced (especially in the first decade). For instance, from 1981 to 2008 tax brackets were reduced from 32 to 5 in Italy, 23 to 5 in Belgium, and 30 to 4 in Spain (Fitoussi and Saraceno, 2010). However, the different developments of disposable income inequality in these countries confirmed that the progressivity of the tax system depends on the combinations of various aspects. In recent years, as reported by Marx and Van Rie (Chapter 10 of this volume), there has been a proliferation of flat tax regimes in the Central and East European countries. Baltic countries had already opted for flat tax systems in the mid-1990s, while Hungary, Bulgaria, and Romania turned to a flat tax system more recently (in 2011, 2008, and 2005 respectively). The Czech Republic and Slovakia introduced flat tax systems in 2008 and 2004 respectively, but they recently introduced a second higher rate. In these

countries, personal income taxes have a limited redistributive capacity (via tax credits), and may even be regressive (in combination with social security contributions). The introduction of flat income tax systems in place of progressive structures would be expected to entail an increase in inequality. Checking for this on net income inequality data is hard as these reforms mostly occurred in ex-communist countries, which suffer from limited data availability. For instance, the Baltic GINI country reports use SWIID imputed data that are not suitable for tracking such shocks (indeed, there seems to be a considerable increase in inequality only in Latvia following the introduction of the flat tax in 1997).

2. The reduction of top marginal income tax rates over the last four decades was remarkable and helps to explain the rise in top income shares since the 1990s (Matthews, 2011). Since the 1980s, top marginal tax rates have been lowered in almost all the countries covered, with the idea becoming widely held that they should not be above 50%. For example, between 1981 and 2008 the top marginal income tax rate changes from 70% to 35% in the USA, 72% to 43% in Italy, and from 65.1% to 27.1% in Spain (Fitoussi and Saraceno, 2010). Correspondingly, from 1971 to 2006, 1% top income shares increased by 10 percentage points in the USA, and from 1982 to 2004 by almost 3 percentage points in Italy and almost 1 percentage point in Spain (Bogliacino and Maestri, 2012a). The effect of lower marginal income tax rates was not purely static (smaller redistribution of income) but may have provided incentives for paying higher incomes. In France, the introduction of a tax shield (a maximum of 60% taxes per taxpayer, which was later eliminated) in the early 2000s explains most of the increase in income inequality between 1997 and 2012 and mostly benefited the top 1% of the income distribution (Frémeaux and Piketty, 2012).

3. Since the 1980s, revenues from employee social security contributions increased in most OECD and European countries, especially in Baltic and Balkan new member states, but with the exception of Spain, Slovenia, and the Netherlands (the latter two from exceptionally high levels) (OECD Revenues Statistics database; Eurostat, 2012). Revenues from social security contributions by the self-employed increased as well, especially in East and Central European countries (e.g. Poland) (Eurostat, 2012). This may be due to an increasing importance of self-employment.

4. Several OECD countries made substantial use of mortgage interest reliefs in recent decades and created a spiral in which they stimulate over-consumption of housing and, in turn, of this form of tax

expenditure. One of the largest and most regressive uses of mortgage deductions is found for the Netherlands (Matsaganis and Flevotomou, 2007). In these countries, as a consequence, the progressivity of personal income taxes is distorted in favour of higher-income homeowners. Indeed, specific reforms in capital income taxes provide high-income earners with a strong incentive to shift earnings to capital income. This is the case for Sweden (as well as other Nordic countries), which in 1991 introduced a dual income tax system, where the tax levied on capital income became flat. The dual income tax reform is seen as one of the drivers of increasing Swedish income inequality since the early 1990s (GINI country report for Sweden). Between mid-1990s and mid-2000s, tax revenues from household capital income decreased in some European countries (e.g. Belgium, Denmark, Italy, Romania) and increased in others (e.g. France, Sweden, United Kingdom). In the Netherlands this taxation was negative throughout the period (Eurostat, 2012). However, these data do not disentangle the increasing importance of capital income from the (increasing) weight of capital income taxation on households.

5. Taxes on consumption did not follow a clear pattern in recent decades, due to the combination of different types of indirect taxes (VAT, excises, etc.). With respect to the 1980s, the importance of indirect tax revenues increased in Europe in particular among Mediterranean countries (OECD Revenues Statistics database) and recently joined Balkan countries (data since 1995 from Eurostat, 2012). During the Crisis consumption taxes have come to the fore with VAT rates in particular on a considerable increasing trend (Eurostat, 2012) and the policy debate going in the same direction.

6. Data on tax evasion trends are very limited so it is difficult to assess the impact on changes in inequality, though evidence on tax offshoring supports the idea of an increasing trend (Henry, 2012).

7. Expenditures on in-kind benefits increased over the last four decades (SOCX database, education excluded), partly due to the ageing of the population (e.g. for health). However, the redistributive effect of publicly provided services was remarkably stable between 2000 and 2007, on average across OECD countries (OECD, 2008). As pointed out by Marx and Van Rie (Chapter 10 of this volume), no country achieves high redistribution with low social spending; as a result efforts to contain social expenditure have a strong regressive effect. In general, benefits are a major contributor, together with capital income, in accounting for the change in inequality from the mid-1990s to the mid-2000s, according to OECD (2011).

The developments illustrated above suggest that taxation, at best, did not keep pace with the increase in gross income inequality and with the changing importance of different income factors. Tax and benefit systems have offset about two-thirds of the increase in primary income inequality (Caminada et al., 2012). Going back a few decades, the main role was played by the sharp curtailments of top marginal personal income tax rates, which have immediate and behavioural effects on inequality, especially at the top. Moreover, the development of tax items (capital and self-employment income, mortgage interests, offshoring) may have reduced the effectiveness of direct taxes. More recent trends suggest an increase in disposable income inequality due to changes in the tax system. This refers to the renewed popularity of flat tax systems, and the increase in social security contributions, specifically for Baltic and Balkan European countries. Recent developments also point to an increase in extended income inequality, following cuts in in-kind benefits and increases in VAT rates, which are not captured by standard measures of inequality.

### 2.2.3 Underlying Causes

The existing literature provides a number of competing explanations behind the trends and the drivers discussed above. We will discuss the more mainstream hypotheses and the more heterodox ones, concluding that all require further empirical scrutiny. However, to better connect the preceding discussions of trends and proximate causes with this broader discussion of interpretations we make two key observations. The story of proximate causes of inequality told above is a mixture of state interventions, capital income, and the labour market. As a result, a coherent story should make empirical predictions regarding the distribution of capital assets, the formation of a policy consensus, and labour market behaviour, whereas hypotheses that primarily focus on the latter are unsuited to provide a comprehensive account (Galbraith, 2007). Secondly, while inequality increased almost everywhere, in some countries this follows a trend, while in some others the increases are episodic and followed by stabilization (Nolan et al., 2013). A theoretical explanation should take on the challenge of explaining both.

TECHNICAL CHANGE

The hypothesis of technical change as a main determinant of change in income inequality has generated a sizeable academic literature. On the one hand, the puzzling increase of the college wage premium in the 1980s and 1990s in the USA (Katz and Autor, 1999)—when there had been a massive increase of college graduates—revived the Tinbergen argument about the race between technology and education (Tinbergen, 1975), namely that technology, acting as a demand shifter (skill-biased technical change, SBTC), counteracts the positive effect of increasing educational attainment. There has been a large theoretical effort in this direction in the mid-1990s and 2000s (Acemoglu, 2002; Aghion, 2002; Acemoglu and Autor, 2011). In the most recent decade, a similar argument has been developed to explain the reduction in the labour share in gross domestic product (e.g. Bentolila and Saint Paul, 2003; OECD, 2012a).

In a nutshell, the argument behind the SBTC hypothesis is grounded in a pure demand and supply framework. If we focus on the dynamics of competitive forces (temporarily leaving aside frictions and heterogeneity in institutional settings), the rapid increase in the supply of skills across the OECD countries (documented by Ballarino et al. in this volume) should operate as an equalizing force. Since wage inequality is increasing, if demand and supply are well behaved as in (representative agent) competitive models, there must have been a demand shifter (Autor et al., 1998). The period since the 1980s has witnessed a rapid increase in trade liberalization, which could be an explanation—based on the tenet of classical theory that international trade will benefit the relatively abundant factor—but it is usually contested because upskilling occurred mainly within sectors and wage inequality increased also in unskilled-labour-abundant countries (Berman et al., 1998; Acemoglu, 2002). As a result, technology seems to be a better candidate.

On the empirical side, the technological explanation is supported by the rich micro evidence showing that labour demand for skilled workers is positively correlated with technological proxies. The literature has been reviewed by Chennells and Van Reenen (2002), who assess the variables and the econometric techniques that have been used, and conclude that the evidence is robust across countries. Of course, the estimation of labour demand has only partial equilibrium implications and we cannot draw firm conclusions at the aggregate level either in favour of or against the hypothesis. At the cross-country level, OECD (2011) shows that R&D intensity is correlated with P90–P10 wage differentials, but at this level the identification of causal channels depends on much more restrictive assumptions.

There is a large consensus on the technological explanation, but the hypothesis has also been challenged. At first sight, Table 2.2 suggests that the pattern of change in wage inequality and the returns to education is much more diverse across countries, and, even in the USA, the college premium stabilizes in the 2000s (Krugman, 2012b)[14] despite the explosion of financial innovation

---

[14] If the source is a technological shock, in the SBTC model (Acemoglu and Autor, 2011) the consequences are the same regardless of the subsequent reaction of the supply of skills: in other words, a breakdown in the 2000s should be justified through a different technological shock from the one occurring in the two decades before. Moreover, across countries the consequences should be the same unless the pattern of comparative advantages is systematically different between e.g. Germany and USA (by comparative advantage we mean the relatively higher

(that was also favoured by the boom in information and communication technology).

One of the critiques addressed to SBTC does not question its existence, but rather its suitability as a main factor. First of all, there is an issue of timing: as can be seen by national stories in the companion volume from the GINI project (Nolan et al., 2013), in many cases (but not by any means all of them) the increase of inequality is concentrated in a short period of time, followed by stabilization at a higher level. Technical change is rarely episodic and one-shot, and thus is unfit in itself to explain this kind of dynamics. Secondly, even in the USA (Card and DiNardo, 2002) the generalized increase in inequality is shaped by different changes in different parts of the distribution at different times: Atkinson et al. (2011) are very sceptical about the role of SBTC in explaining the remarkable surge in top income shares, and most of the change in the 1980s is due to shifts at the lower end of the distribution (DiNardo, 1996), where the wage is more related to the substitution of unskilled labour than with an increasing demand for skilled workers. Thirdly, in countries such as the USA the increase of wage inequality started well before the 1980s, when the increase in the college premium is observed: this implies that for SBTC to hold there must have been an acceleration of technical change afterwards, but the average growth of productivity (both labour and TFP) in the period is at least 1 percentage point lower than during the three decades from the 1950s to the 1970s across all the developed world (Chang, 2010).

Using technical change to explain the change in the labour share has been contested because capital-biased technical change should then have occurred in a period of decreasing real interest rates across the entire time window, which is puzzling in the standard competitive framework.

In both cases—skill-biased or capital-biased technical change—there is very limited literature on the 'trigger' of the SBTC push: Acemoglu (2007) and Acemoglu and Autor (2011) suggest that the exogenous variation of one of the factors may induce technical change directed to complement it. For example, in the models of the economy where innovative machines complement skills, the change in the relative supply of skills modifies the incentives for the profit-seeking innovators, affecting the direction of technological change. Whether the source of SBTC is endogenous or exogenous is a fundamental question, given that in the latter case educational policies are inequality-enhancing and not inequality-reducing. Bogliacino and Lucchese (2011) use a natural experiment and show that the evidence for this version of endogenous skill bias is rather weak. The

---

productivity of a skill in a certain task). This can be true at a more disaggregated level, but not with this level of granularity when skills are measured in two or three groups.

alternative hypothesis on the origin of skill bias is the 'exogenous' version, based on the hypothesis of technological revolutions and cycles (Caselli, 1999; Autor et al., 2003; Aghion, 2002; Krusell et al., 2000), which is not rejected by this empirical evidence.

Finally, on purely theoretical grounds, the technological explanations (skill-biased or the capital-biased version) are based on the assumption that technical change is *directed*. That assumption is defended on the ground that firms aim to save on the most expensive factor (e.g. the factor whose share in total cost is higher). If this is the case, directed technical change rests upon the elasticity of demand, given that the labour share is the product of the wage rate and the quantity of labour and given that they are negatively related (Drandakis and Phelps, 1966). If the elasticity of demand is such that an increase in the wage rate augments the share of the factor, then the economy enters a self-sustaining process where continuously capital- (or skill-) biased technical change feeds on itself. For this to occur, the substitutability among the factors must be relatively high. Whether this is the case or not is an empirical issue.

GLOBALIZATION

Globalization is usually central in policy debate regarding the change in inequality, but it is unclear what specific phenomenon is meant by this term. There are essentially two visions about the relationship between globalization and inequality. The first one is related to increasing integration at the international level, the alternative one to the role of liberalization of capital movements, which is discussed in the next subsection.

As we pointed out above, according to classical trade theory, opening up the economy towards developing countries with lower wages (and less stringent regulation) reduces the bargaining power of unskilled labour and shifts resources towards skill-intensive and capital-intensive sectors, increasing inequality. This hypothesis has been challenged on the grounds of intra-sector movements, where most of the change occurred (see Acemoglu, 2002 for skill premium; OECD, 2012a for decreasing labour share)—although according to modern trade theory most of the international trade is occurring within sectors (Krugman, 1991).

In OECD (2011) the change in the ratio between the ninth and the first decile of the wage distribution does not appear to be correlated with various measures of offshoring, financial integration, or import penetration. However, OECD (2012a) points out that, after controlling for a number of confounding variables, import penetration has a positive effect on the reduction of labour share. The existence of a delocalization effect in industries hit by import penetration is shown by Bassanini and Manfredi (2012). Further evidence is provided by Guscina (2006).

Finally, the increasing integration of the global economy may generate a coupling of the business cycles, and expose economies more strongly to shocks generated elsewhere, increasing uncertainty. The literature on the relationship between macroeconomic shocks and inequality is rather scarce. Maestri and Roventini (2012) analyse the relationship between macroeconomic factors and inequality, finding that the latter series are not stationary; they suggest that permanent effects of recessions on inequality and asymmetric effects of recessions and expansions could be a candidate for reconciling short-term fluctuations of inequality and long-term upward trends. Granger causality tests suggest a mutually reinforcing relationship between unemployment and inequality, underlining the role of adjustment costs in the determination of inequality.[15]

STRUCTURAL IMBALANCES

According to a more heterodox interpretation, the relationship between globalization and inequality is driven by the liberalization of capital movements. From a theoretical perspective, in the presence of behavioural biases, prices do not reflect fundamentals (De Long et al., 1990); as a result, liberalization of capital movement will end up generating bubbles. Scholars of financial crises in developing countries insist that the channel from free capital movement to bubble to financial crises is a very robust stylized fact (Frenkel and Rapetti, 2009; Diaz-Alejandro, 1985).

The two channels through which financial bubbles impact on inequality are through the inflation of the capital share (Dumenil and Levy, 2011; Tridico, 2011; Jayadev, 2007) and the change in top shares: i.e. the existence of rents for companies that allows CEOs and managers to appropriate a part of them (Stiglitz, 2012; Atkinson et al., 2011; Krippner, 2005).

Although the bubbles are created in financial markets, through increases in prices that do not reflect fundamentals, their origin is economic, in the sense that they are rooted in protracted current account deficits, reflecting diverging competitiveness conditions (*structural imbalances*, Servén and Nguyen, 2013). By simple identity of the balance of payments, a structural deficit in the current account implies an increasing external debt, which in the absence of a correct screening will end up inflating the prices of assets.

In the recent experience of GINI countries, we can draw some preliminary evidence from two episodes, one in the USA and the other in the Euro Area. The USA has been running current account deficits since the early

---

[15] The adjustment process can also be influenced by regulation in the labour market. Bargain et al. (2010) discuss the possible effects of labour demand adjustment to a downturn. They explore two scenarios, one based on intensive margin (hours of work) and another on extensive margin (layoffs), using data from Germany. Their empirical estimate suggests that the former has more modest distributional consequences.

1980s. This process was reinforced at the end of the century by the external account policies adopted by middle-income countries and export-oriented economies such as East Asian countries. Those countries shifted to a managed exchange rate regime where appreciation is kept under control to avoid worsening of the balance of payment current account. In the USA, from the 1980s onwards, the shift of income from labour to capital has been remarkable (Figure 2.11), as has the increase in the top-income share (Atkinson et al., 2011). The evidence from the Euro Area is pretty much in line with this: all the periphery of the Eurozone saw a strong increase in external debt because of the deterioration in competitiveness conditions (once the exchange rate no longer operated as a re-equilibrating mechanism). As shown in Sections 2.1 and 2.2.2, all those countries witnessed an increase in top-income shares and a decrease in the labour share. It should be stressed that this occurred even where rather favourable macroeconomic performance improved the condition of the middle class, as captured by a stable (Ireland) or decreasing (Spain, Greece) Gini coefficient. If we widen our perspective to include other countries, e.g. Latin American ones, we find more or less the same pattern in the period that paved the way to the debt crises: during that period inequality was also increasing, but reliable cross-country data on top incomes are scarce (Cornia, 2012).

## THE ROLE OF IDEOLOGY AND FUTURE INEQUALITIES

The period from the 1980s to the 2000s witnessed a clear-cut process of liberalization in all markets (labour, financial, product) and a changing role of taxation and social expenditure. Advocating positive effects on employment, a number of interventions have been introduced in order to make the labour market more flexible, as shown in Figure 2.11.

Top marginal tax rates have been cut. Beyond income, in the last decades there has been a sharp decline in the taxation of wealth and inheritance. Where inheritance tax is still in place, current levels of tax deductions show that in fact inheritance is hardly taxed (Jappelli et al., 2012). Sweden, a typical social-democratic country, abolished any form of wealth and inheritance taxation in 2005.

The effects of these reforms may go beyond a purely static redistributive effect and be associated with higher incentives for wealth accumulation, intergenerational transmission, and growing top incomes (Atkinson et al., 2011).

According to Roemer (2011), the reasons underlying the weakening of redistributive interventions are to be found in the need for material incentives in order to boost growth and creativity, and in an emerging consensus on pro-market reforms. More generally, there has been a detectable effort to downsize redistributive intervention, with the diffusion of neo-liberal ideas

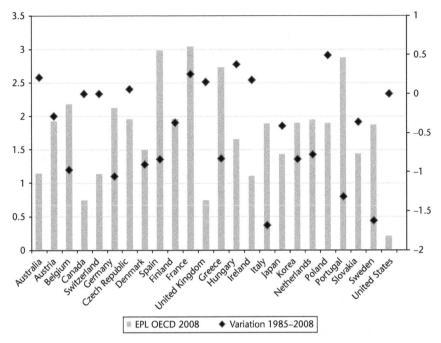

**Figure 2.11.** Level of employment protection legislation in 2008 (left axis) and changes 1985–2008 (right axis)

*Note*: Czech Republic and Slovakia: 1993–2008; Hungary, Korea, and Poland: 1990–2008.

*Source*: OECD indicators on employment protection—annual time series data 1985–2008.

in both left- and right-wing parties, as witnessed by the substantial bipartisan consensus over targeting as a measure of welfare-to-work (Marx and Van Rie, Chapter 10 of this volume), although the extent of its effectiveness is debatable. Increasing efforts to frame public opinion towards a wider acceptance of inequality have been stressed by Reich (2007), Roemer (2011), and Stiglitz (2012). In some cases the development of a new consensus in the economic literature may have played a role. As Mankiw et al. (2009) suggest, the taxation trends in OECD countries over the last decades (lower taxes on capital and on top incomes) seem to be in line with the lessons of the optimal theory of taxation.

This seems to be the case also for reforms in labour markets. The role of labour market reform as a driver of wage inequality has been highlighted by OECD (2011), in line with the evidence for the USA where the change in institutions (especially the minimum wage) is shown to be a main driver of the changes in the 1980s and 1990s especially at the bottom of the distribution (DiNardo et al., 1996; Card and DiNardo, 2002; Lemieux, 2006).

The thesis of policy-reform-driven inequality is partly corroborated by the country reports reviewed in Table 2.2, where we highlighted the role of labour market flexibilization in the majority of countries. Similar evidence can be found for overall income inequality in many countries (e.g. Belgium, Germany, Netherlands, Sweden, etc.) as reported in the GINI project country reports and Nolan et al. (2013).

The role of policy consensus can explain why cyclical downturns may have permanent effects on income inequality.[16] During recessions, the need to boost employment and growth can easily induce labour market flexibility, reduced labour taxation, and cuts in social expenditure. The reforms implemented during the Great Recession confirms this general trend. Most European countries have been recommended to shift taxation away from labour and towards VAT, green taxes, and property (Eurostat, 2012). Social expenditure has been cut (education in UK, massive adjustment packages in Portugal, Greece, and pensions reform in Italy). Although the austerity measures following the 2008 recession include an increase in top marginal tax rates (Callan et al., 2011) the bulk of interventions consisted in increasing VAT and property taxes, as suggested by the Troika and introduced in 2010 (Eurostat, 2012). Similarly, cuts in important social expenditure budget lines reduce the in-kind income derived from these services.

As already stressed, increases in VAT are not visible in standard measures of income inequality, as income does not include expenditures and, consequently, taxes on expenditures. Similarly, standard measures of inequality do not include in-kind benefits as they are generally based on a monetary concept of income. These two facts suggest that policy reforms recently implemented will mean a future increase in income inequality that will not be captured by standard measures of income inequality. A wider concept of economic income that includes tax payments on expenditures and in-kind benefits (and incomes) is necessary in order to track actual changes in the wellbeing of households.

## 2.3 The Economic Effects of Inequality?

Although the greatest debate has focused on the role of economic inequality on a series of societal outcomes (Wilkinson and Pickett, 2009a; Chapters 6 and 7 of this volume), inequality may also be negative for the economy itself. Despite what orthodox theory suggests, namely that inequality is positive

---

[16] Earnings and income inequality are countercyclical. However, the trends of income inequalities are non-stationary, i.e. recessions may have a permanent effect on inequality (Maestri and Roventini, 2012).

because it gives the right incentives, unequal economies may be more unstable, i.e. more subject to crisis. As a matter of fact, some of the main arguments discussed by the literature on the recent financial crisis of 2008 resemble closely the reasoning introduced in the previous two subsections, with particular regards to the role of ideology, lack of regulations, and structural imbalances.[17]

This suggests that inequality may be a cause of financial crisis, or the two may be co-determined or mutually reinforcing. In each case, the relationship suggests that there may be an efficiency argument for preventing increases in inequality, and not just the legitimate (and equally important) arguments in terms of equity.

### 2.3.1 Is There a Political Motive?

Rajam (2010) argues that the increase of inequality put pressures on the political system in the 1980s. Interestingly, in his account, inequality is a product of 'equilibrium' market forces (technical change, trade) and of the difficulty for the education system in keeping pace with the demand for skills. However, in his view this phenomenon generated political concerns; essentially because there was the *correct* perception that the social glue of the opportunity of upwards mobility (the American dream) was becoming rather a myth (OECD, 2008; DeBacker et al., 2013).

Given the difficulty of intervening in educational systems and the political polarization on taxation and other redistributive instruments (the main source of frictions among the parties after the Reagan revolution), access to housing through credit was seen as a relatively easy-to-implement and politically profitable option in the USA. Krugman (2012a) is highly critical of those who blamed the Congress and the *Community Reinvestment Act*, calling this argument *The Big Lie*: bubbles were much more widespread and present in markets where 'Freddie Mac and Fannie Mae'—the state-backed providers of mortgages—had no involvement at all; they were losing market share during the bubble and were also not involved in subprime origination.

Besides this critique, it is also puzzling that in this account the *poor* are at centre stage, in a period in which the capture of the political system by the upper class had been remarked on by many commentators, with increasing concern about lobbying activity (Acemoglu, 2011; Reich, 2007; Stiglitz,

---

[17] The ideology argument comes in various forms, such as the concept of Wall Street culture (Tett, 2009), excess self-confidence by the traders (Patterson, 2010), or in the change of consensus regarding capital markets (Skidelski, 2009). The role of a neo-liberal consensus behind reform is stressed by most of the literature (Krugman, 2012a; Stiglitz, 2010; Skidelski, 2009). Structural imbalances as a main cause have been pointed out by Munchau (2010), Rajam (2010), and Bernanke et al. (2011).

2012). Acemoglu (2011) argued instead that finance should be blamed: poor regulation may be the driver of both non-competitive wages and excessive risk-taking in the financial sector. In his view, SBTC (and offshoring) are the main explanation for what is happening in the bulk of the distribution, but the pathological US inequality is rather related to the excess concentration of income at the very top, which is explained by the rents accruing to CEOs, traders, and other Wall Street superstars.

### 2.3.2 The Keynesian View

According to the Keynesian perspective the inequality story is essentially a story of redistribution from labour to capital, as testified by the generalized evidence on labour share discussed above. Since in the Keynesian theoretical framework the propensity to save out of profits is lower than that out of wages—and the economy is demand-constrained—then redistribution from labour to capital produces a problem of growth potential.

As a result of the fundamental imbalance of the accumulation regime of the post-1980 period, the functioning of the global economy in the last thirty years has been essentially underpinned by the expansion of credit, which sustained consumption beyond the poor evolution of real wages (Tridico, 2012; Krugman, 2012a; Fitoussi and Saraceno, 2010). This dynamic is unsustainable and ordained to collapse. This explanation is, of course, based on the concept of effective demand and on the Minskian hypothesis of financial instability (Minsky, 1975).

Instrumental to this explanation is the shift in income from labour to capital (which is certainly happening) and the divergence between consumption inequality and income inequality documented in Figure 2.6.

It should be recognized that most of the literature on the increase of private debt is focused on the US case, that being the detonator of the financial meltdown. However, the massive increase of private debt directly or indirectly associated with capital flows, boosted by favourable tax treatment and lax regulation, is well documented and has dangerously increased the level of instability (OECD Private Debt databases). In some cases, mortgages and other forms of private debt had two-digit growth (e.g. GINI country reports for Finland, Luxembourg, Netherlands, and Portugal). In some cases it has already paved the way for financial crises (GINI country reports for Spain and Greece). Moreover, consumer debt is also increasing in those countries (such as Italy) that have a relatively low level of (mortgage) debt. Study loans represent a further concern, especially in some Nordic countries. These kinds of loans also have implications for wealth inequality, as discussed by Maestri et al. (Chapter 4 of this volume).

### 2.3.3 Discussion

To the best of our knowledge the only empirical analysis of the relationship between inequality and financial crises is Atkinson and Morelli (2010), which suggests that the evidence (using the two major episodes in the USA) is rather scant. However, this type of empirical analysis is problematic: the idiosyncrasy of financial crises is that they are rare events. To use the Keynesian jargon: it is the sustainability/unsustainability of debt growth and not the Minsky moment that should be used to compute the counterfactuals.

Moreover, financial crisis is normally the results of a complex network of related factors: in particular, as pointed out by Stiglitz (2012), in the USA the initial trigger has been a set of policies. Those policies were in the context of a number of institutional changes that alter the functioning of the financial market. At the international level, we have a complete change of paradigm with increasing liberalization of trade and capital movements (Arrighi, 2008). At the national level—as described by Campbell (2011)—the economy has been shaped by the 1986 Tax Reform Act, which simplified the tax regime for securitization, the repeal of the Glass-Steagal Act that fed the shadow banking system, and, finally, the further impulse towards deregulation during the Clinton administration, which dismissed the initial warning coming after major financial crises in East Asia and Russia (Wade, 2008). These reforms were matched by the changes in corporate governance and remuneration practices that were based on the shared consensus about the efficient market hypothesis applied to the stock market, ignoring self-reinforcing dynamics of financial bubbles (Wade, 2008; Rajam, 2010).

Whatever the initial trigger[18] of this set of policies, the effect was self-sustaining. Indeed, these inequality-increasing reforms transfer money and power to the top 1% of the distribution, inflating its power in the political process through rent-seeking activities (Krugman, 2012a; Stiglitz, 2012; Reich, 2007).

In other words, by changing the distributional patterns that were established during the previous three decades, the paradigmatic shift of the 1980s has also altered the 'political equilibrium'. The result was a self-sustained dynamics of increasing inequality and the freeing up of forces that increase the instability of the economy.

---

[18] Among the proposed explanations, one can find: a change in technological regime (Reich, 2007), a political response of business due to loss of competitiveness (Arrighi, 2008), or a rent-seeking argument, where business foresaw the possibility of reducing the bargaining power of labour (Dumenil and Levy, 2011).

## 2.4 Conclusions

In this chapter we show that income inequality has increased in most of the developed world from the 1980s, although with some variation in timing and magnitude. If we look at the sources of variation, we can see that the overall period of the last three decades can be separated into two main sub-periods: in the first one earnings have been the main driver of increasing inequality in income; in the second one, reduced redistribution by the state and the shift from labour to capital became increasingly important drivers. We show also that increases in inequality at the regional level are sometimes hidden at the national level (Belgium), that increases in top income shares are not always reflected in the standard Gini coefficient (Spain, Japan, Ireland), and that in some cases, such as France, a stable trend is a product of two different tendencies.

In terms of competing explanations, the mainstream literature has focused on globalization and technical change, while heterodox theories identify structural imbalances and the emerging pro-market consensus as main factors. We have tried to assess the correspondence of the empirical predictions of these theories with the stylized facts in terms of trends and drivers. We also discussed the relationship between increasing inequality and the recent financial crises, suggesting that inequality may have contributed to increasing instability. Furthermore, such financial crises are often followed by major fiscal adjustment packages, with the state transferring private losses into the public domain and putting fiscal consolidation in place through increasing indirect taxation and cuts in public spending, all increasing inequality. The Euro Area crisis seems to display such a trajectory.[19] As long as the national and international *fault lines* that created inequality and financial instability persist, such fiscal consolidation will result in higher inequality, without addressing its main underlying causes.

---

[19] This can be seen from the conditional measures to intervention by the IMF, European Commission, and European Central Bank implemented e.g. in Greece, Portugal, and Spain, but also from the general recommendation to countries issued in 2012 as an attachment to the 'Communication on Action for Stability, Growth and Jobs' (European Commission, 2012a).

# 3

# Earnings, Employment, and Income Inequality

*Wiemer Salverda and Christina Haas[1]*

## 3.1 Introduction

In the labour markets of most GINI countries wage inequality has increased (Chapter 2, Table 2.2), and, combined with the observation that the levels of income inequality differ significantly between countries (Chapter 2; Tóth, 2013), this puts on the table the question how the two inequalities relate to each other: '... family earnings inequality need not change in the same direction as individual earnings inequality', according to Gottschalk and Danziger (2005: 247). Potentially, the household distribution can diminish or amplify inequalities in the labour market, which lends the question a political importance beyond its academic significance. Household income is the central measurement unit of income inequality in the public debate and in policy-making, and also in this book. The significant contribution of 'an unprecedented surge in top wage incomes' that has been detected in the analysis of growing top incomes (Atkinson et al., 2011) provides one significant example of the relevance of relating the income distribution to earnings in the labour market, while the much-discussed phenomenon of in-work poverty provides another. A very high percentage of households receive some earnings from labour. Labour income in aggregate is also much larger than any other source of income, such as from enterprise or wealth, though these smaller ones may have important effects at the margin on the

[1] We are grateful to Daniella Brals for her work on SILC data, and to Francesco Scervini, Ive Marx, and Brian Nolan for their comments and suggestions.

overall level of inequality. The importance of labour incomes can also be seen in the impact of its absence, when people are unable to secure employment and the corresponding income, as illustrated by the debate on 'jobless households' that has developed since Paul Gregg and Jonathan Wadsworth (1996, but see also 2001 and 2010; De Graaf-Zijl and Nolan, 2010) started it in the mid-1990s. In assessing the overall impact of labour income on income inequality, differences in access to employment have to be incorporated into the analysis as much as the ensuing differences in earnings among earners. Employment access is an important dimension also for the households that do have a job, as jobs are not evenly distributed—some households having only one member at work while others have two or more. Finally, a job's working hours, part-time or full-time, are an increasingly important characteristic of employment which evidently affects take-home earnings. Working hours may influence household access to employment and also the level of pay, as exemplified by the well-known part-time pay penalty. Consequently, the above question splits into three: how are the two, employment and earnings, distributed over individuals in the labour market, and how do these distributions relate to each other and to the distribution of household incomes?

To answer these questions we compare European countries cross-sectionally for the most recent year for which data are available: 2010, from EU-SILC 2011 wave. The argument of the chapter proceeds in six consecutive steps. First, we briefly consider the literature; next, we explain what we intend to add and we provide some detail about the data. In Section 3.4, we indicate the importance of labour incomes relative to all income in the aggregate income distribution. After that, for the rest of the chapter, we direct attention exclusively to labour earnings, as the prime focus is the within-distribution of household earnings in comparison to that of individual earnings in the labour market. All the analysis is restricted to the working-age age bracket, in the sense that a household will have at least one adult employee below the age of 65.[2] Section 3.5 compares households and corresponding individuals on the basis of the household earnings distribution, and compares both to the dispersion of individual earnings or pay, which is the traditional focus of labour-market inequality. Section 3.6 shifts attention to the employment aspect of these earnings and looks at the role of household type, distinguished by the number of earners in the household, and links to the role of part-time employment. Section 3.7 looks at earnings by household type and concomitant poverty. Section 3.8 concludes.

---

[2] This may bring in a few employees aged 65 or over.

## 3.2 A Tale of Two Literatures

Actually, there is not one but instead there are two extensive literatures, one addressing wage inequality in the labour market and the other income inequality in society. Gottschalk and Danziger (2005: 253) remark that 'Labour economists have tended to focus on changes in the distribution of wage rates, the most restrictive income concept, since they are interested in changes in market and institutional forces that have altered the prices paid to labour of different types. At the other extreme, policy analysts have focused on changes in the distribution of the broadest income concept, family income adjusted for family size. This reflects their interest in changes in resources available to different groups, including the poor.' This confirms eight years on that the conclusion drawn by Gottschalk and Smeeding (1997: 676) that 'an overall framework would simultaneously model the generation of all sources of income... as well as the formation of income sharing units' and is 'the next big step that must be taken', was still a tall order. Yet another five years later, Večerník (2010: 2) observes that 'there seems to be a gulf between the analysis of personal earnings and household income'.

The two literatures differ in focus, analysis, measurement, and measures. Studies of wage inequality focus on individuals, those of income inequality on households. They have also different analytical discourses. The primary interest of the former is in what can explain the level of pay of one individual compared to another. Possible determinants of this include the returns to characteristics of the individual, such as his or her educational attainment, and of the job, such as its occupational level and expertise or its industry and technological content, and much of this literature considers also the effects of labour-market institutions such as minimum wages or unions. Little or no interest was taken, however, in the distribution of aggregate earnings, until this was fuelled recently by the findings showing the rapidly growing income shares of minute fractions of the population at the top of the earnings distribution. Studies of income inequality, by contrast, do focus strongly on the aggregate distribution across households, in a perspective of (in)sufficiency of income—read 'poverty'—and redistribution between households. Their primary interest is in how the disposable income of households relates to their needs. The analysis of wages commonly concerns market income before tax and benefits; the core concept of household income is after tax and benefits and also after equivalization for household size and composition, as a way to control for those needs. Unsurprisingly, these divergences go together with differences of measurement. First, the basis of measurement commonly differs. Household incomes are considered on an annual basis. Wage inequality, by contrast, is examined after controlling for people's efforts, and looks at hourly wage rates—often for full-time earnings.[3] Annual earnings result by definition from wage rates combined with annual hours worked and therefore inevitably incorporate differences in efforts. Equally inevitably, this implies that to enable connection of the two literatures the analysis of labour-market inequality needs to broaden beyond individual wage levels and incorporate individual employment including working hours. As a measure of inequality, decile or percentile ratios are popular in wage analysis but much less so in income analysis, where aggregate measures such as the Gini coefficient are key. Understandably, percentile ratios have less analytical precision here as it is accidental which types of household are found at precise percentiles. Naturally, the gulf is not absolute, as some of the wage-inequality literature pays attention to the household characteristics of individuals as potential determinants of pay, especially when it comes to the labour-market participation of specific groups of individuals—notably married women—but less as a general principle. Similarly, some of the income-inequality literature looks at the sources of income including the earnings from paid labour, the level of pay, or the lack of earnings due to household joblessness, in relation to, for example, within-country inequality growth, in-work poverty, or poverty *tout court.*

There is only a very modest and rather recent literature[4] that explicitly addresses the gulf between the two analyses, meaning here that the distribution of labour earnings is taken into account as such.[5] This trickle of publications has not yet built up into a well-defined body of approaches, let alone stylized facts. Various interesting contributions have been made, though. Gottschalk and Danziger (2005) analyse in an interconnected way the evolution of inequality in four different distributions for the USA over the last quarter of the previous century using CPS data: hourly individual wage rates, annual individual earnings (and therewith annual hours), annual family earnings, and annual family adjusted total income. The first two distributions are found at one side of the gulf, the other two at the other side. Interestingly, they bridge the gulf by ranking individuals for their annual earnings according to the total earnings of their households (p. 247) using consistent samples of individuals. Earnings exclude the self-employed and the analysis splits throughout between men and women. Their approach is very apt in an inter-temporal perspective, but difficult to interpret in a cross-section as it ranks male and female earners according to their respective

---

[3] 'Full-time' and 'full-time-full-year' earnings, used as an approximation in *Divided We Stand* (OECD (2011): 171), are also sensitive to variation in full-time hours, certainly in a cross-country or over-time perspective.

[4] Hardly any of the almost 300 ECINEQ papers to date address the gap.

[5] This differs from (interesting) analyses of effects on inequality of changing household composition (Peichl et al., 2010; Brandolini and d'Alessio, 2001; Del Boca and Pasqua, 2003).

households, which must be largely overlapping sets, concentrated higher up the distribution, to the extent that both male and female in a household have earnings.[6] However, they do not discuss the role of singles nor of possible third earners in the household. They find that 'for females, changes in hours more than offset the rise in wage inequality. The acceleration in male wage and earnings inequality during the early 1980s disappears when earnings of other family members are included' (p. 253). Thus the household mitigates inequality growth in the labour market.

Atkinson and Brandolini (2006), though for the most part considering trends in wage dispersion, compare[7] the Gini of the individual annual earnings dispersion to the Gini of adjusted disposable household income for a set of three Nordic countries, Germany and the Netherlands, and the UK, Canada, and the USA using LIS data around the year 2000. They do so on an annual basis and including part-time and part-year earnings, but leave the distribution of employment out from their analysis, and, consequently, they also do not compare directly to hourly wage rates. In addition, they do not compare individuals and households on the basis of an identical ranking, as is done by Gottschalk and Danziger. They find that the Nordic and Continental countries have similar Gini values for earnings and for incomes respectively, while both are higher for Canada and the USA, and that the UK is European on earnings and North American on incomes (p. 58).

Kenworthy (2008b), observes that 'if every household had one employed person, the distribution of earnings among households would be determined solely by the distribution of earnings among employed individuals' (p. 9).[8] He mentions the possibility that households have different numbers of earners, adding that this number is mainly determined by the number of adults in the household. However, he leaves this aside in the analysis and focuses on the dichotomy between 'some earner(s) or none' (p. 9), which is understandable from his point of view that 'disposable income is more relevant to households than their market income' and the consequent focus on redistribution. On an equivalized basis he does find pre-tax pre-transfer household income inequality to be strongly related to the inequality in individual earnings of full-time employed individuals (his Figure 6). The association to the incidence of households with zero earnings (for the head of household) is less, and to marital homogamy, defined as the correlation between spouses'

---

[6] Consequently, their findings may depend on the differential growth by gender of single-person households.

[7] Consecutively considering six different distributions: gross incomes from working-age employees (1) extending to self-employed (2) and to all non-working individuals (3), then shifting to their disposable incomes (4), subsequently broadening to all ages (5), and finally shifting to equivalized incomes (6).

[8] See Larrimore (2013) for a similar observation.

**Table 3.1.** Earnings of employee households, 2007

|  | CZE | HUN | POL | SVK | AUT | DEU |
|---|---|---|---|---|---|---|
| *A. Shares in household earnings (%)* | | | | | | |
| ▪ heads | 67 | 65 | 65 | 59 | 73 | 77 |
| ▪ spouse | 21 | 21 | 23 | 22 | 17 | 18 |
| ▪ other persons | 12 | 13 | 12 | 19 | 10 | 4 |
| *B. Gini of earnings (levels)* | | | | | | |
| ▪ total | 0.32 | 0.37 | 0.37 | 0.31 | 0.34 | 0.33 |
| ▪ heads | 0.28 | 0.35 | 0.37 | 0.26 | 0.32 | 0.32 |
| ▪ spouses | 0.68 | 0.73 | 0.71 | 0.62 | 0.75 | 0.75 |
| ▪ other persons | 0.86 | 0.86 | 0.86 | 0.8 | 0.88 | 0.93 |
| *C. Decomposition of Gini (%)* | | | | | | |
| ▪ head | 44 | 47 | 52 | 33 | 53 | 61 |
| ▪ spouse | 32 | 29 | 30 | 27 | 29 | 31 |
| ▪ other persons | 24 | 24 | 18 | 39 | 19 | 8 |

*Source*: Calculated from Večerník (2010), Tables 5, 6, and 7.

annual earnings, it is still less. The total employment rate and the part-time employment rate appear to play no role.

Večerník (2010), also using LIS data, considers employees only and does so in conjunction with their households. His focus is the effects of transition in four CEE countries, in a comparison with Germany and Austria. He specifically draws other earners than the spouses in a household into the comparison, and effectively distinguishes multiple-earner households from dual-earner ones. He shows that this category of employee can make an important contribution to household earnings, that earnings inequality among this group is very high in all countries, and that the contribution to overall inequality can also be very substantial (Table 3.1). Slovakia combines the highest earnings share (19%) with a lower Gini coefficient than elsewhere, and a major contribution to overall inequality (39%). This contrasts strongly with Germany, where both the income share and the contribution to overall inequality are the lowest (4% and 8%) and the within-group inequality is the highest (0.93). It seems to suggest that the population of other earners may have a very different character in Western Europe than in the East.

Recently, the OECD's *Divided We Stand* (2011, Part II) has admirably summarized much of the literature and made an important step forward.[9] They compare Gini coefficients for individual annual earnings (including self-employed) with those of households averaged over earners in the household, using LIS data.[10] The result is indicated in Figure 3.1 for eight European

---

[9] Unfortunately, the underlying working paper explaining the approach is not available.
[10] They also compare to household earnings inequality after equivalization.

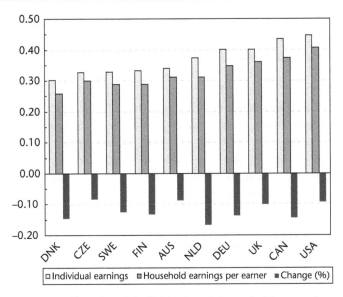

**Figure 3.1.** Gini coefficients of individual and household annual gross labour incomes

*Note*: Years between 2003 and 2005.

*Source*: Derived from OECD (2011, Figure 5.2) (countries reporting gross earnings only), changes added.

countries, Canada, and the USA, which all report gross earnings. On this comparison they find substantial reductions by 8% (Czech Republic) to 17% (Netherlands) in individual earnings inequality as earners join each other in households. Evidently, the effect depends on their averaging of individual earnings within households. Aggregate household earnings inequality would probably be higher than that individual inequality. Note also that individuals are not ranked by their households as was done by Gottschalk and Danziger. Changes in the level of inequality between a first year chosen in the 1980s or 1990s, depending on the country, and 2004, are decomposed with a selective stress on dual earning among households, by male—but not female—earnings inequality, employment rates of both genders, spouses' earnings correlation, and the shift in household structure by size (read the growth of singles). The first is found to be the main disequalizing factor, while rising female employment rates have an equalizing effect.[11] The earnings correlation of spouses as an indicator of assortative mating and the structure of the population of households have only modest effects.

---

[11] Gottschalk and Danziger (2005: 253) find increasing female wage inequality to be more than offset by declining female employment inequality.

In summary we can say that these contributions proceed in different ways. Some include those without work, others do not. Most, but not all, account for the distribution of jobs (and hours) separately from earnings. Some equivalize income throughout, others add this as a separate, final step. Some focus on employees, others include self-employed and/or jobless. A few studies rank individuals consistently with their households. In this chapter we aim to pursue that ranking and see how earnings and employment from the labour market end up among households and contribute to inequality between households. In particular, we will scrutinize how employees combine in households, along the earnings distribution, while we leave out the self-employed and those without work.

## 3.3 Approach, Definitions, and Data

Before continuing we briefly discuss what distributional effects one might expect to occur from the combination of employed individuals and their earnings into households. Taking an ideal, fully symmetrical Bell curve of the distribution of individual (annual) gross unequivalized earnings in the labour market as a starting point, the sorting of individuals over households may work out as follows. If all employed individuals form pairs and no one is left, the outcome depends on the points on the curve from where the individuals combine with each other. If each consecutive household combines two individuals from the opposite tails of the curve, the outcome will be a fully equalized household income distribution: all households receive the same income and the Bell curve shrinks into a vertical line as all households are found at a single level of combined earnings, in the very middle of the curve. This is the maximum possible reduction of individual earnings inequality as a result of household formation. If, by contrast, all individuals match with another person at their own level of earnings, the curve will be linearly lifted up and the level of inequality (as conventionally measured) remains unchanged. Any other combination ends up between these two extremes, or, in other words, inequality will show some decrease. However, this is conditional on the assumption that all earning individuals combine together into households. Obviously, that is not the case in practice, where instead many individuals will remain single and do not match with another earner into a household. Then the outcome depends on the fraction of individuals involved in the matching and on their distributional positions. Now it is possible that the matching actually increases inequality—imagine, for example, that only the best paid match with each other while the rest remain single. Evidently, the curve is not symmetrical either. Consequently, the outcome will depend on the situation and on preceding developments. For example, if historically the mating first concerns those at the top it can at that moment increase the level of inequality, while at a later moment those at lower levels may join the matching and inequality may be diminished.

It is a different question to ask what household labour incomes have contributed to the evolution of income inequality from how the household income distribution compares to that of individual labour earnings, enhancing or mitigating inequality, or, ultimately, shaping each other. For the former question it may be sufficient to know the monetary share of earnings in income, for the latter one needs a direct linking of individuals to their households. For the former a land surveyor's eye may do, measuring with the help of Gini coefficients the heights of inequality on both sides of the gulf between the two distributions without bothering about their possible common origin; for the latter we need a geologist's eye peeling off the 'underground layers' of the distribution to see where the same elements from one side show up at the other side of the gulf. Implicitly this makes household formation, at least partly, endogenous and diminishes its usefulness as an independent determinant that can be invoked as an explanation.[12]

The heights may have grown higher and the gulf wider with the demise of the single breadwinner to the advantage of the dual earners, who get a lot of attention in the literature. However, Večerník's observations on the importance of multiple earners in post-transition countries should make us think twice. Plausibly, these countries had high rates of female employment before transition as part of the Communist approach to (un)employment, implying already high rates of dual and multiple earning. This seems to suggest that the shift from single breadwinners to dual earners may apply particularly to the North and West European countries, where part-time employment grew sharply over recent decades while it remained low and stable in the East. It may also be too easy to think that the number of earners in a household depends on the household's number of adults—certainly a necessary condition but not automatically a sufficient one. Thus, the countries may not all be travelling the same road leading from a single-earner to a dual-earner society, or they might not be doing so in the same direction.

Below, we look first at the importance of households with earnings (Section 3.4). In Section 3.5 we consider how individuals with earnings combine with each other into households across the household income distribution and contribute to income inequality, and how that inequality compares to wage inequality—enhancing it or mitigating? Next (Section 3.6) we consider how

---

[12] Thompson and Smeeding (2012) point to the coping strategy of household size in the USA, while Peichl et al. (2010) make the point that household formation could be partly endogenous, especially in relation to the German tax-benefit system.

this distributes employment opportunities across household types, including the role of part-time jobs. Then (Section 3.7) we look at how the number of household members in employment may be a way of coping with poverty, and at the end we consider how the analysis works out for the five country groups mentioned in the Introduction to this volume. Naturally, the relevance of this is to see whether the answers differ between countries and can contribute to understanding international differences in inequality. It is important to stress that we do not seek an explanation of labour-market inequality in itself. We take it as a given and consider here its relation to household incomes. Neither do we seek to explain household formation and income inequality in their own right, such as the growth in single-person households or dual earning. Again we take that as a given. Thus the fundamental aim of this chapter it to throw up questions for future research.

In this descriptive analysis we restrict ourselves for data reasons to Europe. We aim to complement the GINI country chapters (Nolan et al., 2013) and the underlying GINI country reports (gini-research.org) with a study of the internationally comparative data from the European Union's *Statistics on Income and Living Conditions* (EU-SILC) for a comprehensive and recent cross-country comparison focused on earnings, employment, and income. We focus exclusively on employees and their earnings because the labour market is our prime interest, and other market-income data seem also less reliable, less comparable between countries (Večerník, 2010), and negative values complicate their analysis. We sample households with at least one employee aged less than 65 years, and exclude student households. All remains at the level of gross market incomes, and we leave out transfers, taxation, and equivalization, considered as issues subject to other factors and to be addressed separately, with the exception of what we will say about poverty in Section 3.7. In addition, household incomes are defined on an annual basis, and for consistency the household earnings and individual earnings in the labour market shall both be considered on an annual basis. This annualization brings into play the hours worked over the year. These are increasingly affected by part-time employment and, naturally, they are subject also to the part-year employment of the increasing numbers who are in temporary employment, and of those who enter or leave the labour market, e.g. from school or for retirement. In addition, it should be noted that we focus on households whose most important gross income is from labour earnings. This restriction excludes very low household earnings and higher incomes from self-employment or other sources, and effectively reduces inequality.[13] For two reasons we primarily

---

[13] This restriction diminishes the number of households by 18%, the amount of earnings by 4%, and the S10:S1 ratio by 43%, and slightly increases the Top-10% earnings share (cross-country average derived from SILC (2011)).

use as a measure for inequality the share of the top decile, Top-10% (which can be interpreted as the ratio between the means of the tenth decile and the overall means of the distribution), together with the ratio between the same means and the means of the bottom decile: the shares ratio S10:S1 (it can be interpreted also as the ratio between Top-10% and the Bottom-10% shares). The first reason is that generalized measures of inequality, which depend on a linear ranking by the concept being measured, cannot be used here when comparing the distribution of individual earnings ranked according to a different criterion, in this case corresponding household earnings. Second, the use of percentile ratios in relation to households does not allow a further analysis directed at household characteristics, as it is more arbitrary which characteristics happen to occur at a precise percentile rather than averaged over a decile. In addition, the shares ratio incorporates the 'depth' of the tail deciles, which the traditional P90:P10 ratio ignores. The use of these tail deciles is often thought to be too sensitive to outliers, measurement error, and negative values to be of much use. However, the recent literature on top income shares underlines their systemic nature. The same can be said for labour incomes at the bottom, which are always positive.

We conclude with a few caveats about the data found in SILC. First, Ireland is not available in the latest dataset, and we ignore Cyprus and Malta for consistency with the GINI project. Annual gross incomes and labour incomes are available for the year preceding the survey. Unfortunately, corresponding hours, needed for determining hourly earnings and household employment effects, are not. Therefore we have taken recourse to the (weekly) hours of the same respondents observed at the time of the survey, on the apparent—and mostly plausible—assumption that people will not have changed working hours in the meantime. This ignores people in work in the previous year but no longer during the survey. SILC's observation of hours seems also biased against small hours, implying some underestimation of inequality especially in countries with high part-time employment.[14] To account for part-year employment during the preceding year—people finding a job in the course of the year and still in work during the survey—we multiplied these hours by the number of months that respondents have worked during the preceding year.

---

[14] We use the gross earnings (with negligible omissions) and hours variables for selecting earners in spite of many missing values (10.5%) for self-reported employees in our sample from the dataset, as an extensive analysis has shown that only very few (0.8%) concern people who are not unemployed, in education, in (early) retirement, or otherwise inactive. This may lead to a slight underestimation of the presence of employees and hours in the lower deciles.

## 3.4 The Importance of Labour Earnings in the Income Distribution

We now consider the importance of earnings in household incomes. In national account statistics the major share of incomes is received by labour, the well-known wage share (Atkinson, 2009; OECD, 2012a, Chapter 3). This is no different for household income statistics, though they may differ in important respects (Glyn, 2009). Figure 3.2 indicates the importance of labour households for the European countries for the most recent year available. Other households comprise those with main incomes from other sources such as self-employment, own business, and wealth, or from social transfers, or a pension, which can be either primary or secondary income. Some of these other households may in fact have a labour income, but this cannot be their most important income by definition and will usually be small.

The number of labour households relative to the total number of households in a country varies between the remarkably low levels of 53% and 60% in Greece and Italy and highs of 78% and 79% in Luxembourg and Estonia and 83% in Sweden. Labour households are a majority of households in all

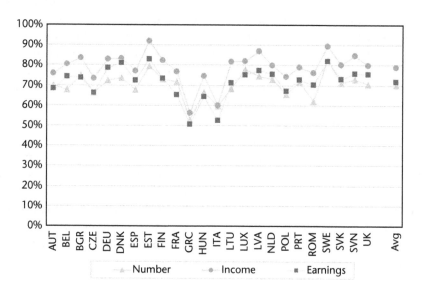

**Figure 3.2.** Labour households: number, income, and annual earnings as a percentage of all working-age households, by country, 2010

*Notes:* Incomes and earnings are gross, before tax. Households have at least one adult aged below 65, and labour households have at least one employee and receive their most important income from labour. The lines here and in Figure 3.4 help to guide the eye of the reader and have no further significance. 'Avg' is unweighted cross-country average.

*Source:* Calculated for the year 2010 from EU-SILC 2011.

countries, 70% on average. Evidently, the country variation corresponds with a complementary variation in the importance of incomes from other sources. Second, the share of labour households' total income—including less important incomes from other sources in addition to earnings—in the income of all households is even larger, again with very low levels for Greece and Italy (56–60%), up to highs of 89–92% for Sweden and Estonia. Third, the chart relays the labour earnings only of these households as a percentage of the total income of all households. Obviously, this earnings share is lower but it still makes up the majority of incomes in all countries, including Greece and Italy with a share just over 50%. The Czech, French, and Polish shares are also relatively low. In Denmark, Estonia, Germany, Latvia, Slovenia, and Sweden, however, main earnings make up more than 75% of aggregate household income. Clearly, the incomes that households draw from the labour market are of overarching importance for a country's total market income in most cases. The largely parallel cross-country variations in the levels seem to imply that the numbers in work drive the importance of the earnings, which in turn are highly correlated with the broader incomes. This establishes the value of looking at wages and earnings in relation to incomes and income inequality.

In addition to this aggregate picture, it is important to realize that labour households are unequally distributed over income deciles from other households (Figure 3.3). The higher up the income distribution the larger is their fraction among households in the income decile. Two notable exceptions are Italy and Greece, where the labour share remains below 70% from the 4th to the 10th decile.[15] Though the pack looks dense, there are notable country differences. In roughly half the number of countries the labour household fraction continues to rise until the very top; in the other half, however, it declines from the ninth to the tenth decile, notably in Austria, Bulgaria, Spain, France, Greece, Italy, Luxembourg, Netherlands, Romania, and the UK. Thus the labour share in the top decile varies between 51% and 55% in Italy and Greece on the one hand and between 95% and 100% in Sweden, Latvia, and Estonia on the other. It implies that other income sources than earnings are more important at the top in some countries than elsewhere. The international disparity is also wide at the bottom. In Romania only 3% of households in the bottom decile have a main income from labour, compared to 62% in Luxembourg. The growth of the incidence over the distribution implies that the top decile for all households comprises more than 10%

---

[15] The countries have many self-employed according to Labour Force data (14%, 21%), but so has Romania (18%). However, Greek and Italian self-employed have also relatively high incomes compared to labour (compare OECD (2012), Figure 5.3).

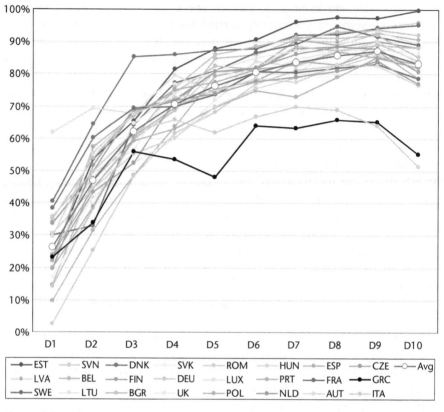

**Figure 3.3.** Labour households: percentage of all households within deciles of total income, by country, 2010

*Note*: See Figure 3.2.

*Source*: Calculated from SILC 2011.

of all labour households (up to 13.5% in Belgium and Romania), with the exception of Italy where it is 9%.

Although it does not necessarily follow from the above, it is no surprise to find in Figure 3.4 that the Gini coefficient of total gross incomes of all households closely resembles that of gross earnings of labour households (correlation coefficient, R2=0.78). Note, however, that these are two distinct distributions, each with its own ranking of households. As another important measure of inequality, the figure also shows the share of the Top-10% in the total income of all households and the role of labour households within this, enabling a direct comparison of the two shares.[16] The top decile shares

[16] Because of data reliability this top is taken over the decile rather than the smaller fractions that are often used, e.g. Top-1%.

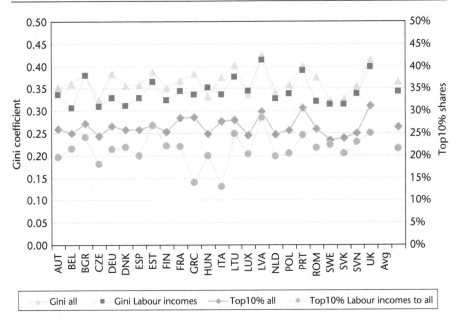

**Figure 3.4.** Gini coefficients and top income shares of all working-age households and labour households, by country, 2010

*Note*: See Figure 3.1.

*Source*: Calculated from SILC 2011.

for all households vary between 23% (Sweden) and 31% (UK); they mimic the variation in the overall Gini coefficients surprisingly well (R2=0.91) (compare Leigh (2009) for a similar observation). For labour households' full incomes (not earnings) there is greater cross-country variation (13% in Italy to 28% in Latvia) and significant differences occur compared to the overall top shares in a number of countries. In most countries, though, top income shares of labour households are over 20% of total income and comprise on average 81% of the overall top shares. The highest levels, of 95–100%, are found in Latvia and Estonia, where virtually all top incomes arise from earnings. This contrasts with much lower labour shares for, again, Italy and Greece (47–49%), which reflect the lower fractions of labour household numbers (Figure 3.3). Nevertheless, we can conclude that on this measure labour households make a massive direct contribution to inequality at the top of the distribution. The share of labour earnings in the overall top-decile share is perfectly correlated to the share of labour household numbers among the top-decile household numbers (R2=0.99). Small deviations, e.g. for Greece and Italy, imply that labour households have a somewhat lower income than other households in this decile. In other words, the role of labour incomes in aggregate top incomes is almost entirely based on their numerical presence at the top of the distribution. Evidently, this does not in itself answer the question of to what extent aggregate income inequality depends on the earnings distribution. OECD (2012b, Figure 5.3) shows with the help of a concentration measure that, on average, earnings account for 79% of the aggregate Gini, varying from around 50% in Italy and Greece to 97% in Estonia. The contributions of self-employment (15%) and capital income (6%) make up for the rest.

## 3.5 The Distribution of Earnings: Households and Individuals

We now turn to (gross) earnings and their inequality over households receiving their main incomes from earnings, and compare them to the individuals who make up the households, distinguishing between the effects of employment and pay levels. First, Figure 3.5 considers the situation from the household perspective, for the cross-country average. The figure ranks households by the cumulative total of annual earnings of the employees among their members, using the means of the ten deciles expressed as a ratio to the level of the bottom decile (D1=1) as an indication of the steepness of the distribution. The top-decile level equals the S10:S1 ratio of top and bottom shares. The graph compares the inequality of these aggregate household annual earnings with that of the aggregate annual hours worked in the same households and the inequality of the corresponding average hourly earnings. Aggregate

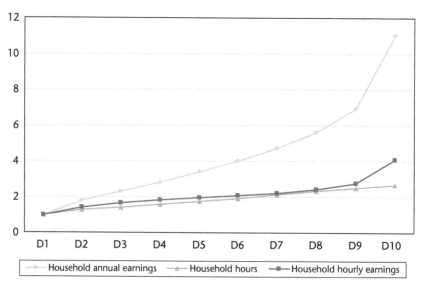

**Figure 3.5.** Ratio of household earnings and hours by decile of household annual earnings, D1=1, 2010

*Source*: Calculated from EU-SILC 2011.

earnings of the top decile exceed those of the bottom decile eleven times. After an almost linear increase up to the ninth decile, the top decile stands out for a sudden further rise. Indicated next, aggregate hours worked show an equal increase, the top-decile household hours being 2.7 times those of the bottom decile: taken together top-decile households work 170% longer hours. Though the rise is much less than for earnings, it is still important to observe that households at the top work more hours and obtain a higher income for that reason too. The two observations are squared with each other by household hourly earnings, the third line in the graph. These increase gradually until they also surge in the tenth decile, up to a level 4.1 times above the bottom. So households move along the distribution by both working more hours and achieving a higher pay level.

Figure 3.6 reports in the same fashion on the average outcomes of the individuals who belong to the households in each decile, ranking them across the deciles in exactly the same way by the total earnings of the households to which they belong. So, now when there is more than one earner in a household the aggregate of their individual earnings is no longer pictured but rather their individual within-household average. In other words, the levels are averaged over the same individuals in the decile and not over the corresponding households as

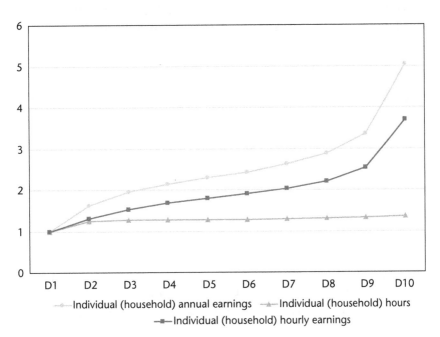

**Figure 3.6.** Ratio of within-household average individual earnings and hours by decile of household annual earnings, D1=1, 2010

*Source*: Calculated from EU-SILC 2011.

was the case above. Individual annual earnings rise five-fold, about half as much as household aggregate earnings. In addition, the average individual hardly works more hours across the distribution, working hours in various deciles including the top decile being only around one-third longer than at the bottom. The ratio of 1.36 at the top is half the above ratio of household aggregate hours. These fewer hours bear the main responsibility for the lower level of individual earnings inequality based on the household ranking. The accumulation of individual earnings in a household doubles earnings inequality among households relative to average individual annual earnings in the household. By contrast, individual hourly earnings are only slightly less unequal than for households, with the top decile at 3.7 times above the bottom. Apparently, households combine individuals with higher pay levels to a modest extent, inciting an only slightly steeper inequality in household hourly earnings of 4.1.

Figure 3.7 adds the principally different individual perspective as viewed from the labour market, ranking individuals solely by their own individual annual earnings, and thus 'unranking' from their households. This chart again lines up annual earnings, annual hours, and resultant hourly earnings for comparison both within the figure and to the other two graphs. The individual annual earnings incorporate the effects of individual annual hours and differ from hourly pay, which is the common focus of labour-market inequality studies. Annual earnings inequality follows much the same path as for households: the S10:S1 ratio of 11 happens to be identical to that of

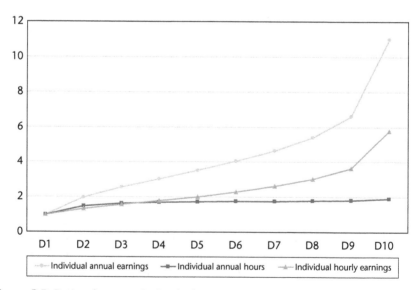

**Figure 3.7.** Ratio of average individual earnings and hours by decile of individual annual earnings, D1=1, 2010

*Source*: Calculated from EU-SILC 2011.

households. Individual hours of the best-earning individuals work are up to 90% longer than for the lowest-earning, compared to 36% when ranked according to their households and 170% for households. Those working few hours will be at the bottom of the individual annual earnings distribution, but apparently many join households that are higher up the distribution. The fact that individual hours inequality exceeds that of individuals ranked by their households implies also that the longest-working individuals do not always join each other in households. The resulting hourly-earnings inequality reaches a much higher level (5.8) than both households (4.1) and individuals ranked by their households (3.7). Apparently, the employees who join each other in households originate from different parts of the individual earnings distribution and taken together attain relatively lower individual average hourly earnings levels in their households.

The comparison of the three presentations tells us that households do mitigate labour-market hourly earnings inequality while at the same time the very combination of employees in households widens it on an annual basis. Taken together the two seem to largely cancel out. These cross-country stylized facts may picture the broad story, but they also hide important country divergences. Table 3.2 summarizes these, focusing on inequality and using the top-to-bottom-decile ratio (S10:S1), which conveniently measures the width of the distribution and for the average is identical to the right-hand ends of the lines in the three figures. Columns 1 to 6 relay the household perspective of Figures 3.5 and 3.6, while Columns 7 to 9 add the pure individual perspective of Figure 3.7.

The household annual earnings inequality ratio ranges from around 8 in Belgium, the Czech Republic, Denmark, Romania, and Slovakia, to an extraordinary 20 in Latvia, followed by 16 in the UK and 14 in Bulgaria and Lithuania. The combination of employees in households leads to a level of household earnings inequality that is 120% higher than for the corresponding individuals (Columns 1 and 2), on average. This gap varies from 100% or less in Finland, France, Greece, and Luxembourg to almost 200% in Slovakia, followed by several CEE countries (Romania, Bulgaria, Hungary, and Slovenia) found between 130% and 150%. The gap seems largely but not fully filled (100% on average) by the hours gap between households and corresponding individuals (Columns 3 and 4). Household working hours inequality moves within a narrow band: from a Polish and Portuguese minimum of 2.1 to a 3.5 maximum in the UK, closely followed by Belgium, Finland, and France at 3.3. However, the relative variation in the gap between households and individuals is substantial, from around 74% in Estonia to 172%, again in Slovakia. Resultant hourly earnings inequalities (Columns 5 and 6) differ remarkably little with a gap of no more than a good 10%, on average. The gap is small in many countries and ranges up to almost 20% for Estonia and

**Table 3.2.** Inequality of household and individual earnings and hours, top–bottom ratios (S10:S1), 2010

| | A. Ranked by households annual earnings | | | | | | B. Ranked by individual annual earnings | | |
| | 1. Annual earnings | | 2. Annual hours | | 3. Hourly earnings | | Annual earnings | Annual hours | Hourly earnings |
| | Households | Individuals | Households | Individuals | Households | Individuals | | | |
| | 1 | 2 | 3 | 4 | 5 | 6 | 7 | 8 | 9 |
|---|---|---|---|---|---|---|---|---|---|
| AUT | 10.3 | 4.6 | 3.1 | 1.5 | 3.4 | 3.1 | 13.7 | 2.1 | 6.5 |
| BEL | 8.0 | 3.7 | 3.3 | 1.6 | 2.4 | 2.3 | 7.6 | 2.4 | 3.1 |
| BGR | 14.3 | 5.8 | 2.7 | 1.2 | 5.2 | 4.8 | 11.2 | 1.6 | 7.2 |
| CZE | 7.9 | 3.5 | 2.6 | 1.2 | 3.0 | 2.9 | 7.7 | 1.7 | 4.4 |
| DEU | 11.1 | 5.2 | 2.7 | 1.4 | 4.1 | 3.8 | 19.1 | 2.6 | 7.4 |
| DNK | 8.2 | 3.9 | 2.8 | 1.4 | 3.0 | 2.7 | 6.5 | 1.6 | 4.0 |
| ESP | 10.0 | 4.7 | 2.5 | 1.4 | 4.0 | 3.5 | 8.6 | 1.8 | 4.7 |
| EST | 11.8 | 5.7 | 2.2 | 1.3 | 5.3 | 4.4 | 11.2 | 2.0 | 5.7 |
| FIN | 9.3 | 4.7 | 3.3 | 1.8 | 2.8 | 2.6 | 7.9 | 2.4 | 3.3 |
| FRA | 11.9 | 6.0 | 3.3 | 1.8 | 3.6 | 3.3 | 11.9 | 2.2 | 5.3 |
| GRC | 9.9 | 5.3 | 2.4 | 1.4 | 4.2 | 3.7 | 8.1 | 1.8 | 4.4 |
| HUN | 11.4 | 4.9 | 2.7 | 1.4 | 4.2 | 3.6 | 9.4 | 1.9 | 5.0 |
| ITA | 10.9 | 5.3 | 2.5 | 1.3 | 4.3 | 4.1 | 9.9 | 1.7 | 6.0 |
| LTU | 14.4 | 6.4 | 2.4 | 1.2 | 6.0 | 5.5 | 15.5 | 1.4 | 10.9 |
| LUX | 10.7 | 5.4 | 2.3 | 1.2 | 4.7 | 4.4 | 12.8 | 2.3 | 5.6 |
| LVA | 20.5 | 9.0 | 3.1 | 1.6 | 6.7 | 5.8 | 18.4 | 2.1 | 8.8 |
| NLD | 11.4 | 5.2 | 2.8 | 1.4 | 4.1 | 3.6 | 12.2 | 2.2 | 5.6 |
| POL | 10.1 | 4.6 | 2.1 | 1.2 | 4.7 | 4.0 | 10.6 | 1.7 | 6.3 |
| PRT | 11.8 | 5.6 | 2.1 | 1.1 | 5.5 | 5.0 | 12.3 | 1.7 | 7.3 |
| ROM | 7.7 | 3.1 | 2.4 | 1.0 | 3.2 | 3.1 | 5.1 | 1.1 | 4.8 |
| SVK | 7.9 | 2.7 | 2.9 | 1.1 | 2.7 | 2.5 | 6.6 | 1.5 | 4.4 |
| SVN | 9.6 | 4.0 | 2.4 | 1.2 | 3.9 | 3.4 | 8.5 | 1.6 | 5.4 |
| SWE | 9.0 | 4.5 | 2.7 | 1.4 | 3.4 | 3.2 | 10.8 | 1.6 | 6.6 |
| UK | 16.1 | 7.2 | 3.5 | 1.6 | 4.6 | 4.4 | 18.0 | 2.7 | 6.7 |
| Avg | 11.0 | 5.0 | 2.7 | 1.4 | 4.1 | 3.7 | 11.0 | 1.9 | 5.8 |

Source: Calculated from EU-SILC 2011

Poland. It seems to imply that though there may be some within-household correlation (homogamy) in hourly earnings capacity, this may be modest and add little to the international differences.

The pure individual rankings attain substantially higher levels of inequality for hourly earnings (Column 9 versus 6) for all countries. For hours inequality (Column 8 versus 4), in contrast, differences are smaller, and the larger ones (Germany, Luxembourg, and UK) seem to point to the role of low-earning jobs that lengthen the individual distribution at the bottom but spread out more evenly over the household distribution. Annual earnings inequalities are always much larger for unranked individuals than household-ranked individuals (Columns 7 and 2) pointing to important equalizing effects of households combining high- and low-earning individuals. However, the latter still make a substantial contribution through joint labour supply, which brings the household annual earnings inequality (Column 1) close to the individual starting point (Column 7). We conclude that labour-market inequality in and of itself is a very important determinant of household earnings inequality. To illustrate, individuals in the top decile of individual earnings in Lithuania earn 11 times more hourly than those in the bottom decile, have 41% longer working hours, and thus earn 15 times more annually. The grouping into households combines individual workers who on average earn 5.5 times more and work 17% longer hours than in the bottom households, bring about more than a halving of inequality. However, the combination of workers makes these households work 142% longer hours than at the bottom and, consequently, increases their aggregate earnings to 14 times those of the bottom households. The combination of employees in households makes an important contribution in all countries. The annual earnings gap between households and individuals (Columns 1 and 2) depends largely on the hours gap between these two categories (R2=0.95) and hardly at all on the hourly earnings gap (–0.10). We consider this in more detail in terms of household earner demographics in the next section, and take the labour-market inequality as given, as was mentioned before.

## 3.6 Households, Individuals, and the Distribution of Employment

We now turn to the allocation of employees over households, and scrutinize what can be called the household earner demographics. How does joint labour supply evolve over the earnings distribution of households? Or, its flip side, how is employment distributed over households along the household earnings distribution? We distinguish households by their number of working-age earners only, irrespective of intra-household relationships. So the presence of two earners or more in a household is not necessarily predicated upon their partnership or marriage but may concern also unrelated adults or a parent and a child. More-person households comprise at least two earners, and within this category we distinguish between dual-earner households, and multiple-earner households with three or more employees. Together with single earners that gives us three types of households.

Figure 3.8a pictures the presence of these types over the household earnings distribution for the country average. Both dual earners and multiple earners are very small categories at the bottom of the distribution. The importance of dual earners grows rapidly over the next deciles and then levels off from the seventh decile at a good 60%; the importance of multiple-earners grows more gradually first but then accelerates towards the top decile, where they make up 30% of all households. By contrast, single-earner households comprise almost 90% of households in the bottom decile, but their share declines continuously, down to 11% at the top. In the aggregate, dual earners and single earners each comprise 44% of all households, while multiple earners have 12%. Clearly, multiple-earner households are more concentrated within the distribution than the other two groups. Figure 3.8b pictures how individual employees range over the household earnings distribution by the three types of households. Because of the much larger role of single earners at the bottom of the distribution, many fewer employees are found there. While 10% of all households are in that decile by definition, only 4.5% of all employees are. Evidently, the distribution of employees is tilted as dual-earner and multiple-earner households have more earners. Consequently, the top decile comprises 15.7% of all employees—three times as much as the bottom decile. A majority of 55% of top-decile employees are found in dual-earner households, while members of multiple-earner households make up 40%, and only 5% are single earners. Thus, multiple earners make up 12% of all households, but they comprise 20% of all employees. Dual and single earners comprise 53% and 26% of employees respectively. Figure 3.8c sharpens the picture by looking at hours worked. Hours shares range from 5.4% at the bottom to 14.5% at the top, which corresponds with the 2:7 ratio of Figure 3.5. The profile has a slightly lower slope than for employees; low-paid individuals may work relatively shorter hours but this seems less obvious for the average individual in households at the bottom of the household distribution, plausibly because of the predominant role of single earners. Clearly, households get to the top of the distribution by combining the hours of their members.

At the same time, the hours picture somewhat mitigates the distribution over household types as those in multiple-earner households work less than average. Their share in total hours is 18%, still 1.5 times their 12% share among households, but less than their 20% share among employees. The dual-earner share of 51% is also slightly below that among employees, while

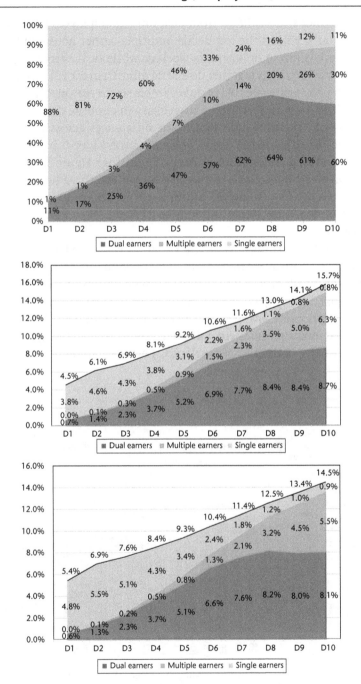

**Figure 3.8.** Households, employees, and hours worked by type of household and household annual earnings deciles, unweighted country average, 2010

(**a.**) Household shares within deciles (**b.**) Employee shares across deciles (**c.**) Shares of hours worked across deciles

*Source*: Calculated from EU-SILC 2011.

71

the single-earner share is lifted from 26% among employees to 30% among hours. Similarly, within the top-decile, multiple-earner households provide also slightly less (38%) of all hours worked, while dual earners (56%), and single earners (6%) taken together do a little more than 60%. Viewed over the three graphs, the aggregate role of dual earners seems reasonably comparable while single earners and multiple earners vary in opposite directions.

These average pictures hide significant differences across the countries, though they do all share the trends of single earners (declining over the distribution), and dual and multiple earners (increasing). Figure 3.9 portrays the distribution of all households with earners over the three household types across the twenty-five countries. Multiple-earner shares vary substantially, from only 4% to 6% in Greece and Italy to 24% to 27% in Bulgaria, Slovakia, and Slovenia.

Within the top earnings decile the variation is even wider. Single-earner shares range from 5% or less in several countries (Romania, Denmark, Slovakia, Slovenia, and Sweden) to a uniquely high share of 29% in Greece, followed by 16% to 18% in Hungary, the UK, and Portugal. Dual-earner shares extend from an exceptionally low 30% in Slovakia to more than 70% in Denmark, Finland, Luxembourg, and Spain, followed by 60% to 70% in Belgium, Estonia, France, Germany, Italy, the Netherlands, Portugal, Romania, and Sweden.

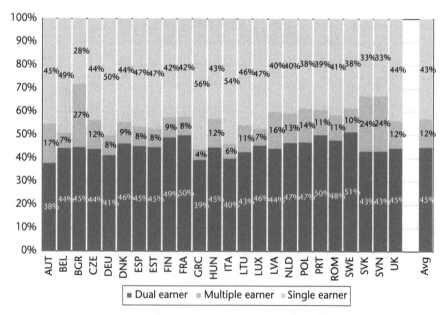

**Figure 3.9.** Shares of household types among households with earnings, by country, 2010

*Source*: Calculated from EU-SILC 20011.

Multiple-earner household shares range from 9% to 12% in Lithuania and Greece to notable quasi-majorities of 49% in Bulgaria and Slovenia and a clear high of 67% in Slovakia. Across the twenty-five countries the multiple-earner shares at the top correlate strongly (0.84) with the annual-hours gap between households and individuals that was found above to be the main driver of the household earnings profile (Table 3.2). It is a clear demonstration of the relevance of household earner demography for the comparative inequality of household employment and subsequent earnings.

The corresponding picture for hours worked (not shown) is similar. The top-decile share in total hours varies around the 14.5% average within a relatively narrow band (13% in Poland and Portugal to 16% in Slovakia). As above, the countries' shares of dual earners stretch over a very wide range, and multiple-earner shares stretch from 18% (Greece) to 77% (Slovakia). Multiple-earner households are always overrepresented at the top and single earners underrepresented; for dual earners this differs between the countries depending on the share of multiple earners. Dual earners are particularly underrepresented at the top in Slovakia, but also in Bulgaria, where multiple-earner shares are very high. A cross-country comparison finds that the shares of these two categories in the top decile are almost complementary ($R2=-0.78$) while their joint complement, the single-earner share, varies rather little internationally. This goes some way towards explaining why before we found the hours gap to be rather similar across the countries in spite of the largely differing shares of multiple earners.

### 3.6.1 Part-Time Working Hours

The structure of working hours is an important dimension of household employment and joint labour supply. Part-time employment has a significant presence nowadays and may bear on the earner demographics, directly for the hours count and perhaps also indirectly as shorter working hours may facilitate the joint supply itself. It has also evolved strongly in recent decades in many countries and shows substantial differences between countries. Figure 3.10 explores the part-time dimension, enriching Figure 3.8 with the distinction between full-time and part-time employment—uniformly defined around a boundary of 35 hours per week. Part-time is a household characteristic if at least one household member works part-time; evidently for single earners this means that they are working part-time themselves while among dual and multiple earners one or more or even all may work part-time.

The most striking feature of the figure seems to be that part-time employment is important across the earnings distribution up to the very top, where still 16% of all households have a part-time working member and 8% of all

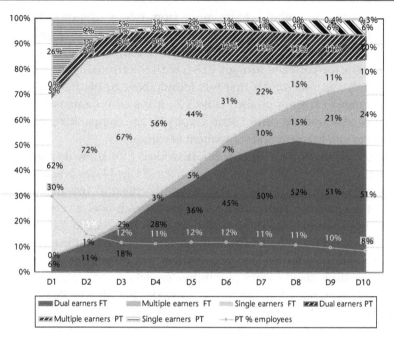

**Figure 3.10.** Full-time and part-time shares of household types within household annual earnings deciles, unweighted country average, 2010
*Source*: Calculated from EU-SILC 2010.

employees work part-time. This is largely due to their importance among dual earners, who comprise 59% of all part-time employees. So although there is some concentration of part-time employees at the bottom of the distribution, it is not excessive and applies to single earners only. Moving up the earnings distribution, part-time employees shift from single-earner first to dual-earner and then to multiple-earner households. In the top decile one-fifth (6% out of 30%) of multiple-earner households have at least one part-time employee, more than dual-earners (16%) and single-earners (3%). Some three-quarters of part-time workers are found in more-earner households, suggesting that a higher level of part-time employment may go together with a greater importance of more-earner households, especially higher up the income distribution.

One tenet of wage inequality analysis is that part-time working individuals show a concentration on low pay and often suffer a pay penalty (see, e.g., GINI country report for the Netherlands); thus, in the wake of part-time employment low-paid employees may be spread widely over the income distribution. Such a spread may help to solve the puzzle (Kenworthy, 2008b, Figure 6, 3rd Panel) that (household) income inequality hardly relates to the incidence of part-time employment in spite of its low pay.

We find strong country differences, ranging from a small 2–3% part-time incidence among top-decile households in Bulgaria, Hungary, Portugal, Romania, and Slovakia, to a 30–40% incidence in Belgium, Germany, Luxembourg, and the UK and a unique 65% in the Netherlands. Countries of the Southeast generally have a much lower incidence (6%) than the Northwest (30%).[17] Leaving the bottom decile aside, the part-time profile for households over the distribution is slowly declining in the East and often slightly increasing towards the top in the countries of Western and Northern Europe. This geographical part-time divide is especially large among multiple-earner households and runs all the way up to the top decile. Unsurprisingly, the cross-country correlation between the multiple-earner shares in the top decile and the individual-household hours gap mentioned above concerns primarily full-time working. Thus the two aspects, household type and working hours, reinforce each other's effects on the international differences in household employment inequality.

## 3.7 Is the Number of Household Earners a Coping Strategy?

By definition, single-earner households have one earner and dual-earner households have two. The limit to the number of multiple earners in a household is its number of relevant adults. On average these households appear to have 3.24 earners with very little international variation (3.15 to 3.36). In the first to the ninth decile household earnings can vary very little across the three household types as they are all bound by the same decile cut-off points. This implies that in the case of more earners their average individual earnings must lag behind those of single earners in the same decile. However, this cannot be said a priori for the top decile as this has no upper bound. Nevertheless, the aggregate earnings of different types of household appear to deviate rather little from each other in this decile too. As a result, average individual earnings of multiple earners equal less than 28% of the top-decile single earners on average (varying from around 20% for the UK, Slovakia, and Bulgaria, to 36% in Portugal and 41% in Lithuania; see Figure 3.11). For dual earners the average fraction is around 47% (from 35% in Denmark and Slovakia to around 60% in Lithuania and Latvia). Apparently, the few single earners among the top-decile households are very well paid in comparison and will largely overlap with the top of the individual earnings distribution. In contrast, more-earner households get to the top of the earnings distribution primarily by combining earners from lower down the individual

---

[17] The main exception is Finland, which, apart from the first decile, has a part-time presence comparable to the Southeast and above-average dual earning with mainly two full-time jobs.

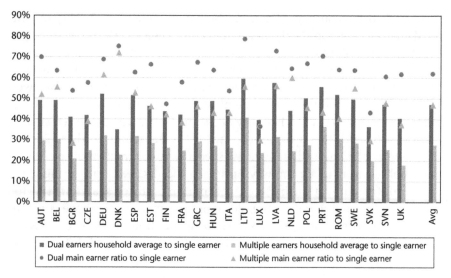

**Figure 3.11.** Average and main earnings in dual and multiple-earner households as a fraction of single earners, top decile of household annual earnings, by country, 2010
*Source*: Calculated from EU-SILC 2010.

earnings distribution. This is underlined by the relative earnings of the *main* earner in dual- and multiple-earner households which are also well below the single-earners level—at 36% (Luxembourg) to 79% (Lithuania) for dual main earners, and 29% (Bulgaria) to 72% (Denmark) for multiple main earners; see Figure 3.11.

So, those employees of more-earner households can indeed originate from deep down the individual earnings distribution. Naturally, when the main earner fraction is relatively high the other employees in the household will come from even further down the earnings distribution either because of a low wage rate or low hours of work. In countries with massive multiple earning this implies a significant transformation from the individual earnings distribution to the household earnings distribution. Note that within-household earnings may still be correlated but clearly the higher levels reached by single earners indicate that the earnings level as such is not the driving force of the presence of a correlated second income.

This raises the question of whether dual and multiple earning may be a coping strategy of household formation aimed at making ends meet and perhaps also escaping from (in-work) poverty. Coping effects of household formation—not necessarily of joint earnings—are suggested by, for example, Haider and McGarry (2006), and by Thompson and Smeeding (2012) in relation to the Great Recession. The European comparative literature on in-work poverty (e.g. Crettaz, 2011; Lohmann, 2008), as far as it pays attention to the role of household joint labour supply, seems to overlook the role of multiple earning.[18] Such coping would make the number of earners and the role of household types in the earnings distribution at least partially endogenous to the national labour market. Note that our definition focuses on earnings as the main source of income and excludes other incomes, such as from pensions. It is not possible to consider the issue here in detail. Nevertheless, the incidence of (relative) poverty across household types may throw some light on this, adopting the common definition of net equivalized household income below 60% of the median[19] (Figure 3.12). In all countries single-earner households have the highest poverty rates; they vary around an 18% average, ranging from Belgian and Finnish lows (10%) to Latvian and Bulgarian highs (26–28%). However, the incidence of poverty is three to six times lower among dual-earner (5%)

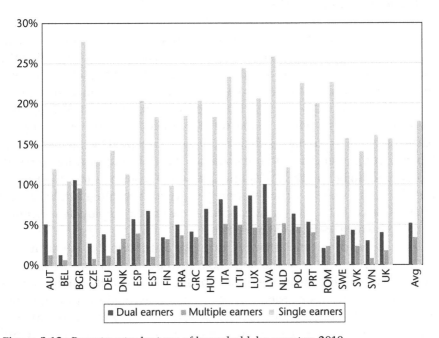

**Figure 3.12.** Poverty rates by type of household, by country, 2010

*Note*: Relative poverty defined as below 60% of median household disposable equivalized income.

*Source*: Calculated from EU-SILC 2010.

[18] Indeed, from the use of European Community Household Panel data (the 1994–2001 predecessor of the SILC data used here) this is understandable as ECHP covered the old EU-15, where the role of multiple-earner households is rather limited (Figure 3.9).

[19] Note that higher household incomes due to more earners may lift the poverty threshold, but only to the extent that the fraction of additional earnings exceeds the fraction of an additional adult added to the equivalization factor.

and multiple-earner (3%) households, and each hovers within a relatively narrow band internationally: 1% to 11% for dual earners and 1% to 10% for multiple earners. Clearly, dual and multiple earning have a great effect on lowering household poverty. In all countries except Denmark and the Netherlands, poverty among multiple earners is lower than among dual earners, quite clearly so in all Eastern European countries, where the third earner often also works full-time. The poverty rate among single earners may give a good indication of the difficulty of escaping poverty with the help of labour-market activity.[20] Evidently, the frequency of multiple earning among working-age households makes an important contribution to the poverty rate. It seems worthwhile to pursue this avenue in future research.

## 3.8 Concluding Remarks

Annual earnings in the labour market are by far the most important contributor to household market incomes. In a cross-country perspective the inequality of these earnings also drives the inequality of household incomes to a large extent (and also for income after transfers, taxation, and equalization, not discussed here). This labour effect concerns the inequality over the distribution as a whole, as measured by the Gini coefficient. It regards particularly the top of the distribution, broadly measured by the share of the top decile of households, because households with labour earnings are over-represented higher up the distribution. In several countries (e.g. the Baltics) the top income share is virtually entirely made up of earnings, while in a few others (Greece, Italy) there is an important role for self-employment incomes at the top, which we have left aside here.

From the starting point that the earnings distribution of labour households is a prime driver of the household income distribution, we have set out to consider how income generated by individuals in the labour market links to that earnings distribution. How does household earnings inequality relate to labour-market inequality? Does the former mitigate or enhance the effects of the latter? The main answer is: households do in fact magnify labour-market inequality, substantially.

We considered this first for households and the corresponding individuals, which means that we looked at the individuals ranked by the total earnings of their households. We find, roughly speaking, that among households inequality is slightly more than twice as large as among their individual members. At the top of the earnings distribution households simply work more

---

[20] Naturally, a country's aggregate poverty rate incorporates the effects of dual and multiple earning.

paid hours. Interestingly, the effect is rather similar across the twenty-five European countries with only a few exceptions. So, household labour does make an important contribution to inequality within all countries. However, because of the roughly comparable size of those contributions, they add relatively little in a cross-country perspective. As a result, between countries the initial individual labour-market earnings inequality is decisive. Its cross-country differences are substantial and these are subsequently amplified by the household contributions. The household contributions rest on two different effects: the combination of labour supply by its members, which adds simply more (annual) earnings to the household, and the correlation of (hourly) pay between those members, which brings higher, or lower, earnings jointly to the household. Both effects are found to contribute positively to household inequality. However, the combination effect is always much larger (+100% on average) than the correlation effect (+10%). The former is largely responsible for the doubling of inequality and also shows more variation (66% to 172%) between countries than the correlation effect (5% to 19%). The two effects happen to compensate each other somewhat over the countries.

Secondly, we considered this in relation to labour-market outcomes of individuals on their own, ignoring their correspondence with households. Viewed on their own, individuals appear to have much more unequal outcomes for annual earnings than when they are related to their households. This is due to the high inequality of individual annual hours worked in the first place. This is largely compensated for by households when they combine individuals with different hours—and restricted to countries where there is a high incidence of part-time employment. For hourly earnings the role is less but still considerable. Viewed in this perspective, households do largely mirror existing (hourly) wage inequality but at the same time they significantly diminish the inequality of annual individual labour market outcomes through their combination effect on hours worked.

In the framework of this book it is interesting to briefly consider how the cross-country patterns relate to the country groupings mentioned in the Introduction to this volume.[21] Though we cover twenty-five countries in detail, the number of observations remains limited in view of the possible variation, even if we disregard within-grouping variation. Though there is a spread between the four groupings, there are hardly any cases where they are all at distinct levels, although regularly, but certainly not always, the North and the East are found at the opposite ends of the range (see Appendix Table 3.A). Most of the time at least two of the four groupings show highly comparable levels, such as for the inequality of household annual earnings (Continental and

[21] We discuss four groupings and exclude the English-speaking group, which comprises the UK only as Ireland is lacking from our data; however, UK results are shown for the sake of completeness.

South), inequality of unranked individual annual earnings (North and South), and poverty among households with earnings (South and East for single earners). Also, the outcomes do not seem to rest on clear distinctions in underlying variables such as hours or hourly pay. Interestingly, the general Gini measure of inequality and also the Top-10% share show little international variation, while by contrast the overall poverty rate does. It is highly interesting to see, however, the large effect that multiple earnings has on the household's poverty. The size of the effect seems similar between East and South but the larger incidence of multiple earnings in the former enhances the aggregate effect.

The findings raise a number of interesting questions for further research. First and foremost, it would be helpful to compare to earlier years. Unfortunately, the European Community Household Panel offers this possibility for a specific subset of countries only (mainly the Northwest, as just presented). The large combination effects certainly put on the table the role of household earner demographics as a contributor to earnings and income inequality in all countries, and underline the importance of accounting for the distribution of employment as a generator of earnings that may be combined in households, in different ways across countries. Improving the joint consideration of working hours and household earner demographics seems desirable. It is important to consider the effects of part-time employment in relation to dual earning, but also a possible structural decline of multiple earning which may be closely related to the growth of the role of earnings in single-person households. This might depend on country circumstances and the possibilities offered by employment to escape from poverty. The role of massive multiple earning in CEE countries as a mechanism of household formation potentially aimed at coping with poor labour-market outcomes contrasts with the possible mitigation of inequality by the lack of such households and the high incidence of part-time employment among them and dual earners in other countries.

In addition, it seems commendable also to analyse the relationship in the opposite direction and look at the effect that the household dimension of labour supply and earnings may have on labour-market inequalities, going beyond the perspective of the individual, which is central to the usual analyses of these inequalities. For example, as a result of household joint labour supply a specific part-time segment of employment (and of the individual earnings distribution) may be growing where a full-time worker 'can no longer go'. Here the rules of competition may differ precisely because of the household environment that can provide new labour supply with the starting point of an existing income situation, which may affect the actual motives of individuals for seeking work in the first place and for the (working hours) extent of that work. Note that workless households were not included in the analysis of this chapter.

Naturally, given the variation found there is also a case for scrutinizing the effects of pay correlation between household members in a comparative framework. The rise in individual educational attainment puts the limelight also on the way this may have affected household labour supply itself, for example by shifting the boundary of household joblessness upwards along the educational distribution if educational homogamy would concentrate labour-market success among a smaller fraction of well-educated households. In that sense household effects may be experienced beyond the distribution of earnings of those actually in work.

## Appendix

**Appendix Table 3.A.** Household and individual inequalities for five country groupings, 2010

| | Continental (a) | Nordic and Netherlands (b) | Mediterranean (c) | CEE (d) | Anglo (UK/IRL only) |
|---|---|---|---|---|---|
| **Gini** | 0.36 | 0.34 | 0.39 | 0.36 | 0.42 |
| Labour households only | 0.33 | 0.32 | 0.36 | 0.35 | 0.40 |
| **Labour Top-10% share** | 21% | 22% | 20% | 22% | 25% |
| **S10:S1 ratios** | | | | | |
| *Household ranking* | | | | | |
| *Annual earnings* | | | | | |
| Households | 10.4 | 9.5 | 10.6 | 11.5 | 16.1 |
| Individuals | 5.0 | 4.6 | 5.2 | 5.0 | 7.2 |
| Gap | 109% | 107% | 130% | 132% | 125% |
| *Annual hours* | | | | | |
| Households | 2.9 | 2.9 | 2.4 | 2.6 | 3.5 |
| Individuals | 1.5 | 1.5 | 1.3 | 1.2 | 1.6 |
| Gap | 95% | 87% | 83% | 110% | 113% |
| *Hourly earnings* | | | | | |
| Households | 3.6 | 3.3 | 4.5 | 4.5 | 4.6 |
| Individuals | 3.4 | 3.0 | 4.0 | 4.0 | 4.4 |
| Gap | 8% | 10% | 11% | 12% | 6% |
| *Individual ranking* | | | | | |
| *Annual earnings* | 13.0 | 9.3 | 9.7 | 10.4 | 18.0 |
| *Annual hours* | 2.3 | 2.0 | 1.8 | 1.6 | 2.7 |
| *Hourly earnings* | 5.6 | 4.9 | 5.6 | 6.3 | 6.7 |
| **Poverty rate** | 9.3% | 7.0% | 13.0% | 11.3% | 9.3% |
| Single earners | 15.1% | 12.2% | 20.5% | 20.4% | 15.1% |
| Dual earners | 4.7% | 3.2% | 6.1% | 5.9% | 4.7% |
| Multiple earners | 2.3% | 3.8% | 3.4% | 3.8% | 2.3% |

(a) AUS/BEL/DEU/FRA/LUX; DNK/FIN/NLD/SWE; (b) UK/IRL; © ESP/GRC/ITA/PRT; (d) Baltics/BGR/CZE/HUN/POL/ROM/SVK/SVN.
*Source*: Calculated from EU-SILC 2011.

# 4

# Wealth Inequality and the Accumulation of Debt

*Virginia Maestri, Francesco Bogliacino, and Wiemer Salverda[1]*

## 4.1 Introduction

This chapter adds to the examination of economic inequality an analysis of the wealth distribution. Chapter 2 pictured a general increase in income inequality over time; the present chapter will show an increase in wealth inequality. The existing evidence on wealth is limited due to the inherent difficulties of analysing wealth distributions and the scarcity of wealth data. We aim to broaden this in several directions by:

- extensively treating the measurement challenges,
- covering as many GINI countries as possible,
- looking at the evolution over time,
- considering both wealth and debt, and distinguishing between types of wealth: financial and non-financial (housing),
- offering an overview of the drivers of cross-country differences in wealth inequality and their trends, and
- analysing the joint distribution of income and wealth across countries.

Thereto we draw on the contributions of GINI project discussion papers, country reports, and the work package 'Drivers of Growing Inequalities', complemented by additional analysis of further available data and the literature.

[1] We are grateful to Abigail McKnight, Frank Cowell, and Brian Nolan for their comments and suggestions, and to Andrea Brandolini, Byung Cheon, Eleni Karagiannaki, Mikko Niemela, and Eva Sierminska for their help with the data for Italy, Korea, the UK, Finland, and Luxembourg respectively.

Chapter 7 includes a more in-depth treatment of housing, which is among other things the major form of wealth for most households and an important contributor to household wellbeing.

The analysis of the distribution of wealth assumes a particular importance, given the increasing weight that wealth has gained over the last decades. Wealth is an important dimension of inequality, but has received much less attention than income or earnings. This is due partly to problems of data availability and quality and partly to the fact that wealth has been regarded as less important than income for the financial wellbeing of households. For example, European poverty policy focuses on disposable income without any reference to wealth. Only a few studies offer a cross-country analysis of the wealth distribution. *Growing Unequal* (OECD, 2008) presents cross-country evidence for eight OECD countries around the year 2000, based on the Luxembourg Wealth Study (LWS). Interestingly, it examines the correlation between net worth and disposable income at the micro level. However, the OECD follow-up study *Divided We Stand* (OECD, 2011) does not deal with wealth inequality. Davies (2009) analyses wealth inequality around the same years for a cross-section of OECD countries based on the LWS and WIDER data. His analysis of the trends is limited to the top-1% wealth share in four countries. He suggests that the role of pensions may explain cross-country differences in wealth inequality. The European Central Bank (2013) recently published very rich evidence on the distribution of wealth and income, based on the new harmonized Eurosystem Household Finance Consumption Survey, which represents an important resource for future research.

In the framework of this book, it is important to say a few things about income and wealth at the outset. Both are related, as the stock of wealth represents the cumulative excess of income over expenditures (savings), augmented by inter-vivos transfers and inheritance. As we will show, the relationship between the two distributions is not straightforward. At the macro level countries with a high level of income inequality do not necessarily have a high level of wealth inequality and vice versa; this raises important questions. At the micro level, whether wealth improves or worsens the economic wellbeing of households depends not only on the wealth distribution itself but on the distribution of assets and debt along the income distribution, another important issue for further scrutiny.

This chapter proceeds as follows. Section 4.2 paves the way with a summary presentation of wealth and income and the growing importance of wealth. Section 4.3 discusses the many measurement issues involved in studying wealth and presents cross-country stylized facts and trends. Section 4.4 discusses drivers of wealth inequality in an internationally comparative perspective. Section 4.5 presents some evidence on the relationship between income and wealth. Section 4.6 concludes.

## 4.2 Wealth, Income, and the Increasing Importance of Wealth

Gross wealth is defined as the sum of financial (savings accounts, bonds, stocks, mutual and investment funds, life insurance, pension assets, etc.) and non-financial (principal residence, investment in real estate, business equity, durable goods, collectibles and valuables) assets. Net wealth is that sum minus liabilities (home-secured debt, vehicle loans, educational loans, hire-purchase debt, etc.). However, there is little consistency in wealth statistics on what is included or excluded (e.g. business equity, valuables and collectibles, private and public pensions), dictated more by data availability than by a lack of consensus on definitions. Wealth and income are very different concepts as they refer to stocks and flows respectively. To add to the complexity, similar terminology may have very different meanings and implications. For example, the difference between gross and net wealth (i.e. debt) is subtler than between gross and net income (direct tax). Households can immediately benefit from their gross housing wealth and fully own it later in their lives, but they can only fully enjoy their net income.

The evolution of wealth holdings relative to income can be represented by wealth–income ratios.[2] According to various sources and depending on the country, the stock of wealth generally amounts to between three and six times the value of disposable income on average (Landais et al., 2011; Brzozowki et al., 2010; Domeij and Floden, 2010; Fuchs-Schündeln et al., 2010; Jappelli and Pistaferri, 2010; Heathcote et al., 2010). Non-financial assets and, in particular, the principal residence represent the largest component of wealth for most households. In Canada, Finland, Germany, Italy, Sweden, and the United Kingdom[3] about 72–87% of total wealth is represented by non-financial assets; financial assets are more important, though, in the USA, where they represent about 35% of total gross wealth (OECD, 2008). Various wealth-to-income ratios are available for a number of countries but need to be treated with some caution because of differences in definitions. Table 4.1 shows the increasing importance of wealth compared to income over the last decades in most of the countries covered; Sweden displays a different pattern and volatile ratios.

---

[2] All ratios of stocks over flows should be used with caution. For the ratio between aggregate wealth on GDP there are two caveats: top wealth shares may be underestimated and the reference population is different between the numerator and the denominator (resident population in one case, versus the economic agents who conduct the economic activity in the national territory in the second). For the median wealth over median income ratio we recall that only the income measure is equivalized.

[3] All data presented in this section from OECD (2008) refer to 1998 for Finland, 1999 for Canada, 2000 for the United Kingdom, 2001 for the USA, 2002 for Germany, Italy, and Sweden.

**Table 4.1.** Wealth–income ratio trends

| | Period | (Net*) wealth–income ratio | Financial–wealth income ratio | Measure of ratios |
|---|---|---|---|---|
| Australia | 1977–2007* | Doubled | Doubled | Total household |
| Canada | 1999–2005* | 5.5 to 7 | <3 to >3 | Total |
| France | 1980–2009* | 3 to 5.5 | n/a | Total private |
| Germany | 1978–2003 | 3 to 3.5 | <1 to >1 | Total |
| Italy | 1965–2009(a)* | Doubled (a) | 1987–2001–2006 | Total |
| | 1987–2006 | 4.5 to 6.5 | 7–9–6 | Median household |
| Netherlands | 1993–2011* | 2.9 to 4.7 | 1.9 to 3.1 | Mean household |
| Sweden | 1978–1992(b) | 3.6 to 2 | 2.3 to 1.2 | Total |
| | 2002–2004(c) | 2.7 to 3 | | |

\* corresponds to net wealth.

*Sources*: GINI country reports for Australia, France, Italy (a), Netherlands; Brzozowki et al. (2010) for Canada; Fuchs-Schündeln et al. (2010) for Germany; Jappelli and Pistaferri (2010) for Italy; Domeij and Floden (2010) for Sweden; (b) and (c) refer to HINK and Statistics Sweden data respectively.

Two main factors may be behind this growth: price developments of financial assets and houses, and macroeconomic dynamics. Regarding the former, many countries have experienced price bubbles in financial and housing markets, which impact significantly on wealth holdings, due to abnormal rates of returns. Inequality can increase when (i) the increased ownership of stocks and houses due to the bubble is skewed, or (ii) the losses are not equally shared across the distribution once the bubble bursts (e.g. because poorer persons enter the market too late due to lack of connections or they are hit more by dropping prices because of lower, less diversified assets). In Italy, for instance, the increase in the wealth–income ratio is explained by the increase in the rate of home ownership and the appreciation of housing and financial stocks. The fall in the financial wealth–income ratio after 2001 is due to falling prices and stock market participation (Jappelli and Pistaferri, 2010). The Swedish wealth and financial-wealth to income ratios track the evolution of real estate prices and the credit expansion following financial liberalization (Domeij and Floden, 2010). After the financial crisis the evidence points to a fall in the wealth-to-income ratios (GINI country reports for Australia and the Netherlands[4]). At the same time, the dynamics of the wealth–income ratio have been affected by the poor macroeconomic performance of many developed countries. As shown by Piketty (2011), the dynamic of this ratio depends on the difference between the rate of return on capital and the

---

[4] In the Netherlands, wealth and financial wealth to income ratios peaked at 5.6 and 3.3 before the recession and then decreased to values still higher than in the early 1990s.

rate of growth of the economy. In periods of growth slowdown, the flow of savings is low and the relative weight of accumulated wealth (transmitted intergenerationally) increases, producing inequality in income (through the return on capital and unequal capital ownership). By the same token, if the rate of return on capital exceeds the rate of growth, the increase in wealth holdings of those who already own assets is larger than the possible acquisitions of assets by those who own very little or no wealth, which also worsens the wealth distribution. In addition, in many countries there has been a shift from public holdings of assets to private holdings. For example, growing pensions and housing both typically represent the largest privately held assets, while large-scale privatizations of publicly held assets in many countries shifted assets from public to private ownership.

However, as wealth has grown since the 1990s, households have simultaneously started to become increasingly indebted. Debt-to-income ratios show the flip side of the increasing importance of wealth. This further discussed in Section 4.3.2.

## 4.3 Mapping Cross-Country Wealth Inequality and Trends: A Measurement Challenge

We now discuss data sources and the properties of wealth data, followed by trends in aggregate wealth, and conclude with a breakdown by assets.

### 4.3.1 Cross-Country Data on Wealth Inequality

Information on earnings and incomes is now commonly collected in household surveys, and over recent decades surveys have become more accurate, and more harmonized internationally (EU-SILC, ECHP). Significant efforts have also been spent on harmonizing secondary data series, such as the Luxembourg Income Study. However, the stock of wealth and its measurement have attracted less interest. There are particular challenges, such as the accurate estimation of market values for certain assets (physical assets, real estate) or of present values for assets providing a future income stream (pensions) or a lump sum (life assurance), or the collection of information on debts in addition to assets. In addition, survey sampling frames need to reflect the fact that the wealth distribution is highly skewed, as we will see, as underrepresentation or even omission of the very wealthy will result in strongly misleading outcomes in terms of wealth holdings and their distribution. As a result, the measurement of wealth inequality is challenged by the limited data availability, in terms of time coverage, cross-country comparability, and asset composition.

Wealth data can be collected through household surveys, tax records, or imputed on the basis of income information. Each country tends to adopt one data source or another, but some countries have information from various sources. Scandinavian countries used to collect tax-based estimates of wealth, but in many countries this is no longer possible when wealth taxes have been abolished. France, the United Kingdom, and the United States used to compile their wealth data based on the 'investment income multiplier',[5] although the United Kingdom has abandoned this method. However, most OECD countries have surveys on wealth (e.g. the USA, UK, Italy). As a result of the lack of or variation in sources, wealth data generally suffer from two major shortcomings: limited time series (compared to income data) and lack of cross-country comparability.

Dedicated wealth surveys provide stepping stones for an accurate measurement of wealth: the American Survey of Consumer Finances (SCF), the Spanish Survey of Household Finances (EFF), the Italian Survey of Households Income and Wealth (SHIW), and the Wealth and Assets Survey (WAS) in the UK are just a few. There have also been several high-level attempts to harmonize wealth data collected from different sources:

- WIDER 2000 by the United Nations University;
- Global Wealth Report (GWR) by Credit Suisse;
- Luxembourg Wealth Study (LWS);
- Household Finance and Consumption Network (HFCN) coordinated by the European Central Bank.

The first two are secondary datasets aimed at providing comparable wealth inequality indicators; the last two are harmonized microdata sources on wealth data. These sources relate to different years and only the GWR refers to the post-crisis period, when both the financial meltdown and the housing market crash dramatically affected the wealth distribution.

Credit Suisse Research Institute recently started collecting comparable indicators of wealth inequality in its *Global Wealth Report* (Shorrocks et al., 2010, 2011). The data are available for 2010 and 2011 and cover all countries in the world. The indicators are imputations based on macro data. The main source is the UN's 2000 database of wealth distribution (WIDER, 2000). The figures for 2010 and 2011 are constructed by taking into account the asset composition of households' wealth by decile and the growth of financial assets, non-financial assets, and debt. The decade that has elapsed since

---

[5] This capitalizes investment income to estimate the value of financial assets (Davies, 2009). Recently, data on wealth inequality for some countries are imputed based on income inequality (for the methodology see Davies et al., 2011).

2000 is characterized by the explosion of debt. Other data sources used are household balance sheet data (HBS), household survey data, and wealth tax records. For the countries for which no data on wealth distribution are available, wealth inequality has been imputed from income inequality, assuming that wealth and income inequality are highly correlated. The GWR wealth indicators are adjusted for (missing) data at the top of the wealth distribution based on information from *Forbes* magazine.

The LWS is an international collection of microdata on household wealth derived from national surveys and register data and harmonized ex-post to a reasonable degree to allow cross-country analysis and breakdowns by key components of household wealth and debt. The availability of wealth information depends on the original national data. The microdata allow the construction of (short) series of wealth inequality. Wealth data are available for a limited number of OECD countries and Cyprus between the 1990s and early 2000s. Data from the ECB's HFCN look promising. The HFCN very recently published the Eurosystem's Household Finance and Consumption Survey, which collects household-level data for the Eurozone on finances and consumption covering real and financial assets, liabilities, private pension entitlements, intergenerational transfers, and gifts. The first survey took place in 2010/11.

ESTIMATES OF WEALTH INEQUALITY
Figure 4.1 shows estimates of wealth inequality based on cross-country comparable data for a time span covering pre- and post-crisis years and the

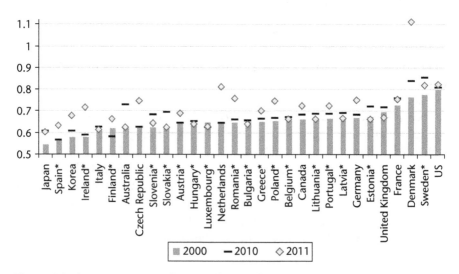

**Figure 4.1.** Are cross-country Gini coefficients for wealth comparable?
*Note*: * corresponds to GWR wealth data which are imputed from income inequality.
*Source*: 2000 WIDER data; 2010 and 2011 GWR.

period witnessing the explosion of the mortgage market. The figure highlights, first, that the level of wealth inequality varies widely across countries. In 2000, the UK, USA, France, and the Scandinavian countries recorded the highest level of wealth inequality (Gini coefficient around 0.7 and higher), while East Asian countries, Spain, Ireland, and Italy had the lowest level of inequality (around 0.6 and lower). Second, some countries show a considerable rise in wealth inequality, especially during the last years: Eurozone bailed-out countries subject to austerity measures, Germany, some Eastern European countries, Finland, Korea, Canada, Denmark, and the Netherlands. The interpretation of these changes for Denmark and the Netherlands will be further discussed under 'inequality and negative values'. The changes reported in the GWR data are so dramatic as to radically modify the position of some countries in the ranking of wealth inequality. In 2011, the Netherlands joins the club of the most (wealth) unequal countries (while the UK leaves it). On the other hand, only Japan and Italy preserve their membership of the (wealth) equal countries club, while Ireland moves from relatively equal to unequal.

The estimates highlight the continuing difficulty of finding comparable estimates not just between countries at a point in time but also within countries at different points in time. These issues of variability and reliability in wealth and wealth-inequality measurement and definition recur throughout this chapter.

WEALTH LEVELS AND WEALTH INEQUALITY

The cross-country comparison of Gini coefficients should be interpreted with caution, as lower average levels of wealth holdings may go together with a higher dispersion. For example, Nordic countries have high levels of wealth inequality but relatively low average wealth holdings and the absolute difference between low and high wealth households is smaller than in other countries. On the other hand, Italy has a relatively high median level of wealth, due to the limited role of debt, but a relatively low level of wealth inequality. In the United Kingdom, the increase in home ownership and house prices between 2000 and 2005 led to a substantial increase in wealth holdings, on the one side, and a fall in wealth inequality, on the other (Cowell et al., 2012).

Figure 4.2 shows a negative correlation between median net wealth holdings and net wealth inequality (Gini coefficient). However, removing Denmark and Sweden (low wealth, high inequality) considerably weakens the correlation. In general, Anglo-Saxon countries have high median wealth and high wealth inequality while Eastern European countries have low median wealth and relatively high wealth inequality.

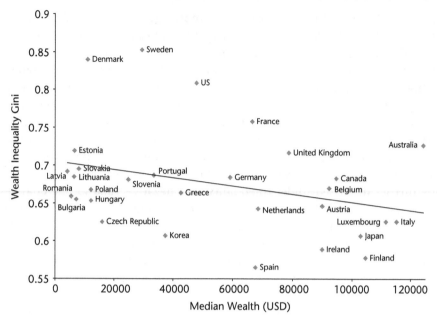

**Figure 4.2.** Median wealth levels versus wealth inequality, 2010
*Source*: Authors' own elaboration based on the data from GWR (2010).

## EQUIVALIZATION AND HOUSEHOLD DEFINITION

Wealth is typically measured at the household level but, unlike household income, it is rarely equivalized. Standard measures of wealth correspond to the total assets and liabilities held by all members of the household. There is no consensus on whether or how to equivalize wealth holdings. No equivalization implies that asset holdings are considered non-rival goods: independently from their number all members of a household are assumed to fully benefit from the total of assets. Demographic differences between countries or within countries over time affecting household composition will influence the wealth inequality measures that result. Relevant demographic factors may be the prevalence of single-headed households, multi-generational households, family size, or the age at which children leave the parental home.

Another dimension affecting the inequality estimates is the definition of households. The high level of wealth inequality in Sweden is partially explained by a (mis)classification of cohabiting individuals who are not married and do not have children as single households (Cowell et al., 2012).

## INEQUALITY AND NEGATIVE VALUES

A major difference between the measurement of income and wealth inequality is the treatment of negative values and the interpretation of ensuing inequality indicators. Net wealth can be negative much more often than income. Although incomes can also be negative, this mostly occurs in the case of market incomes (self-employment losses) or because of measurement errors, and their proportion is much smaller than among wealth, especially in some countries. Moreover, it is common practice for official income inequality series to set negative values to zero. The same procedure applied to wealth is more problematic. However, the inclusion of negative values in the calculation of the Gini coefficient, necessary for some countries, may make its interpretation less intuitive: as the upper bound is no longer 1, the presence of households with negative net worth may make the coefficient larger than in the case of one household owning all assets.

Indeed, there is an important caveat in the interpretation of Figure 4.1 related to this. The upper bound of the Gini is 1 if the variable covered is non-negative (or the number of negative values can be ignored without inducing selection bias). This is the typical case of income data, but usually not for net wealth, particularly for some countries. In that case, as long as the mean is still positive, the Gini can be used but it is no longer constrained to be less than 1.[6] In particular, Denmark and the Netherlands[7] have non-negligible numbers of households with negative wealth. Since the 2010 GWR data discarded negative values, while in 2011 they are included in the calculation of the (modified) Gini coefficient, it is difficult to disentangle the effect of the inclusion of negative values from the change in the distribution of assets and debt between 2010 and 2011, specifically for these countries. The increase in inequality due to the inclusion of negative values implies that previous values underestimated wealth inequality and that Gini coefficients for these countries are no longer comparable with those of other countries. Moreover the high values result from the importance of debt rather than reflecting wealth concentration among richer households. Indeed, we should expect high levels of wealth inequality for countries in which negative net worth is found for a large share of the population and not discarded. In Sweden the bottom three wealth deciles have negative net worth, and in Denmark the bottom four deciles (Domeij and Floden, 2009; Davies et al., 2009). In the Netherlands the bottom decile has negative net worth, while the next two deciles have virtually zero net worth (GINI country report for the Netherlands).

---

[6] If the mean falls to zero, Gini increases to infinity. Here it would be better to use the 'absolute' Gini, i.e. the product between the mean and the Gini (Cowell, 2008). If the mean falls below zero, the Lorenz curve bends the wrong way (see Amiel et al., 1996). We thank Frank Cowell for clarifying this point.

[7] GWR Databook 2010 (p. 8) notes that negative wealth shares for Denmark, Finland, Germany, and Sweden were discarded.

Beyond a fall in asset prices (therefore, specifically for pre-crisis observations), measurement errors can explain a considerable share of households with negative net worth:

1. Young adults living with their parents (who can hold educational loans) and unmarried couples counted as a separate households;

2. Study loans may be accounted for in the stock of wealth but not the present value of resulting human capital;

3. Debt incurred for buying assets not covered in the wealth data (e.g. consumer durables such as vehicles), in particular business debt;

4. Wealth data from tax records may contain the taxable value of wealth (a fraction of market value) and the market value of debt (Davies et al., 2009; OECD, 2008).

As already mentioned, point 1 is an important issue for Sweden, as are points 2 and 3. As to point 2, 25% of Swedish households hold educational loans, designed to assist life-long learning and not only undergraduate studies (Cowell et al., 2012). The impact of student loans is expected to grow substantially in the UK, as thanks to the new system of fees and university grants students may leave university with a debt of around €34,200 (Cowell et al., 2012). For point 3 Swedish data include business debt, which is not common for other countries (Cowell et al., 2012). Scandinavian countries and the Netherlands have usually based their wealth data on tax records or merged survey data with administrative records (point 4).

In addition, negative values may result for other reasons than the measurement imperfections listed above. In the Netherlands the average loan-to-value ratio was already above 110% before house prices fell as a result of the crisis (Vandevyvere and Zenthofer, 2012). Housing mortgages could exceed the value of the asset from the start, e.g. for financing improvements, and tax deductibility of mortgage interest is very generous, enhancing the popularity of interest-only mortgages without redemptions (about 60% of all mortgages in 2010[8]). These features of the tax system and of the credit market may inflate the overall level of debt that is taken.

Therefore, the cross-country comparability of wealth levels is problematic. The main issue seems to be the comparability of Scandinavian countries and the Netherlands to other countries, with respect to the household definition, the data source (tax records versus surveys), and the considerable shares of households with negative net wealth. Nonetheless, different levels and patterns of wealth inequality may be explained by other factors than measurement issues.

---

[8] Vandevyvere and Zenthofer (2012).

POLARIZATION

The role of negative (and nil) net worth is better illustrated by a specific dimension of inequality: polarization. Around 2% to 8% of households hold nil net worth, up to 29% in Germany. A larger share of households have negative net worth: 15% to 20% in Canada, Finland, United Kingdom, and USA, and 27% in Sweden. In Italy and Germany this share is considerably smaller (3% and 9%, respectively), and in Luxembourg it is around 10%. At the opposite end of the distribution, the share owned by the richest households is usually very consistent. The top 10% holds on average around 50% of total wealth, from a minimum of 42% in Italy up to 71% in the USA.[9]

(PUBLIC) PENSION ASSETS

A further measurement challenge regards pension assets. In most of the countries, public pension entitlements are not included in these data. These tend to reduce wealth inequality and their exclusion may lead to an overestimation of inequality (Klevmarken et al., 2003; Davies and Shorrocks, 2000). In Finland, for instance, wealth inequality is reduced by 17 percentage points (in 2005) when future pension benefits are included (GINI country report for Finland). However, most pensions reforms since the mid-1990s have implemented shifts from defined-benefit to defined-contribution systems, which considerably reduces the effect of the inclusion of pension assets in offsetting wealth inequality (Wolff, 2005).

All these aspects highlight the need for analysts to have an informed view of the countries and data they are comparing and, for future research and data collection, to establish an appropriate and uniform measurement of wealth.

### 4.3.2 Trends in Wealth Inequality

The analysis of wealth inequality trends comes at the expense of cross-country comparability. Indeed, efforts at standardization such as the LWS result in short time trends of wealth inequality for a small subset of countries. Instead Figure 4.3 shows non-harmonized trends of net worth inequality in the period 1967–2008 for a set of OECD countries. The data are comparable across the same time series but not across countries.

Although the period covered is not the same for every country, we notice an increase in wealth inequality during the 1980s and the 1990s. Spain reports a decrease in wealth inequality but this refers to only two years in the 2000s, when also other countries report decreasing (UK and Italy) or

---

[9] Data from OECD (2008) around 2000.

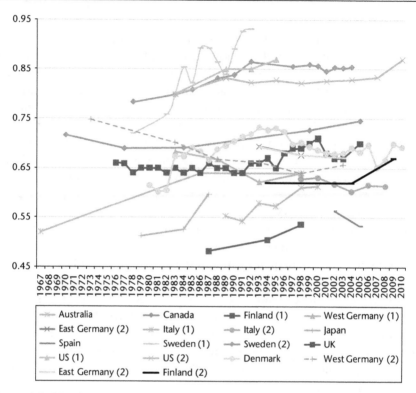

**Figure 4.3.** Non-harmonized trends of net worth

*Sources*: Australia: Kelly (2001); Canada: Morissette and Zhang (2006); Denmark: GINI country report; Finland: (1) Jäntti (2006); (2) GINI country report; Italy: (1) Banca d'Italia (2000); (2) Brandolini et al. (2004); Japan: Takayama (1994); Spain: Bover (2008); Sweden: Domeij and Floden (2009) for both; (1) HINK; (2) SCB; East and West Germany: (1) Hauser and Stein (2003); (2) GINI country report; UK: HM Revenue & Customs: Distribution of Personal Wealth; USA: (1) Keister and Moller (2000); (2) Wolff (2013).

stable (Canada)[10] inequality. Germany is a specific case due to reunification. Inequality decreased in West Germany before reunification, though there are some issues of comparability for the 1983–90 period; after reunification, inequality in West Germany first decreased and then increased, and a convergence with East Germany is taking place. For the country as a whole, net wealth inequality increased by 6 percentage points between the early 1980s and early 2000s. The increase was concentrated between 1988 and 1993, due to the different wealth levels of East and West Germany, although a modest increase occurred also within the West (Fuchs-Schündeln et al., 2010).

---

[10] For Canada, Brzozowki et al. (2010) report stable wealth inequality of net worth between 1999 and 2005.

Between 2010 and 2011 most countries reported a considerable increase in wealth inequality (Figure 4.1). In the Czech Republic, Denmark, Ireland, the Netherlands, and Romania this exceeded 15%. In most countries experiencing a decrease the reduction was small. Only the UK, Slovakia, Estonia, and Australia witnessed important falls in inequality (larger than 6%).

Polarization has increased over recent decades. At one end, the fraction of households with nil or negative net worth increased. For instance, in Germany between 1978 and 2003 this share increased from 6.5% to 10.5%, and for negative wealth only from 3.4% to 5.5% (Fuchs-Schündeln et al., 2010). In Italy, though low, the share with negative net worth grew from 2% to 3% between 1990 and 2010 (Banca d'Italia, 2012). Korea's first quintile's net worth became negative in 2011 (GINI country report for Korea). In the Netherlands the wealth share of the poorest wealth decile turned more negative in the last decade (from –1.9% in 1993 to –3.5% in 2011) (GINI country report for the Netherlands). At the other end, the share of net worth held by the top percentiles increased. In Canada, the top-1% share increased from 16% to 17% between 1999 and 2005 and the top-5% share from 35% to 36% (Brzozowki et al., 2010). In the USA the net worth share of the richest 10% increased from 51% to 59% (1983–2007) (Heathcote et al., 2010). In Japan, the increase in the share of the top 5% is the main driver of increasing wealth inequality over the period 1984–2004 (GINI country report for Japan). In Switzerland the top 5% held 56.6% of the total net worth in 1991, which increased to 58% in 1997 (Dell, Piketty, and Saez, 2007). The Spanish top-1% wealth share (including real estate) grew from 18.5% in 2000 to a peak of 20% in 2002 and fell back 19.7% in 2007. However, financial wealth shares (excluding real estate) show a different picture, with much greater concentration: from 22.7% in 2000 to 25.2% in 2007 (Saez and Alvaredo, 2009). In Sweden the wealth level of the bottom three deciles has been essentially stable, but wealth increased for the top decile by 5% per year from 1999 to 2007 on average (own calculation from GINI country report for Sweden). Finally, in France, the share of wealth held by the top centile has increased by 36% between 1992 and 2010, and the share of the top decile by 4.8% (GINI country report for France).

### 4.3.3 Asset Contributions to the Development of Wealth Inequality

A comparative analysis of the contribution of different assets/liabilities to the trend in net worth is not an easy task, as a comparable breakdown of wealth inequality is not available for all countries. Figures 4.4 to 4.6 show the trends in inequality for housing wealth, financial wealth, and liabilities respectively for the countries for which a comparable breakdown of wealth was available.

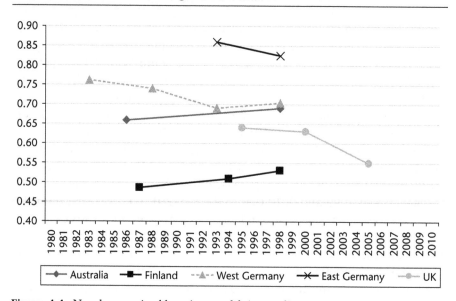

**Figure 4.4.** Non-harmonized housing wealth inequality

*Sources*: Harding (2002) for Australia; Jäntti (2006) for Finland; Stein and Hauser (2004) for Germany; Karagiannaki (2011) for UK.

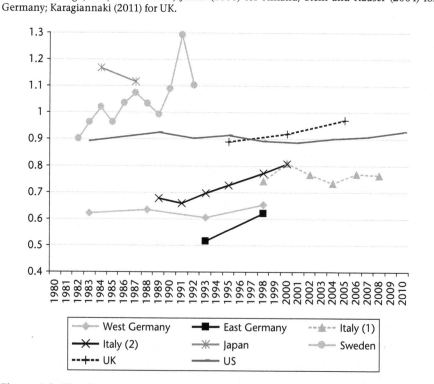

**Figure 4.5.** Non-harmonized financial wealth inequality

*Sources*: Takayama (1994) for Japan; for Italy: (1) Banca d'Italia (2000); (2) Brandolini, et al. (2004, No. 530); for the other countries see Figure 4.4.

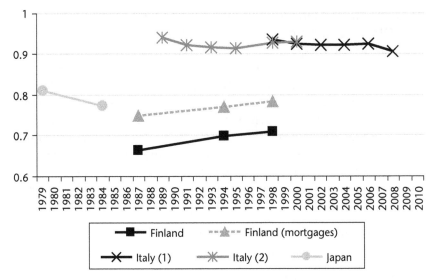

**Figure 4.6.** Non-harmonized debt inequality
*Sources*: See Figures 4.4 and 4.5.

Housing wealth inequality does not seem to drive the general increasing trend in wealth inequality and it generally has an equalizing effect. On the other hand, inequality in financial wealth shows an increase. The booming stock market and the high concentration of stocks among the rich (together with rising transitory labour-market risk) were identified as the determinants of increasing wealth inequality in the USA (Heathcote et al., 2010). In Germany, financial wealth inequality has increased much more rapidly than total wealth inequality, while housing wealth remained stable (Fuchs-Schündeln et al., 2010). Similarly, in Italy total wealth inequality was fairly stable during the 1990s, while financial wealth inequality increased considerably throughout the 1990s (Jappelli and Pistaferri, 2010).

## 4.4 The Drivers of Wealth Inequality: Do Cross-Country Differences Explain National Stories?

### 4.4.1 Cross-Country Differences in Wealth Inequality

Although income and wealth are very different concepts, the relationship between their respective distributions provides interesting results. Internationally, as we showed earlier, the correlation between wealth and income inequality is not straightforward. Countries with relatively high levels of income inequality do not necessarily display high levels of wealth inequality. The Mediterranean countries Greece, Italy, and Spain, and the two richest OECD Asian countries, Japan and Korea, have high income inequality and low wealth inequality. France and particularly Denmark and Sweden are in the opposite situation: low income inequality with high wealth inequality. Some other countries, mostly Anglo-Saxon (USA, UK, Australia, and Canada) combine high levels of both income and wealth inequality. Finally, a set of 'virtuous' countries, such as Finland, the Czech Republic, and Austria, enjoy low levels of both. Figure 4.7 shows how wealth and income inequality combine across countries; the two lines indicating the median levels of the two inequalities show which countries are found above or below.

Cross-country differences in wealth inequality can be explained by four factors which we discuss consecutively:

- Demographic structure of the population
- Institutions (social expenditure)
- Asset composition (private debt)
- Labour market and inheritance.

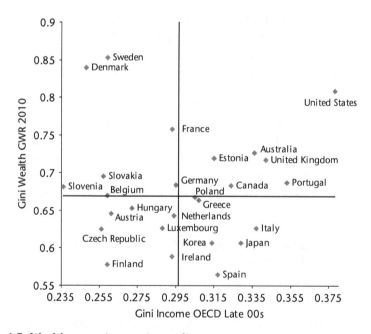

**Figure 4.7.** Wealth versus income inequality

*Notes*: Net wealth and disposable income inequality are used for the calculation of the Gini indices. The vertical and horizontal lines correspond to the median of income and wealth inequality.

*Sources*: GWR 2010 for wealth inequality; OECD for disposable income inequality for the late 2000s.

DEMOGRAPHIC FACTORS

The accumulation of wealth has a clear life-cycle dimension. Not surprisingly age is found to be a main determinant of wealth holdings (OECD, 2008). Cowell et al. (2012) discuss how cross-country differences in household wealth holdings are affected by demographic differences. Countries differ substantially in age profiles of asset ownership. American households are most likely to hold financial debt and this extends to older households headed by individuals over the age of 65. Italian households have an older age profile associated with an ageing population and a later age of household formation. The impact of household structure on wealth inequality links to the fact that standard measures of household wealth are rarely equivalized. Using data from the LWS, Cowell et al. (2013) find that differences between the wealth distributions of Finland, Italy, Sweden, the UK, and the USA cannot be fully explained by differences in age, working status, household structure, education, and income. Unobserved country effects play a dominant role. Indeed, recalculating wealth inequality as if these countries all had the same distribution of characteristics has only a small impact on wealth inequality and does not change the countries' ranking for net financial or net housing wealth. The counterfactual Gini of net worth slightly increases for Italy (from 0.57 to 0.59) and decreases for the other countries, especially for Sweden (from 0.88 to 0.83). Thus the actual distribution of characteristics makes net housing wealth inequality relatively more equal in Italy and unequal in Finland and the USA (Cowell et al., 2013).

INSTITUTIONS (SOCIAL EXPENDITURE)

Some authors suggest a relationship between wealth inequality and the generosity of the welfare state. The high level of wealth inequality in Sweden is thought to be due to the comprehensive pensions system and generous social security, which reduce the need for private household wealth accumulation for life-cycle and precautionary reasons (Domeij and Floden, 2010; Davies, 2008; Domeij and Klein, 2002). Public pensions are considered an important factor in explaining cross-country differences in wealth inequality. However, Davies (2009) notes that Finland has a welfare state similar to Sweden but low wealth inequality, and sees the higher rate of home ownership in Finland and a lower incidence of negative net worth as a possible explanation.

Figure 4.8 correlates wealth inequality and old-age expenditure. Although slightly positive,[11] the relationship between the two is not straightforward. Scandinavian countries, France, Germany, Portugal, and Slovenia in the right top panel confirm the hypothesis that high spending on old age corresponds with high wealth inequality. However, Italy, Finland, and Japan

[11] The correlation also depends on the countries selected. For GINI countries the correlation is positive.

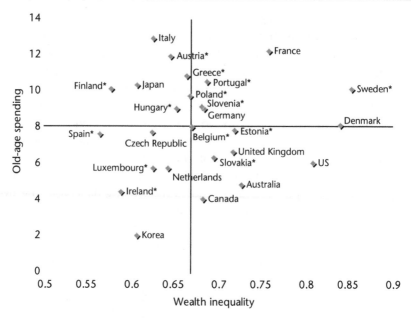

**Figure 4.8.** Old-age expenditure and wealth inequality

*Notes:* Lines correspond to the median values. * corresponds to GWR wealth data, which are imputed from income inequality.

*Sources:* GWR 2010 for wealth inequality; SOCX database from OECD for old-age expenditure.

spend a considerable amount on old age but have relatively low wealth inequality. Anglo-Saxon countries have high wealth inequality despite their low spending on old age.

Social expenditure on housing may affect the wealth distribution similarly, as higher spending may provide less incentive for the accumulation of wealth at the bottom of the income distribution. Means-tested housing benefits and the provision of social housing diminish the need to buy a house for poorer households. Figure 4.9 plots wealth inequality versus expenditure on housing, showing a clear positive correlation between the two. The United Kingdom, France, Denmark, and Germany with relatively high spending have higher inequality, while countries spending less (Italy, Spain) display lower levels of inequality. Ex-communist countries do not follow this pattern, as probably the widespread outright home ownership makes housing expenditure less relevant. It is worth noticing that the same mechanism may be in place in countries with rent controls (Sweden, the Netherlands), although this measure is not included in housing expenditure.

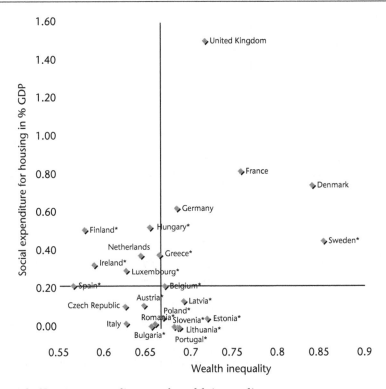

**Figure 4.9.** Housing expenditure and wealth inequality

*Note*: * corresponds to GWR wealth data, which are imputed from income inequality.

*Source*: GRW 2010 for wealth inequality; 2010 ESSPROS data for housing expenditures. We use ESSPROS data instead of SOCX data from the OECD as they maximize the number of GINI countries covered (SOCX data for housing are missing for Japan and Korea).

## FINANCIAL ASSETS AND LIABILITIES

An additional explanation of cross-country variation in wealth inequality is the level of debt. Debts normally include mortgage, consumer, education, and business loans. The extent and the relative weight of the different sources of debt vary across countries, although mortgages are commonly the main component. The level of indebtedness varies widely across countries and may contribute to explaining cross-country differences in wealth inequality. Figure 4.10 shows private debt versus wealth inequality. The pattern is not clear-cut, although measurement problems may play a role. Cowell et al. (2013) show that debt holdings explain a large part of differences in wealth inequality across countries. For Sweden the explanation is again partially linked to a measurement issue that distinguishes it from other countries: the inclusion of household-held business debt contributes to its higher debt holdings. Educational loans are another important factor explaining the high

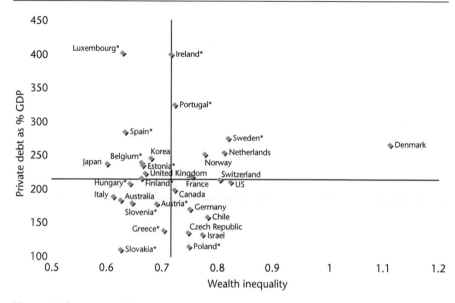

**Figure 4.10.** Private debt and wealth inequality

*Notes*: Gini coefficient for wealth inequality. * corresponds to GWR wealth data, which are imputed from income inequality.

*Sources*: GWR 2011 for wealth inequality and for private debt data are from 2010 OECD households and non-profit institutions serving households in % of gross disposable income.

wealth inequality for Sweden; their exclusion entirely explains the difference in wealth inequality between Sweden and the USA (Cowell et al., 2013).

LABOUR MARKET AND INHERITANCE

Wealth originates from the sum of income in excess over expenditures, inter-vivos transfers, and inheritance. The correlation between earnings and accumulated wealth, though not perfect, is high and remains strong even controlling for differences in observable characteristics. In addition, wealth holdings typically peak around the time of retirement when earnings drop off and this will have some effect on observed correlations. The correlation between income and wealth is stronger for the USA than for other OECD countries (OECD, 2008). In Sweden the correlation between market earnings and net wealth is very low[12] (8%, Domeij and Floden, 2010), further supporting the importance of the Swedish welfare system. In Canada, the correlation between disposable income and wealth was 35% in 1999, compared to 60% in the USA (Brzozowki et al., 2010). Income-poor asset-rich households

[12] As income includes capital income we expect a stronger correlation between income and wealth than between wealth and earnings.

are a reality in all countries, though their share may vary. These house-holds are usually older households living in their own home (owned out-right) but living on a small pension income. Moreover, socio-demographic characteristics have a lower explanatory power for wealth than for income (see Jäntti et al., 2008), probably due to the role played by intergenerational transfers and equivalization. Nonetheless, the correlation between income and wealth at the individual level is still sizeable and more important in the USA (above 50%) than in other OECD countries (between 27% and 36%) (OECD, 2008). This reflects the more unequal income distribution, higher (transitory) labour-market risks and the weaker role of the state in mitigating labour-market risks in the USA.

Inheritance is another important factor driving the accumulation of wealth and its skewed distribution, e.g. in Austria and Luxembourg (GINI country reports). Picketty and Saez (forthcoming) consider microeconomic and macroeconomic factors behind the relative importance of inheritance in the wealth distribution. Criticizing standard economic models of wealth accumulation (e.g. Atkinson and Stiglitz, 1976; Chamley, 1986; Judd, 1999), usually based on a representative agent and perfect markets, they state that heterogeneity in the preferences for bequest and in parental resources gener-ates wealth inequality in addition to labour-market outcomes. Uninsurable shocks due to various imperfections may also deepen wealth inequality. Nevertheless, inheritance may be more important for (un)equal opportuni-ties than for overall inequality.

### 4.4.2 Drivers of Wealth Inequality Trends

If institutional factors seem to better explain cross-country differences in wealth inequality, private debt, financial assets, their fiscal treatment, and the superstar phenomenon[13] seem to better explain the over-time evolution of wealth inequality within countries. In general, trends in net wealth ine-quality within countries can be explained by the evolution of:

- Financial assets
- Debt
- Labour market and inheritance
- Billionaires
- Taxation

---

[13] The superstar phenomenon defines a situation in which very top people in an occupation earn huge pay because performances are widely reproducible.

FINANCIAL ASSETS

As illustrated in Section 2.2, financial wealth seems to be the most important driver of the rise in wealth inequality, together with debt. Indeed, inequality in (gross) non-financial assets (Figure 4.4) seems more stable than (gross) financial wealth inequality (Figure 4.5), while total wealth and net worth inequality (Figure 4.3) were increasing. Asset price changes offer an important explanation for the observed patterns. In general, given the concentration of share ownership among wealthier segments of the population, a rise in stock-market prices tends to raise wealth at the top of the distribution, causing wealth inequality to increase. On the other hand, rising housing prices have a larger proportionate impact on the middle of the distribution compared to the top, causing a decrease in inequality. Changes in stock-market prices can partly explain the rising wealth inequality in the USA since the mid-1980s, as documented by Heathcote et al. (2010). A similar argument is put forward by Klevmarken (2004), who argues that the difference in price changes between the housing market and stock market can at least partly explain the rising wealth inequality in Sweden during the 1990s.

DEBT

Among the drivers of increasing wealth inequality and polarization, one proposed explanation suggests the role of debt. Indebtedness measured as the debt-to-income ratio more than tripled in Czech Republic, from 17.4% in 1995 to 54.2% in the fifteen years up to 2010; in Slovakia it increased by 42.2 percentage points between 1998 and 2000, although data is not available after 2000 (GINI country report for Czech Republic and Slovakia). This seems a general pattern across Eastern Europe. In Estonia the ratio of households' bank loans to GDP multiplied within a decade (2002–10) from less than 10% to 50%; in Poland the number of households with debt holdings grew by 15% in the last decade; and in Slovenia household borrowing also increased in the 1990s, and especially after 2004 (GINI country reports for the Baltics, Poland, and Slovenia). A similar phenomenon is observed in Korea after the Asian crisis (GINI country report for Korea). The high leverage of middle-class families before the Great Recession in the USA is a well-known stylized fact, although wealth inequality increased less than income inequality, perhaps due to the impressive concentration of wealth (GINI country report for USA).

As stressed by the GINI country report for Canada, increasing house prices and the weak performance of wages are underlying causes. Moreover, policies sustaining the housing market were reinforced and exacerbated the household debt problem (GINI country report for Korea). In general, the deregulation of financial markets led to easy credit in various countries and spurred an increasing private indebtedness for housing. The introduction of the euro and its low interest rate also contributed to the indebtedness of households (GINI country report for Portugal). However, the effect of these factors on wealth inequality is less clear-cut. In some countries increasing housing debt had an equalizing role (e.g. in Poland, see the GINI country report), in others it had a disequalizing effect (e.g. in Australia and Denmark in particular in the mid-1990s and late 2000s, from GINI country reports) and in some others it played a different role depending on the time period. In Finland, for example, debt helped to stabilize inequality between 1994 and 2004 but enhanced it in the following five years; overall, both gross and net wealth inequalities increased between the mid-1990s and the end of the 2000s (GINI country report for Finland). Increasing household indebtedness played a crucial role in changing the correspondence between wealth and income distributions, which will be analysed in more detail in Section 4.5.

LABOUR MARKETS

Since wages represent the largest part of income, they are a very important determinant of savings and the distribution of wealth (and also of credit). However, their relative importance among working-age households depends on: (i) how capital income and earnings are dispersed; (ii) the distribution of the propensity to save; and (iii) the average rate of growth of wages with respect to average return on capital. The latter matters because of Piketty's (2011) argument: if the rate of growth is lower than the average rate of return on capital then the weight of accumulated wealth is higher and this increases wealth inequality. Capital income is less equally distributed than labour earnings and the propensity to save is an increasing function of income. Two stylized facts of the last thirty years should be mentioned:

- The labour share in total income has decreased across almost all the developed countries (OECD, 2012a) as wage growth lagged productivity growth (as discussed in Chapter 2 above);

- The rate of growth of the product per capita has been lower than the rate of return to capital in most developed countries (Piketty, 2011).

The former implies that savings out of income have become more concentrated because of the increasing capital share, the latter that accumulated wealth—which is relatively more concentrated than income—has increased its role in explaining the change in the distribution. Both stimulate the concentration of wealth.

As the correlation between earnings and wealth is stronger in the USA than in other countries (Section 4.3), we expected the labour market to play a larger role there in explaining increasing wealth inequality. Heathcote et al.

(2010) explain the rise in wealth inequality partially from rising transitory labour-market risks.[14] However, Kenworthy and Smeeding (GINI country report for USA) report stable wealth inequality between 1983 and 2007 and a sharp rise (+4 percentage points) only after the Great Recession, which conflicts with the labour-market explanation since the mid-1980s. However, it may partly explain the increases in wealth concentration found by others (Wolff, 2006; Kopczuk and Saez, 2004), which are not captured in relative measures of inequality such as the Gini coefficient.

The role of inheritance in explaining overall wealth inequality depends on the average rate of growth. Piketty (2011) constructs a very long-run data series for inheritance in France and finds a flow of inheritances of 5% of GDP during the post-war period of rapid growth followed by an increasingly sharp rise to 15% since the mid-1980s. This is consistent with his view on economic growth and the return on capital, and therefore may apply also to other countries and be enhanced in the coming decades.

BILLIONAIRES

A peculiar channel through which the labour market can explain the rise in wealth inequality is the emergence of 'billionaires'. The increasing concentration of income and wealth at the top of the distribution raised a significant debate in the literature on the 'working rich' and 'superstars' (Rosen, 1981), although the empirical evidence is not overwhelming (Atkinson, 2008). Using the data on billionaires published by *Forbes* magazine since the 1980s, Roine et al. (2012) find striking results. First of all, the top billionaires' resources are considerable (estimated at around 8% of world GDP) and extremely mobile, since the share of total wealth 'residing' in a country different from its citizenship has increased dramatically. Secondly, the billionaires' share of the total has increased as has concentration within the top. European and Japanese shares have declined, while they have increased in the USA and the rest of the world. It is difficult to assess hypotheses on the drivers of these fortunes (sometimes it is difficult to distinguish the individual from the 'dynasty'). However, the share of self-made billionaires has increased globally. While most self-made wealth in BRIC[15] countries was gained from natural resources and traditional manufacturing, much of the American top wealth has been created in high-tech industries.

---

[14] Heathcote et al. (2010) report an increase of 5 percentage points in net worth inequality since the mid-1990s, based on SCF data.

[15] Brazil, Russia, India, and China.

TAXATION

Several tax instruments can influence the accumulation of wealth and its distribution: mortgage interest tax relief, property and inheritance taxation, capital gains tax, capital income tax, and taxation of financial products. These tax instruments have static and behavioural effects.

In the last few decades, there has been a large use of mortgage interest tax reliefs, while housing has enjoyed a favourable tax treatment with respect to other assets. This treatment has had three behavioural effects: increased house prices, increased home ownership also among income poorer (Andrews et al., 2011), and increased debt. The combined effect on wealth inequality has been ambiguous. The static effects are generally assessed over income and point to a failure in terms of redistribution. Mortgage interest tax relief is generally regressive, as higher income earners benefit more (Flevotomou and Matsaganis, 2007). Property taxes have a limited redistributive power (Maestri, 2012b) because home ownership is popular also among lower income households, tax rates may not be progressive, and the tax base may not be updated (Lejeune et al., 2012).

Inheritance taxation has seen a dramatic fall from 0.25% of GDP in 1965 to less than 0.15% of GDP since the mid-1980s, on average across OECD countries (Bogliacino and Maestri, 2012b). This decline can be a candidate explanation for the increasing accumulation of wealth and wealth inequality. Several studies analyse the effect of inheritance taxation on the size of bequests. Jappelli et al. (2012) survey the existing literature on the behavioural effects and conclude that the effect found in the literature is small: an increase in the inheritance tax rate of 10% reduces bequests by only 1%. Nonetheless, they warn that these data cannot disentangle the elasticity of inheritance to taxes from that of tax avoidance. As for the static effects, they suggest that little redistribution can take place via the taxation of intergenerational transfers, as different institutional arrangements generate low and similar tax revenues. D'Addio (2007) reviews the literature on the intergenerational transmission of wealth and concludes it is more important for the top of the distribution. However, inheritance taxation is expected to be more important for social mobility than for inequality.

As for the taxation of finance and inequality, the development of the tax base has been more important than its tax structure. Looking at standard measures of tax revenues may be misleading. The financialization of the economy enlarged the tax base (the 'share' of finance in GDP), which may result in a higher incidence of the tax on GDP for a given tax rate. The role of finance in fuelling the income and wealth of the top earners (Krugman, 2012a, 2012b; Lansley, 2012; Stiglitz, 2012) suggests that the direct and indirect impact of a more up-to-date taxation of finance can be favourable to equality. The widely discussed Tobin tax (a small rate on financial transactions) could have a larger indirect than direct impact on inequality, insofar as the large revenues generated by the huge turnover in financial markets, if not offset by the tax itself, are used for other redistributive policies (Patomäki, 2001).

The last decades have also witnessed a decreased taxation of capital income. Since the late 1980s, Nordic European countries have introduced dual income tax systems, taxing capital income at a flat rate. As indicated in Chapter 2, tax revenues from household capital income have decreased in some countries, and for Sweden the decline in capital income taxation is seen as a major driver of increasing income inequality. A fall in the taxation of capital income may easily translate into a larger accumulation of capital at the top.

Beyond taxation, tax havens are likely to play a role in the effective distribution of wealth and its development. About 8% of global wealth is held in tax havens (Zucman, forthcoming). Almost all this unrecorded wealth will be enjoyed by the world's top 1%, dramatically skewing the distribution of wealth (Shaxson et al., 2012). The take-off of wealth offshoring in the last decades suggests a further (invisible) increase in wealth inequality (Henry, 2012).

In general, these facts suggest that the capacity to tax wealth has not kept pace with the increasing importance of financial and housing wealth (considering also that capital gains realized, for instance, on housing assets are hardly taxed), to the extent that it has not been openly reduced as for bequests and capital income. This makes it increasingly difficult to counteract wealth inequality, to say the least. On the other hand, tax policies have clearly favoured indebtedness with an ambiguous impact on inequality and giving rise to new concerns regarding the measurement and interpretation of wealth.

## 4.5 The Relationship between Wealth and Income Distributions

In this section we describe the link between the distribution of wealth and the income distribution, aiming to assess how important income inequality is for wealth inequality, and vice versa, at the rich top as well as the poor bottom. The joint distribution of both has a particular importance, due to the fact that the availability of a significant amount of assets might shelter households in the lowest income deciles, while a strong exposure to debt may worsen the effect of income inequality.

### 4.5.1 Data Availability and Definition

The joint analysis of wealth and income is hindered even more than wealth analysis by problems of data availability and comparability. We have information for nine countries: Australia, Korea, Luxembourg, and Portugal for one or two recent years; Finland, Italy, the Netherlands, the UK, and the United States for a longer time, spanning from around 1990 to recent years. The data are aggregate and allow no detailed analysis beyond quintiles or (sometimes) deciles of the distribution and exclude the use of sophisticated inequality indices. Data allow only a limited type of analysis, no standard single inequality index for the two dimensions of income and wealth is available, and individual characteristics are not observable.[16]

In practice, analysing the links between income and wealth may be thwarted by important problems of statistical observation. As usual there is a problem of observation of the top tail. Moreover, there are inconsistencies in terms of coverage and definitions: public pension assets are left out from wealth in many countries, while pension benefits are included in income. Following common practice, wealth measures used in this section are not equivalized.[17] Unfortunately, income refers to different concepts: equivalized disposable income for Australia, Finland, Italy; non-equivalized disposable (after-tax) income for Korea, the Netherlands, and the UK; and non-equivalized gross (pre-tax) income for Luxembourg and the USA. As equivalization drastically reduces comparative income levels of larger households, the wealth-to-income ratio will expectedly be amplified in the countries using that income concept relative to others. Non-equivalized and equivalized incomes also rank households drastically differently over income quantiles compared and only low equivalized incomes mirror poverty directly. These are important reasons not to compare levels across countries for which we have different measures of income but to focus on structure and evolution over time within countries using the same income concepts. For most countries the data relate to years (2009–11) and range well into the financial crisis, while only UK data (2005) date back to well before the outbreak of the crisis.

---

[16] Synthetic indicators for the joint distributions are available but are much more complicated to interpret and construct. Among more detailed studies considering household characteristics we cite Jäntti, Sierminska, and Van Kerm (2013) and Cowell et al. (2012), both using LWS.
[17] The Australian Bureau of Statistics also presents wealth after equivalization. This reduces the wealth of the top wealth quintile by 43%, the bottom wealth quintile by 33%, and the wealth Q5:Q1 ratio by 15%.

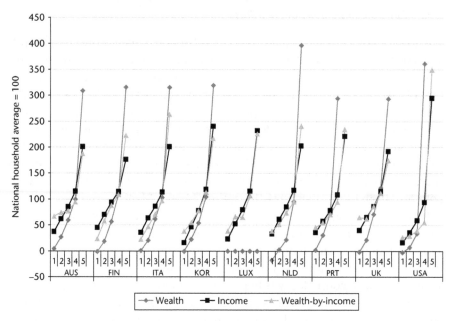

**Figure 4.11.** Wealth, income, and wealth-by-income distributions by quintile, late 2000s

*Note*: Quartiles for the wealth distribution for Portugal and the USA. Gross wealth for Finland. Years: 2005 for UK: 2009 for Australia and Finland; 2010 for Italy, Luxembourg, and Portugal; 2011 for Korea, Netherlands, and USA. Income: before-tax for Luxembourg and USA; disposable income for Korea, the Netherlands, and the UK; equivalized net income for the other four countries. Wealth for Australia excludes superannuation and for the USA retirement accounts.

*Sources*: GINI country reports and BHPS, HWLI, HWWD, IPO, ISFF, LU-HFCS, SCF, SHFLC, SHIW.

### 4.5.2 Aggregate Wealth and the Income Distribution

Figure 4.11 compares for nine countries the three types of inequality that are relevant here:

- The household wealth distribution: mean net worth by quintile of net worth;
- The income distribution: mean income (different concepts as just indicated) by quintiles of income; and finally
- The wealth-by-income distribution: mean net worth over quintiles of income.

Although sometimes the information is available also on a decile basis, the quintile basis allows maximum comparable coverage of countries. The graph presents the quintile levels relative to the national (household) average as a convenient way to compare distributions and not absolute levels.[18]

Clearly, the distribution of wealth is considerably wider than the other two distributions, which in comparison resemble each other remarkably closely. The first wealth quintile (Q1) commonly starts at zero, except for the Netherlands where it is significantly negative (–17% of national average). The upper wealth quintile (or quartile in Portugal and the USA) is always the highest, hovering around 300 in five cases and highest for the Netherlands (400). For the USA the fourth quartile shown implies an underestimation compared to the fifth quintile—the American top decile is lonely at the top with a share in total wealth of 74%, while the Netherlands' top decile ranks second at 60% (Table 4.2). However the first three quartiles of the US distribution are clustered together at very low levels and, consequently, the American top quartile comprises 90% of all wealth. The UK is the only country where middle wealth (Q4) is clearly above the national average, i.e. the 100-line in the graph.

In contrast to the wealth distribution, the bottom quintiles of the income distribution start higher up regardless of the income concept, between 16% and 23% of the national average for Korea, Luxembourg, and the USA, and between 36% and 45% for the other six countries. Those for wealth-by-income start at around 25% for Finland, Italy, USA, and 65% for Australia and UK, with the rest in between. At the same time the top quintiles of these two distributions remain far below the wealth top quintile.

Thus Figure 4.11 indicates clearly that the wealth-by-income distribution is much less unequal than the wealth distribution. Another way to look at this stylized fact is through the analysis of top shares in the three distributions, as presented in Table 4.2. It shows that shares for the American top income decile (44%) as well as the wealth-by-income decile (60%) are lower than for the wealth decile (74%)—though still clearly higher than in the other countries, where they range between 20% and 34%. It is surprising to find the UK at the lower end of both ranges. Thus the American top income decile appears to own 60% of all wealth, a level that strongly exceeds corresponding shares in Finland and the Netherlands, but this may be due partly to the different income concept. The latter countries hover up to about one third, which is where Portugal is found too. The difference is smaller for the top income quintile. Unsurprisingly, the S5:S1 quintile ratios for American income and wealth-by-income (18, 13) are much higher than the European average (3, 9), including Luxembourg, which uses the same gross income concept; Australia and the UK have surprisingly low ratios.

---

[18] Note that average wealth levels seem to be much higher for some countries than for others: Won 245 million for Korea, around €150,000 for Finland, Netherlands, and Portugal, but more than £200,000 for the UK, around $500,000 for the USA, and more than A$700,000 for Australia. The Australian GINI country report attributes this to elevated house prices in the country.

**Table 4.2.** Top shares (%) and ratios for wealth, income, and wealth-by-income, late 2000s

| | Wealth* | | Income** | | | Wealth-by-income | | |
|---|---|---|---|---|---|---|---|---|
| | Share Q5(4) | Share D10 | Share Q5 | Ratio Q5:Q1 | Share D10 | Share Q5 | Ratio Q5:Q1 | Share D10 |
| Australia (2009) | 62 | | 40 | 5 | | 38 | 3 | |
| Finland (2009) | 63 | 44 | 35 | 4 | 22 | 45 | 9 | 31 |
| Italy (2010) | 63 | 46 | 40 | 6 | 25 | 53 | 11 | 35 |
| Korea (2011) | 64 | | 48 | 15 | | 43 | 6 | |
| Luxembourg (2010) | 68 | 52 | 46 | 10 | 30 | 45 | 6 | 27 |
| Netherlands (2011) | 79 | 60 | 41 | 6 | 25 | 48 | 6 | 34 |
| Portugal (2010) | (74) | 53 | 44 | 6 | 29 | 47 | 5 | 33 |
| UK (2005) | 59 | 39 | 38 | 5 | 23 | 35 | 3 | 20 |
| USA (2010) | (90) | 74 | 59 | 18 | 44 | 70 | 13 | 60 |

*Notes:*

* Tiny and often negative levels of the bottom quantile make the Q5:Q1 ratio unfeasible for wealth. Quartiles between brackets for Portugal and USA.

** See Figure 4.11 for diverging income concepts.

*Sources:* GINI country reports and BHPS, HWLI, HWWD, IPO, ISFF, LU-HFCS, SCF, SHFLC, SHIW.

### 4.5.3 Asset Composition

Figure 4.12 pictures the distribution of wealth-by-income ('total') next to the distributions of its two main constituent parts: net housing assets and net financial assets. The panel also adds household debt, which taken together with net worth makes up a household's gross wealth. Definitions are similar to those above. Quite clearly, in the six cases where we have that information, the inequality of financial wealth exceeds that of total wealth while that of housing is clearly less (except for Luxembourg where they equal each other). The inequality of household debt varies across countries. It seems relatively modest in Finland and the USA, but very large in the UK.

Figure 4.13 relates the levels of wealth, broken down by the two main types of assets, and debt to the average income of the household in each of the five income quintiles using the asset-to-income ratio. Table 4.3 adds detail about the top shares and quintile ratios. At the same time it provides a comparison over time, since the mid-1990s, for the five countries where data allow this: Finland, Italy, Netherlands, UK, and USA. In contrast to Figure 4.12, this picture is additive: net housing and net financial wealth add up to total net worth. Debt and net worth are presented separately; they add up to gross wealth, though. Note that income rises over the quintiles and therefore the level of wealth, or debt for that matter, will also rise in case of a stable or increasing ratio to income. We recall that income concepts differ across

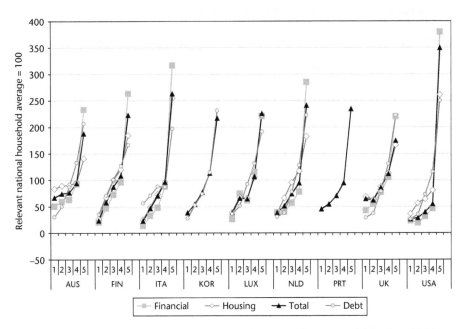

**Figure 4.12.** Wealth-by-income distributions by type of asset, and debt, late 2000s
*See Figure 4.11 for notes and sources.*

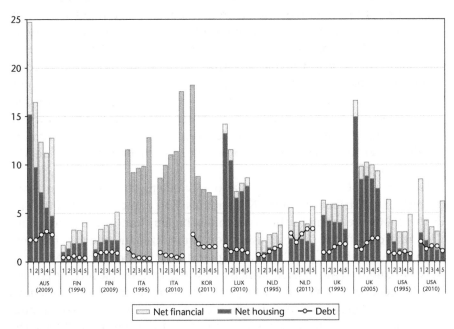

**Figure 4.13.** Wealth-by-income distributions: assets and debt relative to household income since 1994

*Note*: See Figure 4.11. Financial wealth encompasses financial-market claims, business equity, and property equity except own residence (net split is not available for Italy and Korea).

*Source*: GINI country reports and BHPS, HWLI, HWWD, IPO, ISFF, LU-HFCS, SCF, SHFLC, SHIW.

**Table 4.3.** Wealth-by-income top shares (%) and ratios for assets and debt, 1994–2011

| | Net housing wealth | | | Net financial wealth | | | Debt | | |
|---|---|---|---|---|---|---|---|---|---|
| | Share Q5 | Ratio Q5:Q1 | Share D10 | Share Q5 | Ratio Q5:Q1 | Share D10 | Share Q5 | Ratio Q5:Q1 | Share D10 |
| Australia (2009) | 28 | 2 | | 47 | 5 | | 41 | 7 | |
| Finland (2009) | 37 | 7 | 23 | 53 | 13 | 39 | 33 | 5 | 19 |
| Italy (2010) | | | | | | | 39 | 3 | 21 |
| Korea (2011) | | | | | | | 46 | 8 | |
| Luxembourg (2010) | 45 | 6 | 26 | 45 | 6 | 25 | 38 | 5 | 22 |
| Netherlands (2011) | 37 | 5 | 21 | 57 | 7 | 44 | 45 | 7 | 28 |
| UK (2005) | 33 | 2 | 19 | 44 | 5 | 28 | 44 | 8 | 27 |
| USA (2010) | 52 | 7 | 38 | 76 | 16 | 67 | 50 | 9 | 33 |

*Sources:* GINI Country Reports and BHPS, HWLI, HWWD, IPO, LU-HFCS, SCF, SHFLC, SHIW.

countries. Therefore a direct comparison of ratios by quintile across countries for which we have different measures of income is not possible.

For most of the countries, the differences across the quintiles are mainly due to financial wealth, since the profile of housing is flatter. In the case of the USA, Netherlands, and Finland the post-crisis years show an increase of wealth-to-income at the bottom, which may be due to a fall in income and which suggests the relevance of the role of income as the denominator. Whenever we observe a very high wealth-to-income level, the most probable explanation is in housing, as in the case of Australia. Debt relative to income hovers within a narrow band across the seven countries, its quintile profiles are also rather flat, and the changes over time seem modest in the light of the financial crisis.

The pattern of debt-to-income is also very heterogeneous, both in terms of levels and distribution. In the Netherlands, Korea, and the USA at the end of the 2000s the ratio of debt to income is higher than in the other countries, regardless of the fact that using non-equivalized income data for these countries should reduce this ratio (higher denominator) in comparison to Italy, Finland, and Australia for which equivalized disposable income is used. This higher debt is probably due to generous systems of mortgage deductions and other policies favouring private indebtedness. In Italy, Luxembourg, and, more importantly, in Korea and the USA (at the end of the 2000s) the importance of debt over income is particularly high for the bottom income quintile. In Korea this is probably due to the *joense* system, in which a renter makes a deposit of around half the market price to the houseowner for the rental period (GINI country report for Korea). For all the countries for which we have data for the mid-1990s and the late 2000s with the exception of Italy, it is evident how the explosion of the mortgage markets has resulted in an increased debt-to-income ratio. This ratio increased more than the net housing-to-income ratio, especially in the USA and Finland. In the Netherlands, the UK, and the USA this resulted in an increased importance of the debt-to-income ratio particularly for the bottom income quintile (which is for gross income and does not directly correspond to poverty). However, in the USA and the Netherlands, where mortgage interest payments are tax-deductible, the level of the debt-to-income ratio of the bottom income quintile (almost) exceeds that of the top quintiles. In the Netherlands, the rather flat pattern of debt-to-income ratios across income quintiles (with the exception of the second) may be explained by the extreme generosity of the mortgage interest deduction system (interests payments can be deducted with no limits).

The presence of assets at the bottom of the income distribution suggests that the impact of income inequality might eventually be cushioned, but this does not eliminate the worries of increasing inequality. The debt ratio may be high due to low or declining incomes (this is a point-in-time estimate), or debt may be high due to the desired level of consumption, which may be determined endogenously through social comparison. Without a measure of that desired level, it is very difficult to assess the hedging role of assets.

### 4.5.4 More Detailed Measures of Concentration

More detail of the joint distribution is shown for Australia, Italy, and the Netherlands, with a matrix of wealth and income deciles that specifies the number of households, in Table 4.4. In the bottom income decile one-third of all Australian households, one-fifth of Dutch households, and one-tenth of Italian households hold wealth at levels ranging in the upper five wealth deciles. Italian and Dutch low-income households are more often wealth-poor than Australian. The share among households where the top wealth decile and top income decile overlap is similar and modest in Australia and the Netherlands—3.4% of all households (34% of the decile), but income concepts differ—and clearly higher in Italy—5.4% (54% of the decile)—which shares the same income concept with Australia.

Available only for Italy and the Netherlands, the concentration of wealth itself in the same matrix is much more skewed. Over all income deciles 91% to 100% of all wealth is found in the top five wealth deciles for the Netherlands, while for Italy there is a stronger gradient, starting at about 53% in the bottom decile. The Dutch bottom decile even tops the top-decile share with 71% as against 60% in the top wealth decile—as the few low-income households (4%) that do have wealth seem to be euro-millionaires on average. The

**Table 4.4.** Wealth and income deciles, Australia 2009, Italy 2010, and Netherlands 2011

| Found in wealth deciles: | | Income deciles* | | | | | | | | | | |
|---|---|---|---|---|---|---|---|---|---|---|---|---|
| | | 1 | 2 | 3 | 4 | 5 | 6 | 7 | 8 | 9 | 10 | All |
| | | | | | *Household shares* | | | | | | | |
| Australia | % in 6–10 | 36 | 45 | 44 | 40 | 42 | 47 | 50 | 54 | 62 | 80 | 50 |
| | % in 10 | 6 | 3 | 4 | 6 | 8 | 8 | 9 | 10 | 14 | 34 | 10 |
| Italy | % in 6–10 | 9 | 17 | 28 | 34 | 48 | 53 | 65 | 67 | 85 | 93 | 50 |
| | % in 10 | 1 | 0 | 1 | 1 | 4 | 4 | 6 | 9 | 19 | 54 | 10 |
| Netherlands | % in 6–10 | 19 | 23 | 32 | 43 | 51 | 54 | 58 | 64 | 73 | 83 | 50 |
| | % in 10 | 4 | 3 | 4 | 5 | 6 | 8 | 9 | 11 | 17 | 34 | 10 |
| | | | | | *Wealth shares* | | | | | | | |
| Italy | % in 6–10 | 53 | 64 | 67 | 73 | 80 | 85 | 89 | 91 | 98 | 100 | 91 |
| | % in 10 | 7 | 6 | 9 | 10 | 15 | 19 | 20 | 25 | 49 | 83 | 46 |
| Netherlands | % in 6–10 | 91 | 95 | 97 | 99 | 100 | 103 | 104 | 103 | 103 | 102 | 102 |
| | % in 10 | 71 | 36 | 39 | 34 | 35 | 43 | 46 | 49 | 59 | 85 | 60 |

*Sources:* HWWD, SHIW and IPO.

same top-deciles overlap holds 29% of all wealth, and the remaining house-holds of the top income decile hold only 5–6% of all wealth (not shown). The bottom wealth decile is well filled by the lower income deciles in Italy and Australia: 91% and 84% respectively are in the first five income deciles. This contrasts with the Netherlands—here wealth is negative in this decile—where only 30% are found in the bottom five deciles and 70% in the upper five deciles (not shown).

Finally, the evolution of the top-decile shares in wealth of different kinds and debt for the Netherlands and the USA is suggestive of some diminishing of wealth at the top during the recession of the 1990s as well as the current crisis, a lowering of financial wealth concentration at the top, and a slight increase in debt concentration on both occasions.

### 4.5.5 Diverging Top Shares

Finally, the evolution of the shares in total net wealth of, on the one hand, the top wealth decile and, on the other hand, the top income decile shows interesting divergences (Table 4.5), demanding further research.

Focusing on the changes between consecutive observations, the sign of the changes is always in the same direction for both top shares, with one intriguing exception: between 2007 and 2010 the American top-income-decile share falls from 60.5% to 59.6% while the top-wealth-decile share shows a significant increase (71.4 to 74.4%). Also in the Netherlands the top-wealth-decile share increases strongly after the crisis (56.0 to 60.2%) but here the

**Table 4.5.** Shares in wealth (%) of the top income decile and the top wealth decile, 1987–2011

| | Finland | | Netherlands | | UK | | USA | |
|---|---|---|---|---|---|---|---|---|
| | Top income | Top wealth | Top income | Top wealth | Top income | Top wealth | Top income | Top wealth |
| 1987 | 23.0 | 35.9 | | | | | | |
| 1988 | | | | | | | | |
| 1989 | | | | | | | 53.0 | 67.0 |
| 1990 | | | | | | | | |
| 1991 | | | | | | | | |
| 1992 | | | | | | | 51.2 | 67.0 |
| 1993 | | | 33.3 | 60.6 | | | | |
| 1994 | 25.3 | 38.7 | 31.0 | 60.2 | | | | |
| 1995 | | | 30.7 | 57.9 | 26.7 | 49.1 | 51.3 | 67.9 |
| 1996 | | | 30.1 | 59.2 | | | | |
| 1997 | | | 29.0 | 58.2 | | | | |
| 1998 | 32.1 | 42.8 | 29.1 | 60.0 | | | 55.4 | 68.6 |
| 1999 | | | 27.9 | 58.7 | | | | |
| 2000 | | | 27.5 | 58.1 | 24.9 | 45.2 | | |
| 2001 | | | | | | | 58.0 | 69.6 |
| 2002 | | | | | | | | |
| 2003 | | | | | | | | |
| 2004 | 29.9 | 41.8 | | | | | 57.3 | 69.4 |
| 2005 | | | | | 20.4 | 39.1 | | |
| 2006 | | | 34.7 | 57.8 | | | | |
| 2007 | | | 33.8 | 57.2 | | | 60.5 | 71.4 |
| 2008 | | | 36.5 | 56.7 | | | | |
| 2009 | 30.8 | 43.9 | 33.1 | 56.0 | | | | |
| 2010 | | | 33.6 | 59.6 | | | 59.6 | 74.4 |
| 2011 | | | 34.4 | 60.2 | | | | |

*Sources*: HWLI, IPO, BPS AND SCF.

top-income-decile wealth moves up as well (33.1% to 34.4%). At the same time the size of the changes differs substantially, being at one time larger for one top share compared to the other and the other way around the next time. For example, from 1994 to 1998 the Finnish top incomes book a growth of 6.8 percentage points while the top wealth advances by 4.1 percentage points; from 1998 to 2004, however, the former declines by 2.2 percentage points and the latter by only 0.7. Over the limited number of observations this volatility seems to be larger for top-income-decile shares compared to top-wealth-decile shares in Finland and the USA, but there is no difference for the Netherlands and the UK has only two observations. Quite probably debt and financial wealth play an important role in explaining these differences between top incomes and top wealth, and that will be a fruitful avenue of investigation in future research.

## 4.6 Conclusions

The chapter presents extensive evidence on wealth and wealth inequality, their measurement, trends, drivers, and relationship with income, building on the work of the GINI project and fresh analysis of other data sources and literature.

In the last decades wealth has gained importance relative to income in all GINI countries for which we have evidence. However defined, wealth-to-income ratios increased considerably, although more in some countries than in others, and they declined as a first effect of the global financial crisis but are still well above the initial level. The evolution of asset prices and macroeconomic dynamics help to explain this growing importance of wealth.

Wealth inequality increased in most countries during the 1980s and 1990s, with few exceptions. This was strengthened by an increased polarization of wealth: the fraction of households with nil or negative net worth grew and the share of net worth held by the top percentiles increased at the same time. Polarization occurred also when or where aggregate wealth inequality was not increasing.

Though the collection and elaboration of data on wealth and its distribution has been progressing recently, the data situation is still far from satisfactory. We have used different data sources in order to improve the trade-off between cross-country comparability and time coverage. The measurement of wealth and of wealth inequality is also facing analytical challenges posed by the role of debt and of negative wealth shares, the lack of equivalization for internationally diverging household structures, the significance of relative and absolute differences in wealth holdings, and the exclusion of important assets such as public pension entitlements in some countries. We warn that the comparison of data for different countries demands very careful interpretation because of varying definitions and also for lack of wealth equivalization, which hides the role that family-provided welfare may play.

The level of wealth inequality varies widely across countries, with the UK, USA, France, and the Scandinavian countries reporting the highest levels, and the East Asian countries, Spain, Ireland, and Italy the lowest. Recently, the wealth inequality ranking of some countries has changed considerably (e.g. Ireland), although measurement issues play a role in explaining these differences and, in particular for Sweden, the main drivers are to be sought elsewhere. We distinguish between cross-country and over-time drivers, as we think that cross-country differences in wealth inequality do not offer a full explanation of the national stories.

Social expenditure is an important driver of the cross-country variation in wealth inequality. Low expenditures on housing policies in some countries force households at the bottom of the income distribution to accumulate wealth. In other countries, where poorer households are supported by housing policies and subsidies, they do not have such strong incentives to accumulate (housing) wealth. This explanation is weaker for Eastern European countries. Social expenditures regarding old age explain another part of the inequality differences for the same reason. The level of debt (mortgages and educational loans) is yet another important driver of wealth inequality, especially when negative values are taken into account in the calculation of net wealth inequality. Demographic factors play a comparatively small role. The labour market and the distribution of earnings explain the level of wealth inequality in the USA better than in other countries, where inheritance can provide a better explanation.

If institutional characteristics can explain the cross-country variability in wealth inequality, the evolution of capital, financial assets, their fiscal treatment, and the superstar phenomenon seem better at explaining the over-time trends. Debt is an important driver here too. The level of private debt increased in all countries, albeit to a different extent. The increase in debt levels had a (wealth) equalizing impact in some countries and a disequalizing effect in others. The trends in wealth inequality seem better explained by the evolution of capital compared to labour and their respective returns than by the increase in income inequality. The 'superstar' phenomenon of the working rich can explain the increase of top wealth shares. Diminishing taxation of capital income and inheritance may have boosted the accumulation of wealth at the top, but also with unchanged taxation the growing importance of capital incomes and increased wealth offshoring all worked in the direction of increasing wealth inequality; the more favourable tax treatment of housing (at least until recently, and especially in the form of mortgage interest deductions) had an ambiguous and differing impact on wealth inequality across countries.

The chapter has also analysed the important relationship between wealth and income distributions. We identify four groups of countries: (i) low wealth inequality with high income inequality (Mediterranean and East Asian countries); (ii) high wealth inequality with low income inequality (Scandinavian countries and France); (iii) high wealth inequality with high income inequality (Anglo-Saxon countries); (iv) low wealth inequality with low income inequality (Finland, Czech Republic, and Austria), which we define as 'virtuous' countries.

We suggest that an insightful analysis of wealth inequality needs to take into account the income position of households. Indeed, this shows a different picture. The distribution of wealth over households ranked by their income is less dispersed than if ranked only by their wealth, with the exception of the USA. Also the shares in wealth of top-income households are significantly lower than of top-wealth households. Such differences may be explained by the role played by debt, which is more strongly linked to income because of repayment, and the types of assets households possess. Financial assets have the largest income-disequalizing effect as their correlation with income is stronger than for housing assets. Debt seems to worsen the position of the income poorest, especially in most recent years, for example in Italy, Korea, Luxembourg, Netherlands, and the USA. Finally, even some fraction of the income-poorest households is rich in terms of wealth, as we found for Australia and the Netherlands. Nevertheless, the fraction among the income-rich who are also wealth-rich is much larger.

Further improvements are needed in the measurement of wealth, wealth inequality, their relationship with income, and (social and family) welfare systems, for a proper understanding of economic inequality. The explosion of debt and the problems it generates for the interpretation of wealth inequality and its relationship with income calls for further study. Higher debt is not a sign of economic stress and lower wellbeing per se, but may also be a signal of a stronger economic position (workers with a permanent contract, expectations of inheritance, etc.), unless, naturally, the conditions for repaying debts are lax. This calls for a careful comparison of indebted households with households possessing comparable net assets without debt.

## Appendix: Dataset acronyms

| | |
|---|---|
| BHPS | British Household Panel Survey |
| HWLI | Household wealth, liabilities and income. Statistics Finland. |
| HWWD | Household Wealth and Wealth Distribution, Australia, 2009–10. Australian Bureau of Statistics. |
| IPO | Income Panel Survey. Statistics Netherlands. |
| ISFF | Household Finance and Consumption Survey. Banco do Portugal. |
| SCF | Survey of Consumer Finance. Federal Reserve Bank, Washington. |
| SHFLC | Survey of Household Finance and Living Conditions. National Statistical Office of Korea. |

# 5

# Increasing Educational Inequalities?

*Gabriele Ballarino, Massimiliano Bratti, Antonio Filippin,*
*Carlo Fiorio, Marco Leonardi, and Francesco Scervini*

## 5.1 Introduction

As is well known, education is one of the main 'structural parameters' (in the sense of Blau, 1977) governing the life course of individuals in contemporary societies. Both economic and sociological research have widely shown education to be strongly related not just to occupational outcomes, and thus to income, but also to non-occupational outcomes such as health, tolerance, and social and political participation (for a recent review, see Oreopoulos and Salvanes, 2009). At the macro level, the correlation between the expansion of education and economic growth is also well established, although the direction of the causality is still debated (Krueger and Lindahl, 2001; Schofer and Meyer, 2005).

Thus, expanding education has long been a tool of public policies aiming at reducing income inequality. Intuitively, increasing the level of education attained by every individual helps to reduce the gap between high- and low-educated workers in terms of wages and to 'level the playing field' (Roemer, 2000), fostering equality of opportunity. Moreover, reducing educational inequality may also have equalizing effects in terms of income, as long as there is a positive correlation between education and income. Finally, policies aiming at a more equal distribution of education can reduce the role of parental background and intergenerational mobility in educational achievement and job-market outcomes.

While educational policies will be the subject of Chapter 12 of this volume, this chapter focuses on the definition and the measurement of educational inequality. In fact, educational inequality can be defined along two dimensions, inclusion and fairness, as suggested by OECD (2007b). Inclusion implies a minimum standard of education for all and has to do with whether overall levels of provision are sufficient and effective. Fairness implies that personal and social circumstances, such as gender, socioeconomic status, ethnicity, and region of residence, should not be an obstacle to educational success. Given the multidimensional nature of educational inequality, when trying to measure it one has first to clarify what definition of inequality is to be used. The first dimension of inequality can be captured looking at the 'stock' of education individuals receive and measuring how educational levels are distributed across the population. The second dimension is instead related to inequality of opportunities and can be quantified by looking at the extent to which an individual's educational achievement depends on being a member of some social group, defined by socioeconomic background or by some other ascribed feature, such as gender, ethnicity, or being a migrant.

Regarding the first dimension, describing the distribution of education across the population is not trivial and the possibility of computing synthetic indices of dispersion depends on the underlying variables used to measure educational levels. The literature has identified three main indicators of individual education, namely the number of years of schooling completed, the levels and types of qualification achieved, and test scores capturing actual competences. Each of these measures has advantages and drawbacks (a careful discussion of these issues is provided in Meschi and Scervini, 2013) and inequality measures must fit their characteristics.

However, in contrast to the case of inequality, in the literature there is not a set of frequently used and agreed indices of intergenerational mobility. It is possible, indeed, to build several indicators of intergenerational mobility, based on the correlation between parents' and children's position. Two recent examples are Di Paolo et al. (2010), who exploit the differences between fathers and mothers and sons and daughters, and Checchi et al. (2008), who look at the time path of autocorrelation across cohorts. Sociological research has also proposed many ways to measure the association between the education of parents and their offspring, based on log-linear models of mobility tables (Erikson and Goldthorpe, 1992) or on various kind of logit models (Ballarino and Schadee, 2011). The lack of a commonly agreed measure of intergenerational mobility is due to the complexity of the phenomenon on the one hand, and to the small number of surveys including information on two generations of individuals on the other.[1]

---

[1] The present chapter is not an exception from this perspective: most of the analysis focuses on the distribution of education, while a relatively small—but still relevant—space is devoted to intergenerational mobility.

The chapter is organized as follows. Section 5.2 reviews the main issues related to the measurement of education in a comparative framework and describes a new dataset on educational inequality. Section 5.3 focuses on the trends of education expansion at different levels, disaggregated by gender and for several geopolitical areas, and suggests some explanations for the observed trends. Section 5.4 analyses two distinct aspects of educational inequality, namely the intra-generation dispersion of formal education and the intergenerational transmission of competences. Section 5.5 investigates the possible regularities between educational level and educational inequality, while Section 5.6 relates educational inequality to income inequality. Section 5.7 summarizes and concludes.

## 5.2 The Dataset on Educational Inequality

There are three main indicators to measure the quantity of education received by individuals. One is the duration of formal schooling. Its main advantages are that it is measured in years, and therefore is easy to compute, and that it is readily comparable over countries and years. The main drawback is that it is unrelated to the quality of education, both in terms of actual results and in terms of educational careers and achievements.

The second indicator of education is the highest level of formal education achieved. All the educational systems—not just in the countries included in this research—share some common features and analogous structure (see Collins (2000) for the historical origins of this structure). Typically, there are two cycles of education, primary and lower secondary, that are common to all children aged from 5 or 6 to about 14–15.[2] This cycle of basic education is compulsory and is followed by a cycle of upper secondary education, which can have some degree of heterogeneity—with the main distinction being between vocational and academic curricula. Finally, there are post-secondary cycles, which are very heterogeneous with respect to duration, specialization, and formal degrees provided. Some of them, mostly academic, are classified as tertiary and post-tertiary education; others, mostly vocational, are classified as 'post-secondary, non-tertiary' by the ISCED[3] classification. Measuring education by the highest qualification achieved also has pros and cons. The main advantage of this measure over years of education is that it accounts for different durations of analogous school cycles. The main drawback relates to cross-country comparability: levels, types, and duration of specific educational programmes depend on the institutional structure of educational

---

[2] In many educational systems, these two first stages are unified in a single, longer cycle.
[3] ISCED is the International Standard Classification of Education developed by UNESCO in 1976.

systems and, given the degree of differentiation of educational systems across countries and over time, it can be difficult to construct a classification of educational qualification that is valid and comparable internationally.

The third possible measure of education is related to competences. In principle, measuring the competences acquired by individuals is the most direct way to assess the efficacy of an educational system independently of its institutional characteristics. The main drawback is that competences, in particular for adult population, depend not only on the education acquired, but also on socioeconomic background, on job characteristics, on income, on social relationships, and so on. Therefore, competences may be weakly correlated with the educational system.

Most of the available macro-level datasets providing measures of the total quantity of education in a population record the average years of education, or the share of individuals who completed each level of the educational framework, or the average competences acquired by individuals (Barro and Lee, 2012; Cohen and Soto, 2007; Meschi and Scervini, 2013).

Measuring educational inequality poses various challenges. Typical inequality indices, such as the Gini, Theil, and Atkinson measures, can effectively measure the dispersion of years of education, and—in most cases—of the level of competences, but are seldom used for measuring the dispersion of discrete variables, such as the highest qualification achieved. In contrast to income, that is virtually unbounded in the upper tail, education cannot exceed a maximum level represented by postgraduate education and this is relevant for the inequality measure used (Checchi, 2001).

The methodological problems related to the construction of educational inequality indicators are reviewed in Meschi and Scervini (2011). That survey identified significant shortcomings in the available measures of educational inequality, prompting us to create a brand new dataset that constitutes a major advance in the analysis of educational inequality in Europe, and to make it available to the research community. We now briefly highlight the main features of this dataset, although for a detailed description of the procedures and methodologies adopted to build the new dataset and the validation and consistency checks of the measures obtained across surveys one should refer to Meschi and Scervini (2013). Data are available on the GINI project website or upon request to the authors.

This dataset collects measures of educational level and inequality for thirty-one countries over several birth cohorts. Drawing on four representative international datasets (ESS, EU-SILC, IALS, and ISSP),[4] various measures

---

[4] Acronyms stand for European Social Survey, European Union Statistics on Income and Living Conditions, International Adult Literacy Survey, and International Social Survey Program respectively.

of individual educational attainment have been collected and aggregated to generate synthetic indices of educational level and dispersion by countries and birth cohorts. The first step for the creation of the dataset was to merge all the available waves of each survey, in order to increase the sample size, provided the information was consistent across waves. Individuals were then selected according to two criteria: first, only individuals older than twenty-five were included, in order to exclude individuals still (or potentially) in formal education. Second, only individuals reporting no more than thirty years of formal education were included, assuming that is the highest reasonable duration of a complete educational career (from primary school to PhD). The third stage was the aggregation of individuals according to the year of birth, generating thirteen five-year cohorts, from 1920–4 to 1980–4, surveyed between 1992 (first IALS wave) and 2008 (last EU-SILC wave available in 2010).

The length of formal education is available in three of the four surveys, namely ESS, IALS, and ISSP. The variable in EU-SILC is imputed from educational attainment and therefore not considered in the dataset. By construction, each individual's variable is bounded between 0 and 30, and several indicators are provided: the average years of formal education, by country and cohort, a set of inequality indices (Gini, Generalized Entropy, and Atkinson indices), the nine deciles and some decile ratios.

Similar indicators are provided for competences, as assessed by the three waves of IALS surveys. In contrast to years of schooling, IALS scores measure actual skills of individuals and are bounded between 0 and 500. Information on the highest level of education attained by individuals is available in all the four surveys. However, ISSP data were found to be not consistently comparable across countries and years, and therefore only data from ESS, EU-SILC, and IALS were used. Even within these three surveys, in order to ensure comparability and consistency across different countries, different cohorts, and different surveys, the seven standard ISCED levels were aggregated into four broader categories: primary, lower secondary, upper secondary, and tertiary education. For each of these categories, they provided the share of individuals—within each cohort—who attained that level. All the statistics on the quantity of education were computed on the whole sample and divided by gender, while dispersion indicators are provided only for the entire population.

The Meschi and Scervini (2013) dataset presents some remarkable novelties compared to the existing datasets on educational attainment (e.g. Barro and Lee, 1996, 2001, 2010; Cohen and Soto, 2007). First of all, the data are organized by birth cohort rather than by survey years. This allows an increase in the period covered, as it contains information from the beginning of the 1920s, while existing datasets generally start from the 1950s or 1960s (see, for example, Barro and Lee, 2010; Cohen and Soto, 2007). A birth cohort approach allows one to observe the evolution of educational attainment for individuals born in different periods, possibly characterized by distinct institutional features of the school systems, which is particularly useful for analyses of the determinants of educational outcomes. Since formal education occurs mainly in the early stage of life and remains invariant over the life cycle, a cohort approach is less affected by measurement problems of recall data than other variables such as income. Second, by using different data sources to create aggregate measures of educational achievement, this dataset improves on the robustness and reliability of the statistics provided. Third, this dataset presents three alternative (but complementary) measures of education. Namely, besides the standard variable on years of education completed, it also contains information on highest qualification achieved and on individual actual competences, which are often considered better measures of individual human capital (Hanushek and Kimko, 2000; Hanushek and Wössmann, 2010). Fourth, the measure of years of schooling is directly derived from micro-data and therefore based on respondents' answers and not computed by imputation using information on educational attainment, which typically only distinguishes six or fewer categories (see Barro and Lee, 2010). Finally, the dataset is the first one to provide information not only on the educational level, but also on its distribution, using a wide range of indices calculated on years of schooling (namely standard deviation, coefficient of variation, Gini index, Theil index, mean logarithmic deviation, and Atkinson indices with different inequality aversion parameters).

The inequality measures provided in the Meschi and Scervini (2013) dataset describe how much education dispersion is generated at a given moment in a given society. However, there is another concept of education inequality, more closely related to equality of education: intergenerational mobility and equality of opportunity in education. Measuring these kinds of inequality is much more difficult: on the one hand, we need data on education or competences of parents and children; on the other, intergenerational mobility deals with two dimensions: education of parents and education of children. This means that each scalar of an education distribution is replaced by a vector with at least two elements: one for children and the others for at least one parent's education. The most frequently used way to represent intergenerational mobility, inspired by the sociological literature (e.g. Eriksson and Goldthorpe, 1992), is the transition matrix, in which each cell includes the proportion of child–parent with given educational (or competence) levels. To summarize such matrices with a single transition or mobility index is a different issue from inequality measurement. Nevertheless, there are ways to give a rough idea of intergenerational mobility in a society. By looking at absolute levels, one can count the share of individuals who improved (or worsened) their position with respect to their parents. By counting the number of child–parent couples that lay on the main diagonal of the transition matrix, one can immediately assess the level of immobility over generations.

## 5.3 The Expansion of Education

The use of the Meschi and Scervini dataset allows us to provide a description of the process of educational expansion. Figures 5.1–5.6 describe this process, for the three main school levels: lower secondary, higher secondary, and tertiary, using ESS data from waves 2002–8 divided into five-year cohorts of birth. We do not consider primary school, as in most of the countries we observe that participation rate was already close to 100% for the earliest cohorts. For each educational level, we present two graphs by gender: the first pools all the countries together, giving a glimpse of the aggregate process, whereas the second divides the sample into five geopolitical areas: Scandinavia (including Denmark, Finland, Norway, and Sweden); British Isles (Ireland, United Kingdom); Continental Europe (Austria, Belgium, Germany, Luxemburg, the Netherlands, and Switzerland); Mediterranean area (France, Greece, Italy, Portugal, Spain); and Eastern Europe (former Socialist countries: Bulgaria, Czech Republic, Estonia, Hungary, Latvia, Poland, Romania, Slovakia, and Slovenia).[5]

Let us start with the lower secondary level. We focus our attention on the share of individuals who achieved at least the specific level considered. Figure 5.1 plots the share of individuals (on the vertical axis) who completed *at least* the lower secondary cycle, disaggregated by cohort (on the horizontal axis). Overall, the share of individuals with at least secondary education in ESS countries is around 60% for the cohort 1920–4 and almost 100% for the cohort 1980–4. Figure 5.1 shows the typical S-shaped, three-stage pattern of educational expansion (Meyer et al., 1977, 1992; Ballarino et al., 2013). At first, few people participate and expansion is slow. We see only the final part of this stage, as our oldest cohorts show an already high level of participation, starting from over 50% for women and over 60% for men. Then, with the cohorts born in the 1930s and schooled after World War II, the process gets faster, as the proportion of participants increases (the stage of 'explosion'). Finally, a third stage is reached, where expansion gets slow again, approaching a saturation point of near-complete participation, above 90%. We can observe a catch-up process on the part of females: they start disadvantaged,

---

[5] Norway and Switzerland are outside of the GINI frame, but are included in order to increase numbers and detail. However, their exclusion would not change the results.

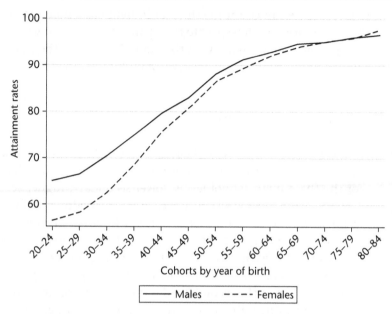

**Figure 5.1.** Lower secondary school, all countries
*Source*: Ballarino et al. (2013), using data from Meschi and Scervini (2013).

but then their curve gets steeper and they catch up with males by the late 1960s.

Figure 5.2 breaks down our sample into the five geopolitical areas described above. A process of convergence can be observed: while in the oldest cohorts the levels of the different geopolitical areas vary substantially, from about 20% to more than 70%, in the more recent cohorts the variation goes from 90% to 100%. Areas starting at a lower level grow faster. The Continental European, the Nordic, and the Eastern areas start at the highest level, above 60%. These areas are those where mass schooling started earlier because of both cultural and geopolitical reasons (Brint, 2006). The Continental European area has a more regular growth, while the Nordic has a flatter curve in the earlier cohorts, then expands with the cohorts born in the 1930s and reaches the saturation point with people born after World War II. The Eastern European area experiences a steeper increase for the cohorts born after 1935, so that it outperforms the Continental European area by the cohort born after World War II. This growth is related to the Communist regimes then ruling the area, which fostered school participation on the part of the lower classes as a means to reach their egalitarian goals. The

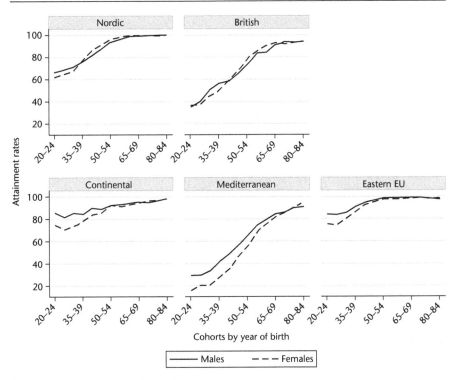

**Figure 5.2.** Lower secondary school, by geopolitical area and birth year
*Source*: Ballarino et al. (2013), using data from Meschi and Scervini (2013).

British Isles area starts at a considerably lower level, and fully catches up only with the cohort born in the 1970s. The same catch-up point can be observed for the Mediterranean area, which starts at the lowest (below 30%) and grows slowly until cohorts born after World War II and much faster afterwards. This could be related to World War II and to specific features such as the Spanish Civil War.

Figure 5.3 shows the pattern of participation in higher secondary school. The S-shaped pattern is much less clear than for lower secondary (for a deeper analysis of this trend, see Ballarino et al., 2013). The growth process gets faster with cohorts born in the 1930s, as at the previous level, but the stage of saturation is reached later, with the cohorts born in the late 1970s, and at a lower level, between 70% and 80%. Also in this case there are some signs of an effect of World War II for cohorts born in the early 1930s. The gender effect is stronger: at the early stage of growth, female disadvantage is stronger than for lower secondary (this could be related to the fact that the early expansion of higher secondary education had a strong vocational

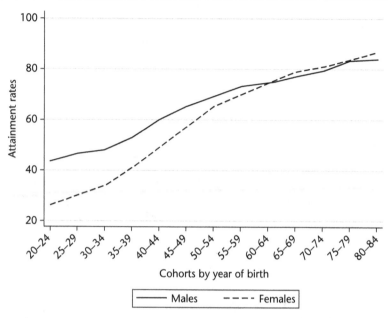

**Figure 5.3.** Upper secondary school, all countries
*Source*: Ballarino et al. (2013), using data from Meschi and Scervini (2013).

component, particularly for males); then the gender difference in the steepness of the second stage is stronger than in lower secondary, so that the catch-up still takes place for the cohorts born in the 1960s. Despite some irregularities, the most recent cohorts show signs of a female advantage in higher secondary achievement.

Figure 5.4 shows the pattern of participation to upper secondary level broken down by geopolitical area. A convergence pattern can still be seen, but not as clearly as for lower secondary, perhaps because of lower saturation effects. In fact, we observe a substantial convergence for the Nordic, Continental, and Eastern areas after the cohorts born in the 1950s, while the British Isles and the Mediterranean area lag behind, even in the most recent cohorts. Concerning gender, we observe different timings of the catch-up process: the Scandinavian area comes first (at the start of the 1950s), followed by the British Isles and the Eastern area in the following decade. In the Continental European area the catch-up takes place later, only with the cohort born in the second half of the 1960s, as in the case of the Mediterranean area, albeit at lower levels.

Finally, Figure 5.5 shows the pattern of expansion of participation in higher education (defined as tertiary education only, excluding vocational

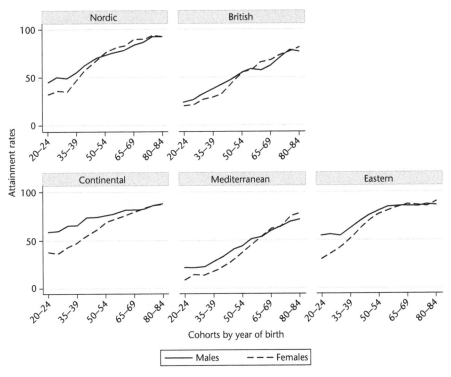

**Figure 5.4.** Upper secondary school, by geopolitical area and birth year
*Source*: Ballarino et al. (2013), using data from Meschi and Scervini (2013).

post-secondary tracks).[6] Both genders show something like a two-stage pattern (Ballarino et al., 2013). For men there is growth for the cohorts born in the 1930s and 1940s (who went to university after World War II), and then the growth stalls, to increase again for the cohorts born in the 1960s and 1970s. Women start lower, see growth as for men with the cohorts from the 1930s and the 1940s, then keep on growing, catch up with men in the cohorts born in the 1960s, and then show growth rates higher than their male counterparts. In general, the gender reversal pattern is stronger at this level than at the previous ones. A two-stage expansion pattern similar to the one we find is to be seen in Schofer and Meyer (2005, Figure 1), who plot the world's higher education students per 10,000 capita in the 20th century.

If we look at the geopolitical areas (Figure 5.6), we see no process of convergence at all: on the contrary, variation among areas appears to increase

---

[6] The relevance of post-secondary non-tertiary education is limited to a small set of countries: Spain, Germany, and the Netherlands are the only countries with more than 5% of individuals achieving this level. In most other countries the share is negligible not only with respect to the whole population, but also with respect to tertiary education achievement.

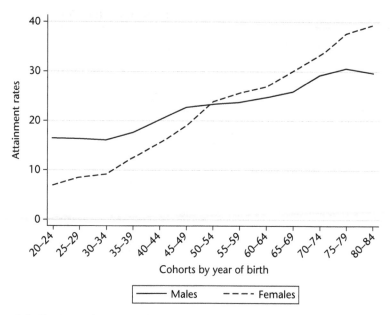

**Figure 5.5.** Tertiary education, all countries
*Source*: Ballarino et al. (2013), using data from Meschi and Scervini (2013).

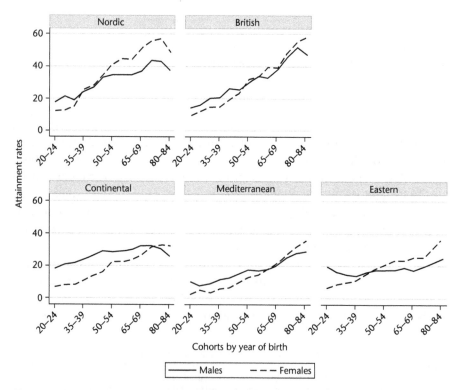

**Figure 5.6.** Tertiary education, by geopolitical area and birth year
*Source*: Ballarino et al. (2013), using data from Meschi and Scervini (2013).

over cohorts. In the oldest cohorts, the Nordic, Continental European, and British areas are those with higher participation, as was the case for the lower levels, but afterwards, the Continental Europe area remains somewhat behind and does not catch up. This difference depends on the educational policies of Germany and German-speaking countries that for many years have constrained access to tertiary education while pushing higher secondary vocational training (Ballarino, 2011). Something similar can be said for the Eastern European areas, where Communist policies tightly controlled access to tertiary education.

The graph also gives more detail on the two-stage pattern of expansion observed in Figure 5.5: the first stage was stronger in the early comers, the Nordic and British areas, while the second was strong in all the areas, but especially in the British and in the Continental European areas. Concerning the gender-reversal pattern, this is stronger in the Nordic and in the Eastern European areas, where females catch up with males as early as the cohort born in the first half of the 1940s. In the British and in the Continental European areas the catch up takes places 20–25 years later, and there is no female bias in the more recent cohorts. In the Mediterranean area there are more irregularities, so it is not really clear when the catch-up precisely takes place, but in the younger cohorts there seems to be a female advantage.

## 5.4 Educational Inequality

As pointed out above, participation in schooling expanded dramatically during the period we observe. What was the pattern of education inequality over the same period? As in the previous section, we continue using the ESS sample from the Meschi and Scervini dataset, but—in order to have a synthetic measure of inequality in school achievement—we measure individuals' years of education. This allows us to compute a Gini index for inequality in this distribution.

Theoretically, the pattern of schooling inequality should present an inverse-U shape, with low inequality at the outset when no one goes to school, then an increase when school is for an élite among the population, and finally a decrease with mass and universal schooling (see, for instance, Ram, 1990; Checchi, 2001; and Meschi and Scervini, 2012). Figure 5.7 shows the general pattern, which is a decreasing one, consistently with theoretical predictions, although here we see only the second part of the curve, with just a glimpse at the first stage of education growth. Then, the downward pattern is almost linear, albeit with some slowing down for the most recent cohorts. Meschi and Scervini (2012) suggest a possible explanation for such a

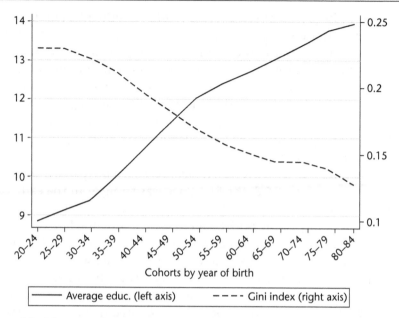

**Figure 5.7.** Educational inequality, all countries
*Source*: Authors' elaboration on data from Meschi and Scervini (2013).

'flattening' of the reduction of inequality. Since the saturation of upper secondary level, the process of educational expansion is being realized through an increase of the length and specialization of tertiary education, leading to a possible increase of inequality. This effect is still rather weak, but there is evidence confirming this trend. The linkage between expansion and inequality is analysed in greater detail in the next section.

The comparative pattern is shown in Figure 5.8, revealing wide variations across different areas. The Mediterranean area stands out, as it shows a much higher level of inequality in school participation. School systems in this area have been more elitist than elsewhere for a long period, with fewer people accessing post-compulsory education. Accordingly, the decrease of the Gini index over time is much stronger here, but convergence is not reached, and in this area we observe more inequality in schooling even in the cohorts born in the 1970s and early 1980s. As we would have expected, the Nordic area is the one showing the strongest reduction over time and the lowest present level of school inequality.

In the previous part of our discussion we considered only institutional education, spanning from *pre-primary* level to *academic* education. However, this is not the only means by which individuals gain competences: 'lifelong learning' is the process of acquiring education and competences even after the exit from formal education. Of course, adults' education may have characteristics

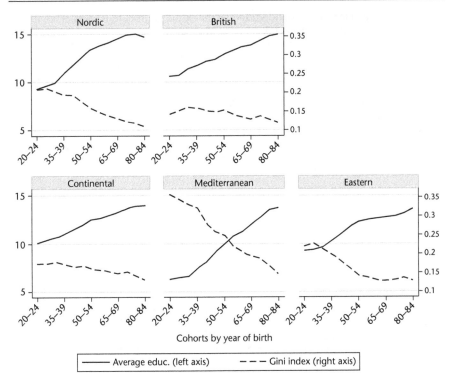

**Figure 5.8.** Educational inequality, by geopolitical area and birth year

*Source*: Authors' elaboration on data from Meschi and Scervini (2013).

and goals very different from the previous 'general' education (i.e. the former is likely to be more focused on the labour market, targeted to specific tasks or competences, while the latter usually gives more general competences and skills), but their importance is not necessarily less. Therefore it is relevant to analyse inequality and heterogeneity also with respect to this aspect.

Data availability prevents us for providing an up-to-date picture of the formation of competences, since the IALS survey was first conducted in 1994–8, it was then followed by a second wave in 2003 (named ALL, Adult Literacy and Life Skills) on a very limited number of countries (six) and no new data is available at present. However, using the Italian sample of ALL data we have found evidence that competences[7] decline with age, and increase with education and labour-market experience, but they still reflect parental education. We also found that formal education plays a partial substitution role in competence formation, as can be easily seen from Table 5.1.

---

[7] Competences are measured through country-comparable standardized tests in four different areas: prose ability, document interpretation, numeracy, and problem solving, measured on a common scale.

**Table 5.1.** Median test score, standardized factor extracted from four areas of adult competences, Italy, ALL survey 2003

| Education attainment of father | Educational attainment of son | | | |
| --- | --- | --- | --- | --- |
| | Lower secondary or less | Upper secondary | Tertiary | Total |
| Lower secondary or less | −0.48 | 0.35 | 0.71 | −0.11 |
| Upper secondary | 0.27 | 0.57 | 0.74 | 0.51 |
| Tertiary | 0.72 | 0.66 | 0.91 | 0.73 |
| Total | −0.42 | 0.41 | 0.76 | 0.00 |

*Source*: Authors' elaboration on ALL data, Italian sample only.

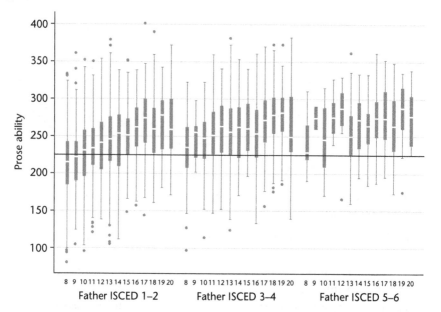

**Figure 5.9.** Distribution of competences (prose ability) by education of father and years of schooling, Italy, ALL 2003

*Source*: Authors' elaboration on ALL data, Italian sample.

Similarly, Figure 5.9, which depicts the distribution of prose ability competences according to years of schooling and parental education, shows that schooling may partially compensate for disadvantages in family background.

One may wonder why we should be concerned about competences. Empirical evidence suggests that, even in regulated labour markets, competence levels make a difference, both in employment probability and in earnings, increasing the employment probabilities of workers. As shown in Figure 5.10, high versus low levels of numeracy or problem-solving ability

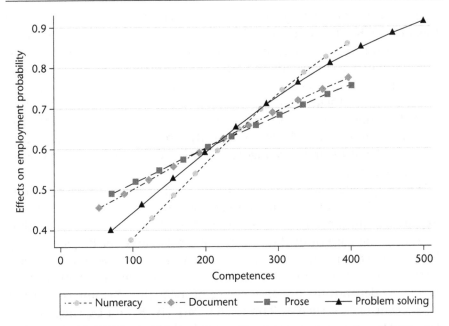

**Figure 5.10.** Marginal contribution of competences to employment probability, net of formal education, Italy, ALL 2003 (gender, age, and regional controls included)
*Source*: Authors' elaboration on ALL data, Italian sample.

substantially increase employment probability. Thus, an additional channel through which income inequality could be reduced is by favouring the accumulation of competences of children from disadvantaged backgrounds, helping the transition to employment and earnings, and reducing the gap associated with social stratification.

## 5.5 The Link Between Expansion of Schooling and Educational Inequality

In the previous sections we analysed separately the trends of schooling expansion and educational inequality. However, the two features of educational distribution are clearly related: given that modern schooling systems have been constantly expanding since the 19th century, the trend of educational inequality over time has to be studied taking expansion into account. Much work has been done on this topic on the part of the sociology of education, in particular trying to establish whether inequality of educational opportunities among social groups (classes, genders, ethnicities) has been decreasing over cohorts, as predicted by modernization theories, or has been stable over time, as predicted by social reproduction and neo-Marxist theories (see Breen and Jonsson (2005) for a review). Concerning inequality determined by family background (parental class or educational level), the first international comparative project found persisting inequality in most of the countries observed (Shavit and Blossfeld, 1993), while more recent work found a slight but significant decrease over time in all countries (Breen et al., 2009; Ballarino et al., 2009). Concerning gender, all studies confirm the pattern observed in Section 5.2 above: an early gap favouring men over women has been closed and in the younger cohorts a reversed gap, favouring women over men, appears.

While sociology has been more interested in inequality of opportunities, research in economics has also focussed on the relationship between expansion and inequality measured as dispersion of years of education, following the pattern of the so-called Kuznets curve for income. Mostly because of lack of data, there are only a few papers that found some regularity between expansion and inequality of schooling. The nature of the regularity depends mainly on the type of inequality measure considered. Less recent papers, such as Ram (1990), Park (1996) and De Gregorio and Lee (2002), found a significant inverted-U relationship using the standard deviation as a measure of educational inequality. However, the standard deviation is not mean-invariant,[8] and therefore is not the best indicator of inequality. Indeed, papers by Thomas et al. (2001) and Castelló and Doménech (2002) found a negative correlation between education expansion and inequality, measuring inequality by the Gini coefficient of years of education. However, all these papers exploit cross-sectional datasets, and so they could not observe the trend of expansion and inequality for different countries, but only one observation for each country, observed at different levels of development.

The main result from the analysis presented in Meschi and Scervini (2012) is that there is no Kuznets curve in education, at least for the countries and periods covered by the dataset. Even if European educational systems were characterized by a decline in inequality and a simultaneous increase in the average years of education, the correlation weakens with educational expansion and reverses after a certain threshold. Indeed, the empirical estimation of the relationship between educational level and educational inequality in a set of twenty-six European countries observed over thirteen cohorts provides evidence for the presence of a U-shaped relationship: after a certain level of education, further expansion is correlated with an increase of inequality.

---

[8] This means that if we multiply the whole distribution by the same coefficient, the standard deviation changes, while inequality indices, such as Gini index, remain unchanged.

The result is consistently found in several specifications and including both country and cohort fixed effects.

Figures 5.11 and 5.12 show how the correlation changed over time and after the education expansion, respectively. In detail, Figure 5.11 splits the sample in two: in the left panel, there are all the observations up to the cohort of people born in 1970–4: a clear negative trend emerges, with a slightly convex shape. In the right panel, there are only observations from the two last cohorts of the dataset: 1975–9 and 1980–4. Apart from the outliers represented by Portugal (with an average lower than 11), there seems to be no clear trend, meaning that further education expansion may not have any effect on the level of inequality. Actually, both from this figure and from the results in Meschi and Scervini (2012), it seems that inequality may increase after further education expansion. This is in line with the evidence provided in the previous sections: the saturation of low levels of education increases the average level of education and makes its distribution more equal; once the low levels are saturated, further expansion can only take place by an increase of the highest levels, generating inequality. This process can generate the U-shaped relationship found in the data.

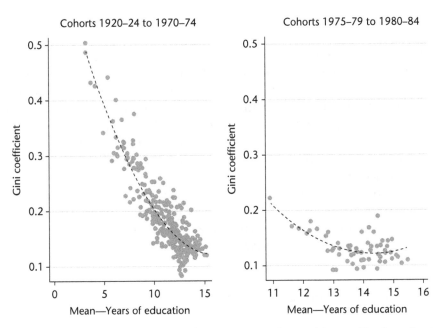

**Figure 5.11.** Correlation between education expansion and inequality, by cohorts of birth

*Source*: Meschi and Scervini (2013).

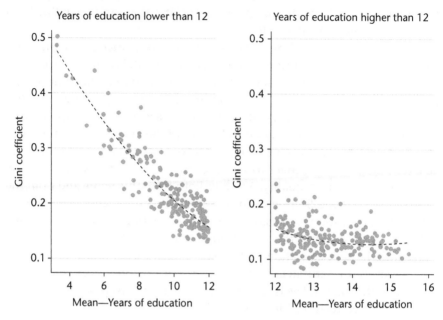

**Figure 5.12.** Correlation between education expansion and inequality, by levels of expansion

*Source*: Meschi and Scervini (2013).

Figure 5.12 considers separately two groups of observations: above and below 12 years of average education. This figure also seems supportive of the process described above: a strong negative correlation for less educated countries by cohort units and almost no correlation for the most educated ones. Combining the two pictures, we can state that all European countries have reached an average level of 12 years of education and that after this point there is no negative correlation between education expansion and educational inequality.

The more detailed discussion in Meschi and Scervini (2012) confirms this evidence, showing that—controlling for countries and cohorts fixed effects—there is a U-shaped curve between expansion and inequality with a turning point at around 15 years of average education.

## 5.6 From Education to Income Inequality

As mentioned above, the acquisition of formal education and competences is tightly linked with labour-market outcomes, in particular individual employability and earning capacity. In this section, we investigate the correlation between individual education and earnings in Europe. To this end, we exploit the EU-SILC 2009 dataset, which includes gross incomes and educational attainment for all individuals in all EU countries.

The analysis focuses only on the active population, which we define as individuals aged between 25 and 65. For every individual we compute market income and educational attainment. The former is the most intuitive economic outcome of human capital endowment. We define market income as the sum of gross incomes from employment and self-employment, excluding capital incomes and in-kind benefits, since these are not available in all countries, and public benefits, because—in principle—these are unrelated to educational attainment. Educational attainment is measured in years of education and represents the best available proxy of the amount of human capital acquired. We computed it through two distinct methods: on the one hand, as the difference between the year when the highest level of education was attained and the year of birth plus six (six being the age at which primary education starts in most European countries);[9] on the other side, using the information of the highest educational attainment and converting this into years of schooling, using the median duration of cycles as conversion values (i.e. 7 years for ISCED1, 9 years for ISCED2, 13 years for ISCED3, 15 years for ISCED4, and 18 years for ISCED5).

Relying on individual observations, we first partitioned the population by five-year birth cohorts and by gender, thus obtaining 522 cells (29 countries × 9 age cohorts × 2 genders), then we computed for each cell alternative measures of inequality for both income and education, i.e. the standard deviation of logs, the Gini concentration index and the coefficient of variation. Figure 5.13 plots the country average of Gini indices in education and income.

As for labour market participation, a proper approach would have suggested modelling the entry decision, but there are no clear identification restrictions to facilitate this. In order to partially overcome this problem, we analyse separately the income inequality indices including or excluding zero incomes. The specific relationship between these two inequality measures depends on the underlying functional form (whether exponential, semi-logarithmic, or linear). In all cases a formal decomposition of inequality by source is not possible when idiosyncratic components contribute to income generation.

We then regressed income inequality on educational inequality, and found a positive and significant correlation between the two, even when

---

[9] Unlike the analyses reported in the previous sections of the chapter, the resulting variable has been censored at 25, in order to increase the number of observations.

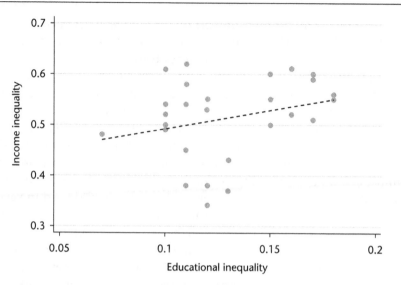

**Figure 5.13.** Scatter plot of inequality in education on inequality in gross income (Gini coefficients)

*Source*: Authors' elaborations on EU-SILC 2009.

**Table 5.2.** Gross incomes and educational (method 1) inequality, OLS estimates

|  | Standard deviation of logs | | | |
|---|---|---|---|---|
|  | Employment incomes | Total incomes | Employment incomes > 0 | Total incomes > 0 |
| Standard deviation of logs (years of education) | 0.665 | 0.403 | 0.665 | 0.403 |
|  | [0.381]* | [0.369] | [0.381]* | [0.369] |
| Observations | 522 | 522 | 522 | 522 |
| R-squared | 0.62 | 0.58 | 0.62 | 0.58 |
| **Gini index** | | | | |
| Gini index (years of education) | 0.611 | 0.517 | 0.502 | 0.585 |
|  | [0.278] | [0.302]* | [0.182]** | [0.171]*** |
| Observations | 522 | 522 | 522 | 522 |
| R-squared | 0.82 | 0.81 | 0.58 | 0.61 |
| **Coefficient of variation** | | | | |
| Coefficient of variation (years of education) | 2.582 | 1.981 | 0.951 | 1.276 |
|  | [0.853]*** | [0.712]*** | [0.315]*** | [0.264]*** |
| Observations | 522 | 522 | 522 | 522 |
| R-squared | 0.65 | 0.63 | 0.44 | 0.41 |

*Notes*: Robust standard errors in brackets; * significant at 10%; ** significant at 5%; *** significant at 1%; standard errors clustered at country level—constant, gender, country, and year controls included.

*Source*: Authors' elaboration on EU-SILC 2009.

**Table 5.3.** Gross incomes and educational (method 2) inequality, OLS estimates

| | Standard deviation of logs | | | |
|---|---|---|---|---|
| | Employment incomes | Total incomes | Employment incomes > 0 | Total incomes > 0 |
| Standard deviation of logs (years of education) | 0.826 | 1.127 | 0.826 | 1.127 |
| | [0.389]** | [0.345]*** | [0.389]** | [0.345]*** |
| Observations | 522 | 522 | 522 | 522 |
| R-squared | 0.62 | 0.59 | 0.62 | 0.59 |
| **Gini index** | | | | |
| Gini index (years of education) | 0.361 | 0.25 | 0.296 | 0.466 |
| | [0.281] | [0.289] | [0.174] | [0.209] |
| Observations | 522 | 522 | 522 | 522 |
| R-squared | 0.82 | 0.81 | 0.57 | 0.6 |
| **Coefficient of variation** | | | | |
| Coefficient of variation (years of education) | 1.873 | 1.489 | 0.489 | 1.165 |
| | [1.016]* | [0.642]** | [0.291] | [0.334]*** |
| Observations | 522 | 522 | 522 | 522 |
| R-squared | 0.64 | 0.62 | 0.41 | 0.39 |

*Notes:* Robust standard errors in brackets; * significant at 10%; ** significant at 5%; *** significant at 1%; standard errors clustered at country level—constant, gender, country, and year controls included.
*Source:* Authors' elaboration on EU-SILC 2009.

controlling for country, cohort, and gender dummies. Tables 5.2 and 5.3 report OLS regressions with standard errors clustered at country level. Even if the significance and the magnitude of the coefficients vary across different models, the data show an overall significant and positive relationship between educational and income inequality. To give an idea of the magnitude of the relationship, we can focus on the second panel of Table 5.2, referring to Gini indices. Depending on the definition of income, coefficients range from 0.502 to 0.611, suggesting that a reduction of 1 point in the Gini index of education (whose sample mean is 0.14) is associated to a reduction of 0.5–0.6 points in the Gini index of income (whose sample mean is 0.36). The relative overall elasticity is then about 1/5. Dummy variables for gender and cohorts, not reported in the tables for space and clarity reasons, are always significant. In detail, income inequality is always lower among males than among females, while the dummies for cohorts exhibit an inverted U-shaped pattern, with an income inequality for the central cohorts higher than inequality among younger and older cohorts.

The results emerging from this simple empirical analysis thus show a significant and sizeable correlation between educational and market income inequality, even accounting for the role of gender and cohort, for labour market participation decisions and for different sources of income.

## 5.7 Concluding Remarks

In this chapter we have described the patterns of educational attainment and inequality in the EU and its main geographical areas, using a newly developed and comprehensive dataset on educational attainment. The dataset allowed us to describe the expansion of education at the different school levels in a more detailed way than when synthetic measures, such as average years of education, are used. Evidence clearly points towards increasing levels of education of the European population. While primary and lower secondary are now universal everywhere, upper secondary is reaching this stage, converging across countries. However, some differences across geopolitical areas (and within them) still can be seen. Differences are quite strong at the tertiary level, where the influence of country-specific institutional design is stronger. In general, there is still much room for expansion at this level.

We described the link between educational attainment and its level of dispersion using standard inequality indices, pointing to the importance of policies to reduce dispersion of education attainment among European citizens. What is not completely clear yet, despite much research, is whether the expansion of educational attainment directly produces a decrease of inequality of educational opportunities depending on family background (be it defined by economic situation, ethnicity, cultural capital, or whatever else). This is a very important topic for educational policies: for instance, the EU Commission's 'strategic framework for European cooperation in education and training (ET 2020)' gives national policies a benchmark according to which the share of 30–34 year olds with tertiary educational attainment should be at least 40% by 2020.

Will such an increase of participation in tertiary-level education decrease inequality of educational opportunities? The evidence we provide does not point in this direction, at least concerning the short-run change. However, most of the research we reviewed, looking at this relationship in the long run, would give a positive answer to the question. The point is that the simple increase of educational participation and attainment is too broad a concept for a clear answer to be given. As Chapter 12 will show, educational policies are not limited to the mere increase of participation: school and university design also depends on political choices, and might interact with increasing participation to produce different outcomes in terms of inequality of opportunities.

In any case, our evidence confirmed that the probability of employment is also strongly determined by the formation of competences, which could be produced outside the formal channels of education. While the discussion of the relations among inequality in educational attainment goes on in Chapter 12, we observed that high levels of education inequality are correlated with high levels of earnings inequality, suggesting that policies aimed at reducing educational inequality might have important effects in improving the standard of living and the distribution of resources among individuals and their families.

# 6

# The Social Impact of Income Inequality: Poverty, Deprivation, and Social Cohesion

*Brian Nolan and Christopher T. Whelan[1]*

## 6.1 Introduction

Rising inequalities in earnings and household incomes may have deep-seated social impacts, and investigating these formed a core aspect of the research carried out under the GINI project. The underlying concern is that increasing inequalities may lead to more divided societies with worse outcomes for all their citizens. The point of departure for this investigation was the substantial body of research already available covering the very wide and diverse range of areas in which such impacts could potentially arise, especially in relation to health and health inequalities, but extending to many other social problems and outcomes. Against this background, the aim has been to assemble and assess evidence on the extent to which such societal impacts of inequality can be identified and, as far as possible, to tease out the key channels of influence. In this chapter we first discuss some general conceptual and methodological issues that must be faced in such an ambitious exercise, and then concentrate on the findings relating to social cohesion in the areas of poverty and deprivation, crime, the family, trust, and social capital; in the next chapter the focus shifts to health, housing, and intergenerational mobility and the transmission of advantage and disadvantage.

[1] We are grateful to the authors of the GINI project discussion papers and country case studies on which the chapter draws, the co-editors of the volume, Daniel Horn (Central European University), Tim van Rie (University of Antwerp), and John Goldthorpe (Nuffield College, Oxford) for helpful comments.

In the contemporary literature on social stratification and social exclusion, the term 'social cohesion' has partly assimilated older terms in sociological analysis such as 'social integration'. Chiesi (2002) suggests that 'social cohesion' can perhaps most usefully be understood as a concept closely related to social integration but allowing for significant diversity in the values of different sub-groups. This usage of the term is consistent with the broad definition of social cohesion adopted by authors such Berger-Schmitt and Noll (2000), incorporating both the extent of key inequalities in life chances and relational connectedness and sense of common membership of a given community. Here we deal first with social cohesion understood as social inclusion/exclusion in relation to access to resources necessary for full participation in society, and focus our attention on poverty, labour market participation, material deprivation, and economic stress. We then turn to social cohesion in the more restricted sense employed by authors such as Friedkin (2004) as involving social connectedness and communal identification, and discuss patterns and forms of family formation, crime and punishment, and what Pichler and Wallace (2009) refer to as general social capital as reflected in levels of social solidarity, trust, and status anxiety. Finally, we focus on overarching subjective measures of wellbeing or 'happiness'.

## 6.2 Identifying and Understanding Social Impacts of Inequality

It is important at the outset to discuss some general issues about the identification of inequality effects and the causal channels through which they may arise. The introductory chapter to this volume has already highlighted the variety of causal channels through which inequality effects could operate, with Wilkinson and Pickett (2009a, 2009b) emphasizing the 'psychosocial' implications of status differences in more unequal societies. Such psychosocial channels could operate through reduced levels of social capital in terms of trust and norms of reciprocity (Kawachi et al., 1997; Putnam, 2000), or the impact on individuals of low social status producing negative emotions such as shame leading to stress (Marmot, 2005; Marmot and Wilkinson, 2006; Wilkinson and Pickett, 2006, 2009a). Wilkinson and Pickett (2009a: 36–40) are also concerned with unhealthy self-esteem, better described as 'threatened egotism' or 'narcissism', deriving from increasing anxieties about how one is seen by others. This hypothesis relating to increasing latent insecurity also underpins some of Wilkinson and Pickett's more general conclusions relating to the undermining of community and social relations and the emergence of mass society and self-promotion. A key element of Wilkinson and Pickett's argument is that income inequality has negative effects for all members of an unequal society. To sustain this case it is necessary to demonstrate not simply that psychosocial factors *mediate* the impact of inequality on social outcomes, but that they *moderate* this impact in that the consequences of, for example, status anxiety are more severe in more unequal societies, thus raising average levels of negative outcomes above what would be expected purely on the basis of cross-national differences in the distribution of such anxiety (Baron and Kenny, 1986).

In contrast, the neo-materialist perspective emphasizes the role of different levels and distribution of resources available within societies, related to varying levels of investment in and development of social and institutional infrastructure (Kaplan et al., 1996; Lynch et al., 1998, 2000). As Layte (2011) observes, the relevant resources include health services, social protection systems, social infrastructure including legal regulation, protections, and controls relating to, for example, employment contracts and minimum wages, and finally the provision of services.

This debate can usefully be framed in broader terms in the context of the long-standing sociological research tradition relating to the consequences of various forms of social stratification (Van de Werfhorst and Salverda, 2012). Assessing the contribution of Wilkinson and Pickett from that perspective, Goldthorpe (2010) emphasizes the need for a satisfactory account of the consequences of inequality to be rooted in a deeper understanding of the social relations in which individuals are in some sense advantaged or disadvantaged. The distinction between class and status as forms of social stratification is crucial and neither can be equated with income or income rank. The status order is formed by social relations of superiority, equality, and inferiority among individuals, whereas social class is based on the objective relations of economic life (Goldthorpe, 2007a: 101–24). Class effects can exist independently of an individual's awareness of their membership of a class. They can also arise from members of such classes pursuing their interests and goals in ways shaped by the constraints or opportunities characterizing their class situation—independently of any class-specific values or norms. Social status reflects the degree of honour attached to positional or ascribed attributes. The associated hierarchy or gradient is reflected in differential association in intimate kinds of sociability and lifestyles of appropriate 'distinction'. Recent attempts to operationalize the concept have focused on the occupational structure of close friendships (Chan and Goldthorpe, 2007: 514–15). Wilkinson and Pickett (2009a) treat social stratification as essentially one-dimensional, with 'class' and 'status' being taken as essentially synonymous and referring to *the* social hierarchy; their comparative analysis focuses on income inequality, and their understanding of the processes and mechanism through which negative social outcomes are generated is crucially dependent on the existence of a close link between such inequality and social status. However, as Goldthorpe (2010) stresses, the link between status and income in modern societies is a good deal weaker than that between class and income, which itself is not a straightforward one.

Reflecting on the relationship between material inequality and status differentiation, Wilkinson and Pickett (2009b) conclude that health and social problems whose frequency is affected by social status are made worse by increased social differentiation. Psychosocial factors could then be *additional* and important routes by which material influences are mediated. If we substitute the term 'social stratification' for 'social status', on this basis it is perfectly possible to consider the neo-materialist and psychosocial perspectives as complementary rather than competing. This makes the need for explicit formulation of hypotheses relating to what Baron and Kenny (1986) refer to as *moderating* and *mediating* mechanisms even more crucial.[2]

In their terms, a moderator is a qualitative (e.g. sex, race, class) or quantitative (e.g. level of income) variable that affects the direction and/or strength of the relation between an independent or predictor variable and a dependent variable. On the other hand, a given variable may be said to function as a mediator to the extent that it accounts for the relation between the independent and dependent variables. Whereas moderator variables specify when certain effects will hold, mediators speak to how or why such effects occur. Moderators reflect interactions whereby the impact of one variable is conditional on the values of the other, whereas mediators play the role of an intervening variable in a (potential) causal sequence. Moderation, as captured by interaction effects in statistical models, is for example the type of effect required to support the Wilkinson and Pickett claim that psychosocial variables have a more pronounced effect in more unequal societies and contribute in this manner to an across-the-board reduction in welfare. The substantive relevance of macro and micro effects, and the role of mediating and contextual effects, would ideally be incorporated in developing and testing hypotheses (Snijders and Bosker, 1999; Hox, 2010). Data constraints mean that this ideal may not often be attainable, and studies conducted within the GINI project draw of necessity on a variety of data sources and cruder forms of statistical analysis, but this framework remains helpful in approaching the various analyses and their findings.

Much of the analysis of social impacts involves comparisons across countries, and in seeking to identify effects of inequality it is critical to be aware of the potential confounding or mediating roles of other macro attributes at country level, and of the danger of falling prey to the ecological fallacy.

---

[2] Evans et al. (2004) label these 'mechanical' and 'external' inequality effects; see also Neckerman and Torche (2007).

The type of multi-level longitudinal individual-level data one would ideally employ are seldom available, but even when they are the choice of appropriate control variables must be based on a theoretical understanding of the role of intervening mechanisms. In that light, methodological issues relating to the forms of analysis likely to illuminate the social impact of inequality need to be addressed. Much of the debate has focused on the bivariate association between the Gini summary measure of income inequality and negative social outcomes, and specifically on the impact on those associations of the particular countries and outcomes included in the analysis, and the extent to which what is involved is average effects across societies or effects observed at variable levels of social stratification (Saunders, 2010; Wilkinson and Pickett, 2010). Establishing the robustness of such associations is clearly an essential first step. In the absence of sufficient evidence of regularities of this kind, there is little point in investing effort in modelling how such associations are created, sustained, modified, or disrupted through the action or interaction of individuals (Goldthorpe, 2007a: 140). As we will show, insufficient evidence exists of such robust associations in some of the key areas that we consider.

Causal interpretation of such relationships, even when such evidence exists, presents formidable difficulties. The use of multi-level models can assist in controlling for a range of associated societal characteristics and help to reduce the risk of ecological fallacy, and analysis of change over time can strengthen conclusions on the direction of causality. However, as Van de Werfhorst and Salverda (2012) emphasize, causal interpretation of the consequences of inequality requires deductive theory-building and hypothesis formulation. In the same vein, Goldthorpe (2001) points to the value of thinking in terms of 'causation as a generative process', involving specifying hypotheses that are derived from a 'causal narrative' at the level of individual actions which can then be put to empirical test. While the available data will not always allow this to be implemented, it remains a useful framework within which to think about the social impacts of inequality, and about distinguishing between potential channels of influence.

## 6.3 Poverty

Poverty represents in itself a key form of exclusion in advanced societies, as well as feeding through to a range of other outcomes, and is thus at the core of concern about the potential social impacts of increasing inequality, sharpened by the current and future effects of the economic crisis. The relationship between income inequality and poverty depends in the first instance, though, on the way poverty is conceptualized and measured. The most common practice in comparative European research is to identify 'the poor' or those 'at risk of poverty' as persons in households falling below income thresholds set at 50% or 60% of the median income in the country in question. Higher/increasing income inequality need not necessarily be associated with more poverty even on this basis—the top end of the distribution could be doing better at the expense of the middle rather than the bottom, for example. In practice, there is a reasonably high cross-sectional correlation among EU or OECD countries between the level of income inequality and such measures of relative income poverty, though the poverty rates of countries with a similar level of income inequality still vary significantly (see, for example, Nolan and Marx, 2009). In terms of trends over time, median-based poverty measures have often risen with overall inequality. OECD (2008) shows that from the mid-1980s to the mid-2000s the poverty headcount using a 50% of median threshold increased in two-thirds of the OECD countries, in most of which inequality was also rising. In the economic crisis from 2007, Jenkins et al. (2012) note that across the EU income inequality has declined almost as often as it has risen; commonly, though not universally, where income inequality has risen so has relative income poverty.[3]

'Anchored' poverty measures, using an income threshold held constant in real terms over time, are also included among the EU's set of social inclusion indicators. OECD (2008) documents that even countries where relative income poverty increased between the mid-1990s and mid-2000s saw significant reductions in such an anchored poverty measure. Jenkins et al. (2012) show that in the first two or three years of the economic crisis, such anchored poverty measures went up even in some countries where relative income poverty rates declined. Whereas the original motivation for including the anchored indicators had been that purely relative measures failed to register progress in raising living standards among the poor in good times, the fact that such measures also fail to reflect real declines in those living standards when a severe negative 'shock' to average income occurs is at least as significant.

Unemployment is clearly a key determinant of poverty risk at individual and household level, with poverty rates among jobless individuals and families much higher than those among working persons/families. The study by De Graaf-Zijl and Nolan (2012) brings out that household-level joblessness substantially increases the likelihood of a working-age person being below country-specific relative income poverty thresholds in EU countries. Increasing unemployment may clearly underpin increasing inequality, as households predominantly in the bottom half of the income distribution are

---

[3] See Tóth's (2013) discussion of the extent to which inequality and poverty measures have moved together over time, based on the country case studies that formed part of the GINI project.

the main losers (see Jenkins et al., 2012). Even in the recent economic crisis, where much attention has been paid to unemployment among professionals such as architects and engineers in countries experiencing property and construction crashes, the risk of becoming unemployed has continued to be highly socially structured. Despite distinctive features of the economic crisis, where it has resulted in substantially increased unemployment this has been in itself a driver of increased inequality (as brought out in a number of the country case studies described in detail in Nolan et al. (2013), notably those for Greece, Ireland, and Spain).

## 6.4 Material Deprivation and Economic Stress

Income has limitations as a sole measure of poverty, and employing only country-specific relative thresholds when assessing progress in promoting social inclusion across the EU has also been increasingly questioned since the accession of the new member states and the onset of the crisis (European Commission, 2011). This has helped fuel interest in incorporating non-monetary indicators of deprivation and developing multidimensional approaches to capturing poverty and social exclusion (Nolan and Whelan, 2007, 2010; OECD, 2008). An indicator of material deprivation based on self-reported enforced lack of a specific set of items was added to the EU's social inclusion portfolio in 2009, and a special module on material deprivation was included in the EU-SILC 2009 wave (see Nolan and Whelan, 2010; Whelan and Maître, 2010; Guio et al., 2009). Such measures of deprivation have been the subject of a good deal of GINI project research, including the volume *Poverty and Deprivation in Europe* by Nolan and Whelan (2011a), which brings out the key role such indicators can play in applying a multidimensional approach.

Whelan and Maître (2012), pursuing this line of investigation, exploit data from the special module on material deprivation in EU-SILC 2009 to provide a comparative analysis of patterns of deprivation across twenty-eight European countries. This identifies six relatively distinct dimensions of deprivation that generally exhibit satisfactory overall levels of statistical reliability. Multi-level analysis reveals systematic variation across dimensions in the relative importance of within- and between-country variation. The dimension termed 'basic deprivation', which relates to rather basic aspects of living standards such as food, clothing, and heating, is seen to be the only one displaying a substantially graduated pattern of variation across countries, has the highest correlations with income and subjective economic stress, and is judged to come closest to capturing an underlying dimension of generalized deprivation that can provide the basis for a comparative European analysis of exclusion from customary standards of living. Multi-level analysis shows that such basic deprivation is related to a range of household socio-economic factors, and controlling for contextual differences in such factors accounted for substantial proportions of both within- and between-country variance in deprivation. At the country level, basic deprivation was found to be significantly negatively correlated (at a level of −0.4) with average national disposable income, while the correlation with the Gini inequality measure was positive as expected, but more modest (at 0.2). However, when average national income and income inequality were added to the statistical model fitted to the micro-data, they contributed little to its explanatory power, with the coefficient for income inequality statistically insignificant. In order to fully understand the role of national income level, it is crucial to consider the manner in which it interacts with a number of key characteristics of the household. The estimated impact of gross national disposable income on deprivation is significantly greater among less favoured socioeconomic groups; the impact of socioeconomic differentiation was significantly greater in countries with relatively low average income levels. Here we find clear evidence of important moderating effects, but they are ones that do not involve income inequality.

Kenworthy's (2011a) comparative study of seventeen OECD countries found that economic growth allowed policymakers to boost benefit levels, impacting on the living standards of those towards the bottom of the income distribution. Such 'trickle down' effects are consistent with Whelan and Maître (2012), whose analysis suggests that higher levels of national income are also associated with a restructuring of the distribution of favourable and unfavourable economic circumstances that has a substantial impact on cross-national differences in levels of basic deprivation. It is necessary to take into account both socioeconomic composition and cross-national variation in social gradients in accounting for such differences.

Deprivation indicators have also been used in a variety of other ways in GINI project research. Calvert and Nolan (2012) take advantage of the fact that aggregate deprivation indicators from EU-SILC are available for most EU countries on a consistent annual basis from 2004 on. These data were used to investigate the key drivers of material deprivation across countries and over time, with a particular focus on the role of changes in average income and income inequality. Over the period between 2004 and 2007, when economic growth was generally strong, many of the countries joining the EU from 2004, with high rates of material deprivation compared to the rest of the EU, saw quite significant decreases in their material deprivation rates. From 2007–10, when the economic crisis impacted so markedly (though unevenly) on economic activity across the Union, the picture was much more mixed. A considerable number of countries saw their material deprivation rate increase—most notably Ireland, where the rate doubled. Some of the new member states, Estonia and Lithuania, also saw a significant increase in deprivation over those years. However, in some other new member states there were substantial declines in deprivation between 2007 and 2010 despite the changed economic climate—including Bulgaria, Poland, Slovakia, and Romania. Multivariate analysis of the pooled cross-sectional and time-series data via fixed effects regression models showed that median income has a substantial role to play in explaining variation in the rate of material deprivation, as might be expected. However, controlling for average income the Gini summary measure of income inequality was also statistically significant and positively associated with material deprivation. An interaction between median income and income inequality is also significant and negative, suggesting that the impact of inequality on deprivation decreases as median income increases, consistent with Whelan and Maître's (2012) finding. These analyses of deprivation employing EU-SILC lend weight to the view put forward by Kenworthy (2011a) that concern with inequality and relative poverty should not lead to neglect of the importance of absolute income levels (and the social spending that higher levels of national income allow) and structural change in studying poverty and deprivation.[4] It also suggests that we should take care in generalizing conclusions relating to the relative importance of income inequality versus absolute income differentials (Goldthorpe, 2010; Lynch et al., 2004; Wilkinson and Pickett, 2009a).

Whelan and Maître (2013) make use of the special module on material deprivation incorporated in EU-SILC 2009 to explore the manner in which national context moderates the relationship between material deprivation and economic stress, the latter being measured by items relating to difficulty in making ends meet, inability to cope with unanticipated expenses, persistent arrears, and burdensome housing costs. Their findings from a range of multi-level models show that the level of basic deprivation was the key dimension associated with economic stress, with national levels of average income and income inequality having little additional effect once this has been taken into account. There is no evidence that material deprivation acts as a mediator for such macro factors. Switching to consideration of the moderating rather than mediating role of macro attributes, the analysis reveals a positive and significant interaction between basic deprivation and gross national disposable income per head. So household material deprivation, rather than having a uniform relationship with economic stress across countries, has a weaker estimated effect when national income is lower. This finding is consistent with the continuing importance of national reference

---

[4] For similar conclusions relating to social mobility, see Erikson and Goldthorpe (1992) and Breen (2004).

groups in evaluating one's own situation. Whelan and Maître (2013) also found that income inequality plays little or no role in moderating the impact of deprivation on economic stress, with no evidence that it exacerbates its consequences. There is no evidence that the experience of such deprivation in a more rather than less unequal society is of greater consequence in contributing to higher levels of economic stress in such societies. These results provide support for the argument of authors such as Torssander and Erikson (2010) and Goldthorpe (2010) that the impact of social stratification is unlikely to be adequately captured by an approach that seeks to conceptualize it in terms of a single status hierarchy, or that fails to take into account the potentially complex interaction between macro and micro attributes.

## 6.5 The Family and Fertility

We now turn our attention from inclusion/cohesion in terms of access to the resources necessary for full participation in society to aspects of social cohesion conceived of as connectedness versus fragmentation, starting with patterns and forms of family formation, a topic that has generated much political and popular debate and the occasional bout of 'moral panic'. There has been considerable research in recent years on the impact of changing family structures on socioeconomic inequality and vice versa. Patterns of family formation and breakdown may respond not only to the general economic climate but also to increasing earnings and job inequalities, with the USA a notable example, as brought out in Kenworthy and Smeeding's chapter in Nolan et al. (2013). Changes in household structures may themselves impact directly on income inequality, notably the rise in lone parenthood, which in the majority of rich countries is associated with a particularly high risk of poverty. Fertility is another element in the picture, with a substantial literature on the role of institutions and policies in influencing fertility (see, for example, Björklund, 2005) but much less research on the relationship with income inequality. Fertility rates have become remarkably uniform across social class and educational categories in developed societies, but there has been little attention to consequences this may have for social inequalities in general. Families with many children are much less common than heretofore. However, there remain national cases where family size is still relevant from a poverty point of view. Family size could have significant implications not only for disadvantage or vulnerability at a point in time but also for transmission of disadvantage across the generations.

Calvert and Fahey (2013) examine the extent to which a range of family indicators vary across countries by level of economic inequality as measured by the Gini coefficient, and then assess the extent of negative social gradients and the implications for the generalization of the Wilkinson and Pickett inequality thesis. They address three important questions in this broad research area:

1. On a point-in-time cross-country basis, is there a correlation between income inequality and variations in family behaviour? This can be regarded as a test of an expanded version of *The Spirit Level* hypothesis as applied to the family.

2. Are there consistent cross-country socioeconomic status gradients in family behaviour, and, if so, do those gradients correlate with the level of income inequality?

3. Over time, is change in income inequality an important influence on change in family behaviour?

The first of these questions is investigated using aggregate data drawn mainly from the OECD Family Database plus other sources (e.g. Eurostat database, European Social Survey), for 2006 or the closest year for which data are available, for OECD countries. It focuses on thirteen aggregate indicators, half relating to partnership (e.g. divorce rate, percentage of children living with lone parents, percentage of births outside marriage) and the other half to fertility (e.g. teenage birth rate, abortion rate, incidence of large families, total fertility rate). Bivariate correlations between each of these indicators and the Gini summary indicator of income inequality are examined for 30–35 countries (depending on the indicator). For twelve of the thirteen indicators examined they do not find a significant positive correlation with the Gini coefficient, the exception being the teenage birth rate, which is higher in more unequal countries (even when four outlier countries are excluded).

The second question addressed by Calvert and Fahey (2013) relates to socioeconomic gradients in family behaviours/outcomes, which they investigate using micro-data for 2006, mainly from the European Social Survey plus some indicators from EU-SILC, covering twenty-three European countries, with the social gradient measured in terms of educational levels. Their analysis revealed a negative social gradient for age at marriage, cohabitation, and births before marriage, but negative social gradients for the incidence of families with many children and lone parenthood were found in less than half the countries, and positive social gradients for partnership stability indicators were seen in most countries.

The third question they explored focused on trends over time. Calvert and Fahey point to the striking fact that the 'second demographic transformation'—involving decline in fertility, instability of partnership, the transformation of the role of women, and the decoupling of sex from marriage—occurred when income differences were falling and were already at an all-time low. More recent trends were assessed drawing together the findings of available national studies, mainly in regard to social inequalities in non-marital childbearing and lone parenthood. The evidence for a link between widening income inequality and widening socioeconomic status differentials in family behaviour is strongest for the USA, with the causality involved being complex and probably running in both directions. Evidence for a similar linkage in European societies is weak, though the data are as yet too limited to conduct robust cross-time and cross-country analysis. The country case studies in the GINI project also highlight examples such as the Baltic states (Masso et al., 2013) where declines in fertility took place at a time when income inequality was increasing, but more broadly based societal changes rather than income inequality per se seem the more likely driver. Even for the USA, often the focus of debate about family trends and inequality, Kenworthy and Smeeding (2013) do not find family-related trends to be consistent with those in income inequality. They note that the fertility rate there fell sharply in the 1970s but then levelled off while income inequality continued to rise, the decline in the marriage rate predates the rise in income inequality, divorce increased sharply in the 1970s but declined in the 1980s, 1990s, and 2000s, and while lone parenthood has risen steadily, that began in the 1960s—well before income inequality began to increase—and slowed from the 1980s. Calvert and Fahey's overall conclusion, having addressed each of the three broad questions set out, is that apart from its current association with early formation, income inequality does not exert a consistent effect on family behaviour and is not a major contributor to differences between countries or changes over time. Trends in income inequality appear to play little role in the changes in family life in affluent societies.[5]

## 6.6 Crime and Punishment

Crime is often seen as a symptom or manifestation of societal fragmentation and breakdown of social cohesion, and has been to the fore in debates about the impact of increasing inequality in those terms. Healy, Mulcahy, and O'Donnell (2013) highlight that charting long-term trends in recorded crime is problematic, not least because of changes in the way the data have been gathered and reported. It is also clear that such police statistics provide only a partial image of crime, being shaped by multiple factors including actual crime rates, demographic trends, reporting patterns, police practices, and legislative changes. This makes comparative analysis or analysis over time

---

[5] For broader reviews of the relationship between fertility, economic growth, and income inequality, see De La Croix and Doepke (2003) and Bloom et al. (2011).

difficult. Victimization surveys provide an alternative perspective, revealing for example that reporting rates for individual crimes vary widely and that disclosure to police may depend on perceptions of police willingness or capacity to provide a remedy. Analysing recent data analysing cross-national variation in reported crime and victimization rates in relation to income inequality, they find a strong negative correlation for crime and a negligible relationship for victimization. The latter finding is in line with existing research and may be explained by the fact that such surveys focus predominantly on minor, non-violent offences, which are not strongly associated with inequality.

Healy et al. do find a strong positive correlation between intentional homicide and income inequality, in line with previous research. A recent meta-analysis also identified clear links between inequality and violent crime (Hsieh and Pugh, 1993). There has been a particular focus in the literature on the social structure of homicide; this is a complex area of research, but there is evidence that lethal violence is related both to poverty and to inequality. One study has claimed that levels of income inequality are sufficient to account for the radically different rates of homicide in Canada and the USA, although the context in terms of gun control is, of course, also very different (Daly, Wilson, and Vasdev, 2001; see also Fajnzylber, Lederman, and Loayza, 2002). An extensive review by Pridemore and Trent (2010) concluded that income inequality appears to be a robust predictor of homicide rates across countries. Pratt and Godsey (2003) found that the amount of public spending on health and welfare in a society mediated the impact of inequality. Halpern (2001) suggested a similar role for the level of self-interest and trust in a society. Thus both psychosocial and material factors may play a mediating role.

Focusing on trends over time, though, recent years have seen substantial and sustained reductions in recorded crime in the USA as income inequality continued to rise (see Kenworthy and Smeeding, 2013). What has been termed the 'great American crime decline' began in the early 1990s and ranged across all regions, all crime types, all demographic groups, and all socioeconomic strata (Blumstein and Wallman, 2000; Zimring, 2007). Other country-specific studies have resulted in some similar findings. For example, Hoare's (2009) analysis of British Crime Survey data between 1995 and 2007 revealed falls in violent crime (down 49%), burglary (down 59%), and car theft (down 65%). The country case studies in the GINI project provide other examples of countries where income inequality has been rising but crime rates falling, notably Australia (see Whiteford, 2013) and in Canada overall (although there violent crime did increase—see Andersen and McIvor, 2013). This picture is replicated in cross-national studies, with Tseloni et al. (2010) in their analysis of trends in criminal victimization referring to the 'universal nature of the crime decline'. (An interesting counter-example is Belgium, where the GINI project case study does report increasing crime rates—but when income inequality was stable; see Marx and van Rie, 2013.) The picture across Western Europe is somewhat less clear-cut, with police data showing falls in homicide and theft but increases in drug crime and non-lethal violence. The explanation offered by Aebi and Linde (2010) for this pattern, in their study of crime trends between 1988 and 2007, is that better household security and increased wealth have reduced the opportunity and motivation for property crime, while a growth in street gangs and episodic alcohol consumption has driven drug consumption and street violence upwards. Notwithstanding difficulties in interpreting the available data, Healy et al. (2013) observe that it seems reasonable to conclude that since the early to mid-1990s, both the personal property and bodily integrity of the citizens of many developed countries have become less at risk of damage through crime.

Imprisonment rather than crime has also been a significant focus of attention, in particular the extent to which punishment regimes vary systematically across countries. Kilcommins et al. (2004) found that 'countries with well-developed, universalistic, generous welfare regimes tend to have lower prison populations than those with low levels of welfare provision' (p. 278). Similar conclusions were arrived at in other studies (Cavadino and Dignan, 2006; Enzmann et al., 2010; Lacey, 2008). In an authoritative review, Lappi-Seppala (2001: 352) observed, 'Looked at globally, increased income inequality seems to produce more prisoners.' The strength of this relationship is noteworthy. Healy et al. (2013) report that levels of tolerance are significantly correlated with inequality, public attitudes towards recidivist burglars are substantially more punitive in societies characterized by higher levels of inequality, and a significant positive relationship between fear of crime and inequality was also found to exist.[6] As brought out in a number of the GINI project case studies, increases in the prison population may well be occurring at a time when crime rates are falling.

## 6.7 Social Solidarity

Turning now to social solidarity, Paskov and Dewilde (2012) focus specifically on solidarity in terms of willingness to support the welfare of fellow countrymen: neighbours, older people, the sick and disabled, and immigrants. Willingness to help others may reflect affective considerations, based upon altruistic feelings of sympathy and moral duty, but could also be a product of

---

[6] See also Van de Werfhorst and Salverda (2012).

'calculating solidarity'—also referred to as 'enlightened self-interest' or 'weak reciprocity'. They hypothesize a positive association between income inequality and calculating solidarity based on the assumption that people recognize the negative externalities originating from inequality, and a negative association with affective considerations based on increased social differentiation and distance. Their analysis is based on the European Values Survey 1999, the only currently available dataset which allows study of the 'willingness to contribute to the welfare of others' as well as people's motivation to do so. Twenty-six European countries are included in the analysis. It appears that Europeans evaluate moral duty and sympathy as the strongest motives to help older people and immigrants, with the general interest of society ranking somewhat lower. Self-interest and reciprocity are also part of people's motivation to help older people and immigrants. However, affective considerations—moral duty and sympathy—come out as the stronger motivations underpinning solidarity. People in Europe are, on average, most solidaristic towards the sick, disabled, and older people, but display much less solidarity towards immigrants.

Multi-level analysis revealed a negative, although rather modest, relationship between income inequality and solidarity in relation to neighbours, older people, and sick and disabled people. In more unequal societies, people are less likely to engage in improving the living conditions of members of the community, older people, and the sick and disabled. In more affluent countries, respondents report more solidarity with members of their community and with immigrants than in poorer countries. This was the case for both low and high income groups and after controlling for levels of social expenditure, welfare regime, and the different socioeconomic characteristics of individuals and households. Paskov and Dewilde (2012) speculate that the reason why the negative relationship between income inequality and solidarity is so weak is that differing motives are pushing people in different directions. The relationship between income inequality and social solidarity is far from straightforward.

## 6.8 Trust

Many of the studies that consider the negative effects of income inequality presume that such effects are mediated by a decrease in social trust (Wilkinson and Pickett, 2009a). A number of studies have reported a negative relationship between income inequality and generalized trust.[7] However,

---

[7] See, inter alia, Knack and Keefer (1997), Uslaner (2002), Zak and Knack (2001), Leigh (2006), Bjørnskov (2007), Rothstein and Uslaner (2005), Berggren and Jordahl (2006), Uslaner and Brown (2005), Fisher and Torgler (2013), Jordahl (2009), Gustavsson and Jordhal (2008).

Steijn and Lancee (2011) suggest a number of reasons why these findings should be treated with caution. First, many do not distinguish sufficiently between the effects of income inequality and the general wealth of a country, although a number of studies have shown the importance of the latter (Alesina and La Ferrara, 2000b; Elgar, 2010; Elgar and Aitken, 2011). Furthermore, the underlying mechanism hypothesized is often unclear. In particular, there is a failure to clarify the relative importance of objective inequality and perceptions of inequality. The former implies larger social distances between people, while the latter may result in higher levels of envy and jealousy, affect optimism about one's chances of advancement (Delhey and Newton, 2005; Rothstein and Uslaner, 2005), and influence egalitarian values (Uslaner, 2002). Finally, there is a possibility that the observed relationships are unduly influenced by a group of non-Western countries characterized by high levels of inequality, with those more unequal countries being essentially different from the remainder.

Steijn and Lancee (2011) provide an analysis based on micro-data from the ISSP 1998 wave and the ESS 2002 wave that takes national wealth into account, distinguishes between objective and perceived inequality, and focuses on a homogeneous sample of countries that nonetheless provided sufficient variation in both trust and income inequality. The ISSP analysis incorporates a Gini coefficient of perceived income inequality based on estimation of incomes for a range of occupations in the ISSP 1999 wave. The ISSP dependent variable based on the question 'Generally speaking would you say that people can be trusted or that you can't be too careful' was dichotomized to distinguish between those who responded 'People can be always/usually trusted' and those who responded 'You almost always/usually can't be too careful in dealing with people'. The ESS trust measure was similar, but asked respondents to choose a score going from 0 to 10. Analysis based on the ISSP revealed a significant negative relationship between income inequality and trust, but with no impact of perceived inequality. However, when national wealth was included in the model income inequality was no longer statistically significant. The results using ESS data were similar.

Olivera (2012) also makes use of ESS data, drawing on the five available biannual rounds implemented between 2002 and 2010. He finds a statistically significant negative correlation between income inequality and trust, and an extremely weak correlation between changes in income inequality and changes in trust. Further analysis employing pooled cross-sectional analysis, taking into account country, time, and country-time specific effects, found that an increase in the Gini inequality measure was associated with a modest decline in the trust score evaluated at sample means, and that was still the case when GDP per capita was included. The positive association between

GDP and trust is in line with the findings of a large literature (Durlauf and Fafchamps, 2004; Zak and Knack, 2001; Beugelsdijk et al., 2004; Knack and Keefer, 1997). Constructing a panel dataset by collapsing the variables of interest in the ESS by country, Olivera is then able to control for country specific characteristics that otherwise could be confused with the impact of income inequality, at which point this panel analysis reveals no significant impact of income inequality on trust. Thus not only is there no evidence of the kind of interaction between income inequality and trust required by the Wilkinson and Pickett thesis, but the bivariate association proves to be less than robust. Given the role that trust has played in their understanding of the role of income inequality, this is clearly an important finding. The GINI country case studies also serve to highlight some particularly interesting experiences in terms of trends over time. These include Australia, where income inequality rose substantially but general social trust was little different in the mid-2000s from the mid-1980s (Whiteford, 2013), and the Baltic states, where levels of generalized trust were initially strikingly low, but increased over time despite pronounced increases in income inequality—in a context where fundamental changes in socioeconomic structures were of course taking place (Masso et al., 2013). Kenworthy and Smeeding (2013) point out for the USA that trust has fallen steadily in the past four decades with a broadly similar trend to income inequality, but the fact that the decline in trust began before the rise in inequality calls into question the direction of causality (see also the discussion on various aspects of trust in Chapter 9).

## 6.9 Status Anxiety

The argument that psychosocial processes are an important contributor to socioeconomic inequalities in health and wellbeing is strongly associated with the work of Wilkinson, Marmot, and colleagues (Marmot, 2005; Marmot and Wilkinson, 2006; Wilkinson and Pickett, 2006, 2009a). They employ a range of anthropological evidence and psychological research to argue that income inequality is but one measure of a status hierarchy in society, which has a more negative impact the more unequal the distribution of income and other scarce resources. People in more unequal societies are understood to have a greater concern with social status and status competition becomes more pervasive (Wilkinson and Pickett, 2006, 2009a). Status anxiety is a concept used to describe people's concerns about their relative position in the social hierarchy. As Paskov et al. (2013) document, status anxiety has been argued to have a variety of negative consequences at both individual and societal levels relating to health, social trust, crime, higher levels of consumption, and even as a contributory factor to the economic crisis by provoking increased debt.[8]

One of the reasons the concept of status anxiety has been capable of being applied to such a wide diversity of phenomena is that it has been used to refer to what appear, at first sight, rather different social psychological states. On the one hand, a key mechanism linking inequality to poorer health via status anxiety is thought to be a sense of inferiority engendered among those lower down the status order in more unequal societies in which status hierarchies and differentials become more important. A somewhat different route is through unrealistic self-enhancement or inflated self-esteem, with Loughnan et al. (2011) suggesting that income inequality is associated with a tendency towards self-enhancement due to increased competition for social superiority arising from economic polarization. Thus, rather than capturing positive self-esteem it should rather be seen as reflecting the need to compensate for status anxiety, an attempt to shore up confidence in the face of insecurities relating to how we are seen and what others think about us (Wilkinson and Pickett, 2009a).

In exploring this issue further, Layte and Whelan (2013) set out to test three separate hypotheses that stem from Wilkinson's concept of social anxiety:

1. that level of social anxiety will be inversely proportional to income position;
2. that the distribution of anxiety will be higher across the income distribution in more unequal countries;
3. that lower income groups will experience more anxiety in more unequal countries.

The same three hypotheses are also examined in Paskov et al. (2013), although they are specified and motivated in a rather different way. Whereas Layte and Whelan see hypothesis 3 as a crucial test of the status anxiety hypothesis, Paskov et al. regard a differential effect of high inequality on lower income groups as offering support to the 'neo-materialist' hypothesis on the grounds that it directs attention to the salience of economic resources. Layte and Whelan (2013) use data from the second wave of the European Quality of Life Survey (EQLS), with a status anxiety measure based on the following item: 'Some people look down on me because of my job situation or income.' Paskov et al. (2013) use five waves of the European Social Survey (ESS), which allows them to examine the longitudinal relationship between income inequality and status anxiety at the country level, using a scale derived from items which reflect the importance that individuals

---

[8] See Elgar and Aitken (2011), Frank et al. (2010).

attribute to respect, admiration, and recognition from others. In both studies, multi-level models controlling for GDP and other factors provide support for the first two hypotheses above: that both income rank and the Gini summary measure are significantly and inversely related to status anxiety, and that higher income inequality is associated with a higher level of status anxiety across the income distribution.

However, the papers diverge to some extent in their results relating to the third hypothesis, that the impact of lower income will be more negative in more unequal countries. Paskov et al. (2013) find a significant interaction, with the impact of income rank being greater the higher the level of inequality. Layte and Whelan (2013), on the other hand, provide more equivocal support for this hypothesis. In their models, the interaction is significant only at medium levels of income inequality and not at higher levels. This divergence could stem from methodological differences between the papers, with Layte and Whelan modelling an ordinal dependent variable using categorical income measures (due to missing values), while Paskov et al. employ a linear model and dependent variable and interact inequality and income as continuous variables; they could also arise from differences in the underlying questions posed and what they capture.

These analyses provide some limited support for the status anxiety hypothesis in that the mean sense of status inferiority at all points on the income distribution is higher in more unequal countries. Although the evidence relating to the crucial implication that individual income is more closely associated with such anxiety in more unequal societies is more mixed, there is some modest support for that hypothesis too. However, issues of interpretation remain. Paskov et al. (2013) take evidence of a stronger influence of inequality among lower income groups as providing some support for the neo-materialist position because of the moderating role of economic resources. This interpretation might be queried on the grounds that advocates of the social-psychological perspective would wish to treat the income rank variable as a proxy measure of status rather than as a measure of economic resources. Paskov et al. (2013) note that the measure of 'feeling looked down on' appears more relevant to disadvantaged groups in society. On the other hand, interpretation of the ESS measure as capturing 'status anxiety' seems to require that we interpret 'status striving' as being motivated by latent status anxiety. The correlation at the national level between these indicators is positive but extremely modest, so they are clearly capturing rather different phenomena. Further investigation is clearly required, broadening beyond income inequality and income rank to fully incorporate social stratification more broadly conceived and measured into the analysis.

## 6.10 Happiness

Increasing income inequality may impact on life satisfaction or happiness in a variety of ways. Via weakening social cohesion it could increase a sense of insecurity and threat, widening gaps in income and wealth could themselves impact on satisfaction via reference group effects, people may have a value-based preference for less inequality, or increased inequality may be perceived as an increase in the risk of worse outcomes. Ferrer-i-Carbonell and Ramos (2012) investigate the main channels of potential influence and survey the limited available empirical evidence. This shows that income inequality has a negative effect on individual self-reported wellbeing or life satisfaction for most Western countries, but not for all. Using the 2008 European Social Survey, Van de Werfhorst and Salverda (2012) find a negative but relatively modest association between income inequality and reported happiness. Importantly, Alesina, Di Tella, and MacCulloch (2004) find that while European respondents' life satisfaction is negatively affected by inequality, this does not hold for American respondents in general—which they interpret as consistent with the prevalence in the USA of the belief that it is a highly mobile society in which effort is an important determinant of income. In Germany, Schwarze and Harpfer (2007) and Ferrer-i-Carbonell and Ramos (2010) find a clear negative impact of inequality on reported life satisfaction using various waves of the German SOEP. Sanfey and Teksoz (2007) use cross-section data from the World Values survey (1999–2002) and find that individuals in higher inequality transition countries report lower levels of satisfaction, consistent with the findings of Grosfeld and Senik (2010) for Poland. However, Eggers, Gaddy, and Graham (2006), in a rare study based on panel data for a transition country, find no effect of inequality on happiness in Russia.

The country case studies in the GINI project also report a varied range of experiences with respect to trends in reported levels of life satisfaction/happiness vis-à-vis inequality. These show that in Finland, for example, the overall level of subjective wellbeing has remained high despite significant increases in income inequality; underlying this average, though, the trend has been for more respondents to report themselves very satisfied or very dissatisfied. For Germany, the period of growing income inequality between 2000 and 2005 saw a decline in life satisfaction, but the variation in satisfaction before and after the rise of income inequality does not suggest a systematic correlation between the two. In the Netherlands life satisfaction has remained stable at a high level since the 1970s, despite periods of increasing income inequality. In Greece, reported levels of overall life satisfaction have remained below the EU average but are very responsive to the economic cycle, plummeting to unprecedented levels since 2008.

## 6.11 Conclusions

In this chapter we have focused primarily on the relationship between income inequality and social cohesion, understood as social inclusion/ exclusion in relation to access to opportunities and resources necessary for full participation in society and, more specifically, in relation to social connectedness and communal identification. We emphasized at the outset that income inequality is only one aspect of social stratification, and that tracing causal relationships with any degree of confidence is extremely challenging. Even where one would expect that relationship to be most straightforward, as in the association between income inequality and exclusion in the form of poverty, the patterns observed are characterized by a good deal of complexity. The empirical relationship between income inequality and poverty depends in the first place on how poverty is defined and measured. When poverty is measured vis-à-vis relative income thresholds, poverty and income inequality are seen to be strongly associated with each other, but one still cannot simply 'read off' trends in poverty in a particular country, or rankings compared with other countries, from conventional summary inequality measures. When the focus is instead on poverty vis-à-vis thresholds fixed in purchasing power terms, or on material deprivation, the major factor accounting for differences across countries and change over time is average income levels. Income inequality contributes little extra to explaining cross-country differences in deprivation once this is taken into account, though changes in inequality over time may have some impact on trends in deprivation.

Increasing unemployment is likely to underpin greater income inequality and increased poverty as households predominantly in the bottom half of the income distribution emerge as the main losers. The relationship between unemployment, poverty, and inequality remains nuanced, with patterns of family and household formation playing a crucial mediating role. In-work poverty is strongly associated with single earnership and low work intensity at the household level, and while joblessness substantially increases the likelihood of being income poor, employment is not a guarantee of avoiding it.

Focusing on subjective economic stress, there is substantial evidence for the impact of average income in the country on such stress, but it also is seen to be important to take into account the manner in which that interacts with material deprivation. There is in addition a statistically significant (weaker) interaction between income inequality and material deprivation in predicting stress, but not of the form one would expect if income inequality played a significant role in exacerbating the consequences of material deprivation for cross-national differences in economic stress. In that case the impact of deprivation would be greatest in more unequal societies, but in fact material deprivation has its most extreme consequences for such stress where national income levels are high and inequality low. These findings point to the continuing importance of national reference groups in relation to absolute living standards, and run counter to Wilkinson and Pickett's claims for the crucial moderating role of income inequality.

Turning our attention to social cohesion relating to social connectedness and communal identification, what emerges is the difficulty in making a case for any uniform impact of income inequality across or within major substantive areas of concern. Family-related features such as fertility, marriage and divorce, and lone parenthood provide good examples. Many of these are not characterized by a distinct and consistent social gradient across countries. Even where they are, income inequality per se does not seem to play a major role in accounting for differences across countries, and trends in income inequality explain little of the dramatic changes in family life seen in many countries in recent decades.

Generalizing about the relationship of income inequality to crime is particularly difficult. This relates partly to problems of cross-national comparison relating to crime statistics, but also to significant differences in patterns of association relating to reported crime and victimization statistics and in relation to sub-groups within such categorizations. The strongest evidence regarding the impact of inequality relates to violent crime. However, it remains the case that many developed countries have seen declines in important aspects of crime during a period when income inequality was increasing, with the United States providing the most striking example. Patterns of punishment bear a much clearer relationship to income inequality and welfare regimes. It is clear that income inequality is only one of a complex set of factors influencing variation in patterns of crime across countries and over time.

Significant bivariate associations with income inequality were observed for a number of social-psychological variables such as social solidarity and trust. However, the introduction of appropriate control variables and the application of multi-level and longitudinal forms of analysis consistently found that relationship to be weak or non-existent. Given the crucial role that such mechanisms are afforded in the causal mechanisms put forward by Wilkinson and Pickett, the cumulative nature of these findings is particularly important. Consistent evidence was found for the association between both income rank and income inequality and status anxiety. However, once again support for the Wilkinson and Pickett claims in relation to the crucial moderating role of income inequality requires evidence for a significant interaction effect, and the evidence for a stronger impact of income rank in more unequal countries was somewhat mixed. While there is some evidence of a negative association between income inequality and happiness, it is relatively limited and far from clear-cut.

Overall, the evidence that income inequality plays the central role some-times proposed for it across a range of social outcomes is relatively weak. However, care should be taken not to generalize from this conclusion relat-ing to income inequality per se to more general processes of social stratifi-cation. Rather, great care is required in considering the relative importance of income inequality, absolute income differences, and socioeconomic dis-advantage, and crucially one also must allow for the manner in which such factors may interact. The need for a broader perspective on social stratification was revealed by the manner in which household disadvan-tage and national income levels contributed to accounting for outcomes such as economic stress. The findings with respect to inequality and vari-ous aspects of social cohesion on which this chapter has focused highlight the importance of seeing income inequality as only one facet of social stratification.

# 7

# Social Impacts: Health, Housing, Intergenerational Mobility

*Abigail McKnight and Frank Cowell*[1]

## 7.1 Introduction

The potential scope for inequalities in income, wealth, and education to reflect into a wider set of inequalities was outlined in the Introduction and Chapter 6 of this book. As has been noted, there is considerable debate about whether any such reflection is due to a causal relationship, joint determination, or is purely spurious. In this chapter we examine the research evidence on the relationship between income, education, or wealth inequality and outcomes in health, housing, and intergenerational mobility. Much of the research in this area has focused on comparing inequality at a point in time with a set of potential outcomes. In this chapter we draw on the new research evidence arising from the GINI project's examination of trends in inequality and wider societal impacts across thirty countries over the last thirty years and a series of research papers also carried out as part of that project. These new findings are put in the wider context of the existing research literature in these areas, but we do not attempt to conduct a comprehensive review.

If we were to provide an informal sketch of the things that principally characterize people's wellbeing in the long term we might identify (i) health, (ii) wealth, and (iii) prospects for the children. Given that the major proportion of household wealth for those of modest means is represented by housing, these three things can be summarized by health, housing, and

[1] We are grateful to the authors of the GINI project discussion papers and country case studies on which the chapter draws, the co-editors of the volume, and to Herman van de Werfhorst and Márton Medgyesi for comments on an earlier draft of this chapter.

intergenerational mobility, as in the chapter title. Some researchers are content to draw strong inferences from simple associations in the data (as brought out in the discussion on Wilkinson and Pickett (2009a) in Chapter 6 of this volume). However, we wish to focus, where possible, on evidence-based discussion of the possible ways in which the impact of inequality is transmitted. As was emphasized at the outset in Chapter 1, the connections between income inequality and social outcomes are complex; there may be several causal mechanisms and in some instances the causal link is in the reverse direction: what we might think of as outcomes are in fact social phenomena that drive inequality. We will see instances of links in both directions in the subject matter of this chapter. The channels through which the impacts of inequality occur may be principally economic, or they may involve social and psychological effects. The economic channels include the differential effects that resources may have on the behaviour of people located in different parts of the income distribution, and the differential effects of the market on people in different economic circumstances.

## 7.2 Inequality and Health

For the first of our three long-term social outcomes there is an extensive literature on the connections with inequality. Several studies demonstrate a relationship between absolute income and health outcomes (see, for example, Subramanian and Kawachi, 2006): this 'absolute income hypothesis' may be a non-linear relationship, steepest among low-income groups (Backlund et al., 1996). In developed economies, enjoying high average levels of income and minimum incomes supported through mature welfare states, some argue that it is relative incomes that matter in terms of health (Wilkinson and Pickett, 2009a; Marmot, 2002). Two further hypotheses have been put forward: the relative-income hypothesis, where an individual's position in the income distribution has a direct effect on that individual's health, and the income-inequality hypothesis, where overall inequality affects average levels of health (Wilkinson and Pickett, 2006). Wilkinson (1996) argues that beyond a certain level of GDP per capita the association between absolute income, health, and mortality weakens, and the distribution of income across society becomes more important as a determinant of outcomes. A number of hypotheses have emerged in the literature to support this theory—social capital, status anxiety, and neo-materialist (Layte, 2012)—but there is by no means anything approaching a consensus that any observed empirical correlation reflects a causal relationship.

Marmot (2002) outlines ways in which income can really matter for health (causal relationship) or simply appear to matter (statistical correlation). He also explains why poverty may be more important than income differences above an income threshold if a certain level of income is required to secure adequate material conditions. The relationship between income and health may be through an indirect effect on social participation and the opportunity to exercise control over one's life. He argues that the problem for rich countries today is inequality rather than absolute poverty and demonstrates this by showing that a gradient is clear across the income distribution. However, he also argues that social factors, particularly social position and social environment are likely to have an important determining role in health outcomes. The Whitehall Study, which followed a group of male civil servants in England, was originally conceived to investigate the causes of heart disease and other chronic illnesses (Marmot et al., 1978) with an expectation that among this group of relatively well-paid employees those employed in the highest-status jobs would experience the highest level of work-related stress and as a result experience the highest risk of heart disease. However, it was found that civil servants working in the lowest grades had the highest death rates, and this sparked a fruitful line of research investigating the relationship between status, working conditions, and health outcomes. While identifying causal relationships is inherently difficult, the evidence suggests that hierarchies have a negative effect on health for those lower down the spectrum. This suggests that higher income inequality (where income communicates status) may give rise to poorer health outcomes where steeper gradients are associated with a greater negative effect on health for those lower down the spectrum.

In the country case studies we found a general improvement in life expectancy over time apart from some CEE countries that experienced temporary falls following transition. We also found evidence in a number of countries that these average improvements masked a steepening of social gradients (Nolan et al., 2013). Here we look behind these aggregate levels and trends at evidence to support a direct link between inequality and health.

In this section we review the findings from recent original contributions to this debate that are innovative either in terms of their approach to the topic or the perspective they take. The three areas we look at are: (i) evidence of socioeconomic gradients in health when alternative measures of socioeconomic status are considered; (ii) cross-national evidence of a relationship between poverty and mortality across rich countries and regime types; (iii) health inequalities in relation to variations in working conditions.

### 7.2.1 Material Deprivation and Health

Many socioeconomic variables exhibit a gradient in health and several studies have sought to understand the extent to which different factors are simply mapping a latent dimension or directly shaping health inequalities. Layte

171

and Whelan (2009) show that class inequalities in smoking (take-up and quit rates), a contributory factor to inequalities in health, are partly shaped by education but more so by enduring economic and social difficulties among the manual working class to the extent that they dominate any direct income effect. Torrsander and Erikson (2010) analyse the relationship between stratification and mortality in Sweden and show that while class, income, and status are all associated with gradients in mortality, they all seem to have slightly different effects. They find net associations between education and mortality for both men and women, but class and income only have independent effects on mortality for men and status is only found to have an independent effect for women. Trying to unpack the overall associations between socioeconomic variables and health to identify those that have a direct impact on health is a lively area of research, not least because of the policy implications.

Blazquez, Cottini, and Herrate (2013) make an important contribution to this debate, examining alternative measures of socioeconomic status. Their study is motivated, in part, by the work of Sen (1985) in understanding the multidimensional aspects of social disadvantage in terms of the failure to attain adequate levels of various functionings that are deemed valuable in society and to examine if comparison effects with societal peers are related to health outcomes. Goldthorpe (2010) outlines how sociologists view social inequality in attributional (ranking individuals in terms of their valued attributes) or relational terms (social class and status), and this study explores both of these views in the empirical analysis. The authors use the Spanish Living Conditions Survey (2005–8) and a measure of self-assessed health. The measure of material deprivation used comprises fourteen indicators grouped according to four domains of quality of life (financial difficulties, basic necessities, housing conditions, and durables). In addition to estimating the direct effect of indicators of material deprivation, they assess the extent to which material deprivation affects self-assessed health depending on individuals' relative position; i.e. relative to that of their societal peers. Measures of absolute and relative income (distance between own income and others' income) are also included in their models.

They find that many of the material deprivation items have a significant and negative effect on health over and above the positive relationship between income and health (income is not significant in the model for women). However, when they include relative income and relative material deprivation, they find that the level of individuals' own income is not significant but relative income and relative material deprivation have negative and significant effects on self-assessed health. In a saturated model, which includes both absolute and relative terms for income and material deprivation, the results are less clear. Income continues to operate only through comparison information with respect to societal peers. In terms of material deprivation, the relative position of women in terms of financial difficulties has a significant and negative estimated effect on self-assessed health, but it is the direct effects of material deprivation in basic necessities, financial difficulties, and housing conditions that have a significant and negative effect on self-reported health.

The findings from this research provide an interesting perspective on the relationship between inequality and health. While individuals' own income is positively related to self-assessed health, when relative income effects are taken into account only relative income has a statistically significant and negative effect on health. This suggests that income inequality is bad for health and supports the relative income hypothesis. On the other hand, the results suggest that it is actual material deprivation that has a negative effect on health rather than own deprivation relative to others' deprivation. These findings for Spain suggest a fruitful area for further research both in terms of comparing countries with different levels of inequality and material deprivation and also within countries where inequality and deprivation have changed over time.

### 7.2.2 Cross-National Variation in Poverty and Mortality

Fritzell et al. (2012) focus specifically on the relationship between poverty and mortality. While Wilkinson and Pickett (2006) state that income inequality is a major threat to population health in modern societies, they summarize that the relation between relative poverty rates and population health indicators is less self-evident. While much of the debate has centred on the relationship between income inequality and health, Fritzell et al. argue that if inequality matters then this should be evident in terms of a relationship between relative poverty (lack of resources and relative deprivation) and health. In rich countries a study of the effect of relative poverty can be informative about the relationship between inequality and poverty. The curvilinear relationship between income and health outcomes, the so-called Rodgers curve, describing diminishing health returns to income as income rises has been used to motivate the argument that reducing inequality through redistribution could lead to improvements in population health because lower-income individuals have a greater health gain than the loss to higher income individuals. Fritzell et al. hypothesize that a curvilinear relationship between income and health should be observable in poorer health outcomes being associated with higher rates of relative poverty at an aggregate level. They set out to explore the relationship between cross-national variations in relative poverty rates and cross-national variations in mortality rates within relatively rich countries.

As evidenced in the GINI project country case studies (Nolan et al., 2013), mortality rates have been falling across rich countries over recent decades (Hungary and Russia are exceptions). The question addressed by this study is whether the incidence of relative poverty has delayed or hindered a fall in mortality. Using data from the Luxembourg Income Study for twenty-six countries covering the period from 1980 to 2005 to provide measures of relative poverty (taking 40% of the median as a poverty indicator), supplemented by data from the Human Mortality Database, they undertake a comparative analysis to estimate the effect of relative poverty on mortality rates among three age groups, namely infants, children, and working-age adults.

In their analysis they separately estimate the relationship between child poverty rates and infant mortality (< 1 year) and child mortality rates (aged 0–17), and between adult poverty rates and working-age adult mortality rates (aged 25–64) for males and females. They estimate pooled cross-sectional time-series models with corrections for autocorrelation and controls for GDP per capita, social expenditure as a percentage of GDP, and welfare regime type.

For infants they find a statistically significant association between relative poverty and infant mortality rates: a one percentage point increase in child poverty is associated with a 2% increase in infant mortality. The inclusion of social spending attenuates the estimated poverty influence by around one-third, reflecting the strong association between social spending and poverty rates. Welfare regime types were found to have significant variation, with higher mortality rates in Central European, liberal, and especially post-socialist regime types relative to Nordic regimes. For children (0–17) they find similar estimated child-poverty marginal effects as for infants. In neither case is GDP per capita significant, but social expenditure as a percentage of GDP is associated with lower mortality. Regime estimates are similar to those found for infants but differences between regimes relative to Nordic regimes is reduced, suggesting that the relative advantage of Nordic countries is lower in older children. In the working-age population the association between poverty and mortality is weaker (particularly for men). There is also a change in the ranking of regime types relative to that observed for children. For women, Central and especially Southern European regime types have statistically significant lower mortality rates than Nordic regimes; for men, Southern European, liberal, and 'other' regimes have significantly lower mortality rates than Nordic regimes.

Sensitivity analysis found that the statistically significant adult-poverty estimates appear to be driven by the higher poverty and high mortality rates experienced in Russia over the period of the study. However, while the results for infants and children are attenuated when Russia was excluded from the analysis, they remain statistically significant.

It is not clear why the Nordic regimes appear to do so much better at achieving lower infant and child mortality but do less well in terms of adult mortality relative to a number of other regime types. It could be that other factors become more important during adult life such as diet, lifestyle, and climate. More research is needed to understand these patterns. The clear findings in relation to infant and child mortality rates lead the authors to conclude that these send out a clear message that national governments should invest to reduce child poverty to limit avoidable infant and child mortality.

### 7.2.3 The Relationship between Working Conditions and Employment Relations and Health

Although the causal relationship between income inequality and health continues to be hotly debated, the relationship between employment, job quality, and individual health status remains surprisingly under-researched. At least part of the explanation for rising inequalities in rich countries over the last thirty years is skill-biased technological change (favouring high-skilled workers over low-skilled workers) and a weakening of labour-market institutions. This is seen to have led to a fracturing in the labour market, creating polarization between 'good jobs' and 'bad jobs'. Therefore understanding the relationship between job quality and health is important for understanding how rising inequality is associated with social outcomes, but also why this may not be uniform across time or countries. Evidence of a social gradient in the risk of experiencing unemployment (Elias and McKnight, 2003) and epidemiological studies that find elevated health risks among unemployed, particularly long-term unemployed, as compared to permanently employed people show that inequalities in the labour market that include the risk of unemployment impact on individuals' health (Morris et al., 1994; Martikainen and Valkonen, 1996; Gallo et al., 2004). The quality of jobs varies considerably, such as in terms of physical working conditions, attributes of workplaces, risks of injury, degrees of autonomy, complexity of tasks performed, and intensity of work. Job quality and working conditions have been researched by social scientists from a number of different perspectives. Rosen formalized a theory of compensating differentials outlining the way wages vary to compensate workers for adverse working conditions (Rosen, 1986). Occupational variation in employment relations and conditions has been used by sociologists as a way of operationalizing the conceptual basis for social classifications (Erikson and Goldthorpe, 1992; Goldthorpe, 2000; Rose and Pevalin, 2003), where occupations form the building blocks for these classifications and are used to allocate people to social positions, signalling their importance in influencing social gradients.

Although relations and conditions of employment implicitly underlie social gradients in health, much of the research on health inequalities by social scientists has focused on the relationship between income or social class and health. However, there is a growing body of evidence for the relationship between employment relations and conditions and health. A whole task group under the Marmot strategic review of health inequalities after 2010 in England was set up to examine the evidence for the relationship between employment arrangements, working conditions, and health inequalities, and to make policy recommendations in the light of their findings. They find that work and employment make a significant contribution to the development of social inequalities and are of critical importance for population health and health inequalities in at least four interrelated ways (Siegrist et al., 2009). *First*, participation in, or exclusion from, the labour market determines a range of life chances, as lack of employment leads to material constraints and deprivations and the experience of unemployment has a direct negative effect on health. As the prevalence of unemployment is unequally distributed, those in lower socioeconomic positions are at higher risk. This fact contributes to the manifestation of a social gradient in health (Kasl and Jones, 2000). *Second*, wages and salaries provide the major component of the income of most people in employment and contribute to income inequalities and associated health inequalities (Kawachi, 2000). *Third*, exposure to physical, ergonomic, and chemical hazards at the work place, physically demanding or dangerous work, long or irregular work hours, shift work, health-adverse posture, repetitive injury, and extended sedentary work can all adversely affect the health of working people. These conditions are more prevalent among employed people with lower educational attainment and among those working in lower, less privileged occupational positions (Karasek and Theorell, 1990). *Fourth*, as the nature of employment and work has changed, psychological and socio-emotional demands and threats evolving from an adverse psychosocial work environment have become more widespread in all advanced societies. Their highest prevalence is found among the most deprived workers, specifically those in 'precarious jobs', defined by a lack of safety at work, by exposure to multiple stressors including strenuous tasks with low control, low wages, and high job instability (Benach et al., 2000). Overall, a social gradient of health-adverse employment and working conditions has been documented in advanced societies, leaving those in lower socioeconomic positions at higher risk.

A report to the WHO on employment conditions and health inequalities by the Commission on Social Determinants of Health noted that although there is abundant literature on specific employment and working conditions and health, the literature rarely focuses directly on the important role played by employment relations and conditions as a key social determinant in shaping health inequalities (Benach et al., 2009).

Monden (2005) extends some of the previous research that has assessed the extent to which the relationship between education and health is partly mediated by working conditions. He examines the extent to which both current and lifetime exposure to working conditions differ between education groups in the Netherlands. He finds that less highly educated men have greater lifetime exposure to adverse working conditions than more highly educated men, and that this lifetime exposure explains around one-third of the health differences he observes between the most and least educated men and has greater explanatory power than current differences in working conditions.

One of the few contributions to the economics literature on this topic, Cottini and Lucifora (2013), provides cross-country evidence for EU15 countries on the links between working conditions, workplace attributes, low pay, and health (both physical and mental) among full-time employees using the 2005 and 2010 waves of the European Working Conditions Survey (EWCS). To capture working conditions they construct indicators to cover psychosocial aspects of work: intensity of work, complexity of tasks, low job autonomy in performing tasks, and working long hours. Exposure to physical hazards is captured by a set of indicators that record if the worker was exposed to the following for half or all of working time: vibrations from hand tools; noise so loud that he/she has to raise his/her voice to talk; high temperature or coldness; repetitive arm movements. These job-quality indicators were summarized into a single job-quality index. Low pay is defined as earnings below two-thirds of the level of median earnings and is used as an indicator of income inequality.

To construct variables indicating poor work-related health they use responses to a question that asks workers to indicate if they suffer from a series of health problems as a result of their work. The health problems identified were: skin problems; respiratory difficulties; stomach-ache; heart disease; depression, anxiety, and sleeping problems. These were divided into mental and physical health problems to construct two indicator variables.

In the raw data they find considerable cross-country variation in job quality and work-related health problems. The results from their statistical modelling show that after controlling for a wide range of personal and job attributes, adverse working conditions are associated with lower health status (physical and mental). In particular they find higher marginal effects of adverse working conditions on the mental health of workers. They also find that low paid work has a significant effect on the physical health of individuals, most likely capturing the relationship between low income and poor health. Although in their analysis they do not control for sorting of workers into occupations and low pay status (endogeneity), recent papers (Cottini,

2012; Cottini and Lucifora, 2010) found evidence of a causal effect of working conditions on the mental and physical health of workers.

## 7.3 Inequality and Housing

From a theoretical perspective widening inequality could affect housing—the second of our long-term outcomes—in a number of ways, but the impact is not straightforward, nor is the direction of causality clear-cut. It is clear that income inequality can affect housing quality and affordability through the same channels that affect the acquisition of other forms of wealth. There is a potential resource effect: those with higher incomes may have a greater propensity to save (they find it easier to 'afford' the investment in home ownership). There is also an inequality effect operating through the market: richer people are less likely to be artificially credit-constrained if they want to buy a house. The housing market here may play both a mediating role, transmitting income disparities through to housing outcomes, and also a moderating role, through the effects of housing tenure on people's creditworthiness (see Chapter 6 on mediating versus moderating processes). The importance of the role of housing not just in people's lives but also in terms of the financial prosperity and stability of nations has been brought into stark relief by the current economic and financial crisis, which began in 2007 arguably sparked by excessive and irresponsible lending in the subprime market in the USA and also across a number of other rich countries.

Widening income inequality could affect access to certain tenures if rising inequality increases house prices effectively pricing lower-income households out of the owner-occupied housing sector. This would be determined to some extent by the shape and size of the housing stock, the extent to which it is segmented, and the availability of other housing tenures. Inequality is also likely to be related to differences in housing quality. This may be considered to be more problematic where the lower-bound housing quality is very poor. Inequality could lead to status competition with households making riskier investment decisions, with an associated greater risk of indebtedness for lower-income households. All of these factors will be influenced by differences in housing regimes, the availability and policy in relation to social housing, financial regulation, housing subsidies, and more generally the emphasis for support for particular tenure types. The literature on income inequality and housing usually focuses on the issues of access, affordability, risk, and quality within the context of housing regime types.

In the country case studies we look within countries at evidence for an association between inequality, housing tenure, and housing costs. Here we focus on research evidence that seeks to establish a direct link between inequality and housing.

In this section we begin by looking at how housing regimes relate to inequality and how housing regimes can directly influence inequality trends in terms of, for example, the direct provision of housing and the redistributive effects of different housing policies. We then look at how inequality and absolute levels of income can affect housing affordability, housing quality, and quantity. We then focus on home ownership, examining how ownership has been seen to counterbalance income inequality across a number of countries but, as ownership rates have tended to converge, the counterbalancing role of ownership has diminished.

Dewilde (2011) examines whether changes in housing regimes, and more specifically the increase in owner-occupation and concomitant changes, have contributed to the upswing in economic inequality—or vice versa—outlining the links between housing inequality and economic inequality. As housing costs (mortgage repayment or rental payments) are typically the single largest item in households' budgets, the cost of housing is intimately linked to the economic wellbeing of households. For homeowners, housing wealth is typically the largest (and sometimes only sizeable) investment they will ever hold. The welfare state also plays an important role through direct provision of housing (social housing) and the redistributive effects of different housing policies (taxes, benefits, intervention in credit markets) on the economic wellbeing of households (Fahey and Norris, 2010). It is also clear that patterns of home ownership can impact on wider economic inequalities. Housing wealth, as with other forms of wealth, acts as a financial buffer during hard times, can be used as security to access credit markets, and once mortgage loans have been paid off housing costs are reduced, particularly in old age.

In many countries home-ownership rates increased in the post-war decades. At the same time as many governments cut back on social housing provision, they invested more in encouraging home ownership (including among low-income households). The timing and pace of growth in home ownership has not been uniform across countries and has been shaped by policies designed to assist home ownership particularly among low-income households, such as the right-to-buy scheme in the UK (where social rental tenants could buy their council houses at discounted values), which took off after 1980, and the mass privatization of the housing stock in the former Communist countries during the 1990s (see, for example, Nolan et al. (2013, Chapter 23) for Romania). However, home ownership is not a positive experience for all. Over-indebtedness, mortgage arrears, and, in the extreme, housing repossession can leave households who overreached (possibly encouraged to borrow beyond safe affordability limits through cheap credit and a poorly regulated financial sector) or fell on hard times (particularly during recessions) with deep scars. Policies encouraging low-income households into home ownership alongside further deregulation of the mortgage market, making it easier for low-income households to attain credit eventually led to the US subprime crisis in mid-2007 (Bratt, 2008).

Dewilde (2011) also reviews the literature that has sought to explain the rise in home-ownership rates, which is now the majority tenure in all EU member states (except in Germany). Fisher and Jaffe (2003) suggest that several factors (legal, economic, political, and cultural) in societies affect not only the costs and benefits of owning versus renting, but also public attitudes and social norms, which in turn affect individual preferences. Government policy aimed at encouraging home ownership and a wide range of other factors have been put forward as determining factors (including property value development, demographic change, mortgage market deregulation, construction costs, and building activities). Some of these factors can be self-reinforcing, such as increases in house prices, which encourage households to invest more in housing, subsequently leading to further increases in house prices. She also considers the political and ideological dimension, including the suggestion that neo-liberal policies encouraging owner-occupation accompanied a shifting emphasis for responsibility for welfare to be borne by individuals and their families and away from the state. Increasing house prices shifted the meaning of home ownership from 'owning a home' to 'owning an investment' and therefore brought about the progressive commodification of housing from a home to an asset (Ronald, 2008; Smith et al., 2008). She explains how home ownership could exacerbate existing inequalities where it is more common in higher income groups and the amassed wealth is subsequently passed on to future generations, but also because it is associated with a wide range of other beneficial characteristics such as favourable geographical location and amenities, the size and quality of the accommodation itself, and that the net benefits (tax subsidies, capital gains) are greater for higher socioeconomic groups compared to lower socioeconomic groups who are restricted in what, if anything, they can afford to buy. Lower socioeconomic groups are more vulnerable during periods of declining house prices, suffering equity losses.

Rising inequality may affect house prices: indeed an increase in inequality can even increase the cost of housing for everyone. Increasing demand for home ownership can lead to higher house prices (where demand exceeds supply) as higher income households can afford to pay relatively more. While increasing house prices usually benefit existing homeowners, for low-income households stretching their incomes to enter the housing market this increase in housing costs can lead to a fall in other consumption or a fall in the quality of the houses they can afford to buy (smaller houses or less favourable location). The empirical evidence from the USA suggests that in the context of a tight housing market an increase in income inequality results in 'the poor' experiencing more overcrowding and some (although weaker) evidence that increasing income inequality pushes up house prices (Matlack and Vigdor, 2008). These relationships are likely to be shaped by how segmented the housing market is in relation to income; spillover effects are likely to be low where different income groups' demand for housing is very segmented.

Dewilde also develops the idea that the increase in home ownership can in turn affect voters' preferences for the level of public spending and the level and nature of taxation, and their preferences for a specific economic climate. Homeowners have a preference for high inflation and low interest rates in conflict with non-homeowners' preferences. Consequently, as home-owners become the dominant group they can in turn influence public policy in their favour and have an impact on the level and trends in inequalities by tenure type.

Norris and Winston (2012) review the debate in the comparative housing literature on convergence and divergence of housing systems across Western Europe and consider what these two strands of the literature predict in terms of trends in home ownership, the relationship between income and access to tenure types, housing quality, neighbourhood satisfaction, and the unequal distribution of risk (burdensome housing costs and mortgage arrears). They then undertake a comparative empirical assessment to examine to what extent the predictions are borne out by the evidence. The first school of thought (the 'convergence' school) is that housing systems are converging to a state where home ownership is the overwhelmingly dominant tenure type driven by the dynamics of capitalism (Harloe, 1985, 1996; Ball, Harloe, and Martens, 1988) or a psychological preference for home ownership (Saunders, 1990). The second school (the 'divergence' school) emphasizes differences between housing systems with cultural, ideological, or political dominance shaping different typologies. Kemeny and colleagues (1981, 1995, 2006; Kemeny, Kersloot, and Thalmann, 2005) identify two contrasting housing regime types under which public policies have modified the balance of costs and benefits attached to different tenure types. One regime is the 'dual' housing system (English-speaking countries, Belgium, Finland, Iceland, Italy, and Norway), where governments support home ownership via subsidies and favourable legal treatment, an unregulated and unsubsidized private rental sector, and a small non-profit social rental sector restricted to disadvantaged groups. Kemeny argues that these arrangements 'push' households into home ownership, which consequently dominates. The second regime is the 'unitary' housing system (Germany, Sweden, The Netherlands, Switzerland, Austria, Denmark, and France), where housing policy is 'tenure-neutral' and social housing is delivered by the third sector and not allocated strictly on the basis of means. Under the 'unitary' system, social and private rental sectors compete, are widely used, and home ownership rates are lower than the norm in the 'dual' system. The two systems reflect ideological and cultural orientations towards individualist or collectivist solutions to social problems. From an inequality perspective, three different types of home ownership inequalities are identified: access to home ownership, housing risk, and standards associated with this tenure (quality of the dwelling and neighbourhood). The predictions are that under the dual system only the poorest households will be excluded from home ownership and will live in social housing, and that as ownership expands governments will limit and target support on low-income households, and those low-to-middle-income households who do not qualify for support will experience poor housing standards and high levels of mortgage arrears and default. Under unitary regimes a more equal distribution of access to home ownership across the income distribution (although lower rates overall), less concentration of rental by income level, high housing standards, and low levels of risk in the home-ownership sector are predicted.

Norris and Winston's empirical examination of the patterns of housing inequality in the various housing regimes as well as home-ownership rates, mortgages, and public subsidization of this tenure in EU15 countries is contrasted with the predictions arising from the 'convergent' and 'divergent' schools of thought and Kemeny's housing regime types. Their research reveals a number of significant shortcomings in the comparative literature on housing regimes. At the macro level there is evidence of convergence in home-ownership rates in EU15 countries; with the exception of Germany, by 2007 home ownership was the majority tenure. However, more detailed analysis reveals that in the majority of Western European countries the growth of home ownership has stalled or reversed since 2000 (even before the current economic and credit crisis). In relation to income inequalities and home-ownership access, risks, and quality, they find marked inter-country differences in many cases in conflict with the suggested typologies. They conclude that Kemeny's typology failed to capture the most significant inter-country cleavages, which they find are between Northern and Southern Europe rather than among the Northern countries of the EU15. They show that in Southern Europe (Spain, Greece, Italy, and Portugal) home-ownership rates are high and evenly distributed across income groups with residential debt per capita and mortgage holding rates below the EU average, with evidence that a decommodified home-ownership regime has emerged. However, they also find that low-income households in these countries also have relatively burdensome housing costs and poor housing standards. Northern EU15 countries are less uniform, and although ownership rates are higher in the dual regimes the patterns of inequality generally did not conform to predictions. Home ownership was only sometimes found to be evenly distributed across income groups in unitary countries, burdensome housing debt was not always common in dual countries, and low-income home-owners were sometimes found to enjoy good housing and neighbourhood standards under both regimes. Despite these differences, Northern EU15 countries typically enjoyed less government support for home ownership, and mortgage debt and mortgage holding rates were generally higher. With a strongly commodified home-ownership system low-income households were less likely to live in this tenure than in Southern Europe. Norris and Winston argue that it is necessary to look beyond housing regime typologies based purely on housing policies to broader social-security policies and more emphasis needs to be put on understanding the different meanings of home ownership across countries and regime types to assess the extent to which it is a commodified tenure.

Dewilde and Lancee (2012) focus specifically on the relation between income inequality and access to housing for low-income households. They estimate multi-level models for twenty-eight countries using EU-SILC data to test the relationships between inequality and affordability, inequality and crowding (size of accommodation relative to household size and composition), and inequality and housing quality. They identify three potential causal mechanisms relating income inequality to access to decent housing for low-income households and private renters:

1. *Absolute incomes*: In more unequal countries, the absolute level of resources held by low-income households is lower than in more equal countries. This could translate directly into restricted access to affordable housing of decent quality and quantity for low-income households. Where a negative influence of income inequality is caused by the absolute level of resources, rather than the relative distribution of income, then the effect of inequality should disappear when controlling for the level of resources;

2. *Rising aspirations*: Inequalities trigger status competition and rising aspirations. Housing has become a status symbol and the increasing affluence of the rich in more unequal societies might have encouraged the middle- and lower-income groups to overinvest and increase their levels of indebtedness. The impact on lower-income households may be mixed, with both affordability problems (larger mortgage costs) and higher quantity and quality;

3. *Pressures on the housing market*: If more households aspire to home ownership and the richer part of the income distribution can afford higher prices then house prices would increase for all. Falling income could

also put pressure on house prices at the lower end of the market. As noted earlier, this will depend on how segmented the housing market is and it is possible that rising inequality could reduce demand for 'inferior' housing. There are clearly important interactions with the private rented sector (specifically investment decisions of landlords) that need to be taken into account.

In the empirical analysis, access to housing is measured by looking at (i) affordability, 'problematic housing costs', consuming more than 40% of disposable household income, (ii) total housing costs, and (iii) the costs of utilities associated with the use of the property (water, gas, electricity, heating). Housing quality is measured in terms of crowding (space relative to household size and composition). For quality, 'housing deprivation' is defined as a dwelling that suffers from two or more of the following: a leaking roof, no bath or toilet, too dark, too noisy, and no hot running water. They find that the effect of income inequality in countries of similar levels of economic affluence runs through the absolute level of resources, while in countries at different stages of economic development, differences in affluence determine access to housing. In terms of affordability they find that relative income differences do not affect the experience of high housing costs, but the interpretation is ambiguous as higher income households spending more than 40% of disposable household income are also classified as 'problematic' according to this definition—even though clearly this may be affordable. They also find that higher inequality is positively related to the likelihood of experiencing crowding for low-income owners rather than an improvement in quality such as the status-competition mechanism could give rise to.[2] One possible explanation put forward for this finding that is consistent with the status-competition theory is that because low-income households feel under pressure to become homeowners they are willing to accept a smaller home. Finally, although they do find evidence that income inequality is positively related to greater housing-market pressures, the fact that inequality remains significant when controlling for a number of housing-market variables leads them to reject this hypothesis. There are clearly measurement and methodological improvements that could be made if the quality of the data was higher, but this paper makes an important step in the direction of defining and testing hypotheses in relation to housing.

---

[2] Increasing housing affluence of the rich might press middle- and lower-income groups to upgrade their perceptions about the type of housing that is required (which may be funded through overinvestment and debt), with an upgrading in the size of houses at all income levels (Beer et al., 2011).

## 7.4 Inequality and Intergenerational Mobility

Our third outcome, intergenerational mobility, is usually seen as a cause rather than a consequence of developments in income distribution. Clearly mobility patterns have an important effect on long-run inequality. But, once again, there are important economic connections from present inequality to future intergenerational mobility. As with housing wealth, we would expect a differential resource effect on behaviour, with the well-off willing to invest relatively more in education, with knock-on effects on mobility. Again, as with housing and other forms of wealth, credit constraints imposed by the market will normally have different degrees of impact on rich and poor.

Cross-sectional inequality highlights divisions between individuals and families in terms of their current standard of living and other dimensions of their lives. Some of these divisions have long-term consequences, such as health and the accumulation of wealth or debt. Studies of mobility provide an assessment of the extent to which inequality at a point in time represents permanent differences between people as well as the extent of fluidity that exists in economic and social positions. The growth in cross-sectional inequality that has taken place across many countries over the last thirty years and the variation in inequality across countries at a point in time have led us to question whether higher inequality is associated with lower rates of mobility. In the UK there is evidence that as cross-sectional earnings inequality increased, earnings mobility fell (McKnight, 2000; Dickens and McKnight, 2008), and this may have a bearing on the relationship between inequality and intergenerational mobility on which we focus here. At the heart of the concept of intergenerational mobility is the relationship between the social and economic position of parents and that of their children. A society is said to be immobile when children's social and economic position is purely determined by that of their parents, and the degree of mobility is determined by the weakness of this link. Economists favour quantitative outcomes such as earnings, income, and educational attainment to measure socioeconomic position; sociologists consider individuals' position in terms of status or class. These two approaches have not always resulted in consistent findings (particularly in relation to changes in mobility over time), partly because they are measuring different concepts and partly because of issues related to measurement.

Children inherit characteristics from their parents that influence their social and economic position, and parents also invest in their children—human, social, and cultural capital—or they might use their own status to influence the position of their children. In addition to parental transfers there is a stochastic element due to the random nature of hereditary features and children's own tastes and aspirations. The state also plays a role: motivated by efficiency considerations as well as equality of opportunity, it has sought to intervene in improving the outcomes of children with less advantaged family backgrounds, effectively trying to even out differences between children so that everyone has the possibility to realize their potential. The demand for individuals' skills and characteristics plays a large part in determining occupational outcomes and earnings. The formation of households brings all of these factors together in a measure of household income. What this highlights is that it is clearly the case that cross-sectional inequality will affect the size of the gaps within a set of parents and within a set of children. However, not all inequality measures are sensitive to the size of the gaps, but they may instead focus on rankings within the distribution. Changes in the occupational structure of employment can also affect absolute rates of mobility.

In terms of the relationship between income inequality and intergenerational mobility, some of the literature has concentrated on trying to establish comparable estimates across countries and comparable estimates across time within countries to test whether higher cross-sectional inequality is associated with lower intergenerational mobility. Despite the development of innovative methodologies and developments in data collection and extraction, it remains the case that the study of intergenerational mobility is limited by data availability. Reliable information is required for two generations (parents and children), and to establish change over time within a country two generational pairs need to be available spanning a period in which cross-sectional inequality changed.

The emphasis in the literature has shifted from the estimation of point estimates summarizing mobility (correlation coefficients and elasticities) across the complete distribution to studies that have focused on mobility for different groups—for example, stickiness at the two tails of the distribution, models of intergenerational transmission that consider different life stages, and the role of different welfare regimes and education policies. While most of the literature focuses on examining associations, there have been some attempts at estimating the causal effects of different components of parental endowments such as income and other factors, for instance educational attainment separate from genetic inheritance (see review in Björklund and Jäntti (2009)).

The relationship between cross-sectional inequality and intergenerational mobility from a theoretical perspective is not predictable. Inequalities between parents in the absence of credit markets and welfare states are likely to be replicated in their children but perturbed by random elements of genetic transmission, children's tastes and preferences, discrimination, and changes in demand for endowments. However, the presence of credit markets, taxation regimes, and the extent to which children from less advantaged backgrounds benefit from welfare-state and public-service programmes will all influence the strength of any relationship (Corak, 2013; Andrews and Leigh, 2009; Solon, 2004; Burtless and Jencks, 2003).

Here, we mainly take an economist's perspective. Sociologists have conducted empirical studies measuring cross-country variation in social mobility and changes in social mobility over time (see, for example, Erikson and Goldthorpe, 1992; Breen and Luijkx, 2004), but they have been less interested in relating any observed differences or trends to inequality variations, at least as they are conceptualized in the GINI project.

### 7.4.1 Measuring Intergenerational Mobility

Blanden (2013) provides a detailed description of standard methodologies used by economists to measure intergenerational mobility and how this contrasts with methodologies adopted by sociologists. The usual approach is to estimate a log linear regression of children's economic position (when they are adults) on that of their parents. So for children and parents in family $i$ the typical formulation is:

$$\ln Y_i^{child} = \alpha + \beta \ln Y_i^{parents} + \varepsilon_i$$

where Y could be income, earnings, or education and $\varepsilon$ is a stochastic error term. The coefficient of interest is $\beta$ (intergenerational elasticity), which reflects the strength of the association between children's and parents' status positions. Attention needs to be paid to measurement error in both the dependent variable (classical measurement error should not bias the estimate of $\beta$, although there is a loss of precision and larger standard errors, but bias may be introduced depending on the age at which the dependent variable is observed (Haider and Solon, 2006—more on this below) and the independent variable (which is likely to lead to a downward bias and inconsistent estimates of $\beta$ (Solon, 1992)). An alternative measure is the intergenerational correlation, which adjusts for differences in variance between the two generations but is more data-demanding to estimate as it requires information on permanent inequality differences in both generations.

Ideally $Y_i$ would be a permanent outcome measure, but data limitations mean that point estimates and sometimes average values of a number of point estimates are typically used. This is more problematic when looking at income and earnings: estimates of earnings early in adults' lives can lead to poor results as lifetime earnings trajectories differ between education and occupational groups, with profiles starting very close in the early twenties but climbing faster and peaking later for the more highly qualified and those employed in higher-status occupations (see, for example, Goldthorpe and McKnight, 2006). This would mean that if children's earnings/income was measured during their twenties but parents' earnings/income was measured during their thirties/forties it would appear that mobility was higher than if children's outcomes were measured at a later age. There are clearly life-cycle effects that shape age–income profiles associated with family formation and earnings trajectories that make the age at which income is measured an important factor in terms of assessing the extent of mobility between generations.

In terms of measuring the effect of changes in inequality on intergenerational mobility, two types of studies approach this issue. Cross-country estimates that compare countries on the basis of differences in cross-sectional inequality can be used to assess whether or not higher levels of inequality are associated with lower rates of mobility. Within-country studies that assess the extent to which intergenerational mobility changed over a period when cross-sectional inequality changed provide a second way of assessing this relationship. Both approaches pose methodological challenges with comparability being the key challenge to meet.

The evidence on cross-country variation in intergenerational mobility suggests a negative correlation between income inequality and intergenerational mobility (Corak, 2013). Blanden (2013), using a number of different measures of inequality and comparing the results from different data sources, shows that nations with relatively high inequality have relatively high persistence (low intergenerational mobility) in income and education. She selects a set of preferred country estimates of intergenerational income/education mobility (elasticities) from the literature and computes the correlation between these estimates and cross-nationally comparative cross-sectional inequality estimates, using a number of different data sources and inequality measures.

By contrast Andrews and Leigh (2009) use a comparative international data series, but are forced to predict fathers' earnings based on retrospective occupational data because there is no information on fathers' earnings when their children were young. This clearly introduces an element of measurement error into the independent variable and, as the variance of children's earnings will be higher than fathers' predicted occupational earnings, estimates of mobility will be downward biased. Also, as fathers' predicted occupational earnings are estimated using earnings data from the year that sons' earnings are observed, no allowance is made for changes in occupational wage differentials over a period of considerable occupational and sectoral change. Overall, they find that intergenerational mobility is lower in countries where the sons grew up in more unequal countries in the 1970s.

Björklund and Jäntti (2009) also select a set of preferred intergenerational income elasticities from several country studies and plot these against cross-sectional disposable Gini coefficient estimates (measured close to the prime age of the parental generation) for eleven developed countries. They conclude that there is a weak tendency for high inequality of disposable income to be related to high intergenerational income elasticity, but confidence intervals are wide for estimates based on survey data, making the exact ranking of countries imprecise.

These findings from cross-country studies showing a negative relationship between inequality and intergenerational mobility suggest that an increase in inequality within a country may be associated with a fall in mobility. As only a limited amount of research has been conducted on trying to explain the observed cross-country variation, it is not known whether country-specific factors explain the observed correlations. In addition, changes in the progressive nature of public policy and returns to skill will also have an impact on intergenerational mobility trends. It is important to seek to establish the relationship between changes in inequality and changes in intergenerational mobility, not least because attitudinal data shows that people are more tolerant to higher levels of inequality if they are accompanied by equal opportunity to succeed (Jencks and Tach, 2006). Due to the even greater data requirements for a study of changes in intergenerational mobility there are only a few studies on this topic. In this section we look at the evidence on trends for the USA and the UK, both of which have experienced large increases in inequality over the past thirty years.

Lee and Solon (2009) review a number of studies for the USA that estimate trends in intergenerational mobility: some studies estimate large increases in intergenerational mobility, some estimate large decreases, but most estimated changes are statistically insignificant. They seek to establish a more reliable set of mobility estimates using the Panel Study of Income Dynamics and a sample of sons and daughters born between 1952 and 1975, using as much of the available data as possible to provide multi-year estimates for parents' and sons'/daughters' family income to proxy for long-run income. Their results suggest that in the USA, for cohorts born between 1952 and 1975, intergenerational income mobility did not dramatically change over time. However, they acknowledge that their estimates, particularly at the start of the period where sample sizes are small, are too imprecise to rule out a modest trend in either direction. Hertz (2007) makes certain refinements to adjust for attrition and age, and reaches the same conclusion that there does not appear to be a long-run linear trend in intergenerational income mobility in the USA over this period.

For the UK, two birth cohorts, for 1958 and 1970, who have been followed periodically since birth, provide the main data source that has been used to

189

analyse intergenerational mobility in the UK and how it has changed over time.[3] Economists and sociologists who have estimated intergenerational mobility using these two birth cohort studies disagree, with economists finding declining income mobility (Blanden et al., 2004) and sociologists finding no such decline in class mobility (Goldthorpe and Mills, 2004). Both 'sides' have sought to reconcile these differences but, not surprisingly, they both reach the separate conclusions that their own findings are superior (Blanden, 2013; Erikson and Goldthorpe, 2010). There clearly are issues around data quality and measurement error that are likely to play a contributory role, but also there are simply different conceptual frameworks, which makes a straight comparison between these approaches difficult.

Much of the literature provides estimates of intergenerational correlations in income or earnings without regard for how correlations may vary according to the parents' relative position in the origin distribution. Björklund et al. (2008) present new evidence on intergenerational mobility in the top of the income and earnings distributions using a dataset of matched father–son pairs in Sweden. They find that intergenerational transmission is very strong in the top of the distributions, more so for income than for earnings. In the extreme top (top 0.1%) income transmission is remarkable, with an intergenerational elasticity above 0.9. They also study potential transmission mechanisms and find that sons' IQ, non-cognitive skills, and education are all unlikely channels for explaining this strong transmission. Within the top percentile, increases in fathers' income are negatively associated with these variables, but wealth has a significantly positive association. Their results suggest that Sweden, known for having relatively high intergenerational mobility in general, is a society where transmission remains strong in the very top of the distribution and that wealth is the most likely channel. Their findings are important, especially as a number of countries have experienced increases in concentration of income, earnings, or wealth at the very top over recent years.

Although plenty of within-country studies show 'stickiness' at the two ends of the distributions (Smeeding, 2013), only one study contains comparable estimates across five nations. Jäntti et al. (2006) find stickiness in both the bottom and top, but there is also variation across countries, with the USA exhibiting the greatest stickiness at the bottom (relative to UK, Denmark, Finland, Norway, and Sweden), while both the USA and the UK are stickier at the top.

Smeeding (2013) argues the case for looking forwards rather than looking backwards to estimate the potential impact of the rise in inequality on

---

[3] In addition, some research on this topic has been conducted using the British Household Panel Survey; see, for example, Nicoletti and Ermisch (2007).

intergenerational mobility, as the birth cohorts most affected by the large increase in inequality have not yet reached the optimal point in their life-cycles to provide reliable estimates of mobility. Smeeding suggests that examining outcomes in factors that help to predict later life outcomes (for example, education outcomes) could provide early evidence about how intergenerational mobility estimates are likely to change in the future. He outlines an alternative approach, which examines in detail how parents contribute to child development and 'success' using a life-cycle approach. The Brookings 'Social Genome' project is developing a dynamic microsimulation model of the process of moving from birth to adulthood, effectively a model of social mobility, which can be used to assess whether individuals reach defined life-cycle stage markers consistent with achieving a 'middle class' life. This can be used to assess how children from different backgrounds vary in the extent to which they achieve these markers and the cumulative positive effects of being born to a more advantaged family. They show how children from less advantaged backgrounds fall behind at every life-stage and highlight the need for positive intervention over the life-cycle (Sawhill et al., 2012). Sawhill et al. also conclude that there are not just large gaps in socioeconomic status (family formation patterns, test scores, higher educational attainment, adult earnings) but these gaps are widening (for test scores and degree attainment), suggesting that social mobility may be falling for more recent generations in the USA.

Financial transfers from parents to children are an important channel of intergenerational transmission of wealth and socioeconomic advantage; it is a mechanism through which the effect of inequality on mobility and vice versa may be self-reinforcing (Champernowne and Cowell 1998, Chapter 10). Olivera (2012) explores the patterns of the division of inter-vivos financial transfers from parents to adult children in a sample of twelve European countries, exploiting two waves of SHARE for those aged 50+. Contrary to previous studies, he finds a higher frequency of parents dividing these transfers equally. He argues that altruistic parents are also concerned with norms of equal division, and hence do not fully seek to offset income differences between their children, but start to give larger transfers to poorer children when the income inequality between the children becomes unbearable from the parent's view. Econometric evidence is presented suggesting how this behaviour operates under different specifications and strategies. The lower frequency of equal division found in studies with American data may respond to the higher inequality and relatively lower pension expenditures in the USA. Alessie et al. (2011), using the same data but a different modelling strategy, examine inter-vivos transfers in money and time between parents and children motivated by altruism and exchange. They outline a model that predicts that an altruistic parent will make compensatory transfers, giving less money to a rich child than to a poor one, but these transfers may be affected by an exchange motive in relation to care given by adult children to elderly parents. They find that parents do not give more to children who have less, rejecting pure altruism in favour of exchange.

Parents can also influence children's outcomes through the wealth effect. Karagiannaki (2012) examines the effects of parental wealth holdings on children's outcomes in early adulthood: parental wealth holdings when children were teenagers are associated with a range of outcomes at age 25. She explores four outcomes: higher educational attainment, labour force participation, earnings, and home ownership. For all outcomes she finds positive associations with parental wealth, which operate over and above the influence of parental education and income. The strength of estimated associations varies across outcomes, with education exhibiting the strongest association. For earnings the association is mainly driven by the indirect effect of parental wealth on children's educational attainment, while for home ownership this is through the direct effect of parental wealth transfers. Further analysis that examines the importance of financial wealth and housing wealth separately shows that housing wealth is more strongly associated with higher educational attainment than with financial wealth. However, important effects are also estimated for financial wealth (especially at low wealth levels), pointing to the importance of financial constraints for low-wealth/financially indebted households.

As noted earlier, there are a number of external influences that affect intergenerational mobility rates across countries. Whelan, Nolan, and Maître (2013) set out to exploit the information contained in the EU-SILC Intergenerational Module to conduct a comparative analysis of the relationship between current poverty and social exclusion outcomes and parental characteristics and childhood economic circumstances. Unfortunately, they uncover a serious problem relating to the scale of missing values and comparability of key variables, which led them to issue a note of caution regarding the findings of this study. However, this paper makes an interesting contribution as it is one of only a few papers that has attempted to assess the manner in which welfare regimes mediate the impact of parental social class and childhood economic circumstances on poverty and economic vulnerability. They find that intergenerational factors have their weakest influence on income poverty in social democratic countries and their greatest consequences in liberal Southern European welfare regimes. When the analysis is extended to consider the joint impact of parents' social class and childhood economic circumstances on income poverty and economic vulnerability, they find that the impact of parental social class on income poverty is weak in the social democratic and corporatist countries and strongest for the liberal and Southern European countries. For economic vulnerability the net impact of social class is generally higher. This is also found to be true in relation to economic circumstances. Despite data difficulties they are able to uncover fairly systematic variation across welfare regimes in the strength of intergenerational influences (particularly in relation to economic vulnerability), and this research plays a useful role in motivating future research in this area while also flagging up real issues in the quality of comparative data available, even within dedicated surveys.

Cross-country differences in the relationship between inequality and intergenerational mobility can be used to highlight differences in the effects of public and private investments. Smeeding (2013) highlights how some countries vary in terms of the degree of mobility relative to that which would be predicted in terms of the level of inequality according to the figures presented in Björklund and Jäntti (2009). For example, Sweden and Finland have slightly less mobility than their levels of inequality would predict, while Denmark has much higher rates of mobility than expected. Italy, the USA and France all have high levels of inequality but with lower levels of mobility than one would predict. He highlights the need to respect parental autonomy and the principle of merit in designing policies to help reduce barriers to intergenerational mobility, but suggests that this is possible through tackling child poverty, early child development programmes, and through the education system.

## 7.5 Conclusions

In this chapter we have examined new evidence under the 'social impacts' theme that assesses the relationship between inequality and health, housing, and intergenerational mobility. These three areas to differing degrees reflect long-term differences between individuals.

In terms of the relationship between income and health, three hypotheses have been put forward in the literature focusing on absolute income, relative income, and income inequality. Three new contributions to this debate have revealed some interesting findings. This new evidence suggests that in rich countries it is relative income (gap between own income and others' income) that is important in predicting levels of self-assessed health—not absolute income. However, it is absolute, not relative, material deprivation that has a negative association with health. There is a significant relationship between mortality and poverty for infants and children and an interesting divergence between regime types in relation to infant/child mortality and adult mortality, with Nordic regimes most effective at reducing infant mortality and to a lesser extent child mortality, but Southern European regimes associated with lower adult mortality rates. This may reflect factors such as climate, diet, and lifestyle that are not sufficiently compensated for in the Nordic regimes. The relationship between working conditions and employment relations and health has received far less attention, but evidence is accumulating to highlight the importance of this dimension. As the rise in inequality has been associated with a fracturing of jobs, the link between job quality and health is important for understanding not just the social determinants of health inequality but also the social impacts of inequality following recent inequality trends. There is evidence that adverse working conditions are related to lower health, particularly the mental health of workers, and that low pay is related to poorer physical health.

Poor housing conditions are detrimental to health, but the overall relationship between inequality and housing is complex and can run in both directions. Home ownership rates have risen across Europe over the last few decades, which appears to some extent to have been encouraged by governments as a means of shifting a greater share of the burden of welfare away from the state. Governments' encouragement of low-income households to become homeowners, coupled with poor financial regulation and cheap credit, are seen as significant triggers of the current economic and financial crisis. Increases in income inequality can drive up house prices and lead to overcrowding among low-income households, and there is some evidence that this has occurred. As housing is typically the largest asset that most households will ever hold, it plays an important role in determining the relationship between parental wealth and children's outcomes both in terms of their education and their adult outcomes. Positive associations have been found between parental wealth and children's higher educational attainment, early adult labour force participation, and earnings. There is also evidence that parental wealth is related to children's home-ownership rates when they are young adults. These associations are examples of how inequalities in one generation can be perpetuated into the next generation.

On the relationship between inequality and intergenerational mobility, the evidence is split between cross-country studies which show a clear relationship between higher cross-sectional inequality and lower intergenerational mobility and the limited evidence available from across-time studies within countries, where the findings are less conclusive. Recent increases in concentration at the top of the income distribution in a number of countries may influence future trends, as 'stickiness' at the top of the income distribution, even in countries such as Sweden with relatively high levels of intergenerational mobility, appears to be leading to rich dynasties. Evidence from the USA examining a number of precursive factors predicts that intergenerational mobility will fall in the future.

# 8

# Rising Inequalities: Will Electorates Go for Higher Redistribution?[1]

*István György Tóth, Dániel Horn, and Márton Medgyesi*

## 8.1 Introduction

Many European countries have faced growing inequalities over the last few decades. With this in mind, the present chapter aims to shed light on some important questions in relation to political impacts. Will these trends induce attitude change and political behavioural responses in various European countries? Does rising inequality lead to increased levels of redistributive claims? Is inequality related to levels of political participation and voting patterns? The early, ground-breaking formulation of the political economy theory of redistribution would predict greater redistributive claims on the one hand, and lower political participation on the other. This appears something of a puzzle, and the actual outcomes are of central importance for the societies involved. Relying on research on the political and cultural impacts of growing inequalities, the present chapter contributes to a more complete understanding of the interplay between inequalities, public opinion on redistribution, and political participation.

Figure 8.1 presents a sketch of our line of reasoning. We take the basic Meltzer–Richard model (1981) as a starting point to situate our analysis in the broader study of the link between inequality and redistribution. While this base model is rather restrictive, it still helps to understand a potential causal relation between inequality and redistribution. We highlight potential mediating mechanisms both on the micro and on the macro levels. Personal

[1] Special thanks are due to Herman van de Werfhorst for his comments and his generous help in computations. The authors also thank Robert Andersen, Brian Nolan, Ive Marx, and Wiemer Salverda for their comments to an earlier version. All errors are ours.

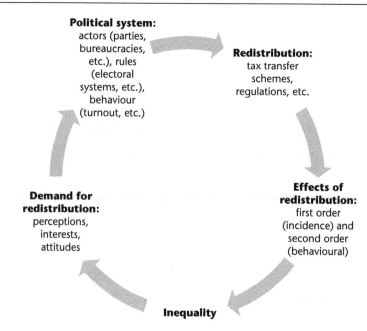

**Figure 8.1.** Theoretical frame of links between inequality, turnout, and redistribution

attributes and perceptions might have an effect on individual redistributive preferences on the one hand and the institutional mechanisms that translate preferences to policy actions on the other. While both the micro and macro mechanisms have an effect on the link between inequality and redistribution (i.e. they are intervening variables), it is likely that both can also be influenced directly by inequality. Next, we analyse the link between inequality and political participation. While the level of redistribution is clearly affected by the level of participation—turnout and the composition of voters and the activity of civil society matter a great deal in policy decisions—inequality in itself can also have a direct impact on the level of participation. Finally, it is clear that the ways in which (and extent to which) attitudes of voters will, via the machinery of politics, shape policies, depend a great deal on various institutions (political and executive alike).

## 8.2 Inequality and Redistribution: The Basic Propositions of the Literature

According to perhaps the most influential of the proposed political economy models, the Meltzer–Richard (henceforth MR) model (Meltzer and Richard,

1981; Romer, 1975), the median voter will have a pivotal role in deciding on governmental policy (in relation to transfers and taxes), assuming a system where majority voting is decisive. The larger the distance between the income of the median voter and the (higher) mean income of the electorate, the greater the pressure on the government to redistribute, assuming those below the mean income will prefer redistribution, while those over it will prefer low or no taxes. The prediction of the model is that more inequality will induce greater redistribution.

The results of empirical tests of this hypothesis vary, to say the least. It commonplace to conclude that the observed negative correlation between inequality and redistribution provides enough proof to refute the theory itself. However, empirical tests of the MR model have often been mis-specified. First and foremost, proper tests would take the distance between the income of the median voter on the one hand and the mean income of the (active) electorate on the other hand, rather than simply taking the relationship of the median income to the mean income of the population. The two may differ significantly, depending upon differential participation of the various income groups at the polls. Second, constructing a measure of pre-tax and pre-transfer inequality (a clear case of the problem of the appropriate counterfactual) is very difficult given the detail of available data in various cross-national datasets. Many studies simply take Gini coefficient values for net (or gross) disposable household incomes. However, both net and gross disposable incomes are second-best proxies, as they incorporate either elements of taxes or elements of social benefits. Finally, many specifications simply take the value of the Gini coefficient as a proxy for income inequality. Given that the Gini (defined as the expected value of pairwise distances of all possible income pairs in the population) is a dispersion-based measure, it is often improperly used as a proxy of social distances between the mean and the median of any given distribution.

Tests with more appropriate specifications show more support for a positive link between pre-redistribution inequality and the consequent redistribution. Milanovic (2000), for example, finds that there is a consistent association between gross household income inequality and more tax/transfer redistribution in a set of twenty-four democracies in the period from the mid-1970s to the mid-1990s. Also, Mahler (2008, 2010) finds support for the MR propositions, after refining definitions of original inequality and redistribution. Kenworthy and Pontusson (2005) find the pattern of cross-country variation broadly consistent with the MR predictions. For reviews of various aspects of the MR model and its propositions, see Borck (2007); Kenworthy and McCall (2008); Keely and Tan (2008); Alesina and Giuliano (2010); Lupu and Pontusson (2009); McCarty and Pontusson (2009); Senik (2009).

In this chapter we focus on a restricted part of a potential causal chain between inequality and redistribution. First, we are interested in the relationship between income inequality and redistributive preferences of the population. This will be followed by an analysis of inequality and political behaviour. Therefore, we do not attempt to reflect the full circle of relationships in Figure 8.1. We proceed on the assumption that the formation of redistributive preferences on the one hand and political participation on the other hand mediate between pre-redistribution inequality and redistribution itself. The main question addressed is whether rising inequality will induce electorates to demand (and vote for) more redistribution as the MR model predicts. We present results of empirical studies that directly address the relationship between income inequality on the one hand and redistributive preferences and political behaviour on the other.

## 8.3 Demand for Redistribution

Predictions of the MR model rest on a series of assumptions about individual behaviour and the nature of the programme that is the object of voting. To start with, it is assumed that voters base their choice of the level of redistribution purely on its effect on their own current wellbeing. Also, it assumes that the issue at stake is pure redistribution of incomes from rich to poor, and that there is no public-good element or other dimension (such as insurance against job loss) that enters the decision about accepted taxes (and, consequently, about redistribution). Another assumption is that voters are fully informed about the relevant aspects of the prevailing income distribution. It does not take compositional differences and their potential effect on redistribution into account (the macro aspects). All these above are strong assumptions. In this section we will go through these assumptions, as well as others, to help unpack the tangled relationship between income inequality and redistribution.

### 8.3.1 Micro Aspects—Individual Attributes

Most studies agree that higher income individuals prefer less redistribution—and this is shown by various studies empirically (Tóth and Keller, 2011, 2013; Corneo and Grüner, 2002; McCarty and Pontusson, 2009; Guillaud, 2013). This argument might be called the 'pure material self-interest' (Tóth and Keller, 2011) or the 'homo economicus' effect (Corneo and Grüner, 2002). From this it also follows that it is not only income that matters, but also that wealth, the material position of the individual, has an effect on her/his preferences towards redistribution. To some extent, this is the logic of the class-based interpretation of attitudes to social policies as well (see Svallfors, 1997; Kumlin and Svallfors, 2008).

Although current material situation is shown to have a significant effect, there are three groups of other important factors that may have an impact on formation of redistributive preferences: expectations, social context/values, and the failure attribution argument (Tóth and Keller, 2011). According to the first, still under the assumption of purely rational, self-interested individuals, people do not only care about their current wealth, but also have expectations about their future material position. If their outlook is optimistic they prefer less redistribution, but if they expect their position to worsen they prefer more redistribution. (One obvious example of this line of reasoning is the so-called POUM hypothesis:[2] see Benabou and Ok, 2001; Ravallion and Lokshin, 2000; Rainer and Siedler, 2008.) The social context/values explanation encompasses all those motives stemming from the complex nature of human motivations. People can be conditioned to egalitarian attitudes that push them towards more redistributive preferences or, on the contrary, based on their socialization, they may oppose redistribution. Further, their experiences with immigrants, with minorities, or with the poor might also shape their individual redistributive demands. Finally, the failure attribution argument states that the way people think about the reasons for poverty—whether it is due to the lack of individual effort or due to pure luck in life—matters in how people think about redistribution.

Tóth and Keller (2011) show that all four aspects are associated with preferences for redistribution. Using the Eurobarometer survey (2009, special survey on poverty), they single out the separate effects of material status, expectations, failure attribution, and the social context/values arguments, and they show that all of these factors have significant and strong relations with the preference for redistribution. Their findings are similar to those found in other studies (showing that individual characteristics besides the material position affect redistributive preferences, e.g. Corneo and Grüner, 2002; Finseraas, 2009; and others reviewed by Alesina and Giuliano (2010) and McCarty and Pontusson (2009)). In sum, it seems that the first assumption of the Meltzer–Richard argument—that income is the sole decisive factor—is oversimplified, but it is also apparent that the empirical evidence testing the link between inequality and preferences for redistribution in fact comes down in favour of the basic political economy model: personal position in the income distribution is negatively associated with preferences for redistribution. This indicates that once inequality increases—i.e. larger numbers of people will fall below the average income—the aggregate measure of redistributive preference will, in turn, increase.

But, still, taxes can be spent in different ways. Welfare spending might be redistributive but it might have other goals as well. As Moene and

---

[2] Prospect of upward mobility.

Wallerstein (2001) argue, welfare policy can be treated as the 'public provision of insurance'. People might support generous welfare policy—and thus higher taxes—to provide protection against risks that private insurance markets fail to cover (Moene and Wallerstein, 2001: 859). This assumption changes the predicted relationship between inequality and the optimal level of taxes. When inequality increases due to a decrease in median income, the demand for redistributive spending might increase (as in the MR model), but the demand for insurance declines, assuming that insurance is a normal good. So the relationship between the level of inequality and the level of welfare spending is less obvious, if we allow the government to spend non-redistributively. Iversen and Soskice (2001) develop this argument by assuming that the individual demand for public insurance depends on the individual skill set, which in turn depends greatly on the institutional structures, the labour market, and the educational set-up.

### 8.3.2 Contextual and Macro Effects

While it is theoretically straightforward that individual characteristics have an effect on redistributive preferences (and not vice versa), it is less obvious how contextual and macro variables affect (or are affected by) individual redistributive preferences. A research question about the impacts of contextual effects on preferences could be framed along the following lines: once absolute material position clearly affects redistributive taste, can we identify a separate effect of a macro constellation such as the overall inequality level or the shape of the distribution? Further, there might be an interaction between individual income position and contextual inequality as well. The question in this respect can be formulated like this: will rich people in highly unequal societies think/behave differently than rich people in less unequal societies? Will the poor define their positions differently if they know how many other poor people there are around? The social (income, educational, wealth, etc.) gradient of voting taste may be stronger or weaker, depending on the shape or extent of overall inequality.

Tóth and Keller (2011) find a positive association between the level of inequality (contextual value) and redistributive preferences. Holm and Jaeger (2011) also test the link between national level contextual characteristics (income and unemployment) and redistributive preferences based on a Danish panel of the European Values Survey. The panel nature of the data and the changing regional level of unemployment allow for a causality test. Their tentative results show that contextual effects are among the probable drivers of redistributive preferences. A figure taken from Tóth and Keller can help explain some cross-sectional contextual determinants of redistributive appetite (Figure 8.2). As is seen, the preference for redistribution is positively related

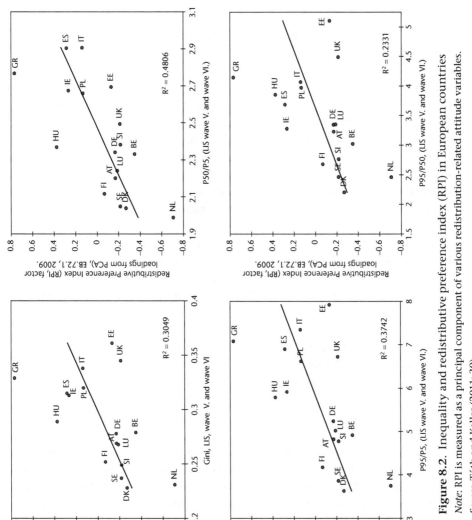

**Figure 8.2.** Inequality and redistributive preference index (RPI) in European countries

*Note:* RPI is measured as a principal component of various redistribution-related attitude variables.

*Source:* Tóth and Keller (2011: 30).

to inequality. The strength of this relationship depends on the measure used, the best fit being found for measures more sensitive to the bottom (such as, for example, the ratio of the median income to the bottom 5%'s income).

Lupu and Pontusson (2011) also argue that it is the structure of inequality, rather than its level, that counts. The 'structure of inequality' logic states that relative distances between various social groups (the internal structure of the distribution) matter, because these translate into 'social affinity' between the poor and the middle and the middle and the affluent respectively. Lupu and Pontusson (2011) argue that 'in the absence of cross-cutting ethnic cleavages, middle-income voters will empathize with the poor and support redistributive policies when the income distance between the middle and the poor is small relative to the income distance between the middle and the affluent' (p. 316). In their argument, a high level of inequality might come from the large difference between the affluent and the median as well as from the distance between the median and the poor. They remain within the median-voter framework—in that it is still the median voter who decides—but allow the median to opt for more or less redistribution depending on her/his distance from both ends.

Tóth and Keller (2011) also test the 'structure of inequality' logic, by looking at the association of material status and preference for redistribution. Their conclusion is in line with the 'structure of inequality' argument: the level of preferences for redistribution is high in high-inequality countries, moderate in middle-inequality, and low in low-inequality countries, while individual material status correlates more with redistributive preference in middle-inequality countries than in high- or low-inequality countries. Thus, according to these results, it seems that although the level of inequality matters, its structure also matters.

### 8.3.3 Institutions

Institutions, understood as aggregate social relationships, are also potential macro factors that have an effect on redistributive preferences. A large stream of research literature analyses the path-dependency of institutions, and the relation of institutions with governmental policies (e.g. Esping-Andersen, 1990; Hall and Soskice, 2001). An example of a clear rational choice based logic connecting institutions with government policy is work by Estevez-Abe et al. (2001) and Iversen and Soskice (2001), where they connect the vocational specificity of educational systems with the level of social protection. Although Estevez-Abe et al. (2001) do not consider preferences for social protection (as a way of redistribution), Busemeyer (2012) does so, by looking at the association between inequality and demand for public spending on education. His results highlight two important points. First, higher economic inequality is associated with greater demand for education spending, but this effect is attenuated by the individual's income position: higher income people tend to oppose spending on education (as expected based on the research highlighted in the previous section, from 'pure material self-interest'). Second, the level of educational inequality also has a positive effect on redistributive preferences—higher inequality is associated with greater demand for spending—but this effect increases with individual income: higher-income people tend to demand more spending on education if educational inequality is larger.

Horn (2012) looks at this argument more closely, and examines how the structure of the education system (its institutions) relates to the demand for educational spending. Selective education systems tend to be more unequal than comprehensive ones. That is, education systems that select children into homogeneous classes, and do so relatively early, tend to have much higher inequality of outcomes, and also display higher inequality of opportunity, compared to non-selective systems (for a comprehensive review, see Van de Werfhorst and Mijs, 2010). Based on this, Horn (2012) argues that in countries where the system of education is selective, and thus helps to reproduce status differences, higher-status people are more likely to demand more spending on education, because they benefit from it. Conversely, lower-status people tend to support less spending on education. So in case of stratified education systems, assuming majority voting, an increase in income inequality will translate into less demand and thus less spending on education.

Another similarly framed logic is Epple and Romano's (1996) 'ends against the middle' argument. Epple and Romano argue that if people can decide between public and private education, that is whether education should be financed through taxes or paid directly by households, both the rich and the poor might benefit more from a separate system of private education (the rich use it, while the poor benefit from the 'unused' taxes paid by the rich for public education), and thus coalesce against the middle, which benefits the most from public education. This logic also highlights that there are instances when it is not the overall level of inequality—the difference between the rich and the poor—that matters.

Further, once more inequality induces greater support for redistribution, how shall higher initial redistribution affect the additional demand for redistribution? Greater initial redistribution may induce inverse processes, if people recognize the negative overall behavioural effects of welfare expansion under certain circumstances (see, for example, Olivera, 2012). Therefore, an increase in inequality might have positive or negative effects, depending on the initial size of the redistribution, on its type, and also on its incidence.

## 8.4 Inequality Perceptions, Values, and Opinions about Inequality

According to the theoretical literature, people might have preferences with respect to levels of inequality for various reasons. People who are aware of the social problems associated with high inequality, or who hold egalitarian values, will have a preference for low inequality (Alesina and Giuliano, 2010). If people have preferences with respect to the level of income inequality, the desired level of redistribution will depend also on the difference between the level of inequality perceived by the individual and his or her preferred level of inequality. Consequently, the information that people have about the level of income inequality and also the values they hold about the acceptable level of inequality become important inputs to the formation of redistributive preferences. Here we review empirical studies that analyse the effect of actual income inequalities on individuals' perception of inequality, their values about the acceptable or 'just' level of inequality, and also their judgements on whether existing (perceived) inequalities are too large.

### 8.4.1. Do People Perceive Levels of and Changes in Actual Inequality?

Empirical studies about people's information or perception of the income distribution have measured individuals' estimates of pay inequality.[3] Osberg and Smeeding (2006), using data from the 1999 wave of the International Social Survey Program (ISSP), find that individuals severely underestimate ratios of CEO compensation to the pay of manufacturing workers in developed countries. While respondents on average estimate quite accurately the pay of workers, they considerably underestimate CEO compensation. According to their data, underestimation of pay ratios is most severe in the case of the USA. Other studies have compared indicators of estimated pay ratios with data on actual wage inequality in a cross-section of countries. Medgyesi (2012) finds a positive relationship in data from the 2009 wave of the ISSP: in countries with higher levels of wage inequality people estimate higher pay ratios on average, but the effect is relatively weak.

Even if estimates of the level of pay ratios can be biased, individuals might be better able to perceive changes of inequality. Studies on post-socialist countries show that during the years of transition to a market economy, characterized by steeply rising earnings inequality, perceived pay ratios also

---

[3] Surveys like the International Social Survey Program (ISSP) or the International Social Justice Project (ISJP) contain a question where respondents are asked about their estimates of actual earnings of a series of occupations. On the basis of the answers it is possible to construct an indicator of perceived inequality.

increased (Gijsberts, 2002; Kelley and Zagorski, 2005). By comparing time series of inequalities and perceived pay ratios for eight developed countries, Kenworthy and McCall (2008) find mixed evidence: in some cases (Norway, Sweden, UK, USA) the trend of the perceived pay ratio was similar to that of actual earnings inequality, while in the case of Germany and Australia, trends in actual and perceived pay ratios were different. Overall, the evidence about perceptions of income inequality is somewhat scarce; we are not aware of large-scale cross-country comparative studies analysing the effect of changes in inequality on perceived levels of inequality. Existing studies serve to highlight that individuals' information about levels of and changes in inequality might be biased, especially in times of rapidly changing income distributions.

### 8.4.2 Actual Inequality and Desired Level of Inequality

Surveys like the ISSP not only ask people's estimation about the actual pay of a series of occupations but also about the amount they ought to be earning. Based on these data researchers have calculated indicators of the preferred inequality level of respondents.[4] Andersen and Yaish (2012) focus on people's opinions regarding the desired level of inequality, which is measured by the Gini index of 'ought to earn' earnings in the 1999 wave of the ISSP study. They find a strong positive effect of the Gini index for actual income inequality on desired inequality in a multi-level model controlling for various individual-level and contextual-level variables. The results suggest that, on average, a 1% increase in the Gini index for actual inequality leads to a 0.5% increase in the level of desired/tolerated inequality.

Kerr (2011) reports results on the effect of inequality change on the level of desired inequality based on three waves (1987, 1992, 1999) of the ISSP study. In his study the desired level of inequality is measured by the ratio of the pay a doctor should earn according to the respondent over that of an unskilled worker. Results from fixed-effect regression models show that respondents are more likely to accept larger pay ratios when inequality is higher. A one standard deviation increase in inequality is associated with a 0.25 standard deviation increase in desired wage differential. Although not explicitly testing the effect of inequality changes, Gijsberts (2002) and also Kelley and Zagorski (2005) document increasing desired inequality in transition countries where inequality levels were increasing substantially during the 1990s. To sum up, studies exploiting cross-country and inter-temporal

---

[4] Some studies use indicators of preferred pay ratios, that is ratios of pay that high-status and low-status occupations ought to be earning. Other studies calculate a Gini index over earnings amounts that different occupations ought to be earning.

variation suggest that increasing inequality is partially accepted by people, in the sense that levels of accepted inequality increase when inequality is on the rise.

### 8.4.3 Judgements about Inequality: Does Inequality Lead to Discontent?

According to Kuhn (2011), individual judgements about the level of inequality might be closely related to demand for redistribution: people are expected to demand more redistribution if they perceive much more inequality than they prefer. Empirical research has followed several strategies to study judgements that people make about inequality. One line of research studies the effect of income inequality on overall satisfaction with life. Another strategy uses direct survey questions on people's opinions about inequality.[5] Studies in the first tradition include Alesina et al. (2004), who analyse the difference in the effect of inequality on life satisfaction between European countries and American states. They conclude that inequality has a negative effect on life satisfaction among both European and American citizens, but the European poor are more negatively affected by inequality than the American poor. Verme (2011) studies the link between income inequality and life satisfaction on a pooled sample of countries from the WVS/EVS. He finds that income inequality generally decreases life satisfaction, but points out that results are highly dependent on modelling assumptions. On the other hand, Zagorski and Piotrowska (2012) do not find a significant effect of income inequality on life satisfaction in models that also control for household income. Grosfeld and Senik (2010) show decreasing inequality aversion during the first years of transition in Poland, but they also show that increasing inequality lowers satisfaction in later years.

Other studies use surveys (e.g. Eurobarometer or the World Values Survey) that directly ask how respondents value actual inequalities—whether they find actual inequalities too large or not.[6] Studies on cross-country data analyse whether in countries with higher income inequality there is more discontent with the actual level of inequality. Earlier studies such as Suhrcke (2001) or Murthi and Tiongson (2008) report a significant effect of the Gini index of income inequality, with higher inequality being associated with stronger discontent with inequalities. However, these studies do not discuss the need to account for the clustering of observations in countries (or multi-level analysis), and thus presumably underestimate the standard error

[5] A third research strategy consists of inferring the discontent with actual level of inequality by analysing how estimated pay ratios differ from pay ratios that the individual deems acceptable.

[6] A standard version of this question asks people whether they agree with the statement 'Nowadays (in our country) income differences between people are far too large.'

of the estimated coefficient on the Gini index of income inequality. Lübker (2004) finds similar results in a country-level regression; however, this analysis fails to control for compositional differences between countries.

The methodological problems in these studies were (at least partially) overcome by Hadler (2005), who performs a multi-level analysis of determinants of opinions about inequality (the 'inequality too large' version) on the ISSP 1999 data, and finds no significant effect of the Gini index of income inequality. Similarly to this study, Medgyesi (2013) finds non-significant effect of cross-country differences in income inequality on the agreement with the 'inequalities are too large' statement in a sample from fifty-seven countries of the World Value Survey. Cross-sectional results should be interpreted with caution however, since these are susceptible to the omitted variable problem: in societies characterized by an egalitarian norm inequality will be lower and individuals will also more often prefer lower levels of inequality. Analysis based on inter-temporal variation in inequality and attitudes might get a step closer to uncovering the 'true' effect of inequality, since in this case time-constant country-level unobserved variables—like an egalitarian norm—can be controlled for.

There are only a few studies analysing the relationship between inequality and judgments about inequality levels based on inter-temporal variation. Earlier studies compare country-level trends in inequality and dissatisfaction with inequality without explicit statistical modelling of the relationship. Lübker (2004) finds that rising inequality was more often associated with an increasing agreement with the statement that inequalities are too large. McCall and Kenworthy (2009) show that contrary to the conventional wisdom that Americans are not really concerned about inequalities, dissatisfaction with inequality increased significantly during the period of rising inequalities in the USA between the late 1980s and the early-to-mid-1990s. Other studies use the World Values Survey/European Values Study, which provide large cross-country datasets. Medgyesi (2013) studies the effect of changes in income inequality on attitudes based on a pooled database comprising all six waves of the WVS/EVS. Results using multi-level models show that an increase in inequality is associated with a stronger agreement with the statement that inequalities are too large (see Figure 8.3). These results are consistent with those of Kerr (2011), who uses models with country fixed effects to demonstrate that acceptance of inequality is influenced by the actual level of inequality. To sum up, studies exploiting inter-temporal variation show that an increase in inequality leads to more agreement that inequalities are too large. Discontent with the level of inequality, however, increases only moderately with the rise of inequality, which might be the result of some increases in individuals' accepted levels of inequality when actual inequality is on the rise (as shown in the previous section).

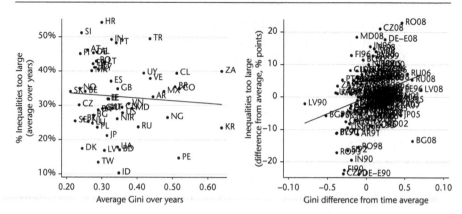

**Figure 8.3.** Cross-country and inter-temporal relationship between income inequality and agreement with the statement that 'inequalities are too large' (pooled WVS/EVS data)

*Source*: Medgyesi (2013).

### 8.4.4 Perceived Inequality and Redistributive Preference

A computation on the basis of the GINI inequalities and poverty dataset (collected from the GINI project country case studies and presented by Tóth (2013)) also confirms that inequality and redistributive preference are related, though much of this relationship is mediated by perceptions of inequality (see Table 8.1).

As the data show, redistributive preference (defined as agreement to the statement that government shall have to redistribute more) correlates with the Gini coefficient if no other variables are included in the model. However, that direct effect is taken away when dissatisfaction with inequality enters the model (as the latter obviously correlates with Gini). Therefore high inequality will lead to redistributive preferences to the extent that people perceive inequalities to be too high.

## 8.5 Inequality and Political Participation

Political participation is one of the most important factors that could have a major effect on the level of redistribution. Voter turnout has been low and steadily declining in European countries throughout recent decades. The average Western European voter turnout was around 85% up until the mid-1980s, but since then has dropped by 10–15 percentage points. The Eastern European turnout level and decline is even worse: it was around 75% at the time of transition and dropped to levels between 50% and 60% after

**Table 8.1.** Inequality and redistributive preference: linear trend in Gini coefficient with country and year fixed effects

|  | (1) | (2) | (3) | (4) |
|---|---|---|---|---|
|  | % agreeing government should redistribute | % agreeing government should redistribute | % agreeing government should redistribute | % agreeing government should redistribute |
| Gini net disposable household income | 1.430* (2.63) | 1.480~ (1.76) | −0.027 (−0.05) | 0.024 (0.02) |
| % agreeing inequality is too large |  |  | 0.883*** (7.60) | 0.905~ (1.72) |
| Gini × % agreeing inequality is too large |  |  |  | −0.001 (−0.04) |
| Observations | 117 | 70 | 70 | 70 |

*Note*: t statistics in parentheses.

~ p<0.10; * p<0.05; ** p<0.01; *** p<0.001

*Source*: Data from country chapters (Tóth, 2013).

2000 (Horn, 2011). Income inequalities have grown during the last couple of decades. A similar trend is observable in more than two-thirds of the OECD countries, independent of the measure employed (OECD, 2008). So is there a link between inequality and political participation?

Taking a closer look at this link is important for two other reasons. Firstly, both of these factors are important outcomes for any democratic society. The level of inequality has always been in the focus of governmental policies, but also the level of political participation can be considered vital for democracy and for the economy.[7] On the other hand, it is not at all obvious whether participation affects inequality or conversely inequality impacts on participation. We argue that both links are possible theoretically.

Most of the literature about social capital treats participation as a single factor (e.g. Uslaner and Brown, 2005). However, political participation is only one of four possible forms of participation, albeit a very important one. One could differentiate between political, social, civic, and cultural participation both theoretically and empirically. But as far as redistribution is concerned, political participation is the key. We treat political participation as a form of engagement in political activities. Party membership, volunteering, giving money to parties, or writing letters to politicians are all different forms

[7] See Chapter 9 and Andersen (2012) on the link between inequality and support for democracy.

of political participation (Uslaner and Brown, 2005). Yet the most straightforward and most widely available proxy is voter turnout. Acknowledging that there are more ways of understanding political participation, we see voting as the most clear-cut—and most easily observable—mode of political participation.

### 8.5.1 Various Propositions to Explain the Inequality–Participation Link

There are two theoretical hypotheses that could guide us in establishing the link between inequality and political participation: the 'psychosocial' (or sociological) hypothesis and the neo-materialist (or resource-based) one (see also Uslaner and Brown, 2005; Lancee and Van de Werfhorst, 2011; Van de Werfhorst and Salverda, 2012). There are many labels for these two hypotheses in the literature, but all point in the same direction. The psychosocial argument states that inequality goes strongly together with factors—such as trust, which can also be seen as a contextual variable, like general trust—that relate to participation, whereas the neo-materialist argument relies on the micro level and emphasizes that differences in individual resources affect individual participation. Note that the two arguments are complementary rather than contradictory.[8]

The most often used variable to proxy the 'psychosocial level' of the society is general trust (Alesina and La Ferrera, 2000b; Uslaner and Brown, 2005; Steijn and Lancee, 2011). The psychosocial argument is that higher inequality leads to lower trust in others and lower trust leads to lower participation. At high levels of inequality people are more pessimistic about the future, which means the level of trust is lower. In a similar vein, if inequality is high, people tend not to share each other's fate, which also means the general level of trust is low. On the other hand, if general trust in the society is high, markets can operate at a lower cost, which means higher growth, and more participation (especially civic and cultural, but also political). Similarly, if trust is higher, people tend to interact more, and that leads to higher social participation. And finally, higher trust could mean closer or more homogeneous preferences that foster engagement in civic and political groups (Alesina and La Ferrara, 2000b). Nevertheless, the link between trust and participation is not a one-way street. Higher participation might easily lead to higher trust as well: '[P]articipation in social groups may lead to the transmission of knowledge and may increase aggregate human capital and the development of "trust"' (Alesina and La Ferrara, 2000a: 849). Uslaner and Brown (2005: 872) list many studies that argue one way or another with respect to the link between trust and participation.

---

[8] See also Chapter 6, this volume.

One might also consider institutional differences between countries when looking at the relationship between inequality and participation. Institutions affect social norms, and norms affect social behaviour. For instance, universal welfare states encourage solidarity but they also encourage (democratic) participation (Lister, 2007). Hence, we observe high voter turnout and low inequality in universal welfare states (Horn, 2011). This argument also highlights a key question on the causal link between inequality and participation: is it not something else (institutions) that drive both?

The neo-materialist argument is rather simple: individual resources affect individual participation—those who have more participate more—or, to put it differently, the poor participate less. We cannot directly stipulate a negative link between inequality and participation using the neo-materialist argument. If, for instance, inequality rises by an increase in income of the rich, overall participation should also increase according to this argument. Thus it is necessary to have inequality increase with a relative decline in the income of the poor to produce a fall in overall participation.

The most often used proxy for resources is income. Studies usually control for income, or some proxies of wealth, in order to control for the obvious resource effect (Horn, 2011; Lancee and Van de Werfhorst, 2011). A trivial but good example for the resource argument is the Downsian rational voter theory (Downs, 1957): people will consider the cost of voting as they decide about the voting, and the cheaper it is the more likely one is to vote. Hence the more resources (the fewer costs) a person has, the more likely she or he will participate. Another good example for the direct link between inequality and participation is the difference in networks (Letki and Mierina, 2012). If people have smaller networks—informal or formal—their ability to rely on them in case of hardship will also be smaller. It is generally assumed that income associates positively with the availability of networks (Pichler and Wallace, 2007), and so using such networks (cf. social, civic, or cultural participation) is much harder for lower-income people. Note that Letki and Mierina (2012) challenge this argument by stating that there are relative differences between countries in how well these networks are utilized by the lower and the upper strata.

Another way of understanding the resource argument is through the status competition or resource competition between different groups in the society. Inequality means differences in power between status groups in affecting policy, which in turn has an impact on future inequality (Uslaner and Brown, 2005; Solt, 2010; Horn, 2011; Van de Werfhorst and Lancee, 2011). Higher inequality means larger differences in status between individuals, which results in larger status gaps. These gaps trigger status competition and this is detrimental to a range of desirable outcomes, including participation (Wilkinson and Pickett, 2009a; Lancee and Van de Werfhorst, 2011). On a resource-based logic one might argue that '[a]s the rich grow richer relative to their fellow citizens... they consequently grow better able to define the alternatives that are considered within the political system and exclude matters of importance to poor citizens' (Solt, 2010: 285). This will, as a result, negatively affect the participation of the lower classes, who find their expected benefit decreased. Mueller and Stratmann (2003) argue in a different direction: if fewer people vote, then relatively more rich people will vote, thus the median voter's income will be higher. Increased median voter income decreases taxes—since richer people want less redistribution—which in turn increases income inequality in the society (see Horn, 2011).

### 8.5.2 Empirics: How Does Inequality Affect Political Participation?

There are only a small number of empirical papers that directly assess the relationship between inequality and political participation. The most comprehensive study is Solt's (2010) testing of the Schattschneider hypothesis (Schattschneider, 1960). In his book, Schattschneider wrote that large economic inequalities lead to low participation rates as well as a high income bias in participation. Using the resource-based logic he argued that the poor are less likely to cast a vote as inequality goes up, since their expected benefit from voting declines. This is a clear neo-materialist argument. Solt (2010) uses American gubernatorial elections data to test the association between turnout and inequality. He uses state-level Gini coefficients calculated for three years (1980, 1990, 2000) to proxy income inequality, while voter turnout is also observed for these very years. The study shows that income inequality is negatively associated with electoral participation, while at the same time higher-income people tend to vote relatively more as inequality rises.

A similar conclusion is presented by Mueller and Stratmann (2003), but with a different theoretical approach. They argue that if the upper classes have higher participation rates than lower classes, if upper classes favour right-of-centre parties and lower classes left-of-centre parties, and if right-of-centre parties adopt policies that benefit the upper classes while left-of-centre parties adopt policies that favour the lower classes, then lower participation rates will lead to higher income inequalities. Hence their conclusion: voter turnout is negatively associated with income inequality, but it is the decreasing participation rate that drives inequalities and not vice versa. That is, their result is the same, but the line of argument is different from that of Schattschneider (1960).

Similar to the Solt (2010) study, Scervini and Segatti (2012) also look at within-country data. They analyse the possible reasons of the dramatic 8% decline in turnout in the Italian elections between 1992 and 2008. Looking at data between 1946 and 2008 they find that besides the obvious institutional suspect—the abolition of compulsory voting in 1993—the increase in social inequalities had a large negative impact on turnout. More precisely, they argue that increasing social inequality had a major impact on less educated voters, while leaving the turnout of the more highly educated unaffected. Note the importance of this statement for the link between inequality and redistribution: if inequality affects the skewness of turnout (in that higher income people are relatively more likely to vote), then the increasing inequality will increase the median voter income, which in turn decreases redistributive demand. If one controls for the skewness and the level of electoral turnout, the relation between inequality and redistribution regains its expected positive sign (see Mahler, 2008).

In a cross-country comparative framework Horn (2011) also looks directly at the link between income inequality and voter turnout using the 2009 European Parliament election. While the negative association between income inequality and voter turnout is supported by the data (although the effect is not very strong), none of the theoretical explanations are substantiated. The status competition argument (within the resource argument) would posit that lower income people will vote less in more unequal countries, while the institutionalist approach of the sociological argument would state that universal welfare states would have lower inequality and higher turnout. When taking into account all commonly used micro- and macro-level factors that explain voting—such as age, education, standard of living, or size of population, type of election system, compulsory voting, GDP, and so on (see Geys, 2006)—none of the above theories are supported by the data. Hence the author concludes that there might be other, untested reasons that explain the negative association between inequality and political participation (see Figure 8.4).

Lancee and Van de Werfhorst (2011) try to disentangle the sociological and resource effects of inequality on civic, social, and cultural participation. Their analysis shows that resource differences do indeed matter. People with larger incomes tend to participate more, but this effect of income on participation is magnified in more unequal societies. It seems that the resource argument explains only part of the negative association between inequality and participation. The authors argue that the unexplained part is probably due to psychosocial (inter-individual or sociological) explanations. Nevertheless, they find strong and significant negative effects of inequality on all forms of participation. Notten, Lancee, and Van de Werfhorst (2012) look at the link between educational level and cultural participation and how it is affected by educational inequalities on the national level. They find support for the sociological argument: in countries with lower levels of educational inequality, cultural participation generates less status for the higher educated, whereas the relation between a person's literacy skills (i.e.

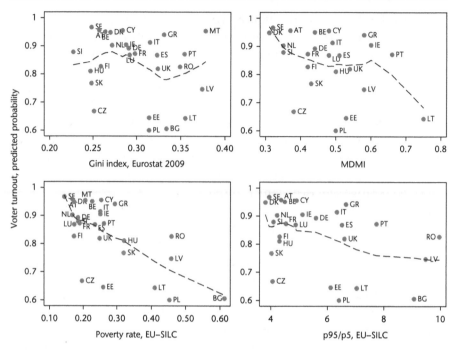

**Figure 8.4.** Association of inequality with turnout, LOWESS smoothed[9]

*Note*: Predicted probabilities are for a 40-year-old man with average income who finished education at age 18. MDMI equals the average of absolute differences from the median. P95/P5 is the ratio of the 95th percentile of the income distribution over the 5th percentile.

*Source*: Horn (2011: 22).

the cognitive aspect of education) and cultural participation remains stable, regardless of a country's educational inequality and thus corroborating the cognitive aspect of the relation between educational level and cultural participation. However, the status-related aspect of cultural participation seems dominant.

Steijn and Lancee (2011) examine the effect of inequality on trust (cf. the psychosocial argument, presented above). Previous studies have shown that income inequality has a negative effect on general trust (e.g. Wilkinson and Pickett, 2009a), but Steijn and Lancee disentangle the reasons behind this link and also restrict their sample to developed European countries to test the association on a more homogeneous sample. They argue that one has to control for the amount of resources (wealth) when looking at the effect of the distribution of resources (inequality), since the two are strongly associated. Moreover, it is important to differentiate between the direct effect of

[9] LOWESS smoothing (locally weighted scatterplot smoothing), provides the strength of association (OLS beta parameter) of the two variables for several subsets of the horizontal axis variable. Its main advantage is that it does not assume any function shape between the two variables.

inequality (stratification effect) and the indirect effect (effect of perceived inequality). Using two independent datasets (the ISSP and the ESS) the authors show that perceived inequality has no significant effect on trust in the first place, probably due to the limited set of countries. Moreover, after controlling for national wealth the association between actual inequality and trust becomes insignificant as well.

Letki and Mierina (2012) study the relationship between inequality and the use of informal networks (cf. the neo-materialist argument, presented above). Previous research has shown income to be positively associated with the availability of networks (Pichler and Wallace, 2007). Letki and Mierina (2012) argue that there are important differences between groups of countries in this respect. This assumed relationship is true especially in post-Communist countries: higher-income people tend to rely on their friends and family more often than lower-income people. In Western European countries the difference between high- and low-income people in their use of networks is less pronounced.

## 8.6 Summary and Conclusions

In this chapter our focus has been the relationship between income inequality, redistributive preferences, and political behaviour. The main question posed is whether rising inequality will induce electorates to demand (and vote for) more redistribution.

First, on the basis of empirical tests, we found that on the micro level the redistributive preference is partially driven by rational self-interest (negatively related to income and material position and with assumptions about future economic prospects of the individuals). The better is the material position and the better are the prospects of the individual, the lower the support for redistribution will be. In addition, however, we stressed that redistributive preference also depends, to a non-negligible extent, on general attitudes related to the role of personal responsibility in one's own fate and also on general beliefs about causes of poverty.

We also reviewed the evidence about macro and contextual determinants of redistributive taste. It was emphasized that larger inequality is associated with stronger preferences for redistribution. In addition, it was also found that the structure of inequality (i.e. the relative distances between the top, the middle, and the bottom income groups) matter for the determination of demand for redistribution. The deeper the poverty is, the larger the redistributive taste is. This adds to the general finding that in countries having a larger level of aggregate inequalities the general redistributive preference (of the rich, of the middle, and of the poor) is higher.

While the empirical backing to show the individual determinants of inequality is fairly convincing, the effect of macro factors on redistributive preferences is less straightforward. The structure of inequality, as well as the institutional setting, can alter the sign of the effect that income inequality has on redistributive preferences. We have argued that the form of redistribution (cash or in-kind, assistance or insurance type, for example), the potential targets (very poor or middle classes, people belonging to majority or ethnic minorities), as well as the institutional setting (education, unemployment benefits, health spending, etc.) all matter for the ultimate effects.

If people have preferences directly with respect to the level of inequality, then their desired level of redistribution will depend also on the difference between the level of inequality perceived and the level of inequality desired. Consequently, the information people have about the level of existing income inequality is an important input to the formation of redistributive preferences. Some empirical studies shed light on people's information about the income distribution by measuring individuals' estimates of the ratio of chief executive to workers' pay. Other studies try to measure whether increasing inequality causes rising discontent with the level of inequalities.

Are people aware of changes in inequality? Studies analysing estimated pay ratios show mixed results. People estimate higher pay ratios in countries with higher wage inequality, and there is also evidence that people's estimated pay ratios rise when inequality increases. On the other hand there is also evidence of underestimation of pay ratios, mostly due to underestimation of high earnings. Other studies use data on discontent with inequalities to see whether people notice changes in inequality. Cross-sectional studies do not find a relationship between inequality and individuals' discontent with the distribution of incomes, but may suffer from reverse causation problems. Results exploiting inter-temporal variation in inequality and attitudes show that attitudes towards inequality seem to respond to changes in actual inequality: discontent with inequalities increases when inequality is rising. Discontent with the level of inequality, however, increases only moderately with the rise of inequality, which might be the result of some increases in individuals' accepted levels of inequality when actual inequality is on the rise

The empirical evidence between inequality and political participation points to a negative relationship between the two. However, whether increasing inequality reduces turnout or diminishing turnout increases inequality is not clear from the reviewed literature. The two complementary theoretical arguments explaining this link are the 'psychosocial' (or sociological) argument and the neo-materialist (or resource) argument. The psychosocial argument states that inequality goes strongly together with factors—such as trust, which can also be seen as a contextual variable, like general trust—that relate to participation, while the neo-materialist argument stays on the micro level and emphasizes that differences in individual resources affect individual participation (poor are less likely to vote). Empirical studies that test the link, and try to argue for a causal chain, usually rely on either or both of these propositions. An example of the neo-materialist argument is that as the rich get richer, and thus inequality increases, they grow better able to define what is on the political agenda, which eventually drives the poor away from the voting booth. Alternatively, since the rich mostly have higher participation rates than the poor, and tend to favour right-of-centre parties adopting policies that benefit them, then lower participation rates will lead to higher income inequality. The link between participation and inequality is negative in both cases, but the causal argument is different.

# 9

# Inequality, Legitimacy, and the Political System

*Robert Andersen, Brian Burgoon, and Herman van de Werfhorst*

## 9.1 Introduction

The main goal of the present chapter is to assess the political implications of inequality at the national level. We do so by providing a brief overview of recent research conducted as part of the GINI research project. The first two sections discuss scholarship on how inequality might influence broad political values within and across nation-states related to political governance at the national and supranational levels. First, with respect to national politics, we demonstrate that inequality has important implications for the values of citizens, including civicness and general altruism, as well as on broad support for and trust in democracy and democratic government. Second, more recent literature suggests that inequality also has important implications for public support for supranational institutions and engagement—from broad support for the European Union to support for general engagement with international institutions and economic contacts. A third and final section considers recent contributions as to how inequality affects not only the values and legitimacy of broad national and international political governance, but also policies of redistribution with respect to both national and international political contexts. Taken together, the three strands of the literature on which this chapter focuses clearly indicate that inequality has important consequences for the legitimacy of political governance and, as a consequence, the functioning of democracies.

## 9.2 Inequality's Domestic-Political Effects: Political Values and Democracy

### 9.2.1 Inequality and Values

A growing body of research indicates that inequality has negative implications for a wide range of factors considered important to democracy, including civic participation, social cohesion, tolerance, solidarity, political trust, satisfaction with democracy, and general trust (Andersen and Fetner, 2008; Andersen and Milligan, 2011; Uslaner and Brown, 2005; Alesina and LaFerrara, 2000b; Rothstein and Uslaner, 2005; Schäfer, 2010; Anderson and Singer, 2008; Lancee and Van de Werfhorst, 2012). Most of this research has been cross-sectional, however, so while we know inequality and attitudes are related, we do not know if inequality has an enduring influence on values relevant to national politics.

More recent work provides new evidence on the possible long-term effects of inequality on values. Specifically, Corneo's (2011) investigation of income inequality in thirty-three modern countries over four decades suggests that inequality does not just shape attitudes in the short term, but it also has a long-term effect on social values. Based on survey data from the European Values Studies and World Values Survey, Corneo estimated the effect of both pre- and post-transfer and taxes inequality on six value sets: work ethic, tolerance, altruism, civicism, obedience, and honesty. Assuming that perceptions of inequality shape values in the long run, he tested not only Gini coefficients for a given year, but also ten- and twenty-year lagged coefficients, and including country fixed effects.[1] Further, as values are particularly internalized during adolescence, Corneo estimated the effects of Gini coefficients on values when the respondent was between 18 and 25. Corneo's findings were mixed. While he found no significant effect of inequality on some values (e.g. obedience, altruism, civicism, honesty), he also found that higher degrees of inequality are positively related to a strong work ethic—a finding that corroborates previous work on inequality and actual working time (Bell and Freeman, 1994; Bowles and Park, 2005). Similarly to Andersen and Fetner (2008), Corneo also found that citizens in countries with more equal incomes tend to hold more tolerant views.

Social trust is another outcome important to legitimacy that is also linked to inequality. Empirical research largely focuses on two types of trust: (i) trust among individuals in society—often referred to as 'generalized trust'—which is typically assessed by survey questions asking whether people can generally

---

[1] Gini coefficients are based on the *Standardized World Income Inequality Database* (SWIID; see Solt, 2009).

be trusted or not, and (ii) trust in government and political institutions, such as the police, parliament, and the judicial system. For the most part, research suggests that both forms of social trust tend to decrease as income inequality rises (Uslaner and Brown, 2005; Newton and Zmerli, 2011; Green et al., 2006). Social trust has been considered an important factor connecting the level of inequality with political participation and other social outcomes such as ill health and deviant behaviour (Kawachi et al., 1997; Kawachi and Kennedy, 1999; Elgar and Aitken, 2011; Elgar et al., 2009). Other research has shown that people rely more strongly on informal networks in highly unequal societies, whereas informal support is less needed in more egalitarian societies (Letki and Mierina, 2012). Inequality may then threaten trust in institutions, and at the same time enlarge the need to find support in an informal way. A lack of trust in national institutions could have direct repercussions for the legitimacy of politics. Some research indicates, however, that the association between trust and legitimacy disappears when GDP per capita is controlled for (Steijn and Lancee, 2011; Olivera, 2012), as discussed in Chapter 6 above.

Summarizing the statistics—especially the Gini coefficients for net disposable income inequality— offered in the country chapters and Chapter 2 (Tóth, 2013) of the companion volume enables us to examine the association between income inequality and generalized trust. Table 9.1 shows results of some regression models, in which different estimations of country and year fixed effects are specified. For each model we estimate parameters with and without controls for GDP per capita (GDP data are taken from the World Bank data, <http://data.worldbank.org>). The dependent variable is the percentage of the population agreeing with the statement that 'most people can be trusted'.

Model 1 demonstrates that higher levels of inequality are indeed related to lower levels of generalized trust. It is important to note that this model

**Table 9.1.** Fixed-effects regressions on generalized trust, with data from the country chapters

|  | 1 | 2 | 3 | 4 |
| --- | --- | --- | --- | --- |
|  | Gini effect | GDP controlled | Gini effect | GDP controlled |
| Gini net disposable household income | −0.784* | −0.266 | 0.369 | 0.037 |
|  | (−2.11) | (−0.54) | (1.55) | (0.15) |
| GDP per capita, PPP current US$ |  | 0.001 |  | 0.000*** |
|  |  | (1.49) |  | (3.63) |
| Country fixed effects | yes | yes | yes | yes |
| Year fixed effects | yes | yes | no | no |

*Note*: t statistics in parentheses

* p<0.05; ** p<0.01; *** p<0.001
*Source*: Data from country chapters of the companion volume.

includes fixed effects for country and year. As Model 2 indicates, however, once GDP is controlled for, the association between inequality and trust is reduced by almost two thirds and is no longer significant. We should also note that a similar pattern occurs when the fixed effects for year are removed (see models 3 and 4). In summary, we find only weak evidence that income inequality is related to generalized social trust, and only when GDP is not considered.

## 9.2.2 Inequality and Trust in Democracy

A particularly important question for democracy is how inequality might affect opinions of the political system, especially public support for democracy. Also relevant is whether large fractions of the electorate feel unrepresented. Overall, the existing literature shows that rising levels of inequality tend to increase dissatisfaction with inequality. Chapter 8 of this volume summarizes research findings in the area, and points to a positive link between actual inequality and people's attitudes and perceptions of inequality. The theory of relative deprivation argues that regardless of whether inequality on the (inter)national level affects one's own economic prosperity, people will tend to dislike rising inequality if their 'distance' to others is increasing (see also Andersen, 2012). As we shall see below, it appears that inequality also affects perceptions of democracy.

The starting point for any discussion of cross-national differences in support for democracy is modernization theory. In short, this theory holds that democracy is spurred on by the process of modernization largely because people tend to become more highly educated and wealthier, leading to higher levels of expression of democratic values (Lipset, 1959; Inglehart and Baker, 2000). Despite a positive link between modernization (usually measured by economic development) and values related to democracy (e.g. Anderson and Fetner, 2008; Kitschelt, 1992; Putnam, 1993), it is clear that not everyone gains equality from economic prosperity, even in modern democracies. Moreover, support for democracy may also be weakening in countries where it has long been well established. For instance, Putnam (2000) has shown that social participation is declining in Western democratic societies; also voter turnout has decreased in these nations (Franklin, 2004). Evidence on trends within countries also point towards a negative relationship between inequality and participation, as is demonstrated in the companion volume from the GINI project (see, for example, the chapter on Canada, which suggests that political participation dropped during times when inequality rose).

Given that these declines in democratic values have occurred despite high levels of economic growth, other factors besides economic conditions may be relevant, such as economic inequality. Theoretical arguments regarding the relationship between inequality and democratic values and actions are conflicting, however. For example, Meltzer and Richard's (1981) classic statement on the issue suggests that inequality should increase political engagement because people feel compelled to protect their interests. This theory fails to consider that people of differing economic conditions do not have equal power in politics. It seems sensible to suggest that inequality may have a positive effect on engagement for the rich but a negative effect for the poor (e.g. Solt, 2008). It is also possible, then, that the growth in inequality in most Western democracies over the past few decades is at least partly responsible for changes in democratic values and actions over this period.

The analysis to follow uses a subset of the 2001 wave of the World Values Survey (Inglehart et al., 2001). Information is used on attitudes of adults (18+) in modern democracies of Europe, North America, and Australia, resulting in a sample of 38,638 individuals from thirty-five countries. Our main goal is to assess the relationship between inequality at the national level—measured by the Gini coefficient for household incomes—and support for democracy. We cannot make strong claims on the causality of this relationship here. Support for democracy is measured on a scale using three survey items: 'Democracy may have problems but it's better than any other form of government', 'I'm going to describe various types of political systems and ask what you think about each as a way of governing this country: Having a democratic political system' (both on a five-point Likert scale), and 'People have different views about the system for governing this country. Here is a scale for rating how well things are going: 1 means very bad; 10 means very good.'

Given its centrality to modernization theory, we also explore the impact of economic development, which we measure by GDP per capita. Finally, given the vast economic, political, and cultural differences between former Communist countries and more established democracies, the analyses are performed separately on these two groups of countries. The experience of a Communist past is thought to be relevant, since former Communist societies tend to be less liberal (Rohrschneider, 2002; Inglehart and Baker, 2000) but also tend to hold low levels of modernization and economic development. Also, as described in several chapters of the companion country-focused volume, levels of trust in parliament in former Communist societies have consistently been low, and in some cases have declined since the transition to a market economy (see, for instance, the chapters on the Baltic states and Bulgaria).

We start by exploring Figure 9.1, which displays the bivariate relationships between average support for democracy and economic development and income inequality in the thirty-five countries.[2] Panel (a) of this figure provides clear support for modernization theory: democracy receives higher

---

[2] See Andersen (2012) for more details on this analysis.

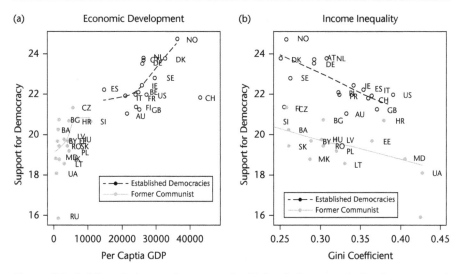

**Figure 9.1.** Public opinion on democracy by (a) level of economic development and (b) income inequality

*Note*: Countries are represented by the International Organization for Standardization's two-letter country codes. Trend lines are LOWESS smooths fitted to the data, with outliers (Switzerland CH and Russia RU) omitted.

*Source*: Andersen, 2012 (with permission).

support in countries with high economic development, regardless of a country's political context (see Figure 9.1a). Nevertheless, consistent with previous research (Solt, 2008; Uslaner, 2002; Andersen and Fetner, 2008), Panel (b) also clearly suggests that inequality matters. Countries with high levels of income inequality have lower levels of support for democracy than countries with low levels of income inequality. Overall, economic prosperity enhances support for democracy while economic inequality—specifically, income inequality—dampens support for democracy.

Further analyses of the individual-level data indicate that an individual's (household) economic position also affects attitudes towards democracy. As we see from Figure 9.2, people with low incomes are less likely than those with high incomes to support democracy. Although this effect is slightly stronger in former Communist countries, it is also clear in more established democracies. Moreover, individual income interacts with a nation's economic level of development. For more established democracies, the difference in attitudes between the rich and poor is most pronounced for countries with low income inequality, though it is important to note that there is a positive relationship between income and support for democracy regardless of the level of income inequality. In other words, the main difference between high- and low-inequality countries pertains to high-income earners, who become even

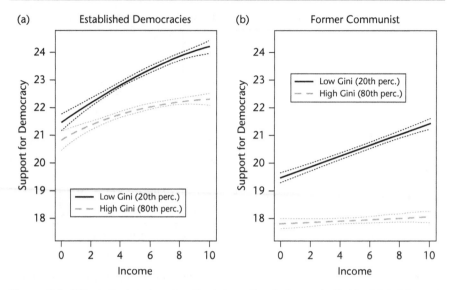

**Figure 9.2.** Effect display showing the interaction between individual-level income and income inequality (measured by the Gini coefficient) in their effects on support for democracy

*Note*: Dotted lines represent 95% confidence bands.

*Source*: Andersen, 2012 (with permission).

more positive towards democracy than others in low-income-inequality countries. In former Communist countries, however, the opposite is true: the relationship between income and attitudes is strongest in high-inequality countries (see Figure 9.2).

In general, these findings suggest that if governments want to facilitate the growth of democracy, policy should take account of not just economic prosperity, but also how prosperity is distributed. If economic growth only benefits the rich, support for democracy could be hampered. Moreover, while the relations between economic conditions, income inequality, and democratic values are similar in both former Communist and more established democracies, there are clear differences between these two types of political context that appear to have little to do with economic conditions. In short, a lingering effect of Communist rule may result in far less support for democracy among people from former Communist societies.

Complementary to these findings, the country report on the Baltic states suggests that inequality may also be related to the importance of bribes and political connections to get ahead in life. Within the Baltic states, Latvia has experienced a consistent increase in the level of inequality during the past decades, whereas income inequality in Estonia, after a very sharp increase, has been decreasing for most of the post-transformation decades. It appears that the Latvian population is more convinced that bribes and political connections matter to get ahead in life than the Estonian population. Arguably the 'shock' of the transformation has not equally led to democratic institutionalization across the Baltic states, leading to situations where income inequality can easily rise through reduced efficacy of the democratic system (Gerber and Hout, 1998).

However, in some societies the legitimacy of national politics is not related to the level of inequality in that society. In Bulgaria, for instance, the level of trust in institutions seems unrelated to the level of income inequality (Tsanov et al., 2013). In Belgium, the rise of anti-establishment political parties, arguably also a sign of criticism of the existing political system, seems unrelated to inequality levels as well (Van Rie and Marx, 2013).

## 9.3 Inequality's Effects on Legitimacy of Supranational Governance

Over the past few decades, political governance has become influenced by supranational institutions. In other words, governance is no longer the exclusive domain of national political authority and institutions. Regional political-economic institutions such as the European Union and broader, more global institutions like the United Nations or the World Trade Organization have become increasingly influential. The multi-level character of modern political life means that any inquiry into inequality's political effects needs also to consider implications for supranational governance, or at least its legitimacy. Scholarship has answered this call in various ways, including work focused on the legitimacy of the EU and support for broader global political-economic engagement—or their opposites, Euroscepticism or the anti-globalization backlash.

### 9.3.1 Euroscepticism among Voters

Euroscepticism may be interpreted as a sceptical or negative attitude towards European integration. For example, people who score high on Euroscepticism tend to display less support for the EU and the associated integration of labour markets. In other words, Euroscepticism is closely correlated to anti-globalization attitudes. Various economic, political and cultural explanations have been offered to account for differences in Eurosceptic attitudes (e.g. Hooghe and Marks, 2005; Lubbers and Jaspers, 2011). The economic explanation focuses on trade liberalization and economic integration, which has different costs and benefits for distinct social groups (e.g. Kriesi et al., 2008). From a political perspective, public opinion on European integration depends on the actions of a nation's political parties and media. Finally, according to the cultural explanation, Euroscepticism is seen as a response to a perceived threat to national identity from the European Union.

Most empirical research on Euroscepticism shows a negative relationship between education and Euroscepticism. More highly educated people tend to hold less Eurosceptic attitudes than less highly educated people for several reasons. In general, the more highly educated experience more benefits from European integration (i.e. globalization), and are thus less concerned about European integration threatening national identity than the less educated. In this regard, Kriesi et al. (2008) argue that citizens with lower skills are increasingly likely to call for protectionist measures to shield national economies from worldwide competition. Several factors have intensified the division between winners and losers of globalization in recent decades.

Following the economic explanation proposed by Kriesi (2008), Hakhverdian et al. (2012) find an increasing gap between the more and less educated in their levels of Euroscepticism over an approximately thirty-year period. They argue that a new political cleavage has emerged in Western European societies. This cleavage has its origin in a structural conflict between groups who can be seen as winners and losers from globalization. Globalization might offer some people (the highly educated; winners) all kinds of opportunities, while others (the less educated; losers) are faced with competition from workers from the new EU member states or see their sector displaced to low-cost countries like India or China. The main hypothesis in Hakhverdian et al.'s study states that education becomes a stronger predictor of Euroscepticism in the Western European member states of the EU. To test this hypothesis, individual survey data from more than 700,000 respondents were obtained by pooling data from more than eighty waves of the Eurobarometer survey across twelve member states of the European Union.

Results show that in the six founding members of the EU,[3] the relationship between education and Euroscepticism is as expected: more highly educated respondents are less Eurosceptic than the less educated. Also, from 1973 onwards, Euroscepticism increases for almost all education groups, but especially among the least educated. In other words, there is an *increasing* educational gap in Euroscepticism. Figure 9.3 shows descriptive trends in French and Belgian Euroscepticism over time for three educational groupings (low, middle, and highly educated). The figure quite clearly reveals the growing tendency of less educated respondents to have more anti-European-integration attitudes than their more educated counterparts. For other countries, trends

---

[3] France, Belgium, Netherlands, Germany, Italy, and Luxembourg.

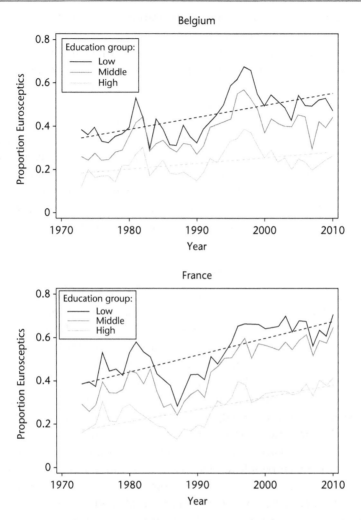

**Figure 9.3.** Rising education gaps in Euroscepticism among voters in France and Belgium

*Source*: Hakhverdian et al., 2012 (with permission).

in Euroscepticism may be less clear, but generally the educational gradient in attitudes tends to grow.

A follow-on study by the same scholars (Kuhn et al., 2013) directly explores whether broader measures of income inequality might directly spur Euroscepticism. Their principal finding is that the rise in ex-ante income inequality, variously measured, is associated with increasing Euroscepticism, particularly among the low-educated. These claims also connect with, and in fact provide individual-level evidence underlying, recent work on the

227

broader backlash against European integration and globalization generally among parties, to be discussed shortly.

The studies of Hakhverdian et al. (2012) and Kuhn et al. (2013), then, demonstrate an increasing role of education in shaping Euroscepticism, largely driven by the fact that Eurosceptic attitudes increase most strongly among the least educated groups. This provides, itself, support for Kriesi's claim that the educational gap in Euroscepticism has increased with time. Most importantly, however, it shows how long-term trends in an important aspect of educational inequality and income inequality can have serious implications for a fundamental aspect of European political legitimacy. If so, we need to consider the possibility that inequalities may have more downstream implications for other political manifestations of Euroscepticism and the backlash against international engagement—an issue to which we can now turn.

### 9.3.2 Anti-Globalization among Political Parties

How inequality shapes the legitimacy of supranational governance is about more than Euroscepticism, but also about broader anti-globalization, or anti-internationalist, sentiment. This broader issue has been addressed by asking how inequality affects political positioning concerning European and also general international openness and globalization.

People perceive globalization in conjunction with stronger domestic labour-market competition. According to an underlying mechanism of 'scapegoating' (Douglas, 1995), citizens can be expected to link their country's global economic exposure and domestic economic situation, where globalization is held accountable for rising inequalities. Further, attribution theory proposes that people tend to blame external sources or agents for negative developments, while positive outcomes are related to internal actions or decisions. Referring to research that established related links between inequality and anti-immigrant attitudes as well as Euroscepticism, Burgoon (2013) focuses on whether political parties, adjusting to voters' preferences, absorb these dismissive attitudes, consequently leading to positioning critical of globalization and internationalization. Furthermore, blame-avoiding party representatives might in any event shift blame for undesirable economic developments such as income inequality onto international interconnectedness. The questions are whether voters and party leaders establish such links, such that the political parties advance critical positions towards international integration.

The evidence of other GINI project scholarship on voter Euroscepticism is suggestive of such links among voters and Euroscepticism, but we need more information about parties and their positioning to complete the picture. Following Burgoon (2013), we can empirically judge such positioning by analysing data from the Comparative Manifestos Project (CMP), which includes indicators of party positioning for various countries over almost five decades between 1960 and 2008. The total sample comprises 200 parties in twenty-two countries[4] based on their participation in national elections. Included in that information are measures of positioning on three issues related to anti-globalization sentiment, measures that can be analysed individually and as a composite: opposition to free trade (net of free-trade support); opposition to (net of support for) international integration and engagement; and opposition to (net of support for) European integration. Based on parties' presentation of positive or negative stands concerning these issues in election-specific manifestos or programmes, these indicators suggest that parties have tended to be pro-globalization in the net: for instance, parties on average (based on party-system means) have tended to be more pro- than anti- with respect to trade, internationalism, and European integration.

An important issue, however, is whether such positions are influenced by inequality. Burgoon (2013) explores whether inequality in market and net Gini coefficients respectively, as measured by Solt (2009), tends to increase anti-globalization position-taking among parties, net of a range of party, national, and yearly conditions, including party identities.[5] As parties are nested within countries, the baseline estimation procedure is based on two level random intercept models.

In line with expectations, net Gini coefficients (measuring post-tax post-transfer income inequality) are modestly but significantly positively related to the anti-globalization composites, suggesting that higher degrees of net inequality come along with backlash positioning of all party families. Figure 9.4 illustrates a rough descriptive-statistic test of a positive relation between a country's Gini means and anti-globalization positioning—smoothing over, hence, the much more extensive within-country and cross-party variation over time in the full data. In the analysis of the disaggregated data (see Burgoon, 2013), furthermore, many control variables such as globalization-exposure, economic growth, unemployment, and political institutions have little effect on anti-globalization backlash.

Since political parties differ in the groups they represent across the income distribution, Burgoon also considered whether inequality has different effects on anti-globalization positioning conditional on partisanship. Indeed, political parties at the left and right wings of the political spectrum were the most anti-globalized—consistent with how these party extremes

[4] Australia, Austria, Belgium, Canada, Denmark, Finland, France, Germany, Greece, Ireland, Italy, Japan, Luxembourg, Netherlands, New Zealand, Norway, Portugal, Spain, Sweden, Switzerland, United Kingdom, and the United States.
[5] (Former) Communist parties, Social Democratic parties, Green parties, Christian Democratic parties, Conservative parties, Liberal parties, and extreme-right Nationalist parties.

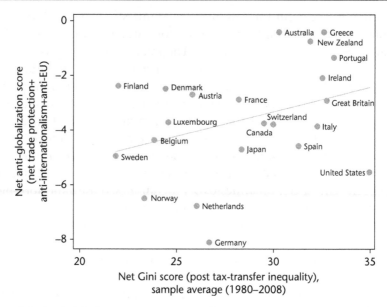

**Figure 9.4.** Anti-globalization positions and income inequality (national means, 1980–2008)

*Source*: Burgoon, 2013 (with permission).

disproportionately represent the poorest and least educated citizens. Further, this backlash positioning applied to a greater extent to extreme-right Nationalist parties than to former Communist parties. Compared to extreme parties, those in the centre of the political spectrum tended to be more pro-globalization in their positioning. Yet, interaction in terms of net Gini coefficients and party family suggest that income inequality has effects on party positioning towards globalization that tend not to vary significantly across party families. Merely one significant interaction coefficient was found for Conservative parties and net Gini, indicating that inequality shapes anti-globalization positioning more strongly among Conservative than other parties.

The main factors that *do* appear to alter how parties respond to inequalities, however, are government taxation and social policies that redistribute income. Such policies tend to diminish any anti-globalization backlash arising from pre-tax, pre-transfer inequality—based on the Solt (2009) measures of 'gross inequality'. Figure 9.5 models this interaction, based on the baseline model of net anti-globalization as a function of existing, gross inequality and existing social-policy expenditures and generosity. The figure summarizes how parties facing higher market inequality tend to respond with more anti-globalization positioning when social spending is modest but not (or in

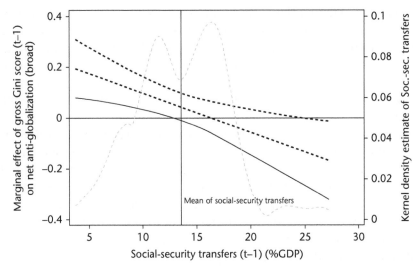

Thick dashed line give 90% confidence interval.
Thin dashed line is a kernel density estimate of social-security transfers

**Figure 9.5.** Social-security transfers mitigate the tendency of gross inequality to increase anti-globalization positioning
*Source*: Burgoon, 2013 (with permission).

any event less so) as social spending becomes more generous. Furthermore, the analysis suggests that the measured extent of actual redistribution—the actual lowering of income differences realized through tax and spending policies—does directly lower anti-globalization positions (results not shown). These results suggest that income inequality is an important but controllable contributor to Euroscepticism, protectionism, and nationalist, anti-globalization backlash generally.

## 9.4 Redistributive Preferences and the Politics of Inequality

Now that we have seen that inequality may well influence support for systems of national and supranational political order, the question is how preferences for redistribution interfere with the relationship between inequality and politics. Whereas the previous chapter was concerned with the relationship between inequality and public opinion on redistributive preferences, this last section of the present chapter addresses the question of how politicians deal with redistributive preferences without losing support from their constituents.

The role of redistributive preferences in the politics of inequality is examined in this section in two ways. First, we discuss that the extent to which political responses to public opinion on redistribution depend on the importance public opinion places on the issue. Second, we explore whether national differences in income distributions are related to income inequalities within countries. We are particularly concerned with whether people's willingness to support developing countries depends on the level of income inequality within their own societies. If it is true that support for development aid diminishes in more unequal societies, politicians can more easily focus on internal politics. Anti-globalization sentiments may then not only be restricted to 'threats from the outside world', but may also be reflected in an unwillingness to help other countries. If on the other hand inequality is not negatively related to the willingness to help developing countries, it may be that anti-globalization sentiments do not stretch to include altruistic motivations to countries in greater need.

### 9.4.1 Salience of Redistribution and Political Power

Melzer and Richard (1981) provide a common baseline model for understanding the link between inequality and redistributive politics. As discussed in the previous chapter, this starts with the premise that the median voter has a lower income than the mean voter due to the positive skew in the income distribution. This putatively results in a positive relationship between inequality and support for redistribution. Empirical assessment of the theorem has yielded inconsistent results. Like the work of some scholars (e.g. Finseraas, 2009), evidence in the previous chapter supported the model, suggesting that more inequality is related to stronger demands for redistribution. Nevertheless, a larger body of research fails to find support for the Melzer–Richard model (see Kenworthy and McCall, 2008; Lupu and Pontusson, 2011; Lübker, 2007).

An important explanation proposed for the possible weakness of the Melzer–Richard model is that electorates from different parts of the income distribution are not equally involved in politics. If the poor are less likely to be politically active than the rich, their interests are less likely to influence the political decision-making process. As discussed in detail in the previous chapter and in other studies (Van de Werfhorst and Salverda, 2012; Scervini and Segatti, 2012), a rise in income inequality tends to strengthen the association between social position and political participation. Although Brady's analysis (2003) reveals a decreasing relationship between income inequality and participatory inequality among US states between the 1970s and the 1990s, most scholars suggest that high levels of income inequality fuel inequality in political participation

(Beramendi and Anderson, 2008; Solt, 2008; see also McCarty, Poole, and Rosenthal, 2003).

Relative power theory supposes that those at the bottom of the income distribution are the most uninvolved, as they do not perceive political engagement as an option that can improve their fates. They feel powerless and think their needs are disregarded regardless of their involvement, leading to concentration of political power within the higher ranks of society (Solt, 2008). Using cross-sectional data from the European Election Study 2009, Horn (2011) reaffirms the negative link between inequality and turnout in national elections. Further, he finds modest evidence that 'larger differences in income between the very rich and the middle decrease overall turnout' (Horn, 2011: 20). Such voting outcomes may yield lower aggregate support for redistribution. If low-income voters retreat from political participation, it seems sensible to suggest that they become less important to left-wing parties (Pontusson and Rueda, 2008; 2010). That is, catering to low-income earners—who are less engaged than others—makes it difficult to achieve electoral victory. So, even though the Melzer–Richard model would predict that the political arena would aim at redistribution if inequality is high, the power resource theory (Kenworthy and Pontusson, 2005) implies that the salience of redistributive preference may be low in unequal societies due to low turnout of the low-income groups.

Yet, even after considering political participation, it remains disputable whether inequality is the main determinant of redistributive preferences. Hakverdian and Van der Meer (2011) shed some light on the relationship between redistributive preferences and left–right self-placement. Employing cross-sectional data from the European Social Survey 2008 and the European Election Study 2009 on all twenty-seven European Union countries, they find a relationship that is at odds with the median voter model (Figure 9.6). Specifically, regressing left–right self-placement on a set of policy preferences (redistribution, same-sex marriage, law and order, immigration, EU), they find that the association between attitudes towards redistribution and left–right self-placement is lower where inequality is higher. In other words, their findings indicate that redistribution is less important for individual left–right positioning in countries where incomes are more unequally distributed.

How can this puzzling finding be interpreted? It seems sensible to suggest that societal norms regarding inequality—e.g. acceptance and justification of inequality—shape the priority of redistribution in the light of rising inequalities across countries. Indeed, this argument is in line with Andersen and Yaish's (2012) finding that higher levels of inequality are related to less egalitarian views within societies (see Chapter 8 of this volume). The authors argue, however, that the findings are an issue of reverse causality: if redistribution becomes a dominant aspect of left–right self-placement, it shapes

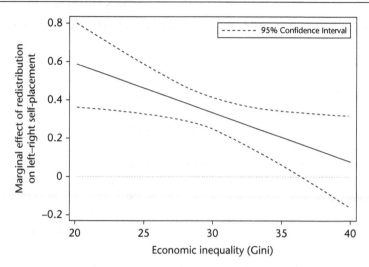

**Figure 9.6.** Marginal effect of redistribution on left–right self-placement
*Source*: Hakhverdian and Van der Meer, 2011 (with permission).

people's political priority and becomes a political matter. Consequently, redistributive policies are implemented, leading to lower levels of inequality. The Melzer–Richard model of the median voter theorem thus needs adjustment for the salience of redistribution in determining political positioning.

Analyses that focus on trends within countries make a clear distinction between four groups of countries, the details of which can be found in the country chapters of the companion volume. First, some countries experience consistently high demands for redistribution by the government, but also a tendency for such demands to be unable to halt rising inequality levels. Austria, France, Sweden, Spain, and Greece are examples of such a combination. Second, in some countries it appears that rising inequalities are matched by rising concerns for redistribution. Populations in this group of countries, which includes Germany, Canada, and Poland, are responsive to rising inequalities, but they have been unable to counter the trends they try to combat. For these two groups of countries, a lack of salience (or political representation) could well explain why preferences for redistribution have not lowered inequalities. An alternative theory, however, is that changing inequalities are explained by market forces beyond the influence of politics, even if salience had been high. A third group of countries, including the United States and the United Kingdom, shows that rising inequalities are not matched with increased concerns with redistribution, even if those concerns were rather low from the beginning. A fourth group of countries did not see inequality rise, but saw declining support for redistribution and trust in the government (examples are Italy and Portugal). Such cross-country patterns, combined with the analysis of left–right partisanship and redistribution, point to the complexity of and recursive relationship between inequality and redistribution—well beyond the initial Meltzer–Richard expectations.

### 9.4.2 Redistribution from Rich to Poor Countries: The One-Way Street of Anti-Globalization

Noël and Thérien (2002) propose that people living in low-inequality countries will be satisfied with the given level of domestic redistribution and favour more international redistribution. In contrast, domestic redistribution could be perceived as a priority under circumstances of high inequality rather than redistributing from richer to poorer countries. Hence, a negative relationship between people's demand for domestic and international redistribution is suggested, rooted in a positive relationship of domestic income inequality and demand for domestic redistribution, and a negative relationship between income inequality and international redistribution. Further, on an individual level the poor might have less comprehension that their government supports people abroad, while people living within the country deserve financial support as well. It is suggested that this effect should be more pronounced under conditions of high inequality, as people with low incomes in highly unequal societies may perceive international redistribution as unfair while they are the most affected by domestic income inequalities.

Haas's (forthcoming) investigation of the relationship between inequality and people's approval of international redistribution is also insightful. Based on an analysis of cross-sectional unbalanced panel data from the Eurobarometer survey for sixteen countries over seven waves between 1983 and 2002, it finds that national-level income inequality is positively related to support for development aid. Further, although lacking statistical significance, national expenditures on development assistance are positively related to attitudes. Both educational level and household income significantly increase the support for development aid, even though the impact of educational level is much stronger. Moreover, women give greater priority to development aid than do men, while political right-wing self-placement is related to lower concern regarding development aid.

Haas's results are consistent with the conclusion that, although anti-globalization and anti-EU standpoints of political parties are affected by income inequality, this does not mean that governments respond to inequality with a reduced willingness to help those in poorer parts of the world. In other words, while inequality increases political will to protect workers against globalization, contrary to some earlier probes into this issue (Noël and Thérien, 2002), it does not diminish—and in fact may increase—the willingness of citizens of Western countries to support development aid. So, the anti-globalization backlash seems to be a one-way street, where protection of own workers is emphasized, but not at the cost of restricting financial aid to countries in greater need.

## 9.5 Conclusions

This chapter discussed the relationship between income inequality and the legitimacy of the political system in Western societies. Our main goal was to highlight important findings about that relationships that come from the Growing Inequalities' Impacts research project funded by the European Commission. Supplementing these findings with insights from related studies, we focused on three sets of correlates to inequality: (i) those related to values and legitimacy relevant to national governance (relating to attitudes towards democracy and civic values), (ii) those related to supranational governance (anti-globalization standpoints of political parties, and Euroscepticism among European populations), and (iii) those related to national and international redistribution. The evidence clearly demonstrates that rising inequality could have important repercussions on the legitimacy of democracies in European and other Western societies. In short, inequality is systematically related to both public opinion and the orientations of political parties.

We started by demonstrating that inequality is negatively related to social trust and attitudes towards democracy. Public opinion towards democracy tends to be more negative the more unequal a society is. We also found a positive relationship between individual-level income and support for democracy that holds regardless of the level of income inequality in the country. Interestingly, in established democracies, the gap between rich and poor in terms of their support for democracy increases as inequality rises. This increasing polarization occurs not so much because the poor are less supportive of democracy than the rich in unequal societies—there is only a slight difference between them—but mainly because the rich are much more supportive in equal societies. This finding has implications for electoral politics. If governments hope to increase democratic values, they must convince the richest income earners that a high level of inequality is no better for them than for the poor.

We also showed that as inequality rises, people tend to be less concerned with societal responsibilities such as politics and civic participation and have less social trust—both of which are important for the extent and quality of democracy. On the other hand, there is also evidence that people embrace or develop a hard-work ethic as inequality rises, that is, inequality may well encourage awareness that responsibility for 'the good life' rests on themselves, affecting an orientation towards hard work. In unequal societies people seem to consider the responsibility for wellbeing to rest with individuals themselves rather than with government or society as a whole. Although it is difficult to determine the direction of causation—and it may, in fact, be reciprocal—these findings are consistent with the idea that the level of income inequality in a particular society largely reflects public opinion. That is, high levels of income inequality are largely a function of limited policies on redistribution, which in turn reflects the idea that individuals should work for their living rather than receive 'hand-outs' from the government.

This chapter also directly explored the relationship between income inequality and public opinion on redistribution. It is evident, both from research in the GINI project and beyond, that the salience of the redistribution issue is of paramount importance. Inequality appears to influence public opinion on redistribution only when the issue is salient. Salience is not guaranteed, however, because those who benefit most from redistribution—i.e. low income recipients—often feel they have little say in politics and thus tend to be less engaged. This lack of engagement can, in turn, result in redistribution having little salience in political discussions. Of particular concern to the salience issue is legitimacy. The gap in participation between the rich and poor, or between the well-educated and the poorly educated, is larger in unequal societies than in egalitarian societies. It is plausible, then, that the gap between popular opinions on redistribution and actual decision-making on this issue is particularly high in unequal societies. A misrepresentation of public opinion (especially of people belonging to the lower parts of the income distribution) could invoke further gaps in political participation between the advantaged and the disadvantaged, a pattern that is found to happen in Italy (see the companion volume). In short, as income inequality rises, politics could become more strongly the domain of the well-educated and the better-off.

Finally, we also explored how transnational forms of governance may be affected by inequality. In this regard, it is clear that inequality has direct repercussions both on how political parties position their public platforms and commitments, and on public opinion on European integration. Political parties tend to be more concerned with the protection of workers against globalization when inequality is high. Globalization has winners and losers, and the 'losers' (i.e. low-skilled workers) need protection. Not surprisingly, there is evidence that the 'losers' have become increasingly critical towards European integration. Particularly interesting is that parties on the far-right of the political spectrum have become especially affected by inequality. Centre-left and centre-right parties, however, have become less protectionist or nationalist, illustrated by more modest anti-globalization positioning irrespective of the level of inequality. The general effect of existing inequality, however, has been to dampen enthusiasm of parties and publics to embrace supranational integration.

Together with the range of other findings, the bottom line of the GINI project research is that inequality poses substantial dangers to democracy and openness in national political life, enhancing the importance of policies and regulations that might redress inequality.

# 10

# The Policy Response to Inequality: Redistributing Income

*Ive Marx and Tim Van Rie*

## 10.1 Introduction

If limiting income inequality, especially compressing the lower end of the income distribution, is desirable, in its own right or as a means of mitigating the potentially negative consequences of inequality, how is it then best done? This chapter focuses on policies that seek to redistribute income in a direct and immediate way, while the next chapter will address policies that seek to reduce economic inequalities in more indirect ways. Primary attention here will go to policies to redistribute income towards the bottom of the distribution in an effort to reduce or eradicate income poverty. Rather than attempting to review and summarize a massive literature, our aim is to address a number of questions that loom large in current debates. These questions include:

- Does effective redistribution require high levels of social spending and taxation, or can much be done with well-targeted redistributive efforts?
- Are social safety nets that offer adequate protection against poverty affordable and achievable?
- Should we expand and augment existing redistributive mechanisms or should we put our trust in new redistributive policies, notably earned income supplements?
- Does redistribution have to come with more strings attached?

We start this chapter with a discussion of trends in the share of taxes and benefits in rich countries, and we briefly review how the redistributive impact of taxes and transfers has evolved over the past decades. The remaining sections deal in turn with the questions just listed, and a final section concludes.

## 10.2 Trends in the Share of Taxes and Transfers

Public social expenditure is the most commonly used proxy variable for the size of the welfare state. While this indicator has certain limitations for welfare analysis,[1] both conceptual (Esping-Andersen, 1990) and methodological (De Deken and Kittel, 2007) spending clearly matters, not least in a context of general budget austerity. The share of public social spending in GDP ranges widely across OECD and EU countries, as shown in Figure 10.1.

Average social expenditure in the OECD rose rather strongly from the early 1960s to the mid-1990s, and then remained rather stable up to the Great Recession. Through its major impact on both expenditure and GDP, the current crisis has once again driven up social expenditure levels. Among industrialized countries there is a well-documented tendency for public social spending levels to converge (Wilensky, 1975, 2002; Schmitt and Starke, 2011; Caminada et al., 2010). In the EU, that convergence has grown stronger since the recent crisis (European Commission, 2012b). This is quite remarkable, in the light of the gaps that opened between EU member states in terms of (un)employment and overall living standards.

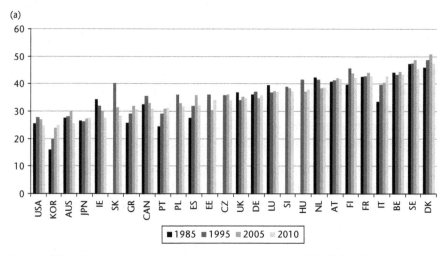

**Figure 10.1a.** Public social expenditure as percentage of GDP, 1985–2010
*Source*: OECD SOCX.

---

[1] The conceptual critique states that welfare expenditure may give some indication of the total size of the welfare state, but fails to provide information on key dimensions such as rights and distribution of benefits. In the words of Esping-Andersen (1990: 21), 'it is difficult to imagine that anyone struggled for spending per se'. The methodological critique relates to cross-national comparability of data. For example, it appears that there have been cross-national inconsistencies in the coding of mandatory cash benefits provided by employers.

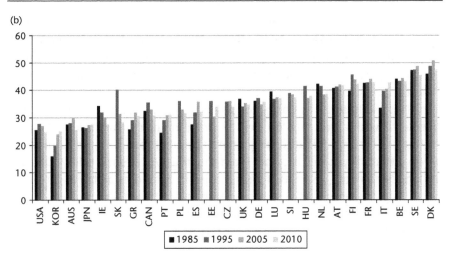

(b)

**Figure 10.1b.** Tax revenue (including social security contributions) as percentage of GDP, 1985–2010
*Source*: OECD SOCX.

If the level of spending is to a large extent driven by socio-demographic and economic parameters, its composition may shed some light on shifting policy priorities (Castles, 2009). In most industrialized countries, cash benefits represent a larger share of public social spending, compared to in-kind benefits. The latter had been growing in relative size in a large majority of countries, with healthcare spending playing a leading role. The recent crisis did, however, trigger an absolute and relative increase in cash spending in many countries, further underlining the role of income transfers as automatic stabilizers.

In terms of welfare functions, there is little indication so far that expenditure on new policy priorities, such as childcare and active labour-market policies, is crowding out funding of more traditional welfare functions, including old age pensions or unemployment benefits (Vandenbroucke and Vleminckx, 2011; Meeusen and Nys, 2012). Across the European Union, means-tested benefits represent approximately one-tenth of all public social expenditure. Since the mid-1990s, this share has remained fairly stable overall, but with considerable variation in national trajectories (Marx and Nelson, 2013).

It should be noted that more sophisticated analyses highlight the need to jointly analyse benefit and tax policies. Conventional measures of (gross) social expenditure tend to overestimate the cost of welfare in Denmark, Finland, and Sweden, where a significant amount of benefit spending is clawed back through taxation. Conversely, in the Czech Republic and Slovenia, a substantial share of social spending takes the form of tax breaks for social purposes rather than cash transfers (Adema et al, 2011).

Immervoll and Richardson (2011; see also OECD, 2011) find shifting dynamics of income redistribution in OECD countries. Across the industrialized world, market income inequalities among the population aged below 65 increased particularly strongly between the mid-1980s and the mid-1990s. Over this period, there has also been a substantial increase in income transfers. This evolution was partly automatic, as pre-existing welfare systems interacted with a growing 'burden' of rising market inequalities. The public transfer systems failed to fully contain market forces, resulting in rising inequality of disposable income. From the mid-1990s to the mid-2000s, the dynamics changed, as market inequalities increased at a slower rate than previously. However, social spending stagnated and public transfer systems proved far less effective at redistributing income. As a result, the dispersion of disposable household incomes occurred at an even faster rate than in the previous decade.

Beyond general trends, there is considerable variation across countries and cash benefit functions, as well as over time. Van Mechelen and Bradshaw (2012), for instance, observe that throughout the 1990s child benefits for working families had generally escaped the welfare erosion that marked many other cash benefits. Since 2000, however, the size of the child-benefits package, expressed as a percentage of net disposable income, has declined in the majority of countries awarding these benefits.

In many cases, tax reform effectively exacerbated underlying rises in inequality over the course of previous decades. Country reports from the GINI project observing a strong decline in redistributive effect of public revenues include cases as diverse as Austria, Canada, Finland, France, Japan, Luxembourg, and Australia. The report on Germany, for example, documents how the tax system actually became less progressive during the period 2000–5, especially as a consequence of the income tax reform enacted in various steps by the government. Recently, there has been a proliferation of (semi-)flat tax regimes in Central and Eastern European Countries. Estonia introduced such a scheme in 1994, followed by the two other Baltic states in the mid-1990s, Slovakia (2004, but partly reversed in 2013), Romania (2005), the Czech Republic and Bulgaria (2008), and Hungary (2011). While these shifts annul progressivity of tax scales, their overall effect also depends on (intended) improvements in tax collection and concurrent shifts in the tax mix. The Danish country report shows that it is possible to reduce the overall marginal tax rate of income tax without affecting its distributive effect. Spain is an example where taxes have become more redistributive over time, through a broadening of the tax base and increased progressivity.

Benefits have a much stronger impact on inequality than social security contributions or taxes, despite the much bigger aggregate size of direct taxes. Redistribution policies have often been less successful at counteracting growing income gaps in the upper parts of the income distribution. In what follows we turn to the four questions posed at the start and consider more closely the link between the size of the welfare state and inequality and poverty outcomes.

## 10.3 How Much Does Redistributive Effort Matter?

Several studies have established a strong empirical relationship at country level between the overall level of social spending and various measures of inequality and inequality reduction, including (relative) poverty. This is arguably one of the more robust findings of comparative poverty research (Nolan and Marx, 2009; Kenworthy, 2011b; OECD, 2008; Immervoll and Richardson, 2011; see also Figure 10.2). A number of countries for which internationally comparative data became available recently (the Czech Republic, Slovakia, and Slovenia, as well as Korea) do combine fairly low levels of social expenditure with low relative poverty rates and income inequality. For the Central European countries, part of the explanation might lie in a reliance

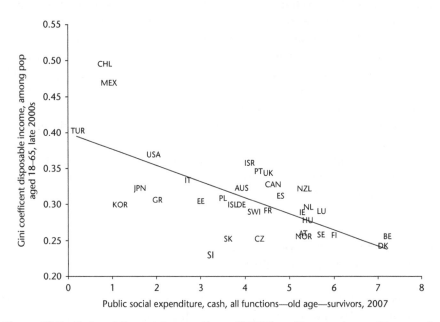

**Figure 10.2.** Cash public social expenditure (%GDP) and income inequality at working age in OECD countries, late 2000s

*Note*: Gini coefficient of equivalized disposable household income among the population aged 18–65.

*Source*: OECD, 2011 (income inequality); OECD SOCX (social expenditure).

on tax breaks as social policy tools (which are not captured in gross social spending indicators). Moreover, cohabitation in multi-generational households may also play a role (European Commission, 2012b).

The relationship at the country level between the level of cash spending and poverty reduction probably does not simply reflect the direct impact of transfers: high-spending countries typically have other institutional features that contribute, notably high levels of minimum wage protection and strong collective bargaining compressing wages (hence limiting overall inequality), more extensive public and subsidized employment, as well as active labour-market programmes and higher levels of public spending on education. Indeed, the Danish country report identifies a combination of success factors: equal access to education, wage compression in the public sector, progressive incomes taxes, and a comprehensive system of (means-tested) cash transfers. The Italian report, by contrast, argues that a weak state implies not only a lack of effectiveness in redistribution, but also contributes to larger market inequalities ex ante.

Disentangling the effect of these various factors is inherently fraught with difficulties. There may in fact be mechanisms of mutual reinforcement between these factors. Barth and Moene (2009) argue that a more equal wage distribution leads to welfare generosity through a process of political competition. In turn, more income redistribution produces more equality. The authors hypothesize that this 'equality multiplier' operates mainly through the bottom of the income distribution: the amplification occurs where wages near the bottom of the distribution are compressed, not where higher incomes are compressed. They find empirical support in their analysis of eighteen OECD countries over the years 1976–2002.

While in theory low or moderate levels of social spending could produce low poverty rates if resources were well-targeted, the reality is that very few advanced economies achieve low (relative) poverty rates, or high levels of redistribution, with low levels of social spending. This raises important questions regarding the efficiency of expenditure.

## 10.4 Can More Be Done with Less?
## On Targeting vs. Universalism

There is a long-standing controversy in welfare-state literature on whether targeting benefits towards the lower part of the income distribution enhances the redistributive impact of social transfers. This issue is of far more than academic importance. In its 2011 report on inequality, the OECD states that 'redistribution strategies based on government transfers and taxes alone would be neither effective nor financially sustainable'. In this context the

OECD (2011) calls for 'well-targeted income support policies' while adding that 'policies for more and better jobs are more important than ever'. Organizations such as the IMF and the World Bank have long advocated targeted benefits. The issue of targeting will probably gain even more traction in a post-crisis period marked by continued and in some cases increased budget austerity.

The debate on targeting is still marked by opposed views. On one side are those who think that a welfare state can only fight poverty effectively and efficiently (i.e. cost-effectively) when benefits are mainly targeted on those most in need. The straightforward argument here is that selective benefit systems are cheaper, as fewer resources are 'wasted' on recipients who are not poor. Lower public expenditures imply lower taxes, which in turn are said to be conducive to economic growth. Economic growth, the argument proceeds, benefits the poor directly (although not necessarily proportionally so) and at the same time increases the fiscal base for redistributive policies.

This view of selectivity has never been commonly shared. Two sorts of argument underpin a more critical stance. First, there are technical considerations. Van Oorschot (2002) sums up the most important dysfunctions associated with means-testing. To begin with, targeting tends to entail substantial administrative costs. Establishing need or other relevant criteria requires monitoring, whereas universal benefits allow for less complex eligibility procedures. Furthermore, the distributional effectiveness of means-tested benefits is hampered by non-take-up, often due to stigmatization issues. Finally, and perhaps most importantly, targeted benefits can give rise to poverty traps, where benefit recipients have little incentive to take up work. In such a case, modest and volatile earnings from work do not outweigh the loss of income replacement benefits that employment entails.

A second line of counter-argument is that proponents of selectivity pursue a 'mechanical' economic argument that abstracts from the political processes governing income redistribution. In this view, selective welfare systems garner less widespread public support, resulting in smaller welfare budgets. As a consequence, the redistributive impact of selective systems tends to be smaller. To put it differently, some degree of redistributive 'inefficiency' (what is sometimes called the 'Matthew effect') is required to foster robust political support for redistribution, including to the most needy. A universal welfare state creates a structural coalition of interests between the least well-off and the politically more powerful middle classes, i.e. the median voter. By contrast, a selective system entails an inherent conflict between the least well-off, by definition the sole recipients of social transfers, and the better-off, who fund the system without the prospect of getting much out of it.

The juxtaposition outlined above forms the starting point for Korpi and Palme's (1998) highly influential 'paradox of redistribution'. Their article presents empirical evidence in support of the hypothesis that targeted systems paradoxically redistribute less, simply because they are generally smaller systems.

Some scholars have expressed reservations because of the rather rudimentary character of the research methods in Korpi and Palme's analysis (Bergh, 2005). The degree of redistribution, for example, is measured by comparing the actually observed degree of income inequality with a rather unsophisticated 'counterfactual' distribution. In theory this counterfactual ought to accurately reflect the income distribution that would prevail in the absence of social transfers, taking into account people's responses in terms of work effort or family formation. However, the construction of this counterfactual is hampered by theoretical and practical problems. In most cases, including Korpi and Palme's paper, pre-transfer income is simply calculated by deducting observed social transfers and re-adding observed taxes, ignoring any behavioural effects that such a dramatic change would entail.[2] While patently less than perfect, the reality is that no satisfactory method exists to adequately model such behavioural effects, except for very specific programmes and settings.

A further critique has been formulated by Moene and Wallerstein (2003), who have argued that redistribution needs to be analysed at a disaggregated level, rather than 'the welfare system' as a whole. The determining redistributive principles may differ substantially for, say, unemployment, healthcare, or pensions. Some schemes may rely heavily on the insurance principle, while others may put more weight on the need principle. From this perspective, universality and selectivity can coexist within one system. Still, Moene and Wallerstein (2001) concur that universal provisions provoke the largest political support, due to higher probabilities for middle class citizens to become beneficiaries. Some opinion-based studies also confirm that universal welfare schemes enjoy broader support (Forma, 1997; Kangas, 1995).

Recent studies, however, claim that the link between redistribution and universal provision has substantially weakened, or even reversed over time. Kenworthy (2011b) reproduces and updates Korpi and Palme's analyses, which related to the situation in eleven countries as of 1985. Redistribution is measured by the difference between the Gini coefficients with and without tax-transfers relative to pre-transfer income; this corresponds to the difference of the Gini coefficients of market and disposable income relative to that of market income.

---

[2] Still, as documented in Chapter 2, the behavioral impact of taxes is not clear-cut.

Targeting is captured through a concentration index (see, for example, Kakwani, 1977; Lambert, 2001; OECD, 2008; Whiteford, 2007). This measure takes into account both the size of transfers and the extent to which they benefit different sections of the income distribution. A concentration coefficient equal to the Gini coefficient suggests redistributive neutrality of transfers. Values below Gini indicate that units with the lowest (market) income gain more from the transfers. When the concentration coefficient exceeds the Gini, cash is transferred from the poorer to the richer.

Kenworthy's replication confirms that countries with more universal benefits achieve more redistribution (measured in the size of redistributive policies in the budget) between 1980 and 1990. By 1995, the image becomes less clear. Data for 2000 and 2005 indicate that there is no longer any association (either positive or negative) between the two variables. Evidently, the findings are based on a small number of cases, which make them particularly sensitive to outliers. A trend towards more targeting in Denmark, in conjunction with an evolution towards more universal benefits in the USA, is largely responsible for the shift in conclusions. Moreover, the new findings may be driven to some extent by the growing share of pensions in social spending. Kenworthy (2011b: 58) writes, 'This by no means settles the question, but it does suggest additional reason to rethink the notion that targeting is an impediment to effective redistribution.'

Marx, Salanauskaite, and Verbist (2013) consider additional evidence, including a larger set of countries, alternative data sources, and different methodological specifications. Figure 10.3a, taken from this study, supports the thesis of a weakened—even non-existent—relationship between targeting and redistribution.

The term 'targeting' may suggest that these outcomes are due solely to characteristics of the system. However, the distribution of benefits also depends on the traits of the underlying population, including socio-demographic structure, income inequality, and composition of income. Assume, for instance, a benefit that is designed in such a way that only children are eligible. If all children are situated in the bottom quintile, this policy may appear as targeted towards low incomes, even though its design did not include any means-testing or needs-based criteria. Strictly speaking, one should not derive policy intent from the concentration coefficient.

Figure 10.3 indicates that transfers are concentrated most strongly among low-income households in Australia, the United Kingdom, and Denmark. Yet, the redistributive impact of the transfers differs quite substantially across these countries, being strongest in Denmark. Moderate concentration coefficients (–0.2 to 0) can be observed in highly redistributive systems (Sweden and Finland), as well as in states that reduce inequality to a very limited extent (the USA, Canada, Israel, and Switzerland). For countries with positive

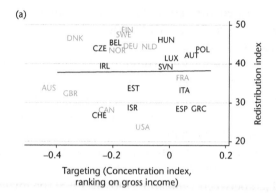

**Figure 10.3a.** Concentration index of cash transfers (ranking by gross income) and redistributive impact of taxes and cash transfers, mid-2000s

*Notes*:

1) Due to data availability, disposable instead of gross incomes are used for Belgium, Greece, Hungary, Slovenia, and Spain; part of 'gross' incomes are reported net of taxes for Italy and France.

2) The countries included in Korpi and Palme (1998) are in grey font.

*Source*: Marx, Salanauskaite, and Verbist (2013) on the basis of the Luxembourg Income Study.

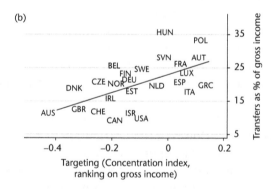

**Figure 10.3b.** Concentration index of cash transfers (ranking by gross income) and generosity, mid-2000s

*Note*: Due to data availability, disposable instead of gross incomes are used for Belgium, Greece, Hungary, Slovenia, and Spain; part of 'gross' incomes are reported net of taxes for Italy and France.

*Source*: Marx, Salanauskaite, and Verbist (2013) on the basis of the Luxembourg Income Study.

targeting coefficients the relationship tends to be negative, especially in the countries with the weakest pro-poor spending (Greece, Spain, and Italy). In the latter, the concentration coefficient shows segmentation between 'insiders' who are fairly well-protected and 'outsiders' receiving little or no financial support.

(c)

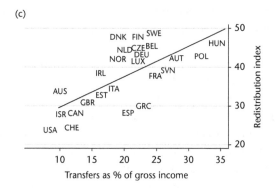

**Figure 10.3c.** Reduction in inequality due to taxes and transfers compared with size of social transfers (expressed as a share of gross income), mid-2000s

*Note*: Due to data availability, disposable instead of gross incomes are used for Belgium, Greece, Hungary, Slovenia, and Spain; part of 'gross' incomes are reported net of taxes for Italy and France.

*Source*: Marx, Salanauskaite, and Verbist (2013) on the basis of the Luxembourg Income Study

Why does a similar degree of targeting, as captured by the concentration index, produce stronger redistributive outcomes in Denmark as compared to the UK and Australia? Similarly, why do similar (quasi)-universal systems yield such different redistributive outcomes across countries? The pattern suggests that design features matter a great deal. It is notable that the relationship between the extent of targeting and the size of the system remains strong. There are exceptions: Denmark combines a strong degree of targeting with a high level of social spending.

The strongest redistributive impact is achieved by countries that combine moderate (Sweden and Finland) to strong (Denmark) targeting with comparatively high levels of spending. This suggests that the most redistributive systems are characterized by what is called 'targeting within universalism'— that is to say, systems in which many people receive benefits but where the poorest get relatively more. Other studies yield similar results. Corak, Lietz, and Sutherland (2005), for example, find that universal child-related benefits that also have some degree of targeting at the poorest protect best against income poverty. Their conclusion is echoed by Van Mechelen and Bradshaw (2013) for child benefits for working families, while similar patterns have been found for social assistance benefits (Van Mechelen and Marchal, 2013).

Why then did the strong relationship between targeting and spending weaken over time, as documented by Kenworthy (2011b)? Arguably, strong work disincentives and (perceived) family formation incentives reduced political support for means-tested systems, which made them vulnerable to cuts. The last decades have seen an intensified attention to such incentives.

To address these concerns, earnings disregards have been introduced for recipients who make a (partial) transition from complete benefit dependency to part-time work.

As a result, means-tested benefits are no longer aimed exclusively at people who are not in employment. The French RSA (Revenu de Solidarité Active) scheme is a good example of a new-style means-tested benefit scheme that offers integrated support for the non-employed and (part-time) low-paid workers alike. The RSA was introduced in France in 2008 with the specific aim of remodelling the incentive structure for social assistance beneficiaries, and particularly to make work or returning to education a more lucrative financial prospect. The previous minimum income system (Minimum Integration Income—RMI) was based on a one-for-one trade-off of benefit for earned income. Under RSA a 62% slope (taper) is applied. Additional, non-monetary efforts have been made to encourage beneficiaries of RSA into employment, for example through assisted employment contracts and (improved) insertion mechanisms. In addition, the RSA has simplified the provision of social protection by combining several previously separate schemes into a single sum. A household with no earned income is eligible for the 'basic RSA', which is defined at the household level and takes into account the composition of the household. The 'in-work RSA' acts as a top-up for households with low earnings.

This demonstrates that targeted, means-tested systems look very different today from those present in the 1980s. Whereas the old systems were the focus of harsh welfare critiques, especially from the political right, the new targeted systems are lauded as the essential gateways from welfare to work. In the United States, the Earned Income Tax Credit—a transfer programme for households on low earnings—has become the country's pre-eminent welfare programme (Kenworthy, 2011b). The system appears to enjoy far broader and more robust political support than earlier American anti-poverty programmes. The system also is less strongly targeted than earlier provisions and it caters to larger sections of the electorate, including the (lower) middle class, and this may account for that expansion. But an equally if not more important factor may well be that the system is perceived to encourage and reward work.

## 10.5 Are Effective Income Protection Arrangements Affordable and Feasible?

Much comparative poverty research that has sought to link observed variation in income inequality and poverty across countries to policy has relied on government (social) spending statistics as indicators of policy 'effort'. As we have seen, the relationship across countries between the level of social spending as a percentage of GDP, or some related indicator, and observed inequality or poverty levels is in fact by and large a rather strong one. This is in a way surprising because the level of spending mirrors as much the number of people receiving benefits as the level, and thus potential adequacy, of those benefits. A high level of spending may be achieved by providing very generous benefits to a limited section of the population, while it may also be the result of small benefits to a large number of people.

Likewise, measured outcomes, for example pre- versus post-transfer differences in inequality or poverty, also depend on a host of factors that are independent or only indirectly influenced by policy: contextual and compositional factors, including labour-market conditions (unemployment, employment patterns, wages), household composition (patterns of cohabitation, marriage, divorce, childbirth, etc.), and policies that influence these dynamics (education, ALMPs, childcare, etc.).

If we want to understand variations in outcomes, we need more sophisticated and accurate measures of policy effort and policy design than spending indicators. So-called institutional indicators aim to be directly reflective of policy intent and design. In this section we will focus solely on institutional indicators of minimum income protection. Such a focus is necessary because the design features of tax and benefits systems, and especially the way various programmes interact in specific situations, tend to be so complex that they are not accurately and validly captured in a limited number of parameters that allow for valid cross-country comparisons. Entitlements to social insurance benefits are particularly difficult to simulate because these depend on past wages, employment histories, and contribution records.

A further reason to focus on minimum income protection provisions is that adequate protection against severe financial poverty is arguably the first duty of the welfare state. It is also an explicitly stated priority of redistributive and policy efforts in many countries, and at the EU level where a poverty reduction target is part of the Europe 2020 strategy. Additionally, minimum income protection provisions mark the floor for other income maintenance provisions; minimum social insurance levels and minimum wages are almost always above the level of the social safety net. In that sense, indicators of minimum income protection also tell us something about the generosity of other income maintenance provisions.

In this section we draw on the CSB Minimum Income Protection Indicators (MIPI) dataset (Van Mechelen et al., 2011). In this dataset net income packages are calculated using the so-called model-family approach, where the income package of households in various situations (varying by household composition and income levels) is simulated, taking into account all relevant benefits for which such households are eligible as well as taxes. While providing valuable information about what policies are aiming to achieve in terms of the scope and level of income protection, it is worth pointing out that such institutional indicators have their limits. They are calculated for a limited number of family types and situations. The assumption is that there is full take-up of benefits and that people effectively and immediately receive what they are entitled to. In the case of minimum wages, the assumption is that these are fully enforced. However, this is not always the case, and this is one reason why the observed relationship between generosity levels as reflected in these indicators and outcomes is relatively weak (Nelson, 2012).

The importance of adequate social safety nets really hit home when an economic downturn of a magnitude unseen in decades struck after 2007. Despite some differences between individual countries, unemployment levels generally surged, causing dramatically increased demands for income protection. The impact of the crisis has been quite varied in Europe, not only in terms of its immediate effect on employment and wages, but also in terms of its impact on household living standards. As Jenkins et al. (2013) write, 'Although GDP fell during the Great Recession, the real disposable income of households, as measured in national accounts by Gross Household Disposable Income (GHDI), actually rose between 2007 and 2009 in 12 countries of the 18 for which we have data (there was no change for Ireland, despite the large fall in GDP). The household sector was protected from the impact of the downturn by both automatic stabilisers and additional support of governments through the tax and benefit system.' A host of new research papers document the role of tax and transfer systems, as well as labour-market institutions, in cushioning households from the recession (e.g. Dolls, Fuest, and Peichl, 2011, 2012; Figari, Salvatore, and Sutherland, 2011). The GINI country reports provide further illustration. Finland and Sweden (in the early 1990s) and the United States (during the Great Recession) emphasize the initial stabilizing role of cash income distribution, but also its political and fiscal challenges in the aftermath.

Safety nets have particularly important roles as the final barrier against severe poverty and the disruptive consequences thereof, including the potential impact on children, their development, and opportunities for education. Given the surge in non-standard work in the years before the crisis, minimum income schemes may have gained in relative importance (Immervoll, 2012).

Van Mechelen and Marchal (2013) analyse patterns and trends in the level of minimum income protection for able-bodied citizens in European countries. The chief focus is on means-tested benefits providing minimum income protection, usually in the form of social assistance. These general means-tested benefits provide cash benefits for all or almost all people below a specified minimum income level. In some countries separate schemes exist for such groups as newly arrived migrants or the disabled. The study shows that the minimum income benefit packages for the able-bodied at working age have become increasingly inadequate in providing income levels sufficient to raise households above the EU at-risk-of poverty rate, defined as 60% of median equivalent income in each country (Figure 10.4). The overall tendency for the 1990s was one of almost uniform erosion of benefit levels, relative to the development of wages. This downward trend in the relative income position of families in receipt of social assistance changes somewhat in the 2000s, when the erosion of the level of benefit packages came to a halt in a number of countries. In the first years of the crisis a small number of countries took extra steps to increase protection levels (Marchal, Marx, and Van Mechelen, 2011). Despite a number of positive developments, net incomes of minimum income recipients continue to fall well short of the EU's at-risk-of-poverty threshold in all but a few EU countries (Figure 10.4). The size of the gap between the level of the social safety net and the poverty threshold varies across countries and family types, but it is generally quite substantial.

This poses the question: why are social safety nets not more (potentially) adequate? Let us briefly consider two potential impediments: first, 'adequate

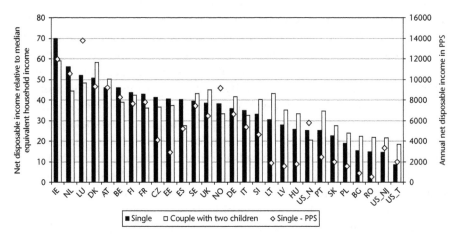

**Figure 10.4.** The adequacy of minimum income protection packages for people at working age not in work, 2012, EU plus Norway and three US states

*Note*: In some countries, such as the USA, Italy, and Bulgaria, time limits apply, either formal or discretionary. In order to avoid additional assumptions, the levels displayed do not take these time limits into account. Where minimum income protection is a regional or local responsibility, levels refer to the situation in a large city or region (for Spain: Catalonia; for Italy: Milan; for Norway: Oslo; for Sweden: Stockholm). Poverty thresholds as available on Eurostat, 2011, referring to income 2010 (exception: Ireland: 2011 not yet published).

*Source*: CSB-MIPI (Van Mechelen et al., 2011); Eurostat, 2011; U.S. Bureau of the Census and Bureau of Labour Statistics, 2011.

social safety nets are not affordable', and second, 'adequate social safety nets undermine the work ethic and people's willingness to work'.

Are adequate social safety nets too costly? Final safety net provisions (social assistance schemes) generally constitute only a fraction of total social transfer spending (the bulk of outlays going to pensions, unemployment and disability insurance, child benefits, and other benefits). Vandenbroucke et al. (2013) have made tentative calculations of the redistributive effort required to lift all equivalent household incomes to the 60% of median level. In most European countries, this expenditure amounts to less than 5% of the aggregate equivalent household income that is above the 60% threshold. Nowhere is it higher than 9%. The countries that would have to make a relatively large effort are Southern and Eastern member states. Such a mechanical calculation ignores incentive effects and behavioural change (more poor people may prefer social assistance to low-paid jobs; the non-poor may reduce their work effort). The real cost of such an operation is probably higher than the mechanical effect, and the calculation may be seen as indicating a lower boundary for the distributive effort that is required. Still, the calculation also illustrates that the cost of an adequate social safety net is not necessarily outside of the realm of the conceivable.

Are adequate social safety nets compatible with work incentives? Despite recurring concerns over the potential work disincentive effects of social safety nets, empirical studies tell a more nuanced story (Immervoll, 2012; Marchal and Van Mechelen, 2013). The income gap between the situation of full-time dependence on minimum income benefits and a full-time job at the minimum wage (or the lowest prevailing wage) is in fact quite substantial in most European countries, especially for single persons. In some countries and under certain circumstances, particular groups, such as lone parents with young children, gain relatively little from moving into a low-paid job, especially when childcare costs are accounted for. Partial transitions into work—moving to a small part-time job—also do not pay in certain circumstances. But generally speaking, long-term dependence on social assistance benefits is not an attractive financial situation relative to a full-time minimum-wage job in most of Europe. The hypothetical Europe-wide introduction of social assistance minimum levels equal to 60% of median income would, however, create a financial inactivity trap in many countries, as is brought out by Vandenbroucke et al. (2013) and Marchal and Van Mechelen (2013). In countries such as Bulgaria, Estonia, Slovenia, and Lithuania, the net income of a single benefit recipient would be between 25% and 30% higher than the equivalent income of a single person working at minimum wage; in Spain and the Czech Republic, the relative advantage of the benefit claimant would amount to around 15%. This implies that if such countries wished to move towards better final safety net provisions then minimum income floors would have to be raised at least in step.

This would require quite substantial increases in minimum wages, or in effective wage floors. In 2013, twenty member states of the European Union have a national minimum wage, set by government, often in cooperation with or on the advice of the social partners, or by the social partners themselves in a national agreement. In addition, a host of other labour-market institutions have an impact on effective wage floors (Lucifora and Salverda, 2009). The Nordic countries, for example, do not have statutory national minimum wages, but wage setting is highly institutionalized and coordinated, resulting in comparatively low levels of overall wage inequality, especially at the bottom end of the distribution. Governments can have an important indirect impact on wage inequality by making wages set through collective bargaining generally binding (OECD, 2004).

As is illustrated in Figure 10.5, presenting data for 2010, only for single persons and only in a number of countries do net income packages at minimum wage level (taking into account taxes and individual social security contributions, but also social benefits) reach or exceed the EU's at-risk-of-poverty threshold, set at 60% of median equivalent household income in each

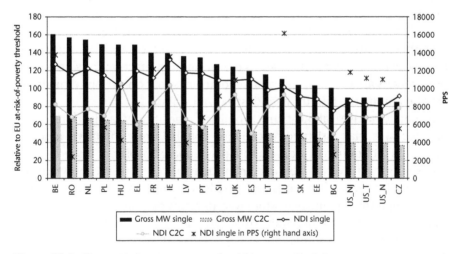

**Figure 10.5.** Gross minimum wages and net incomes at minimum wage as a percentage of the relative poverty threshold, 2012, selected EU member states plus three US states

*Legend*: MW: minimum wage; C2C: couple with two children; NDI: net disposable income.

*Note*: Poverty thresholds as available on Eurostat, 2011, referring to income 2010 (exception: Ireland: 2011 not yet published).

*Source*: CSB-MIPI (Van Mechelen et al., 2011), Eurostat, 2011; U.S. Bureau of the Census and Bureau of Labour Statistics, 2011.

country. For lone parents and sole breadwinners with a partner and children to support, net income packages at minimum wage are below this threshold almost everywhere, usually by a wide margin. This is the case despite shifts over the past decade towards tax relief and additional income support provisions for low-paid workers (Marx, Marchal, and Nolan, 2013).

When it comes to the question of whether and to what level minimum wages and hence minimum income benefits in general could be increased, opinions clearly diverge. The debate over whether minimum wages destroy jobs, or stifle job growth, is as old as the minimum wage itself. A wealth of empirical evidence has been amassed by labour economists and it seems fair to state that the measured effects of actual changes (rather than the hypothetical increases needed to ensure poverty relief effectiveness among workers) have sometimes been positive, sometimes negative, sometimes neutral, but never very large (Dolado et al., 1996, 2000; Freeman, 1996; OECD, 1998, 2004; Kenworthy, 2004). As the OECD's Martin and Immervoll (2007) state, 'On balance, the evidence shows that an appropriately-set minimum wage need not have large negative effects on job prospects, especially if wage floors are properly differentiated (e.g. lower rates for young workers) and non-wage labour costs are kept in check.'

Concerns about work disincentive effects of social safety nets are legitimate, as are concerns over potential negative employment effects of minimum wages, especially if these were to be set at levels high enough to keep households solely reliant on that wage out of poverty. The fact remains, however, that countries like Denmark or the Netherlands combine what are comparatively among the highest levels of minimum protection for workers and non-workers alike with labour-market outcomes that on various dimensions are also among the best in the industrialized world.

Elaborate active labour-market policies, specifically activation efforts directed at social assistance recipients, coupled with intensive monitoring and sanctioning of non-compliance, appear to play a key role here. The strength of overall labour demand may also be a key contextual factor for such associated policies and practices to effectively result in low levels of long-term dependence. Moreover, in terms of quality of employment, Denmark and the Netherlands are clearly among the best performers in Europe (European Commission, 2008; Leschke et al., 2012), with relatively few workers in low-quality jobs (Eurofound, 2012). Replicating the activation, empowerment, and sanctioning aspects associated with comparatively generous systems may well be difficult enough in itself. Replicating a context where job growth is strong and where jobs are sufficiently rewarding and attractive may be even more difficult. It that sense we may not want to be overly optimistic about the possibilities of introducing similarly generous minimum income protection provisions in other settings.

## 10.6 Do We Need New Redistributive Mechanisms?

It is increasingly argued that more effective redistribution will not come from augmenting/expanding the traditional channels of income support, for example more generous social insurance or social assistance levels, or from higher minimum wages. These are seen not only as failing to address today's social risks and needs, but as exacerbating underlying problems such as exclusion from the labour market and entrapment in passive benefit dependency. They are considered by some as standing in the way of innovative mechanisms of social protection that are proactive and self-sufficiency-enhancing, such as active labour-market policies and services such as childcare and improved education and training.

Therefore, the option is to consider other forms of (targeted) income supplements for households that provide some level of income protection but that are also conducive to labour-market participation. Kenworthy (2011b: 44) observes, 'Given the importance of employment and working hours for the market incomes of low-end households, policy makers must guard against programs that provide attractive benefits without encouraging or requiring employment. An ideal transfer would be one that both boosts the incomes of low-earning households and promotes employment by able working-aged adults. As it happens such a program exists. Referred to variously as "in-work benefit" or "employment-conditional earnings subsidy", it is best exemplified by the Working Tax Credit (WTC) in the United Kingdom and the Earned Income Tax Credit (EITC) in the United States.'

Under these schemes households with low earnings do not pay taxes but instead they receive additional money through the tax system. In the United States, the 1993 expansion of the Earned Income Tax Credit (EITC) turned it into the country's pre-eminent anti-poverty programme for families of working age. The United Kingdom has also implemented and extended several schemes (and in fact did so earlier than the USA), now to be integrated with other means-tested benefits into Universal Credit. Clearly, Anglo-Saxon-style negative income taxes have been garnering increased interest of late. Immervoll and Pearson (2009: 16) remark, 'Even in the mid-1990s, twenty years after such schemes were first introduced in the United Kingdom and the United States, they were being seen as interesting but unusual schemes... it seems reasonable to conclude that IWB schemes are now mainstream policies in many countries.'

That is perhaps somewhat of an overstatement. Several European countries have contemplated introducing Anglo-Saxon-style tax credits, or have done so in some form. Yet the reality is that most of these schemes exhibit only a faint resemblance to the American EITC or the British WTC. Sweden has a scheme that goes by the same name in English as its American counterpart the EITC. It was introduced in 2007, and subsequently reinforced. The stated motive of the reform was to boost employment; in particular, to provide incentives for individuals to go from unemployment to, at least, part-time work. The Swedish scheme is different from the American scheme in that it is a non-refundable tax credit. Also, because the tax unit in Sweden is the individual and not the household, it works in effect as tax relief on low individual earnings. In that respect it is similar to measures elsewhere in Europe that target low-paid workers rather than low-earnings households.

Interest in EITC-type schemes remains strong, however, in the public debate and in the academic literature (Marx and Verbist, 2008; Kenworthy, 2011b; Figari, 2011; Allègre and Jaerhling, 2011; Crettaz, 2011; Marx, Vanhille, and Verbist, 2012). That interest seems entirely legitimate. The empirical evidence shows the American EITC, in combination with other policy reforms and several increases in the minimum wage, to have produced some significant results, including marked increases in labour-market participation and improvements in living standards among some segments of the population, especially single-parent households (Hotz and Scholz, 2003; Eissa and Hoynes, 2004). It needs to be noted, however, that these initial results happened in favourable economic circumstances, including strong labour demand and low unemployment. The relatively strong increases in labour supply of lone mothers in the American setting also resulted from welfare reform, notably the transformation of the social assistance scheme into a temporary support system with time limits on the duration of benefits. This clearly provided a strong push incentive, with the EITC acting as pull incentive. Not all who were forced out of passive dependence found their way to work (Grogger, 2003, 2004).

There are potential downsides to subsidizing low-paid work. While the EITC is intended to encourage work, EITC-induced increases in labour supply may drive wages down, shifting the intended transfer towards employers. Rothstein (2010) simulates the economic incidence of the EITC under a range of supply and demand elasticities and finds that in all scenarios a substantial portion of the intended transfer to low-income single mothers is captured by employers through reduced wages. The transfer to employers is borne in part by low-skill workers who are not themselves eligible for the EITC. There is some empirical evidence that corroborates the potential wage erosion effect of the EITC (Leigh, 2010; Chetty et al, 2013).

Yet whether EITC-type schemes can work elsewhere, as Kenworthy (2011b) and others suggest, is not self-evident. The socio-demographic make-up of the USA differs from that of most European countries; there are more single-parent households in the USA than in many European countries.

The dispersion in earnings is also much more compressed in most European countries, where, in addition, benefits are generally higher relative to wages (including minimum wages) and less subject to means-testing if they derive from social insurance. This also implies that benefit entitlements of household members are less interdependent, possibly weakening the potential impact on labour supply. Many countries have individual taxation, and the trend is away from joint taxation of couples.

In order to be effective as an anti-poverty device and at the same time affordable within reasonable limits, such measures need to be strongly targeted. However, strong targeting at households with low earnings is bound to create mobility traps, which can only be avoided if tapering-off rates are sufficiently flat. That comes at a very considerable cost if the lower end of the household earnings distribution is densely populated, as is the case in many European countries. This cost can only be avoided by making the amount of the tax credit itself smaller, but in that case the anti-poverty effect is reduced. Simulations in a wide range of European countries cast doubt on the applicability of EITC-type systems in other settings. In an earlier study, Bargain and Orsini (2007) investigated the effects on poverty of the hypothetical introduction of the British scheme (as it was in place in 1998) in Germany, France, and Finland, using EUROMOD for 2001. They found that the anti-poverty effects of a UK-type tax credit (similar in design and relative overall spending) would be very small in these countries, especially relative to the budgetary cost. For Belgium, the hypothetical introduction of the UK's WTC is shown to yield a limited reduction in poverty at the cost of possible weakened work incentives for second earners (Marx, Vanhille, and Verbist, 2012). Figari (2011), simulating application in Italy, Spain, Portugal, and Greece, notes that the presence of extended families in Southern Europe does not allow for such policies to be well targeted at the very poorest. Bargain and Orsini (2007) have concluded that 'interest in such schemes is destined to fade away'. Whether that is true remains uncertain and indeed doubtful, but EITC-type tax credits are not obviously suitable for wholesale emulation throughout continental Europe. In Germany, for example, the labour market has undergone some profound changes over the past decade. Low-paid employment has become far more prevalent and in-work poverty seems to have increased. It is not unlikely that a simulation like the one performed by Bargain and Orsini on 2001 data would yield different results today.

Clearly, simulations demonstrate that in-work benefit schemes that work well in certain settings do not necessarily perform equally well in a different context. Family composition, individual earnings distributions, and family income structures drive outcomes in a very substantial way. It remains to be explored whether alternative designs are conceivable that have better outcomes in continental European settings and that are realistically affordable.

## 10.7 Should Benefits Come With Strings Attached?

Making cash benefits conditional on certain behavioural requirements is a policy strategy that has gained prominence in many developing countries and that is also gaining increased attention in the developed world. The European Commission, for example, is calling on EU member states to pursue 'simple, targeted, and conditional' social investment policies (European Commission, 2013).

In the developing world such conditional cash transfers (CCTs) are increasingly used to promote human-capital accumulation or preventive healthcare for children (school enrolment, regular attendance, regular medical examinations, vaccinations). Some programmes in particular, such as Progresa in Mexico or Bolsa Escola in Brazil, have garnered much attention and debate. Organizations such as the World Bank have taken a leading and influential role in promoting and evaluating CCTs. In OECD countries, conditional cash transfers are mainly used within the context of labour-market policy (activation measures, job-search requirements). More rarely, yet increasingly, developed countries apply conditional cash benefits to human-capital accumulation for children.

Conditional cash transfer programmes have been subject to evaluations of effectiveness using experimental or quasi-experimental methods. Several meta-reviews are available. Rawlings and Rubio (2005) argue that evaluation results 'reveal successes in addressing many of the failures in delivering social assistance, such as weak poverty targeting, disincentive effects, and limited welfare impacts'. They argue that there is clear evidence of success from the first generation of programmes in such countries as Colombia, Mexico, and Nicaragua in increasing enrolment rates, improving preventive healthcare, and raising household consumption. However, it remains less clear whether programmes that work well in one setting are transposable to other settings with equal results—contextual factors seem to matter in determining outcomes. It is also clear that CCTs have their limits in terms of addressing the broader range of challenges facing poor and vulnerable populations, and in preventing the intergenerational transmission of poverty.

Conditional cash transfers are part of a new line of thinking in social policy that seeks to understand and remedy the economic and psychological complexities in the lives of poor people, informed by social experiments and field observations. Banerjee and Duflo (2011) are its most prominent advocates. In a self-proclaimed effort to find a 'new way of doing economics', they focus very strongly on micro-level interventions. Their preferred policies entail small reforms at the margin, also informed by experiments—specifically randomized control trials (RCTs).

In a strong critique of such RCTs, Ravallion (2012) notes, '[T]he question of *why* the intervention did or did not have impact in that population remains most often open. Nor is it clear whether the intervention would have similar impacts in some other population.' The issue of potential limits to upscaling initiatives that work well in controlled experimental or quasi-experimental settings seems especially pertinent, particularly since RCTs only control for unobserved variables within the setting of the experiment, not for the unobserved factors beyond that setting.

Perhaps Ravallion's most trenchant critique concerns the fact that, almost by implication of their approach, Duflo and Banerjee only focus on small-scale policy aspects. These can probably only go some way to explaining why some countries have been far more successful than others in combating poverty and promoting higher levels of education and development among their populations. Pointing to the contrast between India and China, Ravallion writes, 'Along with many developing countries, China's leaders came to realise (in the late 1970s) that their reform agenda had to be based on evidence...but while China's reformers were selective and cautious, there was nothing "small" about their reforms.'

This is very much in tune with what comes out of comparative poverty research, namely that macro-variables, such as sheer social spending levels, are strongly correlated with poverty outcomes, even though these may be partially driven or reinforced by other (macro-)correlates such as wage bargaining structures and spending on other items than social programmes.

Focusing on OECD countries, Medgyesi and Temesváry (2013) review the results of conditional cash transfer programmes to promote human capital accumulation. The authors review evidence concerning the impact of such programmes on human capital investments (enrolment, absenteeism from school, participation at health exams). They differentiate between 'scholarship-type' benefits, which entail education-specific benefits, and 'sanction-type' programmes, where non-compliance with regulations (e.g. truancy) implies (the threat of) discontinued benefit provision. For many of the interventions under consideration, impact assessments show statistically significant (positive) effects with regard to health and educational outcomes. To some extent, this finding echoes those in developing countries. Similarly, quite a few assessments in Medgyesi and Temesváry's review show mixed results, and a number of important questions remain. First, the effect of the interventions tends to vary, with some groups (for instance, girls) more responsive than others. Second, there remains uncertainty regarding the long-term effects of the interventions. Under certain conditions, granting conditional rewards might even be harmful, crowding out intrinsic motivation. Third, there is no conclusive answer as to which interventions are more effective: programmes that apply positive or negative sanctions, focusing on performance or input. The exact design of the schemes varies substantially and appears to matter a great deal for the observed outcomes.

A crucial question regarding conditional cash transfers, then, is whether the effect of the interventions justifies their (administration) cost, and whether more beneficial outcomes could be obtained by other means, for instance investing in quality of service provision. These methods need not be mutually exclusive, and combining conditional transfers with improvements in service provision may yield better outcomes in terms of poverty reduction (as pointed out by Bastagli (2011), based on a literature review for Latin America). It should be clear, however, that conditionality of cash transfers cannot by itself be a 'silver bullet' or an adequate substitute for social provisions.

## 10.8 Conclusion

For all the rhetoric of permanent austerity, social spending has trended upwards rather than downwards over the previous three decades in the majority of industrialized countries. In most countries, cash benefits continue to represent the lion's share of this expenditure, driven to a large extent by 'automatic' factors such as growing market inequality and population ageing (the latter also having an impact on a secular trend of rising healthcare expenditure). Across countries, there remains a negative and strong association between (active age) social expenditure and measures of income inequality. However, the redistributive strength of tax-benefit systems appears to have weakened in many countries over the past two decades. While growing market-income disparities were the main driver of inequality trends between the mid-1980s and mid-1990s, reduced redistribution was often the main reason why inequality rose in the ten years that followed.

The underlying causes of the rises in market income inequality are complex and there is also considerable variation across countries in the relative importance of various drivers. Yet it is striking that one major potentially compensatory trend—the rise in labour-market participation levels—did little to dampen income inequality or to reduce relative income poverty, as the next chapter will set out in more detail. This points to the key importance of adequate direct income support provisions for workers and non-workers alike. The crisis has certainly also added urgency to the issue of minimum income protection adequacy.

Minimally sufficient levels of minimum income protection are in theory not necessarily prohibitively expensive; in most countries additional redistribution equivalent to a couple of percentage points of GDP would suffice to eradicate relative income poverty altogether. Yet very few countries actually have social safety nets that are high and wide enough to provide effective protection against poverty. The main barrier to adequacy is not first-round cost. Far more problematic is the fact that the hypothetical introduction of an income support floor equal to 60% of median income would create serious financial inactivity traps in many countries, simply because this floor would then exceed the minimum wage or the effective wage floor. Such inactivity disincentives could also be overcome by increasing minimum wage floors quite considerably. This is not self-evident as an option, however, especially in the short run, and particularly when unemployment is high. Countries that have relatively adequate social safety nets and that manage to keep chronic dependency levels low at the same time also have elaborate active labour-market policies, counselling, and other accompanying services attached to minimum income provisions. There is also intensive and continuous monitoring of recipients and sanctioning in case of noncompliance. Such accompanying policies are not only costly, but they also require considerable administrative capacity and expertise.

Increasingly, the search is for new forms of (targeted) income supplements for households that provide some level of minimum income protection but that are also conducive to labour-market participation. Ideally such transfers boost the incomes of low-earning households and promote employment by able working-age adults at the same time. Employment-conditional earnings subsidies as exemplified by the Earned Income Tax Credit (EITC) in the United States are seen by some as the way to go in redistributing income to households at working age. This may be the case, but programmes that work well in one setting do not necessarily work well in other settings in the same shape and form. Further analysis is needed to see if and in what modified form such systems are implementable and potentially effective elsewhere. This similarly applies to conditional cash transfers, the effect of which appears to depend to a large extent on the broader context in which they are deployed.

Finally, all the evidence suggests that adequate poverty relief requires more than well-targeted minimum income provisions in the form of generous social safety nets and/or negative income taxes and the like. It requires substantial social spending channelled through various programmes. New evidence sheds doubt on the now widely accepted social policy tenet that 'systems for the poor become poor systems'. Korpi and Palme's influential claim that 'the more we target benefits at the poor, the less likely we are to reduce poverty and inequality' no longer holds as a robust empirical generalization. Transfer systems that cater disproportionally for the poor are generally associated with higher levels of redistribution, if overall spending is high enough. The reality remains that the countries with the most redistributive systems combine a relatively strong level of targeting with a relatively high level of effort spending. In other words, 'targeting within universalism' appears to yield the best results if the aim is to maximize redistributive effects. This said, in current social policy discourses the status of systems for direct income redistribution has become somewhat unclear. While the general tendency is to acknowledge the continuing importance of traditional social security and social assistance arrangements, more direct redistribution is not generally seen as the way forward in countering (growing) inequalities at the market income level. Instead, employment and social-investment-based policies are seen as offering more structural, sustainable, and affordable responses. These are the focus of the next chapter.

# 11

# The Policy Response: Boosting Employment and Social Investment

*Ive Marx and Gerlinde Verbist*

## 11.1 Introduction

By the turn of the century the idea that having more people in paid work was key to improved social inclusion, poverty, and equality outcomes had become central to policy reform in many OECD countries. This notion was at the core of influential new policy doctrines at the time, for example the 'Third Way'. Disproving fears of a future characterized by 'jobless growth' and 'the end of work', the fifteen years prior to the crisis of 2008 were marked by strong net employment gains so that just prior to the crisis employment rates had reached historically high levels in many countries. Yet it also became clear that employment growth in and of itself had not produced the expected social improvements. Marked increases in employment rates had for the most part gone accompanied with rising or stagnant relative poverty rates for the working-age population. Income inequality had mostly increased.

Despite this, and the crisis, employment growth ambitions remain strong. The Europe 2020 growth strategy has the objective of reaching an employment rate of 75% by 2020. Following its two high-profile reports on income inequality, the OECD (2011) has stated that 'policies for more and better jobs are more important than ever'.

Yet it is also increasingly recognized that job growth alone may not suffice to make sure that everybody has its share of prosperity if this is not actively supported by government investment in human capital and in services that make it easier for people to realize their earnings potential. The OECD (2011) stresses the crucial importance of human-capital investment in the fight against growing inequality and poverty. By the same token, the European

Commission (2013) has launched a 'Social Investment Package' also emphasizing human-capital investment. Publicly provided or subsidized services of
various kinds, and particularly education and care services, are seen as key
instruments in this package.

All this is in tune with thinking among a number of scholars
(Esping-Andersen et al., 2002; Vandenbroucke et al., 2011; Morel et al., 2012;
Hemerijck, 2013; Nolan, forthcoming; Cantillon, 2013). Some advocate a
radical shift from cash to care/social investment. In an influential report to
the Presidency of the European Union, Esping-Andersen et al. (2002) called
for a radical overhaul of welfare-state architectures in Europe, stating, 'As the
new social risks weigh most heavily on the younger cohorts, we explicitly
advocate a reallocation of social expenditures towards family services, active
labour market policy, early childhood education and vocational training, so
as to ensure productivity improvement and high employment for both men
and women in the knowledge-based economy.'

In view of the centrality of activation and human-investment strategies
in current policy discourse, this chapter specifically considers the empirical
evidence on the redistributive impacts of such policies. First we consider the
role of activation and employment policies in promoting more egalitarian
societies. Special attention is paid to the links between individual employment outcomes, household work intensity, and poverty. We then investigate
the distributive role of the services that are often seen as an instrument 'par
excellence' for fulfilling the social-investment strategy. We examine whether
the various services—including education, health, childcare, and other
social services—foster egalitarianism, thereby distinguishing between first-
and second-order redistributive effects.

## 11.2 Does High Employment Foster Egalitarianism?

### 11.2.1 Introduction

Observing the debate, it is striking that widely different, in some cases diametrically opposed, assumptions are entertained about the relative merits of
alternative courses of action for policy when it comes to reducing inequality
and poverty. This is perhaps none more true than with respect to the link
between work and poverty. An important section of opinion basically holds
that more people in work equals fewer people in poverty and, by implication,
that an elaborate welfare state with large-scale redistributive efforts is not a
prerequisite for a low level of poverty.

The idea that, ultimately, the best and most sustainable anti-poverty strategy is a work-based strategy has long been advocated. There is some intuitive

appeal to the notion that 'the best protection against poverty is a job'—a ubiquitous political slogan with popular appeal. People who are not in work tend to occupy the lower strata of the income distribution. If more jobs become available and low-income people take up these jobs and improve their income position, the result is a selective rise of incomes at the lower end and thus a reduction in income inequality and the share of the population in poverty relative to the median. The important proviso, of course, is that work pays more on average than remaining inactive.

An alternative view holds that we are effectively confronted with a trade-off between employment (that is, *non-government* employment) and income equality. The idea here is that high levels of non-subsidized employment can in present-day economic circumstances only be achieved at the cost of a large low-paid (service) sector and increased, though perhaps temporary, 'poverty in work'. Deindustrialization, economic globalization, and technological progress play a central role in arguments that the industrialized economies are increasingly faced with a choice between more structural labour market exclusion or more low-paid employment, unless government is willing to provide adequately paid employment. Iversen and Wren (1998) called this the 'trilemma of the service economy'. The contrast is drawn with the golden years of welfare capitalism when manufacturing industry provided stable, well-paid employment even for those with little or no formal education. As Esping-Andersen et al. (2002) put it, 'We no longer live in a world in which low-skilled workers can support the entire family. The basic requisite for a good life is increasingly strong cognitive skills and professional qualifications...Employment remains as always the sine qua non for good life chances, but the requirements for access to quality jobs are rising and are likely to continue to do so.' In a similar vein, Bonoli (2007: 496) states, 'Postindustrial labour markets are characterised by higher wage inequality with the result that for those at the bottom end of the wage distribution, access to employment is not a guarantee of a poverty-free existence.'

Such statements are in line with an important stream in the academic and popular literature on the devastating effects of economic globalization and skill-biased technological change on the labour-market position of less qualified workers in rich countries. Research by labour economists shows that this picture of a uniform shift away from low-skilled work needs nuance (Autor et al., 2003). The impact of technological change, real as it is, has not simply entailed a demand shift away from lower-skilled labour and towards more highly educated workers. Studies have shown that there is growth in employment in both the highest-skilled (professional and managerial) and lowest-skilled occupations (personal services) with declining employment in the middle of the distribution (manufacturing and routine office jobs). Goos et al. (2009) document this trend towards 'job polarization' throughout

Europe, albeit with varying intensity. This research does, however, provide legitimate concern about a possible rise of low-paid work (Lucifora and Salverda, 2009). We also refer back to the findings reported in Chapter 3 in this volume, which details developments in labour markets.

### 11.2.2 The Activation Drive

The period before the current crisis saw a strong rise in employment levels in the EU. These did not come about by accident (Van Rie and Marx, 2012). In most EU countries a marked policy shift had taken place towards boosting labour-market participation levels and reducing benefit dependency among those of working age. Many examples can be found in the country case studies in the companion volume from the GINI project. The Netherlands stands out as one of the most striking earlier examples of a radical turn towards activation. Later on many countries followed suit. The German Hartz reforms provide another much discussed illustration.

Some countries pursued macro-economic policies to foster job growth, such as the Netherlands, where a policy of sustained wage moderation was central to boosting labour participation levels—and with considerable success, it must be added. In other countries, changes in macro-economic conditions (low interest rates following the EMU and euro membership) had major impacts on employment performance, as for example in Spain, where unemployment dropped spectacularly prior to the crisis.

At the same time, an increased policy emphasis on micro-level activation has become evident in many European countries, certainly at the level of rhetoric, and gauging by some indicators also in terms of actual policy (Barbier and Ludwig-Mayerhofer, 2004; Kenworthy, 2008a; Immervoll, 2012; Marchal and Van Mechelen, 2013; Weishaupt, 2013). Within the broad set of activation strategies deployed, an important number specifically target the long-term unemployed, including social assistance recipients. The general purpose is to get these people into a job, in the private market or in the subsidized sector. Most of these are relatively low-paid/minimum-wage-level jobs. In the case of Belgium, for example, the main activation measure for social assistance recipients is a public employment scheme offering temporary employment at the minimum wage. Similar programmes exist elsewhere. Employment subsidies and employers' social security contribution reductions also generally aim to stimulate the creation and take-up of relatively low-paid jobs.

From a poverty perspective, it matters who is targeted for activation into such low-paid jobs and under what conditions this is done. If activation measures stimulate single persons to move from long-term benefit dependency into minimum-wage jobs, this will impact positively on poverty if minimum wages (and net incomes at minimum wage) exceed poverty thresholds and when benefits for the long-term unemployed (be it social insurance or social assistance) are below poverty thresholds. Similarly, if such measures stimulate potential second earners into low-paid jobs there may also be a positive effect on (in-work) poverty, provided they are living in a household with a disposable income not far below the poverty threshold. There may be an indirect effect, however, in that poverty thresholds may be pushed up if these jobs are mainly taken up by people in households with disposable incomes already in the middle and upper ranges of the distribution. This could then cause median equivalent income and hence the relative poverty thresholds to rise, other factors held constant.

If, however, single parents are the target of activation efforts, without there being affordable/available childcare, there is a potential problem in that they may be forced to take part-time jobs. This may imply that they remain stuck in financial poverty. Even a full-time minimum-wage job may not suffice if the minimum wage is not sufficiently high relative to the poverty threshold, or if taxes and social security contributions cause net disposable income to drop below the poverty line. Similarly, unemployed sole breadwinners with a dependent spouse and children (and possibly others) to support may not be lifted from poverty if they are forced to take up a low-paid job unless there are supportive measures such as child benefits or in-work benefits. Hence, the potential impact in each country will depend on compositional factors (the household composition of the non-active population) and contextual factors (minimum wage levels, the presence of child benefits and childcare facilities, the presence of in-work benefits, or earnings disregards).

## 11.2.3 Employment, Income Inequality, and Poverty

The notion that 'a job is the best protection against poverty' was key to efforts to boost activity rates in the EU and elsewhere (Cantillon, 2011). So how did employment growth affect the economic position of people at the bottom of the distribution? Figure 11.1 shows employment rates and Gini coefficients for overall income inequality and relative poverty rates as averages for the EU countries over the period 1995–2010. Between 1995 and 2008 the employment rate increased on average by about 7 percentage points in the EU-15. For all EU member states we present data from 2000 and onwards. In this larger group of countries the increase in employment was particularly pronounced in the mid-2000s. Yet, as the figures clearly show, this increase in employment is not reflected in a corresponding decrease in income inequality or in the relative income poverty rate. At the very minimum it can be said that highly significant net employment gains did not yield lower household inequality levels and that in more than one instance employment growth was in fact

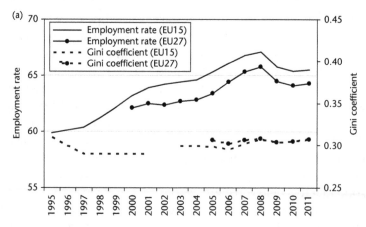

**Figure 11.1a.** Rising employment, stagnant inequality, EU, 1995–2010

*Source*: Eurostat.

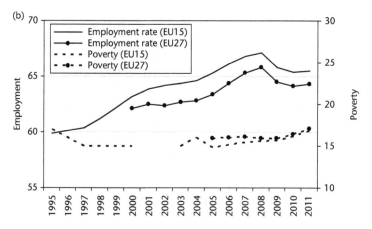

**Figure 11.1b.** Rising employment, stagnant relative poverty, EU, 1995–2010

*Notes*: The poverty threshold is 60% of the equivalized median household disposable income. The poverty rate is for the population less than 65 years of age. The employment rate is for the population 15–64 years of age.

*Source*: Eurostat.

accompanied by rising inequality and relative income poverty, as is extensively documented in the country chapters in Nolan et al. (2013). Projections of the probable poverty impact of the Europe 2020 employment-rate target of 75% produce a picture that is in line with past experience; net gains in the number of people employed will result only to a very limited extent in reductions in the number of people in relative poverty (Marx, Vandenbroucke, and Verbist, 2012).

In its report *Growing Unequal*, the OECD (2008) performed a comprehensive analysis of the role of earnings and employment trends in income inequality trends at the household level. Amid a considerable degree of variation across countries, the general pattern was for increases in male earnings inequality, while the wage gap between men and women narrowed. The growth of non-standard employment did, however, contribute to a widening in the dispersion of personal earnings. This increase in earnings inequality was partially offset by higher employment rates and the continued proliferation of dual-earnership.

Distributive outcomes result from a large number of often complexly interrelated factors, and many factors not immediately related to labour-market trends account for observed inequality and poverty trends. There are three principal reasons why past job growth did not produce poverty declines: (i) because past job growth did not sufficiently benefit poor people, while at the same time the adequacy of minimum income protection deteriorated, (ii) because getting a job does not always raise income enough to escape poverty, and (iii) because median equivalent income shifted upwards in association with job growth and the policies that stimulate job growth. There are many other factors, often country-specific, that play a role, as is documented elsewhere in this volume and Nolan et al. (2013), but we restrict our discussion here to three main mechanisms.

First, most at risk of poverty are persons living in so-called 'workless households', i.e. households where no adult at working age has an attachment to the labour market (OECD, 2009; de Graaf-Zijl and Nolan, 2011). People of working age living in such workless households face the highest poverty rates by far and they also tend to experience the most severe financial hardship, including their dependent children if any. More generally, poverty at working age is more strongly associated with work intensity at the household level than with individual labour-market status, for the obvious reason that a non-employed person may well live in a household where others have earnings. A household where no one has earned income, or very little of it, is almost always reliant on transfer income.

Household joblessness tends to be higher than the distribution of individual non-employment risks would lead one to expect (Corluy and Vandenbroucke, forthcoming). The concentration of non-employment within the same households may be due to many factors (Gregg, Scutella, and Wadsworth, 2010). A correlation between the employment statuses of household members may reflect a tendency for individuals who share common characteristics to live together. Since persons with fewer educational qualifications typically experience higher unemployment and non-employment rates, households whose members all have a low level of educational attainment are likely to be overrepresented among workless households. Household members are usually looking for work in the same local labour market and a depressed labour market will have a common impact on them. The disincentive effects of tax and benefit systems can also play a role. It is often the case that if one person in the household gets a benefit, another is penalized if he or she accepts a job. To get out of this dependency trap, all members of the household must find a job simultaneously, which may be particularly hard if both partners have low educational attainment. This problem may be more severe in countries with extensive means-testing of welfare benefits based on family income.

In this light, it is perhaps not altogether surprising that employment growth did not produce commensurate drops in workless household rates. In many countries job growth resulted in more double- or multi-earner households, but only to a more limited extent in fewer no-earner households (Corluy and Vandenbroucke, forthcoming). While the position of households that acquired additional income improved, the relative income position of (near) jobless households deteriorated because of the general erosion of minimum income protection levels, certainly at the level of social assistance, but also in some cases at the level of social insurance. For a discussion of direct income support trends we refer back to the previous chapter and to the country chapters in Nolan et al. (2013).

A second reason why employment growth does not necessarily result in less poverty is that a job may not pay enough to escape poverty. This is what is commonly referred to as 'in-work poverty'. What poor jobless persons often require is not just a job, but a job that pays significantly more than their benefit. In the case of non-employed poor persons living in a household with already one earner, the additional income required to escape financial poverty may be quite limited. Indeed, a small part-time job may suffice (Maître, Nolan, and Whelan, 2012). For sole breadwinners the required income gain is often quite substantial. From an anti-poverty perspective, the issue is not just 'making work pay' (i.e. tempting people to move out of dependency), but to make work pay sufficiently to ensure that a move from dependency to work also implies a move from poverty to an adequate living standard. The living standard of poor households with weak or no labour-market attachment is often so far below the poverty threshold (especially in the case of single parents and child-rich households) that it is quite possible that a job that pays significantly above the minimum wage will not suffice to lift them from poverty (Marx et al., 2013).

A host of recent comparative studies have documented patterns and trends of in-work poverty in rich countries (Andress and Lohmann, 2008; Crettaz, 2011; OECD, 2009; Fraser et al., 2011; Maître, Nolan, and Whelan, 2012; Marx and Nolan, 2013). As many as a quarter to a third of working-age Europeans living in poverty are actually already in work. In most EU member states the majority of children living in a financially poor household have at least one working parent.

It is not the case, however, that in-work poverty rates are higher in countries with more elevated employment levels. It is also not the case that in-work poverty increased most strongly in countries where employment increased most strongly. In fact, despite across-the-board increases in employment in the pre-crisis decade, in-work poverty remained stable in most European countries (Marx and Nolan, 2013). That may have something to do with the way in-work poverty is conventionally measured. The 'working poor' as conventionally defined in the statistics are those individuals who have been mainly working during the reference year (either in employment or self-employment) and whose household equivalized disposable income is below 60% of the median in the country in question. Combining two levels of analysis—the individual's labour-market status and the household's income (adjusted for household size)—inherently complicates interpretation, since the labour-market status of other persons in the household, rather than that of the individual being considered, may be crucial, as may the number of dependent children if any. This definition/measure makes it difficult to identify the different factors potentially underlying the phenomenon and thus the locus(es) of policy failure, which could include low (household) work intensity, inadequate out-of-work benefits, inadequate earnings, inadequate earnings supplements, the number of dependent people (children) relative to income, etc.

It may be more relevant to ask whether high-employment countries have more households at full work intensity unable to make ends meet. A number of studies have looked at poverty and poverty trends through the lens of work intensity at the household level. These studies show that zero and very low work intensity households face much higher poverty risks than households with very high levels of work intensity, i.e. households in which all adults of working age put in significant work effort. The difference is in fact quite significant, with workless households often facing poverty risks of around 40% and upwards. For households with at least some work intensity, that risk is much lower, from around 5% to 15%. At the same time it is the case that because relatively high-work-intensity households make up such a large part of the working-age population, poverty at working age is to a very considerable extent concentrated among high-work-intensity households. As can be seen from Figure 11.2, in a significant number of EU countries, people in relatively high-work-intensity households actually make up the majority of poor persons at working age. A significant share of poor people of working age in each country live in full-work-intensity households, i.e. households where every work-able adult in that household works full-time.

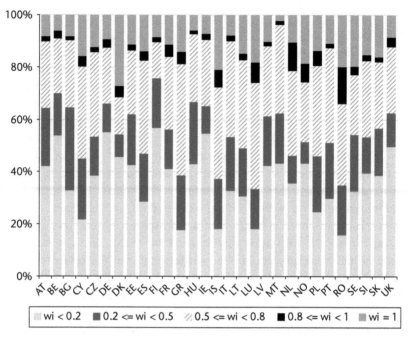

**Figure 11.2.** The distribution of household work intensity in the working-age population (20–59) living in relative income poverty

*Source*: EU-SILC (2010). Calculations by Vincent Corluy.

A third reason why past employment growth did not translate into lower relative poverty rates is because of the poverty line dynamics associated with employment growth and, more indirectly, the policies, particularly at the macro level, that stimulate job growth. The difference can be seen when poverty trends are considered using an anchored-in-time poverty line. With this approach the poverty threshold does not increase in line with median living standards, it only adjusts for increases in prices. Clearly, against a fixed poverty line, countries experienced much sharper drops in poverty prior to the crisis than was the case within a relative poverty framework (see also Chapter 6 of this volume). Note, however, that even against a fixed threshold, employment gains never resulted in proportional drops in poverty. As we have already indicated, the main reason why the poverty-reducing impact of employment growth is limited is because the first beneficiaries from employment growth tend to be people who do not live in poverty in the first place. Everything depends on where in the overall income distribution the newly created jobs end up, and in the past that has not always predominantly been in the bottom half of the distribution. If employment growth results in rising median living standards, but not in rising living standards in the lower segments of the distribution, the effect may well be a rise in relative income poverty. This is in effect what we observe in a number of countries. The poorest did not manage to take full advantage of growing demand for labour where and when this happened, and their plight was further exacerbated by the fact that passive protection levels, as provided through social insurance and social assistance, were eroded relative to wages and living standards.

### 11.2.4 What Can Policy Do to Promote a Better Linkage between Work and Poverty Reduction?

Which policy action, or set of policy actions, is most appropriate cannot be seen as entirely independent from normative notions that underlie the various ways in which the causes of working-age poverty in relation to work can be construed. Take, for example, a two-adult household with three dependent children and only one adult working. The breadwinner, in this particular example, has a low-paid job, yet is paid well above the minimum wage. Child benefits are modest in the country where they live. The household finds itself living in financial poverty. Whether, and to what extent, their poverty status is construed as a problem of insufficient breadwinner earnings, or as a problem of partner non-participation, or as a problem of insufficient child support makes a fundamental difference as to what type of policy action is to be examined and possibly favoured. In the case of traditional breadwinner-type households with insufficient earnings, the preponderance of opinion appears to be that this is to be seen as a matter of partner non-participation or under-participation. But other cases may be less clear-cut. Even if in-work poverty is construed as largely a problem of low household work intensity, the question arises as to what can be deemed a sufficient level of work intensity. It is not self-evident that this shall require all working-age, work-capable adults in the household to be in full-time work the whole year round. Societal norms may differ across countries. In the Netherlands, for example, four-fifths of a job per adult appears to be closer to the norm of full-work intensity. Also, household composition may be deemed to matter. It is not self-evident that a lone parent with young children is expected to work full-time all year before additional income support is to be considered legitimate if his or her earnings fall short of the poverty threshold.

Poverty is to a large extent, yet not exclusively, associated with low work intensity at the household level. This brings into view a wide variety of potential policies that can help households to increase, if not maximize, their work intensity. These include policies aimed at boosting the demand for workers, and particularly the demand for people with low levels of education or little work experience. Employer subsidies or reductions in employers' social-security contributions are an example here.[1] On the supply side, policy can stimulate (e.g. through fiscal reform) or support (e.g. through childcare) people to take up work or to increase working hours. What mix of policies will work best in a given context will depend on the composition of the low-work-intensity population and on the underlying causes of low work intensity.

Yet, and this is crucial, it must be recognized that even if such policies succeeded in getting every single non-employed person into work, or every household to a level of full work intensity for that matter—and all empirical evidence to date suggests this to be highly unlikely—this would not guarantee the elimination of poverty. What policy can do to help households in these circumstances is again likely to depend on such factors as the institutional and policy context in place, labour-market conditions, and the profile of the population in need of support.

Minimum wages can play an important role. In some countries minimum wages remain non-existent or low relative to average wages. As we have seen in Chapter 10, minimum wages in a range of countries do suffice to keep single persons out of poverty. Thus it would appear sensible for countries with non-existent or very low minimum wages to contemplate introducing or increasing these. However, the route of introducing minimum wages or boosting their level (relative to average earnings) to the upper ranges currently prevailing in advanced economies would, even in the absence of negative employment effects, not be sufficient to eradicate in-work poverty. Even in countries where minimum wages are comparatively high they do not suffice to keep sole-breadwinner households out of poverty, especially when there are dependent others or children. Minimum wages have probably become inherently constrained in providing minimum income protection to sole-breadwinner households, especially in countries where relative poverty thresholds have become essentially determined by dual-earner living standards.

For low-earnings households, only direct household income supplements offer a reasonable prospect to a poverty-free existence, especially when there are dependent children. Such 'in-work benefits' are now often associated with Anglo-Saxon-type 'tax credits' such as the EITC in the United States and the WTC in the United Kingdom. In Chapter 10 we have emphasized that

---

[1] Employer subsidies account for a significant share of expenditures on active labour-market programmes in Europe. There are basically two types of subsidy. First, there are subsidies aimed at boosting the employment prospects of very specific groups, such as the long-term unemployed. These tend to be quite substantial, but are provided only for a limited time. Second, there are subsidies (or social security reductions) aimed at low-skilled workers in general. These tend to be permanent, but they also tend to be more modest in magnitude compared to highly targeted subsidies. Empirical evaluation studies include Card et al. (2010) and OECD (2009).

the socio-demographic, economic, and institutional context varies widely across other advanced countries and that such 'tax credits', while demonstrably effective in particular settings and for particular groups, do not appear to offer a model for wholesale emulation. Moreover, Anglo-Saxon-type tax credits are strongly targeted, which implies a potential cost in terms of mobility 'traps' and wage erosion. From the perspective of public support, there may also be limits to such strongly targeted measures. By contrast, less strongly targeted income supplements, such as child benefits, can have an immediate impact on poverty among those at high risk (i.e. 'child-rich' households) without adversely affecting work incentives between workers and non-workers, although an income effect may have a dampening effect on labour supply among both categories. But for such benefits to be effective across the board as an anti-poverty device they need to be high, even when to some extent categorically differentiated (e.g. higher benefits for lone parents) or income-modulated. This inevitably comes at a significant budgetary cost. This fact is important because increased spending on direct income support runs contrary in many respects to current policy discourses. There it is argued that policy should focus less on compensating people for their low incomes and more on making sure that people are capable of economic self-reliance in the first place. We now turn to such social-investment policies.

## 11.3 Services, Social-Investment Strategy, and Inequality

Within the social-investment strategy, services are a key instrument (Morel et al., 2012: 13). This is advocated very explicitly by Esping-Andersen et al. (2002), who recommend a reallocation of social expenditure towards services, and then especially those services that support families in coping with the work–family life balance, and those that enhance human capital. The social-investment strategy intends to sustain the knowledge-based economy, which 'rests on a skilled and flexible labour force, which can easily adapt to the constantly changing needs of the economy but also be the motor of these changes' (Morel et al., 2012: 1). This investment through services should improve productivity and employment levels by creating a 'healthy, well-educated and more productive and mobile work force' (European Commission, 2012b: 177). The underlying idea is that advantages will be found at two levels: namely an increase of economic efficiency and employment, as well as a reduction in inequality and poverty (Nolan, forthcoming). The focus on investment and work in the social-investment strategy, however, risks relegating the distributive aspect to the background: both among researchers and policymakers the question of redistribution tends to be ignored (Cantillon, 2011). To some extent, this is understandable, as services do not have vertical redistribution as their primary aim. But as social inclusion is to be enhanced through this strategy, it is important to study the equalizing properties of social investment through services, which we aim to do here.

The inequality impact of services is far from clear. Le Grand (1982: 137), for instance, claimed that '[p]ublic expenditure on health care, education, housing and transport systematically favours the better off and thereby contributes to inequality in final income', while Esping-Andersen and Myles (2009) conclude 'that services are generally redistributive in an egalitarian direction, albeit less so than are cash transfers'. But gauging the distributive characteristics of services is difficult, as they do not only affect net disposable incomes, but also shape market incomes. A typical example is how service-intensive Nordic welfare states have defamiliarized caring responsibilities for children and the elderly, which resulted in virtually identical employment rates for men and women. Consequently, the Nordic countries have low child-poverty rates even before social benefits are taken into account. Ignoring these indirect effects of publicly provided social services on the distribution of market incomes risks seriously misjudging their real distributional impact (Verbist and Matsaganis, 2013). Hence, it is important to distinguish between first- and second-order distributive effects of publicly provided social services. With first-order effects, we mean that one tries to estimate the value of these benefits for individuals and households in order to have values comparable to cash transfers, and then perform a pre-post analysis, i.e. what would inequality be if the value of these services were incorporated in the income concept. These effects are the topic of Section 11.3.2. In this approach no account is taken of any possible second-order effects, such as behavioural reactions or long-term effects; these will be discussed in Section 11.3.3. But first we look in section 11.3.1 at the importance of services in social spending in OECD countries. We start from an overall picture of total publicly provided social services, and then focus on the most visible social-investment services, notably education and childcare.

### 11.3.1 The Importance of Services in Social Spending

Increased spending on services is often seen as an indicator of commitment to a social-investment strategy. It is undeniable that services constitute an important part of government social spending (see Figure 11.3). Spending on publicly provided services corresponds to around 13% of GDP on average across the thirty-four OECD countries, which is more than spending on cash social transfers (11%). The evolution of these shares is difficult to capture for all OECD countries. For the EU-15 (the European Union member states prior to 2004) a longer statistical series is available, which shows that spending on

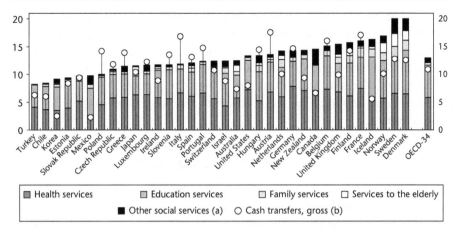

**Figure 11.3.** Public expenditure for in-kind and cash transfers, in percentage of GDP, 2007

*Notes*: Countries are ranked in increasing order of total expenditure on all social services. 2005 data on education services for Greece, Luxembourg, and Turkey.

(a) Social services to the elderly, survivors, disabled persons, families, unemployed, as well as those in respect of housing and social assistance.

(b) Cash transfers to the elderly, survivors, disabled persons, families, unemployed, as well as those in respect of social assistance.

*Source*: OECD (2011), data from OECD Social Expenditure database <http://www.oecd.org/els/social/expenditure> and OECD Education database <http://www.oecd.org/education/database>.

social services as a share of GDP has on average increased by one percentage point between 1998 and 2008, while spending on cash decreased by one percentage point. Also, in the 1990s relative service investments increased for these countries (Kauto, 2002).

As Figure 11.3 shows, there is considerable cross-country variation in in-kind spending, ranging from close to 8% of GDP in Turkey and Chile to 20% in Denmark and Sweden. In-kind expenditures consist mainly of healthcare (6% on average) and education services (5%). Care services to the elderly and to families represent together more than 1% of GDP, but there is more variation in spending across countries than there is for the two major categories. Care services are particularly important in the Nordic countries, Australia, and Japan. Kauto (2002) found three different groups of countries in terms of cash versus services redistribution strategies in 1990s, and Figure 11.3 suggests that this categorization still applied just before the financial and economic crisis. The first group is called the 'service approach' group and is characterized by high service effort and average or high cash-transfer effort. As in Kauto (2002), countries belonging to this group in 2007 are Denmark, Sweden, Norway, Finland, France, Germany, and the United Kingdom, but now also Belgium, Austria, and Hungary have joined this group. The 'transfer approach' group is characterized by high cash-transfer effort, and average or low service effort. Southern European countries belong to this group, as well as Poland and Slovenia. The third group in Kauto (2002) combines low service effort and low cash-transfer effort, with Turkey, Chile, Mexico, and Korea as main examples. Given the (increasing) importance of services in social spending, let us now turn to a discussion of their distributional impact.

### 11.3.2 First-Order Redistributive Effects of Social Services

Most studies on the redistributive impact of the in-kind benefits from social services deal with first-order effects, i.e. the impact on inequality of incorporating these benefits into the income concept. This literature strand stemmed from the observation that most empirical studies on cross-national differences in the levels of inequality and poverty use cash incomes only. Given that more than half of social spending in OECD countries is provided through non-cash benefits in the form of publicly provided services, and that there is wide variety across countries in their relative share of cash and in-kind spending, such 'cash-income-only' studies miss an important part of welfare-state efforts, and might give a misleading picture of redistributive outcomes. As both in-kind and cash transfers have an impact on the inequality of living standards, a measure that includes these in-kind benefits is theoretically superior to the more conventional cash-income measures (Atkinson et al., 2002; Callan et al., 2008; Canberra Group, 2011).

Incorporating the value of publicly provided services in household income raises a range of methodological issues (see, for example, Aaberge et al., 2010a, 2010b; OECD, 2008, 2011; Verbist et al., 2012). How should one value the benefits households derive from these services (valuation)? How should we distribute the aggregate value of these services among individuals (allocation)? How should the equivalence scale be adapted to take account of the needs associated with these services (equivalence scales)? As public services are provided outside market settings, there is no market price valuation, which makes the valuation of these services particularly difficult. In the literature, the standard practice is to value the benefit deriving from public services at their production cost, i.e. its measurement is based on the inputs used to provide these services rather than on the actual outputs produced (see, for example, Aaberge and Langørgen, 2006; Marical et al. 2008; Smeeding et al., 1993). This means, however, that it does not necessarily reflect the user's valuation of the service. Another problem with using the production cost is that it does not take account of the quality and efficiency in the provision of these services.

The second question relates to the allocation of these benefits across individuals: who are the beneficiaries to whom the value of public services is attributed? The literature distinguishes two approaches, namely the 'actual consumption approach' and the 'insurance value approach' (see, for example, Marical et al., 2008). The actual consumption approach allocates the value of public services to the individuals who are actually using the service; it can of course only be applied if actual beneficiaries can be identified. This approach is typically used in the case of education services (Antoninis and Tsakloglou, 2001; Callan et al., 2008), childcare services (Matsaganis and Verbist, 2009; Vaalavuo, 2011; Van Lancker and Ghysels, 2012), and social housing (Verbist et al., 2012). For healthcare, most empirical studies use an insurance value approach, imputing the value of coverage to each person based on specific characteristics (such as age and sex). It is based on the notion that what the government provides is equivalent to funding an insurance policy where the value of the premium is the same for everybody sharing the same characteristics (Smeeding, 1982; Marical et al., 2008). The insurance value approach also incorporates the value of access to this type of service.[2]

As the needs of a household grow with each additional member in a non-proportional way, equivalence scales are commonly used in distribution analyses to take account of such economies of scale. But as some types of non-cash income may have needs associated with them that are unmeasured in usual equivalence scales, using a cash-income equivalence scale when non-cash income components are included in the income concept may give rise to what Radner (1997) has called the 'consistency' problem. Service-related needs do not necessarily depend on economies of scale as captured by a standard cash-income equivalence scale, and may therefore require an alternative approach. Recent studies that experiment with such alternatives are Aaberge et al. (2010a, 2010b) and Paulus et al. (2010). A comparison of the empirical application of these two approaches can be found in Verbist et al. (2012).

Over the past decades the number of studies investigating the first-order redistributive impact of social services has grown considerably (for overviews, see, for example, Marical et al., 2008; Vaalavuo, 2011; Verbist et al., 2012). These studies differ in terms of country coverage as well as types of services studied. Pioneering work was done by Smeeding (1977, 1982), who

---

[2] The actual consumption approach has also been used for public healthcare services, based on detailed data on the effective use of healthcare services by individuals (see, for example, Evandrou et al. (1993) and Sefton (2002) for the UK). Marical et al. (2008) have applied the insurance value and the actual consumption approach for healthcare services in eight European countries. On average, the reduction in inequality when including healthcare expenditures in the income concept turned out to be considerably lower on the basis of the actual consumption approach than with the insurance value approach. This rather surprising outcome is largely due to the effect of re-ranking (see Marical et al. (2008) for more details).

investigated the poverty impact of in-kind food, housing, and medical-care benefits in the United States.[3] Evandrou et al. (1993), Sefton (2002), Lakin (2004), and Jones (2008) look at the United Kingdom, and Harding et al. (2006) at Australia, with a focus on healthcare, education, and social housing. For Norway, Aaberge and co-authors (Aaberge and Langørgen, 2006; Aaberge et al., 2010a, 2010b) investigate the distributive impact of municipal services, while Caussat et al. (2005) look at healthcare spending in France, and Spadaro et al. (2012) in Spain. The outcomes of these (and other) national studies are not directly comparable to one another due to differences in methodology and data; but in general it appears that these services have an inequality-reducing effect.

International comparative evidence is on the increase, starting with Smeeding et al. (1993), who study the distributive effect of healthcare, education, and public housing in seven countries (Australia, Canada, Netherlands, Sweden, United Kingdom, United States, and West Germany), using the LIS (Luxembourg Income Study) data for years between 1979 and 1983. Garfinkel et al. (2006) supplement this analysis by using more countries (including also France, Belgium, and Finland) and more recent LIS data (2002 or earlier). More recent evidence is presented in Paulus et al. (2010), who investigate the inequality effect of the same three services in five EU countries, as well as in OECD (2008) and OECD (2011), which present the widest country coverage. OECD (2008) investigates for fifteen OECD countries the inequality impact of the three services that have received most attention in the literature: public healthcare, education, and housing (for more details, see also Marical et al., 2008). OECD (2011) extends the analysis both in terms of number of countries (twenty-seven OECD member states) and type of services, as it also studies childcare and long-term elderly care (for more details see Verbist et al., 2012). The outcomes of these studies all go in the same direction: including the value of publicly provided social services has a considerable equalizing effect on the income distribution. We now illustrate this with empirical material from the most recent OECD publication on this topic (OECD, 2011; Verbist et al., 2012).

Table 11.1 shows the first-order impact of incorporating social services in the income concept on the Gini coefficient when moving from cash to extended income. The difference between cash and extended income consists of the monetary value of five types of publicly provided services, namely healthcare, education, social housing, childcare, and long-term

---

[3] Wolff et al. (2005) provide a broader picture by looking at total public expenditure to households (so not only social spending). A similar broad scope is found in O'Higgins and Ruggles (1981) for the United Kingdom.

elderly care.[4] The first-order inequality reduction of services is important: on average across the countries considered here, the Gini coefficient is reduced by about one-fifth when moving from cash to extended income. Even though this is less than inequality reduction through cash transfers (which is about one-third), it is still considerable (OECD, 2008, 2011; Verbist and Matsaganis, 2013). For all countries healthcare and education services are by far the most important contributors to inequality reduction; the impact of early childhood education and childcare (ECEC), long-term elderly care, and social housing is much smaller, mostly because their size is much more modest than the two 'big' services.

The five types of service considered here should contribute to a 'healthy, well-educated, and productive workforce', and can thus be seen as instruments of social investment. But as investment in human capital and family policy as a productive factor are essential ingredients of this strategy (Cantillon, 2011; Morel et al., 2012), education and ECEC services stand out as its most direct manifestations. We therefore pay more attention to the extent of inequality reduction in these two categories. For education, the redistributive impact is likely to vary across education levels. Compulsory education can be expected to be more redistributive than higher education, since the former is supposed to benefit equally all school-age children.

Inequality reduction through education services stems indeed mainly from compulsory education, which reduces inequality by 5% on average (Table 11.1, measured by Gini coefficient). In budgetary terms, the total of primary and lower secondary education (ISCED 1 and 2) carries most weight of all education categories, corresponding to more than 6% of disposable income on average (while total education expenditures correspond to 12%; Figure 11.4). This is one reason why inequality reduction is strongly related to spending on this education category. But a more important driving factor is the socio-demographic composition of the beneficiary population, namely children in primary and lower secondary education. Pupils in compulsory education tend to be more concentrated in the lower parts of the income distribution, which is shown in Panel B of Figure 11.4. The bars (Q1/Q5) represent the share of all beneficiaries located in the bottom income quintile over that in the top quintile. On average, the bottom quintile contains about 23% of compulsory education pupils of this education category, compared to only 14% for the top quintile, resulting in a Q1/Q5 ratio of 1.6. This pattern is strongest in Austria, Hungary, and the Czech Republic, where the

---

[4] The value of publicly provided education, childcare, and social housing is allocated on the basis of the actual consumption approach. For public healthcare and long-term care an insurance value approach is used. Incomes are equivalized with the square root of household size (for more details, see Verbist et al., 2012).

**Table 11.1.** Impact on the Gini coefficient of including public services in the income concept, 2007

| | Gini | | % change in inequality (Gini) | | | | | | | |
|---|---|---|---|---|---|---|---|---|---|---|
| | Cash | Extended income | All services | Healthcare | Education | ECEC | Long-term care | Social housing | Compulsory education | Tertiary education |
| AUS | 0.312 | 0.260 | -16.6% | -10.3% | -6.6% | -0.4% | | | -5.7% | -0.1% |
| AUT | 0.267 | 0.219 | -18.0% | -10.5% | -6.3% | -1.4% | | -0.3% | -5.0% | 0.0% |
| BEL | 0.264 | 0.209 | -21.0% | -14.3% | -4.4% | -1.5% | | -1.5% | -2.9% | 0.1% |
| CAN | 0.319 | 0.259 | -18.7% | -9.6% | -9.1% | -1.2% | | | -5.7% | -1.3% |
| CZE | 0.261 | 0.207 | -20.7% | -13.3% | -5.1% | -1.6% | | -0.8% | -4.7% | 1.1% |
| DEU | 0.300 | 0.249 | -16.9% | -10.4% | -5.1% | -1.2% | 0.1% | -0.3% | -3.3% | -1.1% |
| DNK | 0.250 | 0.194 | -22.3% | -10.0% | -5.7% | -1.1% | -5.0% | | -1.2% | -3.8% |
| ESP | 0.310 | 0.248 | -19.9% | -11.6% | -6.4% | -1.4% | -0.8% | -0.4% | -5.6% | 0.1% |
| EST | 0.338 | 0.280 | -17.1% | -11.3% | -6.0% | -1.0% | -0.3% | -0.1% | -4.1% | 0.4% |
| FIN | 0.266 | 0.218 | -18.2% | -10.8% | -4.3% | -1.0% | -2.5% | -1.1% | -2.2% | -1.3% |
| FRA | 0.264 | 0.209 | -21.0% | -13.0% | -5.8% | -1.8% | -0.8% | -1.1% | -4.4% | -0.4% |
| GBR | 0.330 | 0.252 | -23.6% | -12.5% | -7.0% | -0.7% | -1.6% | -4.6% | -5.2% | -0.5% |
| GRC | 0.342 | 0.288 | -15.9% | -9.6% | -5.9% | -0.5% | | 0.0% | -3.7% | -0.5% |
| HUN | 0.262 | 0.201 | -23.3% | -10.5% | -8.2% | -2.8% | -1.3% | -0.5% | -6.1% | 0.5% |
| IRL | 0.317 | 0.242 | -23.5% | -12.5% | -10.1% | -0.1% | | -3.4% | -7.5% | 0.0% |
| ISL | 0.291 | 0.227 | -22.1% | -11.4% | -7.9% | -2.5% | -3.1% | -0.5% | -5.8% | -1.5% |
| ITA | 0.320 | 0.262 | -18.2% | -9.2% | -7.8% | -1.5% | 0.0% | -0.5% | -5.0% | -0.3% |
| LUX | 0.275 | 0.220 | -20.1% | -10.7% | -7.6% | -2.3% | | -0.3% | -6.1% | |
| MEX | 0.475 | 0.375 | -21.1% | -11.2% | -11.5% | -1.3% | | | -10.9% | 0.4% |
| NLD | 0.272 | 0.220 | -19.0% | -8.1% | -6.4% | -1.8% | -2.9% | | -5.4% | -0.7% |
| NOR | 0.242 | 0.193 | -20.2% | -9.1% | -5.8% | -1.1% | -4.6% | -0.4% | -3.5% | -2.4% |
| POL | 0.317 | 0.259 | -18.2% | -8.6% | -9.9% | -1.1% | | -0.1% | -7.1% | -0.2% |
| PRT | 0.370 | 0.291 | -21.3% | -13.6% | -8.0% | -0.9% | | -0.5% | -6.5% | 0.0% |
| SVK | 0.251 | 0.204 | -19.1% | -12.1% | -6.7% | -0.6% | | 0.0% | -4.1% | 0.2% |
| SVN | 0.236 | 0.196 | -17.2% | -11.3% | -5.8% | -0.9% | -0.1% | -0.1% | -4.6% | 1.0% |
| SWE | 0.237 | 0.181 | -23.4% | -12.4% | -5.6% | -1.5% | -4.2% | -0.1% | -3.1% | -1.7% |
| USA | 0.372 | 0.303 | -18.5% | -9.8% | -9.0% | -0.9% | | | -6.7% | -0.6% |
| OECD-27 | 0.298 | 0.239 | -19.8% | -11.0% | -7.0% | -1.3% | -1.9% | -0.8% | -5.0% | -0.5% |

*Notes:* Averages are calculated over countries with non-zero values only. Due to data limitations no estimates for long-term elderly care are available for Australia, Austria, Belgium, Canada, the Czech Republic, Denmark, Greece, Ireland, Luxembourg, Mexico, Portugal, Poland, Slovakia, and the United States. For six countries, no estimates of the impact of social housing are provided, namely Australia, Canada, Denmark, Mexico, the Netherlands, and the United States. Education includes primary, lower secondary, upper secondary, post-secondary non-tertiary, and tertiary education. ECEC includes both childcare services and pre-primary education. Compulsory education is here defined as the total of primary and lower secondary education.

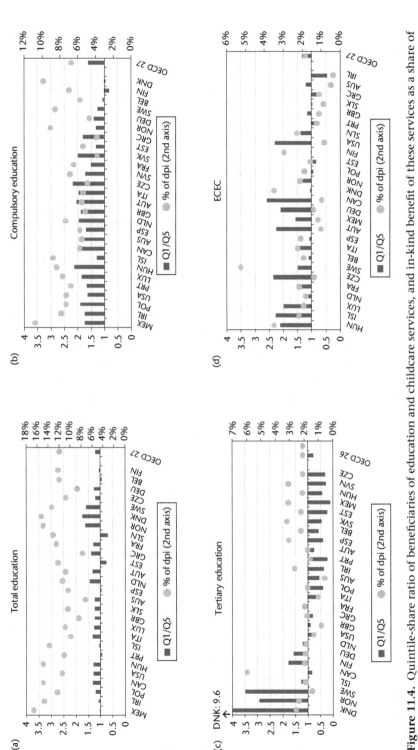

**Figure 11.4.** Quintile-share ratio of beneficiaries of education and childcare services, and in-kind benefit of these services as a share of disposable income

*Notes*: Countries are ranked in decreasing order by relative inequality reduction of the service category (see Table 11.1). 'Q1/Q5' is the share of beneficiaries located in the bottom income quintile over that in the top quintile. '% of dpi' is the share of the in-kind benefits in disposable income.

*Source*: Authors' calculations based on Verbist et al., 2012.

share of pupils in Q1 is about twice that in the top quintile. Much more even distributions, indicated by a Q1/Q5 ratio close to 1, are found in the Nordic countries and Belgium. The position of these children in the income distribution is closely related to how successful countries are in combating child poverty, either by changing market income through high employment or by well-designed tax-benefit policies. These outcomes confirm the better performance in this domain of the Nordic countries, and the challenges other countries face to better protect children against income poverty and social exclusion (see, for example, Gornick and Jäntti, 2012).

Outcomes for tertiary education services are quite different: inequality reduction is very limited (on average 0.5%). In most countries, inequality is hardly affected at all, or it even increases after the inclusion of the value of tertiary education. Again, these outcomes are largely driven by the distribution of participants in education, with some countries having very regressive patterns, as indicated by an interquintile ratio well below 1 (Panel C of Figure 11.4), and very progressive patterns in the Nordic countries. In Denmark, Norway, and Sweden the bottom quintile accounts for around half of the participants in higher education, resulting in very high Q1/Q5 ratios. Consequently, in these countries inequality is reduced when including the value of these services in the income concept. These participation patterns reflect both socioeconomic differences that are important in terms of access to higher education, and also institutional differences in, for example, the structure of earlier levels of education (in terms of preparation for the labour market or for higher education), affordability, etc. The Nordic countries are characterized by accessible and affordable tertiary education institutions, which translates in to high enrolment rates (Usher and Cervenan, 2005; Vaalavuo, 2011). An issue that complicates the interpretation of these outcomes, however, is the fact that many students live away from their parents in the Nordic countries and are thus classified as a separate household. Due to their low incomes, students are often concentrated in the poorest 20% of the population. This partly reflects cultural differences, but is from a poverty perspective also partly an artefact, because students living away from their high-income parents have temporary low incomes during their student years, while the literature on the returns to education indicates that their probable position in the earnings distribution later will be towards the top (Callan et al., 2008). But even when controlling for this artefact, Vaalavuo (2011) finds that Sweden and Norway still have the most equal distribution of tertiary education expenditures.

Spending on early childhood education and childcare (ECEC) services is associated with an average decline of the Gini by 1.3% (Table 11.1). When looking at Figure 11.4, Panel D, we see again how compositional factors drive these outcomes: in countries like the Czech Republic and Hungary the bottom quintile makes up around 30% of beneficiaries, while in Ireland the poorest quintile is heavily underrepresented. In contrast to compulsory education, where almost all children of that age group are in school, the pattern is also driven by differential use of ECEC services. Table 11.2 provides an indication of whether poorer or richer households are more likely to enrol their young children in public ECEC facilities. In most countries, children in higher-income households are more likely to be enrolled than those in lower-income households. The difference between childcare and pre-primary education is relevant in this context: for the youngest age group (0 to 3 years) enrolment is much more stratified along socioeconomic lines, with dual-earner couples (and hence higher incomes) making relatively more use of childcare (Förster and Verbist, 2012; Van Lancker, 2013). For children

**Table 11.2.** Actual ECEC beneficiaries as a share of potential beneficiaries (children aged 0–5), by income quintile

|         | Q1    | Q2    | Q3    | Q4    | Q5    | Total |
|---------|-------|-------|-------|-------|-------|-------|
| AUS     | 33.0% | 35.0% | 50.8% | 39.3% | 42.4% | 40.1% |
| AUT     | 38.1% | 44.7% | 46.6% | 42.8% | 47.7% | 43.2% |
| BEL     | 54.2% | 69.9% | 71.6% | 75.7% | 79.0% | 69.2% |
| CAN     | 30.9% | 32.9% | 29.2% | 27.5% | 26.3% | 29.8% |
| CZE     | 44.1% | 45.6% | 46.9% | 40.0% | 40.7% | 43.8% |
| DEU     | 65.8% | 59.9% | 67.9% | 61.0% | 57.1% | 62.8% |
| DNK     | 80.1% | 80.4% | 86.0% | 86.8% | 84.6% | 83.8% |
| EST     | 56.1% | 48.0% | 54.2% | 53.3% | 48.4% | 52.0% |
| ESP     | 64.7% | 66.4% | 66.9% | 68.0% | 72.7% | 67.6% |
| FIN     | 42.2% | 45.2% | 55.2% | 69.5% | 66.1% | 54.0% |
| FRA     | 63.4% | 56.9% | 63.4% | 63.2% | 70.8% | 63.0% |
| GBR     | 33.7% | 38.8% | 45.7% | 52.2% | 53.1% | 43.0% |
| GRC     | 33.2% | 37.6% | 38.1% | 50.8% | 43.8% | 40.7% |
| HUN     | 53.0% | 52.2% | 54.9% | 57.2% | 55.7% | 54.2% |
| IRL     | 15.1% | 26.7% | 31.5% | 31.4% | 43.0% | 28.9% |
| ISL     | 59.3% | 70.4% | 67.4% | 74.6% | 66.8% | 66.8% |
| ITA     | 55.3% | 57.4% | 57.4% | 57.4% | 68.9% | 58.5% |
| LUX     | 52.2% | 63.3% | 64.3% | 63.3% | 75.6% | 61.6% |
| MEX     | 15.2% | 15.9% | 16.2% | 15.5% | 16.1% | 15.8% |
| NLD     | 66.2% | 64.8% | 66.8% | 69.1% | 85.5% | 69.4% |
| NOR     | 48.6% | 57.2% | 60.2% | 58.9% | 67.6% | 57.5% |
| POL     | 17.4% | 17.2% | 20.6% | 24.5% | 31.5% | 21.8% |
| PRT     | 46.5% | 45.3% | 54.8% | 68.1% | 68.3% | 56.2% |
| SWE     | 70.6% | 70.6% | 72.6% | 70.0% | 69.6% | 70.9% |
| SVK     | 29.3% | 33.4% | 56.1% | 42.4% | 64.8% | 43.2% |
| SVN     | 56.2% | 64.1% | 62.0% | 57.7% | 62.7% | 60.4% |
| USA     | 29.6% | 27.7% | 29.5% | 28.8% | 28.5% | 28.9% |
| OECD-27 | 46.4% | 49.2% | 53.2% | 53.7% | 56.9% | 51.4% |

*Source*: Förster and Verbist, 2012.

aged 4–5 years, pre-primary education is much more widespread, with often very high enrolment rates when getting closer to the age of compulsory schooling. An important element in this context is that pre-primary education is in general free of charge, while parents have to pay a fee for childcare use. Even though in many countries these fees are income-dependent in order to limit the private cost of childcare for low-income families, the use of childcare is still often biased towards higher incomes. A number of studies have shown that availability of childcare places is often more important than its price (see, for example, Wrohlich (2011) for Germany; Vandelannoote et al. (2013) for Belgium).

Summarizing, we find a substantial first-order redistributive effect of services, also for those services that are key instruments in the social-investment strategy. This sizeable redistributive role of services in Western societies is an important finding, especially given the fact that inequality reduction is seldom a primary aim of delivering most of these services. Note, however, that in line with their universal coverage, services such as compulsory education are in most countries substantially more egalitarian than tertiary education and ECEC.

### 11.3.3 Second-Order Effects on Inequality of Publicly Provided Services

So far we have only discussed first-order inequality effects of publicly provided services. But these are only part of the story. Services (as well as cash transfers) also have other effects, relating to behavioural reactions and long-term impacts. Trying to study the second-order inequality effects of public policies empirically is, however, a hazardous task because finding a pre-government counterfactual is problematic (Jesuit and Mahler, 2010): we do not know what the distribution of market income would be without cash and in-kind transfers. The few studies that try to take account of such second-order effects (e.g. Jesuit and Mahler, 2010; Doerrenberg and Peichl, 2012) concentrate on cash redistribution only. Nevertheless, the second-order effects due to services merit further attention as they are at the heart of the social-investment strategy. Preparing individuals for the knowledge-based economy and increasing their employability are central themes in the social-investment rhetoric. But, interestingly, despite the fact that social inclusion is also part of this rhetoric, a recent book on social investment (Morel et al., 2012) hardly discusses the poverty and inequality effects of services or other key instruments in the social-investment paradigm. It is rather assumed that a well-implemented social-investment welfare state will be egalitarian by increasing employment. But that this is not an inevitable outcome already became clear in Section 11.2. We therefore think it is important to try to grasp these second-order effects, and we now turn to consider short-run and long-run second-order effects of education and ECEC services.

In the short run, education services can often have negative effects on labour supply. As the public provision of education stimulates participation in both compulsory and non-compulsory education, these participants obviously cannot spend their school time on the labour market. There is little question in the literature that primary and secondary education in the longer run consistently increase labour supply, so not surprisingly these types of education are heavily subsidized in almost all OECD countries and are to a large extent compulsory. They provide the human capital that society deems to be the absolute minimum to be attained. The expectation that job training programmes would have similar positive effects is not corroborated by empirical evidence. The vast literature on evaluating such programmes shows only modest gains in terms of labour supply and earnings (Currie and Gahvari, 2008). It is argued that this is due to the fact that these programmes are often too short and too superficial to generate a more substantial impact (Lalonde, 1995).

How education services impact on income inequality in the longer term is difficult to assess, and until now hardly any studies have undertaken this difficult task, mainly due to conceptual and methodological limitations, as well as lack of information. Exceptions are Sylwester (2002) and Bergh (2005). By combining data on public education spending between 1960 and 1969 with changes in Gini inequality indicators for later years (between 1970 and 1990), Sylwester demonstrates that a country with higher education expenditures (as a share of GDP) has lower income inequality in later years. Bergh (2005) then shows that this equalizing effect is entirely due to public spending on primary and secondary education. The effect of public higher-education expenditures, in contrast, is either not significant or even negative. Intuitively, one would expect higher public spending on tertiary education to lead to higher enrolment rates and subsequently lower income inequality. Bergh and Fink (2008), however, show that if public subsidies raise the incentive to enrol in tertiary education, this in the first instance increases inequality if the group enjoying the wage premiums associated with higher education is small. As enrolment increases, this effect will become less and eventually will be egalitarian.

For childcare services, Currie and Gahvari (2008) assert that they have short-term positive effects for the parents, in particular for young mothers. Childcare services reduce the relative price of childcare and should facilitate employment of parents, especially mothers. The European Commission (2009) reports evidence from country studies according to which the availability of childcare facilities intensifies mothers' labour-market participation rates. On the basis of a literature review, however, they conclude that there is little empirical evidence that these positive short-term effects will offset the deadweight loss associated with the tax system (studies examining the elasticity of maternal employment include Bassanini and Duval (2006), Blau and Currie (2006), and Gelbach (2002)). Moreover, if the use of childcare is biased against vulnerable socioeconomic groups (such as low-skilled mothers), then investment in ECEC will not necessarily be inequality-reducing (Van Lancker, 2013). One may expect larger long-term effects than short-term, as these services may limit potential losses in future earnings stemming from longer career interruptions. But stimulating maternal employment is not the only channel through which childcare services should foster social inclusion in the longer run. They also aim to enhance school readiness of children, in order to have a positive impact on human-capital formation of young children and their potential wages later in life. There is empirical literature that offers some support for the idea that in-kind transfers to children may be productivity-enhancing in the long run. The Perry pre-school programme and other similar initiatives highlight the beneficial effects of high-quality early-intervention services targeted at underprivileged children (for an overview, see Karoly et al., 2005). It is not straightforward, however, to simply transfer these American interventions to a European context where inequalities in child conditions are less extreme. Nevertheless, these results illustrate that such early-intervention programmes can be effectively equalizing, as they support the most vulnerable groups (Esping-Andersen, 2008). Various studies demonstrate that the quality of childcare provision is an important condition in order to derive beneficial effects from pre-school programmes (for an overview, see Esping-Andersen et al., 2012). Moreover, a comparison of programmes in Denmark and the United States (Esping-Andersen et al., 2012) indicates that investment in high-quality services is not of itself sufficient. This should be connected to the quality of the subsequent school system, parental leave arrangements, and broader welfare programmes (Van Lancker, 2013).

The long-term effects of both education and childcare services may provide a justification for the more paternalistic arguments that are traditionally seen as underpinning the provision of public services over cash transfers. Provision in kind steers families towards education and childcare, which might not be the case if the value of these provisions was given in cash to families. According to Currie and Gahvari (2008), such paternalistic arguments become more powerful 'when the intended recipient of a transfer program is a child but the transfer goes to parents. Parents may not take full account of the utility of their children when making decisions or they may neglect to factor in externalities. For example, suboptimal spending on children's education may lead not only to poorer individual prospects, but also to slower future economic growth.'

## 11.4 Conclusion

In current policy discourses higher levels of employment, together with 'social investment' in human capital, are increasingly seen as the way forward in bringing about structural and sustainable social progress. What can we expect from activation and social-investment policies if our concern is with inequality and poverty?

A first important point is that while giving more people access to work is important for a wide range of reasons, increasing the proportion of people in work does not automatically translate into less poverty and inequality. This is what past experience teaches us and also what projections suggest. Part of the problem here is that those most in need of extra work and income do not tend to be the first beneficiaries of an increased demand for labour if and when this happens. The prime beneficiaries tend to be people with the strongest profiles in terms of age and skills. These tend to be school-leavers or new entrants not living in poverty in the first place. Another problem is that gaining access to a job does not necessarily imply a significant move up the income ladder and out of poverty. Even if policy succeeded in getting every single person into work, or every household to a level of full work intensity for that matter—and all empirical evidence to date suggests this to be highly unlikely—this would not guarantee the elimination of poverty. This points to the key role of direct income-support policies, including for those in work. What policy can do to help households in these circumstances depends on such factors as the institutional and policy context in place, labour-market conditions, and the profile of the population in need of support.

Introducing or boosting effective minimum wages to the upper range of those currently prevailing in OECD countries (relative to average earnings) would, even in the absence of negative employment effects, not be sufficient to eradicate in-work poverty. Minimum wages and other wage regulation mechanisms have probably become inherently constrained in providing minimum income protection to sole-breadwinner households, especially in countries where relative poverty thresholds have become essentially determined by dual-earner living standards. For low-earnings households, only direct household-income supplements may offer a reasonable prospect for a poverty-free existence, especially when there are dependent children. Such 'in-work benefits' are now often associated with Anglo-Saxon-type 'tax credits' such as the EITC in the United States and the WTC in the United Kingdom. However, it is important to keep in mind here that socio-demographic, economic, and institutional contexts vary considerably across the rich countries. While demonstrably effective in particular settings and for particular groups, tax credits do not offer a model for wholesale emulation in other settings. Child benefits are an alternative or complementary way of offering direct income support. These can have an immediate impact on poverty among those at high risk (i.e. child-rich households) without adversely affecting work incentives between workers and non-workers. But for such benefits to be effective across the board as an anti-poverty device these need to be high, and this inevitably comes at a significant budgetary cost. Increased spending on such forms of direct income support is not self-evident in view of current calls for more spending on indirect support policies, in the form of what is now referred to as social investment.

Even though services are a key instrument of the social-investment strategy, researchers and policymakers often neglect their impact on income inequality and poverty. To some extent, this is understandable, as income redistribution is not the primary aim of these services. Moreover, there are many methodological challenges if one wants to assess both first- and second-order inequality effects of services. Interestingly, when bringing together empirical literature on this topic, it is clear that services matter for making societies more egalitarian. If we take the example of compulsory education, then empirical outcomes from both a first- and a second-order perspective are unequivocal: this type of investment in children is good for income equality. Probably the compulsory character is of high importance here: within the relevant age group, almost all children participate, and hence acquire a minimum level of skills. Empirical evidence on tertiary education and ECEC services tells a different story, with a variety of experiences across countries. In most countries these two types of services are more socially stratified, with often relatively more beneficiaries towards the top of the income distribution. Consequently, simply increasing spending on these services will not be enough to foster egalitarianism. The wider social context is important, and crucial parameters, such as access, availability, and quality of the services, need to be considered and integrated into the policy perspective. If, for example, childcare is provided almost free of private costs, then this may still not guarantee that more vulnerable groups will benefit if there are not enough places available. So this may call for extra policy efforts in this domain targeted at these groups. Moreover, if quality of childcare is not similar within a country and low-income families typically mainly use lower-quality care, then this may hamper egalitarian outcomes in the longer run. So investment in equal quality is also important, as well as connections with other policy domains, e.g. complementary parental-leave systems and the quality of the regular school system.

Particularly relevant for the wider socioeconomic context are the dramatic decreases in labour demand associated with the crisis. This puts the social-investment strategy in a different perspective: a call on childcare for (young) parents who do not have any job prospects at all may then not be the first policy priority for countries hit by very high (youth) unemployment rates. The policy priority in such a context must surely lie with providing adequate direct income support. A balanced approach is needed at any rate. As Vandenbroucke et al. (2011: 14) put it, 'We know that egalitarian societies are more successful in implementing social investment policies. The fact that it is a precondition urges us to remember the merits of traditional social protection and anti-poverty programmes, and suggests that reducing income inequality should remain high on the social investment agenda. Hence, there is a need for a balanced approach, with an "investment strategy" and a "protection strategy" as complementary pillars of an active welfare state.'

In sum, it is clearly important to think about effective policies that prevent situations of need arising in the first place. However, one also needs to be cautious about radically shifting resources towards policies that seek to impact on inequality and poverty in a structural but indirect way, at the expense of social policies of proven effectiveness in terms of direct poverty alleviation and inequality reduction, especially in times of high unemployment. The best performers among the rich countries in terms of economic, employment, social cohesion, and equality outcomes have one thing in common: a large welfare state that does several things at the same time, investing in people, stimulating and supporting them to be active, and also adequately protecting them and their children when everything else fails.

# 12

# The Policy Response to Educational Inequalities

*Daniele Checchi, Herman van de Werfhorst,*
*Michela Braga, and Elena Meschi*

## 12.1 Introduction

In order to analyse the role of educational policies with respect to observed inequality in earnings and incomes, one needs to investigate separately the relationship between educational policies and educational achievements, and the relationship between educational achievements and the distribution of earnings and incomes. In this chapter on the policy response in the field of education, which complements Chapter 5 of this volume on educational distributions, we examine the relationship between educational policies, the distribution of education in terms of attainment and achievement, and the distribution of income and earnings. By focusing on both attainment and achievement, we make the conceptual distinction between quantity of education (i.e. the level of educational attainment) and the quality of education (i.e. student achievement on tested skills). The broad research question that guides our overview of recent scholarship on the matter is this: to what extent is there evidence of a relationship between educational policies, the quality and quantity of education, and the distribution of income?

In the following Section 12.2 we examine policies that may help to combat educational inequalities in the competences achieved (i.e. quality of education). In this section we also demonstrate the relationship between several institutional characteristics of educational systems and student achievement, including early tracking, vocational orientation, and forms of national standardization. Due to the lack of data over time, these relationships are examined using cross-sectional variations across countries.

Then, from Section 12.3 onwards, we take a more longitudinal approach to educational policies. In this section we describe various policies to combat inequality in educational attainment, both in terms of distributions and in terms of inequality of educational opportunity by social groups. This section presents measures of educational policies across time for most European countries, mostly relying on published work by Braga et al. (2013). We distinguish between the following types of policy, partly relying on a classification of Krueger and Lindahl (2009): the structure and length of pre-primary education; length of compulsory education; school tracking; school autonomy; school accountability; teacher qualification; student funding; university autonomy and selectivity. It is shown to what extent policies have changed across Europe.

Then, in Section 12.4, we examine how educational policies and institutions come about. How can we explain why certain policies emerge? Following a framework borrowed from Iversen and Stephens (2008), the importance is examined, among others, of political factors such as the colour of government.

Section 12.5, finally, encompasses the relationships between the whole set of educational policies, educational distributions, and income inequality. By complementing contemporary EU-SILC data on educational and earnings attainments with comparative student achievement data from the 1960s onwards, we examine to what extent educational policies affect the quality and quantity of education, and how these educational distributions relate to the level of income inequality.

The concluding section discusses the potential opposition to the implementation of these policies.

## 12.2 Policies to Reduce Inequalities in Competences

We start by a general discussion of how the educational institutional structure in a society is related to the level of inequality in the quality of education, measured by competences possessed by students or adults. In this section, we cannot exploit temporal variation, because surveys on competences are relatively recent, and we are therefore forced to rely on cross-country variation. Most of what is presented here derives from Bol and Van de Werfhorst (2013a, 2013b). It should be noted that the number of countries that are analysed is sometimes larger than the pool of countries under investigation of the larger GINI project.

The field of comparative stratification has made a distinction in three broad dimensions on which educational systems may differ (Allmendinger, 1989; Kerckhoff, 2001; Shavit and Müller, 1998). First, educational systems differ between countries, and across time within countries, in the extent to which students are separated into clearly distinct educational curricula during secondary education. The most evident form of separation is in the form of *tracking*, in which students are sorted into different tracks catering for students of different learning abilities. The age at which such tracking occurs varies substantially between countries.[1] Tracking may have severe consequences for the distribution of skills, both with regard to the mean and the dispersion.

Second, it has been considered relevant to distinguish the standardization of the educational system. Standardization is a general term referring to the extent to which education meets the same standards nationwide. It can include standardization of *input*, in the form of curricular standardization, standardization of teacher quality, or standardization of resources across schools. Standardization of input has also been referred to as *centralization* (Horn, 2009), or as an antonym of school autonomy. Standardization can also refer to standardization of *output*, most clearly marked by the existence of central exit examinations (sometimes called *accountability*) (Horn, 2009). These two types of standardization can have very different impacts on the distribution of skills. Standardization of input is generally assumed to equalize performances of students across different schools, thereby reducing the variance, and possibly also reducing the average performance of students. Standardization of output may, however, also increase competition between schools, certainly if school performance is used to hold schools accountable for their performance. This may lead to enhanced variability between students, and increased average performances.

Third, educational systems have been classified according to the vocational orientation of the system. Vocational orientation often refers to the upper secondary school system, where some countries have educational systems with vocational schools with strong links to the labour market, whereas other countries lack such an occupationally relevant orientation.

For the assessment of the relevance of educational institutions on the distribution of quality of education (mostly based on student surveys at the mid-teen age—TIMSS, PISA), we initially review some of the existing literature with a cross-country perspective, and then provide additional new evidence. Earlier research has interpreted the association between average student performance and the dispersion in performance as a trade-off between equality

[1] In Germany children are separated as early as the age of ten, in the Netherlands at the age of twelve, and in Finland and Sweden much later at the age of sixteen. Countries have sometimes also changed their level of tracking, most notably in the 1960s and 1970s, and these changes are exploited for identification in the following paragraphs. For instance, in Finland, France, and England an early tracked educational system was abolished and replaced with comprehensive secondary education in the 1970s.

and efficiency (Hanushek and Wössmann, 2005; Micklewright and Schnepf, 2007; Van de Werfhorst and Mijs, 2010). Such a trade-off would exist if higher average performances would coincide with larger dispersions. If evidence is found for such a trade-off, educational policy may have to choose between enhancing the average skill level and reducing inequality among students.

If the relationship between average performance and dispersion in performance is examined using cross-sectional data on a large number of countries, there is little evidence for the existence of a trade-off (Hanushek and Wössmann, 2005; Brown et al., 2007; Micklewright and Schnepf, 2007). In Figure 12.1 achievement scores are displayed, both in terms of country averages (standardized at mean=0 and standard deviation=1 across all individuals) and country standard deviations. This is done for mathematics collected in the PISA 2006 data among 15-year-olds, and on literacy among 16–35-year-olds in the International Adult Literacy Survey of 1994–8, for the countries that are covered in the GINI project. The figure shows that there is no association between a country's average position on mid-teenage mathematics achievement and the dispersion across students. With regard to adult literacy we even see a negative relationship between averages and dispersions. So there is no evidence for the trade-off hypothesis that higher average performance can be achieved by allowing for greater dispersions.

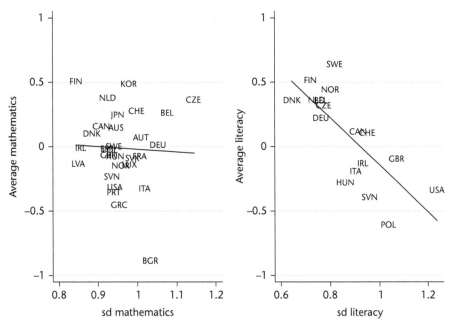

**Figure 12.1.** The association between equality and efficiency in mid-teen mathematics and adult literacy

*Sources*: Mathematics: PISA 2006; Literacy: IALS.

So how do the three dimensions of institutional variability relate to inequalities and average performances? First of all, the evidence on the association between educational policies aimed at the tracking of students and the dispersion in test scores is mixed. Although the most authoritative studies point to higher dispersions (inequalities) in countries with more strongly tracked educational systems, including when a difference-in-difference design is used to study change between primary and secondary school (Hanushek and Wössmann, 2005; Huang, 2009), some other studies have found evidence to the contrary (Duru-Bellat and Suchaut, 2005; see Van de Werfhorst and Mijs (2010) for a review).

When we consider alternative inequality measures in relation to tracking age, we find mixed evidence. Using PISA 2006 data for twenty-nine countries, Figure 12.2 shows bivariate relationships at the country level between the age at which tracking starts[2] and the standard deviation in mathematics performance, the average mathematics performance, and the mathematics performance at the 25th and 75th percentile. It appears evident that only the standard deviation is statistically significantly related to the age of selection; countries with later tracking have lower standard deviations. The average performance is not enlarged, nor is the 75th percentile. So whereas proponents of tracking may claim that education can be organized more efficiently by tracking in order to maximize performance (or at least maximize performance at the top), we do not see evidence of this in a cross-sectional design for either the average or the top performers. There is, however, another form of inequality in learning that is strongly related to tracking: inequality of educational opportunity by social origin. Generally, it has been reported that systems in which students are tracked earlier have larger skill inequalities between students of different origins than systems with comprehensive education (Brunello and Checchi, 2007; Bol and Van de Werfhorst, 2013b; Marks, 2005; Horn, 2009; Schütz et al., 2008).

With regard to the relationship between standardization of input and skill distributions, the pattern is similar to what is seen in Figure 12.3 over the same sample of twenty-nine countries. Standardization of input is measured by aggregating school principals' responses to the PISA questionnaires to the country level. Questions are asked about who decides about the textbook used, who determines which courses are offered, and what is taught in these courses. One of the answer categories to these questions was that the state or country decides on these issues. Using a dichotomized version of the variables (state/country versus other), the country-level aggregations of these items can be taken, after which a scale can be produced using factor

---

[2] Tracking age is assessed through the OECD Education at a Glance database, and is referring to the cohort that is analysed.

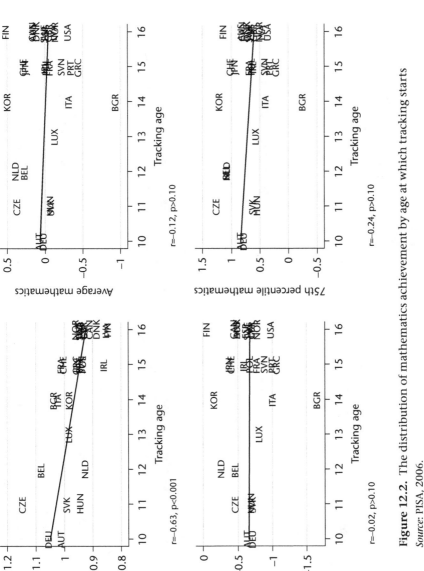

**Figure 12.2.** The distribution of mathematics achievement by age at which tracking starts

*Source:* PISA, 2006.

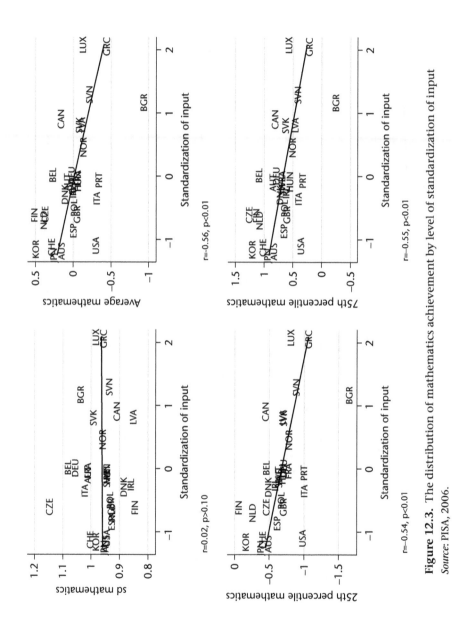

**Figure 12.3.** The distribution of mathematics achievement by level of standardization of input

*Source:* PISA, 2006.

analysis. The average skill quality and the skill level at the bottom and the top of the distribution are negatively correlated to standardization. Other research has demonstrated similar findings using difference-in-difference designs that capture changes in regulations on school autonomy. School autonomy (i.e. a lack of standardization of input) is found to enhance average performance because it leads to efficiency gains due to stronger competition between schools (Hanushek, Link, and Wössmann, 2013). The dispersion in student achievement (as measured by the standard deviation) is not related to the level of standardization of input in the cross-sectional data depicted in Figure 12.3, because the entire distribution is shifted.

Finally, the distribution of skills is assessed in relation to the existence of central exit examinations. Following earlier work (Bishop, 1997; Bol and Van de Werfhorst, 2013a), we define central exit examinations by the joint occurrence of the following conditions: (i) exams have real consequences, rather than just being symbolic; (ii) the qualifications given after successful examination are tested against an external standard; (iii) the standardized exams are organized by subject; (iv) the exam does not simply have a pass/fail outcome, but has various potential outcomes on a continuum; and (v) the exam is meant for secondary school students, and a large majority of the secondary school population is covered. Most countries score either a 0 (no central exit examinations) or a 1 (with central examinations), except countries in which there is regional variation in the existence of central exams. For these countries we took the proportion of regional entities (provinces, states) in which there are central exit examinations. The variable can be constructed for thirty-six countries. Figure 12.4 shows the statistical relationships with average performance, the standard deviation, and performance at the 25th and 75th percentile. From the figure it emerges that only the standard deviation in mathematics achievement is significantly related to the existence of central exit examinations; in countries with centralized exams the dispersion in mathematics achievement is lower. Average performance and the performance at the bottom and the top are unrelated to whether a country has a centralized examination system. It should be noted that other research has found a positive association between centralized exams and the average performance (Jürges et al., 2005; Wössmann, 2003, 2005).

The relevance of the vocational orientation of the system for the distribution of skills should be investigated at a later age than the standard mid-teenage tests of PISA or TIMSS. The vocational orientation is usually assessed by the proportion of students within upper secondary education that is enrolled in vocational education. In Figure 12.5 we therefore relate the vocational orientation of educational systems to the distribution of literacy as assessed in the International Adult Literacy Survey data of 1994–8. These data are rather

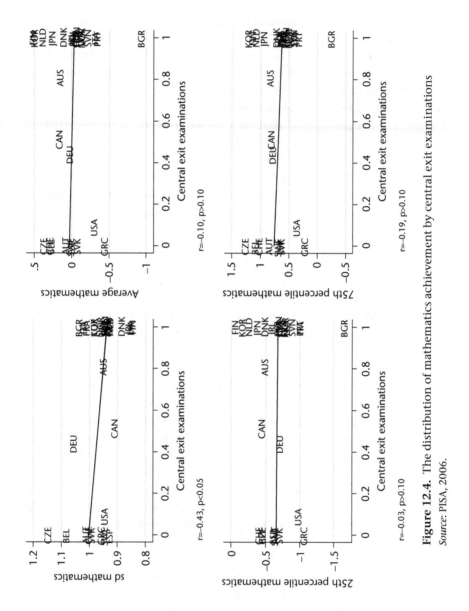

**Figure 12.4.** The distribution of mathematics achievement by central exit examinations
*Source:* PISA, 2006.

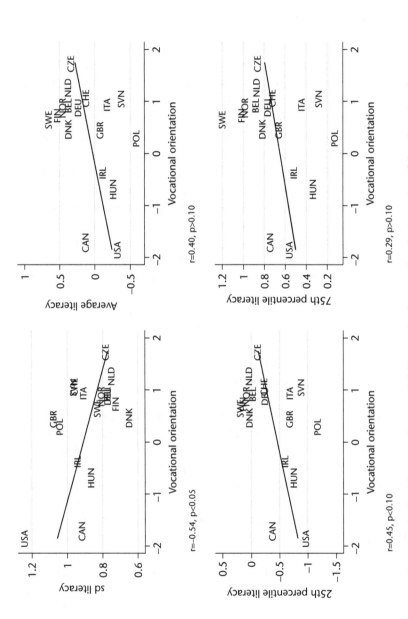

**Figure 12.5.** The distribution of young adult literacy by the vocational orientation of the educational system

*Source:* International Adult Literacy Survey (IALS).

old, but at least available for a reasonable number of countries that have been investigated in the GINI project. The relationship between vocational education and the dispersion of skills appears to be quite strong. In societies with a strong vocational sector, the dispersion is lower, particularly because the bottom of the skills distribution performs rather well. This finding substantiates that vocational education can function rather inclusively, by promoting achievement of the lower part of the distribution. A similar conclusion has been reached by Brunello and Checchi (2007), where they consider early tracking as harmful to social equality, whereas vocational education promotes equality of opportunity.

Some evidence has also been presented on the relevance of school system characteristics for other types of outcomes than academic ones. For instance, Janmaat (2011) has shown that the between-school variance in civic engagement is larger in tracked educational systems than in comprehensive educational systems. Van de Werfhorst (2007a) has examined civic participation among young adults, and found that the educational gradient in participation is stronger in strongly tracked educational systems. Also the average level of civic participation is lower in these countries (Bol and Van de Werfhorst, 2013b). Koçer and Van de Werfhorst (2012) examined the relationship between tracking and vocational orientation of educational systems and opinions on income redistribution. Their study showed that early tracking is related to larger dispersions in the people's orientations towards redistribution. Potentially this could threaten the realization of consensus on important political issues concerning the income distribution in societies whose educational systems are tracking students at 'formative ages' when attitudes are formed.

Summing up the results of this section, we identify three main messages. The first is that there is no evident trade-off between average achievement in competences and its dispersion, at least during the period of schooling, whereas some negative correlation could emerge later in life. The second message is that postponing the age of tracking may contribute to a reduction in dispersion of competences, while raising the degree of standardization of inputs (i.e. reducing the degree of school autonomy) and/or introducing central examinations seems less effective in reducing educational inequality in competences. Finally, the vocational orientation of the secondary school system, by retaining in schools the least motivated students (who often coincide with students with poorer cultural backgrounds), reduces the dispersion in competences in the adult population. Overall, these findings together may lead to the conclusion that early tracking is harmful to equality and shapes antagonized interests, whereas a strong vocational sector in the education system functions to foster inclusion rather than divergence.

## 12.3 Policies to Reduce Inequalities in Educational Attainment

While the previous section took a cross-sectional approach to the study of the relationship between educational systems and policies on the one hand and the quality of education on the other, it should be stressed that educational policies can and do change across time within countries. In the remainder of this chapter we take a longitudinal approach to educational policy, and study changes in policies (this section), how the emergence of policies can be explained (Section 12.4), and how policies, educational distributions, and income distributions are related. In this section we mostly rely on the analysis which led to the published version of Braga et al. (2013). The existing literature on the expected impact of educational policies on the distribution of educational attainment as measured by years of schooling is reviewed, mainly focusing on cross-country studies.

We classify the institutional characteristics of school systems into eight categories: structure and length of pre-primary education; length of compulsory education; school tracking; school autonomy; school accountability; teacher qualification; student funding; university autonomy and selectivity. For each of these characteristics of the school system, we shall discuss their expected impact on educational attainment and on educational inequality, thus highlighting potential trade-offs between equity and efficiency (see also the related discussion in Wössmann, 2008).

### 12.3.1 Pre-Primary Education

The economic literature seems to agree on the positive effects of pre-school education on both the efficiency and equity of the education system. The theory behind this idea is explained in various models developed by James Heckman and co-authors describing the technology of skill formation (see Cunha et al., 2006; Cunha and Heckman, 2007, 2008, 2009). Building on the traditional theory of human capital, they model the formation of skills as a life-cycle process that exhibits both recursive productivity and dynamic complementarity. Recursive productivity means that the skills acquired at one stage are inputs into the learning process of the next stage, while dynamic complementarity implies that the stock of skill acquired in a period makes the investment in the next period more productive. Therefore investment in education at one stage raises the skills not only directly attained at that stage, but also indirectly the productivity with which educational investments will be transformed into further skills in the next stages. This implies that investments in early education are more productive than those at later stages and can thus increase the efficiency of the following learning process.

The empirical literature, mainly based on US studies, confirms that interventions in early childhood are generally efficient, especially when targeted at disadvantaged children, and that the positive effects are persistent over time (see surveys in Currie (2001) and Waldvogel (2002)). Results for other countries are fewer but tend to reach similar conclusions. The cross-country evidence on the topic is significantly more scant. Esping-Andersen (2004) shows that the impact of family background is smaller in countries with extensive pre-school daycare. Schütz et al. (2008) find that the length of a country's pre-school education system is positively associated with cognitive performance in middle school. They also show that more extensive systems of pre-school education—in terms of both enrolment and duration—significantly increase equality of opportunity, as measured by a lower dependence of eighth-grade students' test scores on their family background.

### 12.3.2 Expansion of Compulsory Education

Few cross-country studies have investigated the impact of compulsory schooling legislation on the actual educational attainment of the population. Brunello, Fort, and Weber (2009) exploit the exogenous variation provided by minimum-school-leaving-age laws to identify the effect of education on earnings using data from twelve European countries. They find that compulsory school reforms significantly affect educational attainment. Murtin and Viarengo (2011) study the expansion of compulsory schooling in fifteen Western European countries over the period 1950–2000 and investigate the effectiveness of this policy to increase average education in post-war Europe. They regress the average years of schooling in the over-15 population in a given country and period onto lagged compulsory years of schooling and show that the increase in compulsory schooling is a robust determinant of current changes in school attainment.

### 12.3.3 School Tracking

School tracking is a specific aspect of school stratification (or differentiation). A school system is characterized by tracking when children are allocated—at some stages of their career—to different tracks, characterized by different curricula offered (generally distinguishing between academic or vocational education) and different average ability of the enrolled students. School tracking introduces, therefore, a selection in the schooling process either in the form of self-selection or in the form of admission based on ability tests (Brunello and Checchi, 2007). National school systems differ widely in the amount of ability tracking of students they provide in school: in the age at which the selection takes place, in the degree of differentiation, in the share of students attending one track, and in the vocational orientation of the more labour-market-oriented tracks. In the majority of OECD countries, tracking takes place at age 15 or 16, but in other countries the first tracking occurs much earlier (at age 10 in Austria and Germany; at age 11 in the Czech Republic, Hungary, and Slovakia; at age 12 in the Netherlands and Belgium).

The empirical evidence has generally confirmed the inequality-enhancing effect of early school tracking, while the evidence on efficiency is more mixed. Both Hanushek and Wössmann (2006) and Ammermuller (2005) adopt similar identification strategies (differences-in-differences approach using PISA and PIRLS), finding that tracking increases educational inequality. Similar conclusions are reached by Schütz, Ursprung, and Wössmann (2008), who estimate the effect of different education policies, including school tracking, on equality of educational opportunity in fifty-four countries. All these analyses are based on student samples surveyed in the last decade or so.

When looking at lifetime consequences of tracking, Brunello and Checchi (2007) show that the negative effect of early school tracking on equality of opportunity persists beyond the school age, reducing intergenerational mobility. More recently, Hanushek, Wössmann, and Zhang (2011) have shown that having attended vocational schools (at secondary or tertiary level) provides an advantage in the short run (represented by a higher probability of employment), which decays during the course of life; for some countries, vocational education is also associated with a wage penalty. Overall, the cross-country literature suggests that early tracking accentuates the role of family background on pupils' attainment and therefore increases educational inequality. It also points to the disequalizing effect of tracking beyond school age, affecting labour market transition and lifetime income. In contrast, we are not aware of robust evidence finding beneficial effects of tracking as a means to increase average performance.[3]

### 12.3.4 School Autonomy

School autonomy (or decentralization of decision-making power) is expected to exert positive effects on student outcomes, because local decision-makers tend to have superior information to central government. On the other hand, where their interests are not strictly aligned with improving student achievement, local decision-makers may act opportunistically unless they are held accountable for the achievement of their students (see Wössmann (2005)

---

[3] These results are largely confirmed by the empirical evidence based on country-specific studies: see, for example, Dustmann (2004) for Germany; Bauer and Riphahn (2006) for Switzerland; Meghir and Palme (2005) for Sweden; Pekkarinen et al. (2006) for Finland, and Galindo-Rueda and Vignoles (2004) for the UK.

for a discussion of this topic in a principal–agent framework). Few empirical papers have studied the role of school autonomy in a cross-country framework, possibly because of the difficulty of measuring school autonomy in a comparable way across countries. Wössmann et al. (2009) show that students perform significantly better in schools that have autonomy in process and personnel decisions (such as purchase of supplies, budget allocations, hiring and rewarding of teachers, textbook choice, instructional methods, and the like). Similarly, students perform better if their teachers have both incentives and opportunity to select appropriate teaching methods. By contrast, school autonomy in budget formation and teacher autonomy over the content to be covered in class—two decision-making areas that are probably subject to substantial opportunism but little superior local knowledge—are negatively associated with student achievement. Wössmann et al. (2009) also find that the effect of school autonomy depends on the extent of accountability that affects the incentive for opportunistic behaviour. In particular, when they interact measures of autonomy with measures of accountability, they show that school autonomy is negatively associated with student achievement in systems without external exit exams (low accountability), but the association turns positive when combined with external exit exams. No clear results are obtained over the distribution of test scores.

### 12.3.5 School Accountability

Pupils' educational attainment can also be affected by the extent of school accountability, generally proxied by the presence or not of external exit exams. Cross-country evidence indicates that introducing accountability by externally testing and making students' and schools' exams public creates incentives to improve educational performance (see Bishop, 2006). The results of centralized standardized exams, by being more comparable, are more valuable as signals to the job market than the results of non-central examinations. In addition, student test results can be also used to monitor teacher and teaching quality on a regular basis and the reputation of entire schools can be based on the achievement of their students, with good schools attracting good students when the results of the tests are made public. Over the last decades, forms of accountability have been introduced in many countries to raise school performance. However, the impact of these policies in terms of inequality and aspects other than performance are not yet clear.

Hanushek and Raymond (2003) review the literature discussing the unintended consequences that accountability has produced: (average) teachers have reacted by narrowing their teaching focus to better performing students, ignoring other aspects of pupils' development. More importantly, public disclosure of school performance has increased their exposure; schools have become more selective, and aim at choosing the best students in order to improve school scores, not necessarily changing the quality of the teaching. If school accountability policies are ill-designed, namely based on performance levels rather than value-added, they may give undue advantages to schools serving students from more privileged socioeconomic backgrounds. Even in the case when they are based on value added, schools may still have an incentive to exclude disadvantaged students from official exams and place them in special education or counsel them to be absent on the days of testing. These mechanisms have clearly negative consequences in terms of equity, since they imply more exclusion, higher dropout rates, and a narrowing of the curriculum. However, there is a scarcity of empirical works that have specifically looked at the impact of accountability on educational inequality. Cross-country evidence is provided by Wössmann (2005): using student-level data from three international student test surveys (TIMSS, TIMSS repeated, and PISA), he analyses the impact of external exit exams on student performance and finds heterogeneous effects depending on students' backgrounds, students' ability, and schools' specific settings, as well as increasing effects over the course of secondary education. Also, using quantile regressions to estimate the effect of central exams on student performance for students at different points on student ability distribution, he finds that the positive impact of central examinations in performance is stronger for high-ability students, which would tend to widen the achievement distribution.

### 12.3.6 Teacher Qualifications

Measuring teaching quality is complicated because the most common observable characteristics of teachers (such as gender, age, qualifications, or experience) appear to be relatively uncorrelated to (unobservable) teachers' quality as estimated from students' testing scores, once family and school effects are taken into account (Rivkin, Hanushek, and Kain, 2005). There is a large literature that investigates the role of teacher quality and teacher incentives in improving educational outcomes, considering test scores as the outcome of interest (Hanushek and Rivkin, 2006).

Most of the recent policy recommendations to improve educational systems point to attracting, motivating, and retaining good teachers. The possibility of attracting better applicants into the profession, combined with stimulating their effort through appropriate wage policies, explains the observed correlation between teacher pay and student performance observed in a cross-country perspective (Dolton and Marcenaro-Gutierrez, 2011).

### 12.3.7 University Autonomy and Selectivity

Most European countries experienced a significant expansion in tertiary education enrolment in the recent decades, without sizeable changes in the internal organization. The vast majority of European universities are centrally organized and financed, and this reduces the degree of internal competition, especially when compared to US universities. Jacobs and van der Ploeg (2006) have clearly described the outcome of such a framework:

> European universities seem more comfortable providing a decent education for all with not much selection based on national exams and/or interviews or exams set by the universities themselves. Of course, abstaining from selection may be a legitimate policy choice, but it hurts efficiency and excellence. One big consequence is that there will be less competition on academic excellence among secondary schools, especially if there is no national exam or the national exam only sets a minimum standard. (p. 557)

They advocate a greater internal differentiation among European universities, in terms of mission, funding, and student selection. This can be accomplished by shifting funding to students and diminishing governmental control. Less attention is paid to the implications of increased university autonomy on student access. By observing the American market for tertiary education, it is an easy prediction that increased autonomy/competition among European universities will lead to increased selectivity in admission to better universities, which will probably be accompanied by rising tuition fees as well as expected wages (for a review of the US experience, see Hoxby, 2009). Less clear is the overall impact, since a rise of the signalling value of tertiary degrees may be accompanied by a rising number of applicants and/or by a rising number of places. Even more uncertain may be the implications with respect to equality of opportunities.

### 12.3.8 Student Financial Support

Several studies have suggested that liquidity constraints may prevent the children of poorer households from proceeding in their educational career up to secondary and tertiary levels (for a recent review of the literature, see Lochner and Monge-Naranjo, 2011). The empirical difficulty in assessing the extent of constraint is related to disentangling the contribution of other factors (either biological and/or cultural) to generating intergenerational dependence of children's choices from parental conditions. Oliveira Martins et al. (2007) review the existing student-loan situation in most OECD countries, showing that, when available, loan systems are designed not only to limit individual financial risks but also to provide a direct subsidy (through interest-rate subsidization, high income thresholds for repayment, and long amortization period). Despite this, in many countries the take-up rate remains low, students preferring part-time work as an alternative source of funding. The alternative of student grants has universal coverage only in a limited number of countries (USA, Scandinavia, Netherlands). They also show that the ratio of direct costs to available funds from alternative sources (loans, grants, family income) is a significant predictor of graduation rates in a panel sample of nineteen OECD countries over the period 1992–2002.

### 12.3.9 Summary of the Literature and Additional New Evidence

If we focus on the impact of the reviewed policies on school inequality, we can summarize the main findings of the previously reviewed literature in Table 12.1. We notice that some policies (such as expansion of compulsory education or financial support to college) have a clear impact on reducing inequality, mostly through the raising of the bottom tail of the distribution of intended attainments, while others (especially those aiming to expand autonomies of educational institutions) may have more uncertain effects on inequality, since they foster differentiation among schools and universities, thus boosting the attainment of better endowed students at the risk of leaving behind students from weaker backgrounds.

In Braga et al. (2013) we have collected data on reforming activities in nineteen educational areas by European governments over the last century, then aggregated in six dimensions of policy action that mostly overlap with the reviewed literature. The cross-country averages of these measures are shown in Figure 12.6. These measures are upward trended, since by construction each reform is summed (subtracted) to another if it has the same (opposite)

**Table 12.1.** Educational reforms and expected impact on educational attainment

| Area of reform | Expected impact on schooling inequality |
| --- | --- |
| Pre-primary education | reduction (through increased educational attainment of students from disadvantaged background) |
| Expansion of compulsory education | reduction (through increased educational attainment of students from disadvantaged background) |
| School tracking | ambiguous (vocational tracks have shorter duration, prevent academic enrolment, but have lower dropout rates) |
| School autonomy | ambiguous (adaptability to social environment, increased competition in presence of centralized control) |
| School accountability | increase (school differentiation, screening and sorting of students) |
| Teacher qualification | ambiguous (better quality benefits students from poorer backgrounds but allows for greater differentiation) |
| Student financial support | reduction (increased enrolment of students from poorer backgrounds) |
| University autonomy and selectivity | increase (increased signalling value of tertiary education requires a more intensive selectivity in university admissions) |

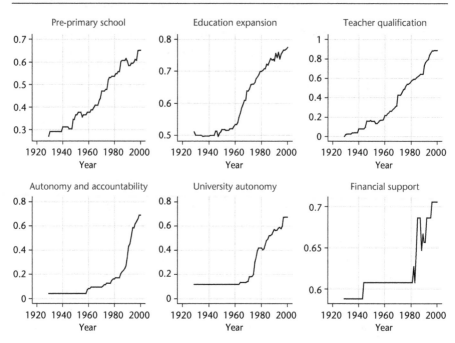

**Figure 12.6.** Temporal evolution of reform summary indices averaged across countries and rescaled in the (0,1) interval

*Source*: Braga et al., 2013, figure 7.

orientation. However, one can notice a clear sequence in the activity. The initial waves of reforms among European countries in the aftermath of World War II involved pre-primary schooling, teacher qualification, and expansion of access. The latter intensified in the following decades, when many countries raised the leaving age for compulsory education and/or increased the comprehensiveness of their secondary school systems. Widening school access required recruiting more teachers, which led to reforms raising the qualification requirements to enter the profession during the same period. At the beginning of the 1980s the pressure for increasing the access to universities led many countries to widen admission rules and/or to introduce grant policies for financially constrained students. Another common trend experienced by European countries is towards increased autonomy for universities, which took off at the end of the 1970s and continued during the 1980s and 1990s. Eventually, by the end of the 1980s, we also witness greater emphasis towards the accountability of the educational systems, which pushed many countries to establishing national assessment agencies.

These proposed measures of reforming activity were then used as regressors to account for schooling inequalities across age cohorts in European countries. Educational inequalities are measured along two dimensions: *within-cohort dispersion in years of schooling* (captured by the Atkinson index ($\varepsilon = 2$) because it incorporates an inequality aversion focussing on the bottom tail of the distribution) and *across-cohort persistence* (measured by the correlation between parental education and children attainment—it can be considered as an index of inequality of opportunities in schooling).

The main results of our analysis are reproduced in Figure 12.7, where we have reported the impact of a unitary variation of the policy activities on inequality in educational attainments (horizontal axis) and on intergenerational persistence in education (vertical axis), as estimated in the original paper. Solid lines are used when both coefficients are statistically significant, while dashed lines correspond to cases when at least one of the coefficients is statistically insignificant. Figure 12.7 represents a sort of 'menu of policies' available to governments: they clearly show that 'expansion of access' policies (which include expansion of compulsory education and de-tracking) accomplish the simultaneous goals of reducing the dispersion in the distribution of years of schooling and increasing intergenerational mobility in educational attainment. In contrast, policies addressed to tertiary education tend to reinforce intergenerational persistence (at least according to what has been experienced in European countries over the last century). However, 'financial support' policies reduce educational inequality, whereas 'university autonomy and selectivity' policies tend to increase it. Remaining policy measures (pre-primary schooling, teacher qualification, and school

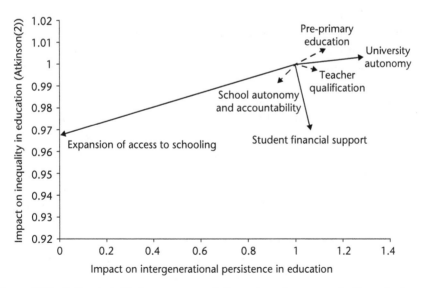

**Figure 12.7.** Estimated effects on mean and dispersion of summary indices of reforms
*Source*: Braga et al., 2013.

autonomy and accountability) exhibit smaller impacts, which do not achieve statistical significance.

There are clear potential complementarities between reforms that we do not explore here and that may increase or reduce the effectiveness of specific policies: expanding pre-primary and/or compulsory education requires more teachers; autonomy of schools should be accompanied by strengthening of their accountability, which may require the introduction of student testing; more autonomy for universities may imply greater freedom in setting tuition fees, which in turn requires stronger financial support for students; teacher autonomy should be enhanced by an increasing degree of teacher qualification; and so on. In the literature previously reviewed the usual approach is to correlate the change of *one* single policy instrument with some educational achievement (either competences or attainments). Neglecting the possible clustering of policies leads to an overestimate of the impact of each single policy.

Educational policies are clearly expensive, but some are more expensive than others. Given the fact that schooling is a highly labour-intensive process, we expect most access/expansion policies to be more costly, because in general they require the hiring of more teachers, at all levels. In contrast, policies that increase schools' and teachers' autonomy by decentralization of responsibilities affect the internal organization of the production technology, and can be relatively less expensive; however, they require the financing of potential incentives, as well as the creation of assessment agencies in order to increase the accountability of the system. We thus aim to explore the cost dimension of the reforming activity of governments. Expanding the access to schools or universities, providing financial support to students, hiring better qualified teachers, all these actions imply additional public expenditure. On the other hand, each reform generates a change in mean and variance of educational attainments. As long as they translate into GDP points, via growth regressions, they generate benefits accruing to the entire country.

In principle, one would like to assess whether the cost of each reform outweighs the benefits, in order to provide a full evaluation of the relative convenience. Unfortunately, proper data on costs of education with cross-country coverage are unavailable. One of the best sources going back to the beginning of last century is Flora et al. (1987), which unfortunately groups educational expenditure with social expenditure. Another source (Barro and Lee, 2010) contains data on a quinquennial basis, but starts only in the 1960s, excludes expenditure on tertiary education, and takes the form of expenditure per student (primary or secondary) over GDP per capita. Finally, the Unesco Institute for Statistics database <http://www.uis.unesco.org/Education/Pages/education-finance.aspx> covers almost all countries on a yearly base, but starts only from the 1970s.

Aiming to provide an order of magnitude of potential costs of reforms, we evaluate costs and benefits in terms of GDP points. The aggregate expenditure on education can be decomposed into expenditure per student, student enrolment, and age composition of the population. In fact:

$$\frac{\text{expenditure in education}}{\text{gross domestic product}} = \frac{\text{expenditure}_{\text{prim}} + \text{expenditure}_{\text{sec}} + \text{expenditure}_{\text{ter}}}{\text{gross domestic product}}$$

$$= \left( \frac{\text{expend}_{\text{prim}}}{\text{pupil}_{\text{prim}}} \cdot \frac{\text{pupil}_{\text{prim}}}{\text{popul}_{\text{prim}}} \cdot \frac{\text{popul}_{\text{prim}}}{\text{popul}_{\text{tot}}} + \frac{\text{expend}_{\text{sec}}}{\text{pupil}_{\text{sec}}} \cdot \frac{\text{pupil}_{\text{sec}}}{\text{popul}_{\text{sec}}} \cdot \frac{\text{popul}_{\text{sec}}}{\text{popul}_{\text{tot}}} \right) \cdot$$

$$\frac{\text{popul}_{\text{tot}}}{\text{GDP}} + \frac{\text{expend}_{\text{ter}}}{\text{GDP}}$$

$$(1)$$

If we consider that duration of primary and secondary school are of comparable length in most countries, we can rewrite this as:

$$\frac{\text{expenditure in education}}{\text{gross domestic product}} \cong \left( \frac{\text{pupil}_{\text{prim}}}{\text{popul}_{\text{prim}}} \cdot \frac{\dfrac{\text{expend}_{\text{prim}}}{\text{pupil}_{\text{prim}}}}{\dfrac{\text{GDP}}{\text{popul}_{\text{tot}}}} + \frac{\text{pupil}_{\text{sec}}}{\text{popul}_{\text{sec}}} \cdot \frac{\dfrac{\text{expend}_{\text{sec}}}{\text{pupil}_{\text{sec}}}}{\dfrac{\text{GDP}}{\text{popul}_{\text{tot}}}} \right) \cdot$$

$$\frac{\text{pupil}_{\text{prim/sec}}}{\text{popul}_{\text{tot}}} + \frac{\text{expend}_{\text{ter}}}{\text{GDP}}$$

$$(2)$$

The variable enclosed in brackets in equation (2) is available in the series provided by Barro and Lee (2010). We can therefore study the relationship of public expenditure in schooling with the summary indices of reforms, after computing their five-year averages in order to match the frequency of expenditure data. Not surprisingly, we find that reforms expanding access (that normally require hiring additional teachers) are more expensive than organizational reforms concerning accountability or teacher recruitment. Taking the estimated coefficients at face value, and weighting a pupil cohort one-tenth of the entire population (since our constructed dependent variable should be reweighted by the incidence of a primary/secondary school cohort on the entire population), they suggest that pre-primary reforms may cost 2.3 GDP points, while expansion reforms may cost 1.7 GDP points (this is an underestimate because we do not have information on tertiary expenditure). Reforming teacher recruitment or school autonomy does not reach one percentage point (see Table 12.2).

Moving to the benefit side, a back-of-the-envelope calculation suggests that additional years of education increase the average human capital of

**Table 12.2.** Cost of educational reforms, OLS

| Variables | Expenditure in education over GDP | Estimated impact on GDP (β/10) |
|---|---|---|
| Pre-primary index | 0.228*** | 0.023 |
| | (0.067) | |
| Expansion of access index | 0.170*** | 0.017 |
| | (0.026) | |
| Teacher qualification index | 0.083*** | 0.008 |
| | (0.012) | |
| School autonomy index | 0.099*** | 0.010 |
| | (0.019) | |

*Note*: 93 observations referring to 15 countries—reforms are included separately—country fixed effects included.
*Source*: Braga et al., 2013.

**Table 12.3.** Benefits of educational reforms, OLS

| Variables | Years of education | Estimated impact on GDP (β*0.05) |
|---|---|---|
| Pre-primary index | 1.321*** | 0.066 |
| | [0.357] | |
| Expansion of access index | 0.566*** | 0.028 |
| | [0.178] | |
| Teacher qualification index | 0.172** | 0.008 |
| | [0.073] | |
| School autonomy index | 0.735*** | 0.037 |
| | [0.147] | |

*Note*: 329,102 individual observations, referring to 24 countries—reforms included separately—country and year fixed effects included.
*Source*: Braga et al., 2013.

employed workers and therefore total factor productivity. We abstract from distributional effects, which may reinforce the growth impact. Using reported estimates from de la Fuente and Ciccone (2002, table 1), one additional year raises GDP by 4 (macro) up to 6 (Mincerian) percentage points among European countries (as in our sample). If we take a conservative view of 5% as the rate of return, we obtain the values shown in Table 12.3.

Thus a full pre-primary reform (from 0 to 1) would raise GDP by about 6.5 points, while expansion reform would yield 2.8 GDP points. In both cases gains exceed costs. Reforming teacher recruitment produces 0.85 GDP points, almost in line with costs. Finally, school autonomy reforms yield 3.6 points. This is the most cost-effective reform, with pre-primary reform reaching similar cost-effectiveness.

We can now conclude this section by summarizing the main points concerning schooling inequalities and educational policies. The first message is that policies are effective in shaping the distribution: both the cursory review of the literature and our new evidence agree on this point. The second message is that some reforms are more effective than others in reducing inequality, irrespective of whether inequality is measured within generations or across generations. In particular, we have shown that policies that widen the access to secondary and tertiary education are the most effective in reducing inequality. We have also highlighted the possibility of policies that increase existing inequality because they raise selectivity in admissions. The third message concerns cost-effectiveness: while more detailed data would be necessary to realize a proper cost–benefit evaluation, we have offered rough estimates that nevertheless provide an order of magnitude of these dimensions.

## 12.4 What Drives Educational Policies?

In previous sections we have shown that earnings inequality is shaped, among other things, by inequalities in educational attainment and in competences. The question now is what accounts for country differences in educational policies. In the companion volume, country chapters indicate that the expansion of secondary schooling has been pursued by almost all countries, while differences emerge about their strategies in widening or restricting access to tertiary education. Some countries are enlarging the access (Greece, Korea, Baltics, Sweden), while others are restricting it, or at least not encouraging it (Slovenia, Spain). This may be due to several factors, among which one may list:

a) different (ideological) opinions about the target for a college-educated workforce;
b) different (ideological) opinions about the desired extent of public subsidization;
c) different degree of state indebtedness;
d) different (equilibrium) labour-market return to education.

While the fourth explanation goes beyond the goal of the present chapter, because it involves the analysis of phenomena such as skill-biased technological change and globalization (Acemoglu and Autor, 2011), we now provide some cues to a better understanding of the other three points.

Iversen and Stephens (2008) offer a general framework of analysis. They emphasize the mutually reinforcing relationships between social insurance, skill formation, and spending on public education, identifying *three distinct worlds of human-capital formation*: a first one (referred to as 'Coordinated Market economies with proportional representation and Social Democratic governments') characterized by redistribution and heavy investment in public education and industry-specific and occupation-specific vocational skills; a second one (referred to as 'Coordinated Market economies with proportional representation and Christian Democratic governments') characterized by high social insurance and vocational training in firm-specific and industry-specific skills but less spending on public education; and a third one (the traditional 'Liberal Market economies with majoritarian representation') characterized by heavy private investment in general skills but modest spending on public education and redistribution. While the first group of countries invests more public resources in higher education, the other two are rather similar in terms of spending less. However, the general skills of the population at the bottom end in the second group are significantly better. They attribute this difference to the incentives for general skills acquisition in vocational education (specific skills) systems for those not intending to pursue higher education. As a consequence, earnings inequality is lowest in the first group and highest in the third one, with vocational education acting as an inequality-reducing institution because it raises the level of competences of the least-endowed individuals, who are also most likely to end up at the bottom of the earnings distribution.[4]

Iversen and Stephens (2008) also provide evidence of the importance of political orientation of governments in selecting the level of expenditure on educational policies. In the same vein, Braga et al. (2013) show that the type of educational reforms is correlated to the political orientation of governments. They test the assumption that parties with a left-wing orientation are more supportive of educational expansion policies (which they term 'inclusive' policies, because they raise the mean and lower the variance of attainments), because they benefit the lower tail of the educational attainment distribution, where their supporters are largely overrepresented. In addition, they may expect a more intense political participation from lower-class people, which should translate in stronger electoral support. Conversely, conservative parties are assumed to be more reluctant towards any generalized

---

[4] 'Information age literacy is strongly to very strongly related to all policy variables...In addition, it is extremely strongly and negatively related to the degree of inequality, measured here by the Gini index for disposable household income among households in which the household head is aged 25 to 59 years old. The correlations between information age literacy and the 5th and 95th percentile scores indicate that variations in information age literacy are primarily a product of variations at the low end of the distribution, and it is there that the inequality factor plays a large role as indicated by the fact that the national average 5th percentile score is very strongly related to inequality, whereas there is virtually no relationship between the average 95th percentile score and inequality' (Iversen and Stephens, 2008: 621).

expansion of schooling, for at least two reasons: firstly, educational expansion requires an expansion in public expenditure; secondly, expansion raises people's expectations with respect to future lifetime incomes, which may translate into higher wage pressure and rigidities. In both cases, policies are undertaken under varying external circumstances, concerning growth and availability of public resources. Parties' differences may have been attenuated in recent years due to reduced ability to finance public expenditure (Korpi and Palme, 2003).

Our main results are reported in Table 12.4.[5] From this table one may observe that educational reforms classified as *inclusive* tend to be negatively correlated with a right-wing attitude of parliaments. This is always true under any specification for access expansion policies, while reforms of pre-primary schooling and teacher qualification change sign according to the policy measure we use. In contrast, *selective* policies exhibit positive correlation with right-wing parliaments (in all cases but the school autonomy index). It is then clear that the political orientation of the parliament matters for the type of educational policies undertaken. The other regressors

**Table 12.4.** Educational reform and political variables, OLS, 1950–2000

|  | 1 | 2 | 3 | 4 | 5 | 6 |
|---|---|---|---|---|---|---|
|  | Pre-primary | Expansion of access | Teachers | School autonomy | University autonomy | Financial support |
| Right-wing orientation of parliament | −0.006* | −0.026*** | 0.033** | 0.016 | 0.029** | 0.030** |
|  | [0.004] | [0.004] | [0.015] | [0.015] | [0.012] | [0.013] |
| log GDP per capita | 0.190*** | 0.189*** | 0.202* | −0.363*** | −0.552*** | 0.467*** |
|  | [0.036] | [0.044] | [0.122] | [0.113] | [0.109] | [0.101] |
| Government share | 1.131*** | 0.778*** | 2.340*** | 0.117 | 4.528*** | 4.942*** |
|  | [0.181] | [0.239] | [0.868] | [0.776] | [0.831] | [0.770] |
| Observations | 843 | 843 | 843 | 843 | 770 | 770 |
| $R^2$ | 0.901 | 0.899 | 0.871 | 0.864 | 0.893 | 0.828 |
| Countries | 24 | 24 | 24 | 24 | 17 | 17 |

*Notes*: Robust standard errors in brackets. * significant at 10%; ** significant at 5%; *** significant at 1% constant, country and year fixed effects, country-specific time trend included.
*Source*: Braga et al., 2013.

[5] Data on policy orientation of political parties elected to parliament and selected cabinets are taken from ParlGov database (Döring and Manow, 2010), which codes each party elected on a 0–10 scale, ranging from 0 (most left-wing) to 10 (most right-wing). By taking seat-weighted average of parties elected to a legislature or supporting a cabinet, we obtain a measure of the *political orientation of policymakers*. External circumstances are controlled for using data from Penn World Tables v.7.0.

suggest that inclusive educational policies are more likely in richer countries/ periods, given the positive association with per-capita income, while public expenditure in value added seems to favour reforms. It is worth noticing that reforms associated with school autonomy and accountability do not exhibit statistically significant correlations with either the ideological orientation of parliaments nor with the availability of resources, but tend to be negatively correlated with (log of) GDP per capita. Given the inclusion of country-specific time trends, this suggests that these policies are more likely to occur in recession years.

Despite the set of controls for confounding factors, it is impossible to claim the existence of causal links between electoral outcomes and reforming activity of governments, since reverse causality is a real issue in this type of analysis (that is, people may vote following promises that are implemented later on). However, finding significant correlations with ideological inclinations of parliaments reinforces our claim that the reforming activity variables are truly exogenous for individual educational choices, and therefore they matter in shaping the distribution of educational attainment in the population.

Some further understanding of the political process underlying the selection of educational policies can be obtained by surveys on people's attitude towards public expenditure in education. Busemeyer (2012) shows that high levels of socioeconomic inequality enhance the conflict between the rich and the poor over public investment in education. By contrast, when access to higher levels of education is effectively restricted, the rich are more likely to support spending on public education. This is because higher levels of educational stratification ensure that further public investment in education benefits the rich relatively more than the poor, who in turn become less willing to support this kind of public spending.

## 12.5 How Are Educational Policy, Quality and Quantity of Education, and Income Inequality Related?

Now that we have seen that educational policies are related to the quality and quantity of education in a society, and that we have studied how policies have emerged, an important question in the light of this book is how educational quality and quantity are related to the level of income inequality. It is well known that education and earnings are related (see Card (1999) and Heckman et al. (2006) for reviews of the Mincerian approach). Less attention has been devoted to the relationship between the distribution of schooling and the distribution of earnings (see Peracchi (2006) for a notable exception), probably because causality may go in both directions. An increase in earnings inequality may prevent educational investments when households are liquidity-constrained (Galor, 2011), but may also represent an incentive to acquire further education. General equilibrium models should account for the relative speeds of expansion of demand and supply for skills (the so-called 'Tinbergen race'; see Acemoglu and Autor, 2011).

More recently, a few studies have investigated the relationship between earnings inequality and the distribution of education, distinguishing between quantity (typically measured by the years of schooling) and quality of educational attainments (measured by level of competences). As a consequence, inequality in earnings may depend on the distribution of years of education and of competences. Blau and Kahn (2005) were among the first to study this problem using micro-data from IALS.[6] They claim that the greater dispersion of cognitive test scores in the United States plays a part in explaining higher US wage inequality.[7] In the same vein, using the Canadian version of the same survey, Green and Riddell (2003) show that the impact of literacy on earnings does not vary across quantiles of the earnings distribution, while the interaction of schooling and literacy is statistically insignificant. Their result can be interpreted as a signal that competences provide an autonomous contribution to observed inequality, conditional on identical school attainment.

A different approach has been followed by Bedard and Ferrall (2003), who study the correlation between the distribution of competences and the wage distribution of workers in the same age cohorts. They show that Lorenz curves for a cohort's wages always lie above of the cohort's test score Lorenz curve. However, in their analysis, they do not take into account the mediating role played by schooling, which is intertwined in a complex way with parental background (see again Chapter 5 in the present volume). Therefore, in Checchi and Van de Werfhorst (2013) we have replicated a similar exercise, extending the sample size and including the distribution of the years of schooling, in order to consider inequality along both the quantity and quality dimensions.

In Chapter 5 of this volume various measures of inequality in educational distributions were presented. It was shown that the dispersion in attained level of education is reduced across time, while elsewhere in this volume it

---

[6] IALS is a survey collecting information on adult literacy in representative samples for some OECD countries. It was implemented in different years–1994, 1996, 1998–for different countries using a common questionnaire. The central element of the survey is the direct assessment of the literacy skills of respondents, but the background questionnaire also includes detailed information on individual socio-demographic characteristics. For more information, see <http://www.statcan.gc.ca/dli-ild/data-donnees/ftp/ials-eiaa-eng.htm>.

[7] They write, 'For example, a one standard deviation increase in test scores raises wages by 5.3 to 15.9 percent for men and 0.7 to 16.2 percent for women, while a one standard deviation increase in education raises wages by 4.8 to 16.8 percent for men and 6.8 to 26.6 percent for women.'

has been demonstrated that income inequality has been on the rise in many countries. Even though we will show positive relationships between educational dispersion and income inequality, it must be borne in mind that rising earnings inequalities are to a large extent due to rising within-education-group inequalities (Lemieux, 2008; Van de Werfhorst, 2007b).

Drawing on the study by Checchi and Van de Werfhorst (2013), we can bring together measures of inequality in years of educational attainment, inequality in mathematics test scores (all tested in Grade 8, around the age of 14), and income inequality, for cohorts born around 1950, 1966, and 1981. Overall, we possess an unbalanced panel covering twenty countries with sixty-four observations (32 country/cohort × 2 genders). Figure 12.8 shows the plot of the relevant data.

From the graph we can observe that there is a positive correlation between inequality in quantity and inequality in quality of education for the country/gender/cohort cell available (north-west panel). The quality of education is also positively correlated with earnings inequality (computed over employees—north-east panel). In the south-east panel we contrast earnings inequality for dependent employees and for total employment: the relationship between the two is altered by the extent of self-employment, labour-market participation (which varies significantly across countries in accordance with gender), and unemployment and early retirement (which are both computed at zero incomes).

Checchi and Van de Werfhorst (2013) have regressed earnings inequality measures onto corresponding inequality measures for years of schooling (quantity measured over the same population on which non-negative/positive earnings are available) and for mathematics test scores when the same cohort was fourteen years old, controlling for country fixed effects. The results confirmed that inequality in quantity and inequality in quality of human capital are related to the observed earnings inequality.[8]

Further analyses of Checchi and Van de Werfhorst (2013) took a more elaborate perspective on the relationship between educational policy change (the data in Section 12.3, based on Braga et al. 2013), the distribution of skills and educational attainment, and income inequality. Using an instrumental variables design to instrument educational quality and quantity on educational policy indicators, adding country and birth-year fixed effects, Checchi and Van de Werfhorst (2013) showed that inequality in years of education is reduced in countries which expanded pre-primary education or raised the leaving age for compulsory education. Conversely, inequality in test scores is

---

[8] This is not evident from the south-west panel of Figure 12.8, which however is considering only a bivariate comparison for a subset of country/years. For wider evidence on this, see also Chapter 5.

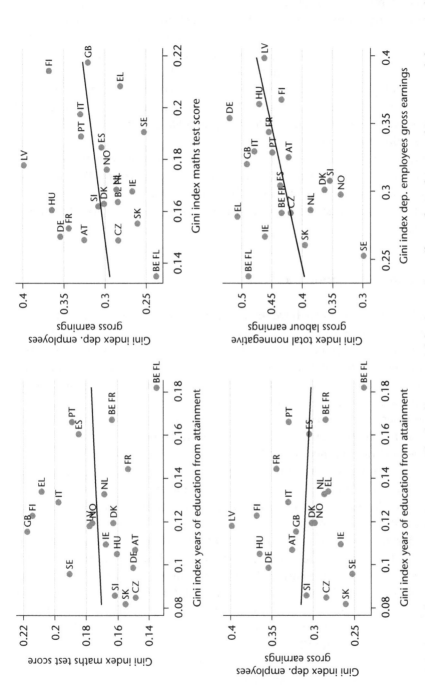

**Figure 12.8.** Inequality in competences, years of schooling, gross labour earnings (from dependent employment and from total employment)

*Source:* Checchi and Van de Werfhorst, 2013.

reduced by reforms introducing standardized tests and/or reinforcing school accountability, while it is enhanced by late tracking and reforms that expand university access. Figure 12.9 plots the bivariate association between two educational reforms (years of compulsory education and university access policies) and inequality in education. Both types of inequality (in educational quality and quantity) are then positively correlated with earnings inequality, even when instrumented. Figure 12.10 shows the equivalent of a reduced form, where inequality in dependent employment earnings is scatter-plotted against educational reforms.

Thus, there is evidence that inequality in education affects inequality in earnings along both dimensions, quality and quantity. Furthermore, inequality in quality (as measured by student test scores) and inequality in quantity (as measured by years of schooling) respond to educational policies.

## 12.6 Concluding Remarks

Overall in this chapter we have seen that educational reforms exhibit a complex relationship with income inequality, especially when considering inclusive policies. These policies are effective in reducing earnings inequality, but they are also more expensive. Other things being equal, they exacerbate the conflict over the allocation of the public budget. We can therefore observe the equivalent of multiple equilibria, depending on initial conditions.

Countries characterized by low income inequality support a high level of investment in education, both from private and public sources. Low inequality in education and income in the parent generation implies lower inequality of opportunities for the offspring generation, as well as reduced conflict in the selection of (redistributive) public expenditure in education. This in turn yields lower inequality in educational attainments, which reinforces the stability of this configuration.

A different configuration occurs in countries with high initial inequality in incomes. This prevents parental investment in children's education for poor families, as well as exacerbating the internal conflict on public expenditure. The resulting equilibrium results in lower public investment in education and greater inequality in educational outcomes. Once in the labour market, the offspring generation experiences higher earnings inequality, which again reinforces the stability of this alternative equilibrium.

The transition from one equilibrium to the other is not easily identifiable, despite variations in political attitudes observed in many European countries. The social desirability of one or the other outcome should also be evaluated

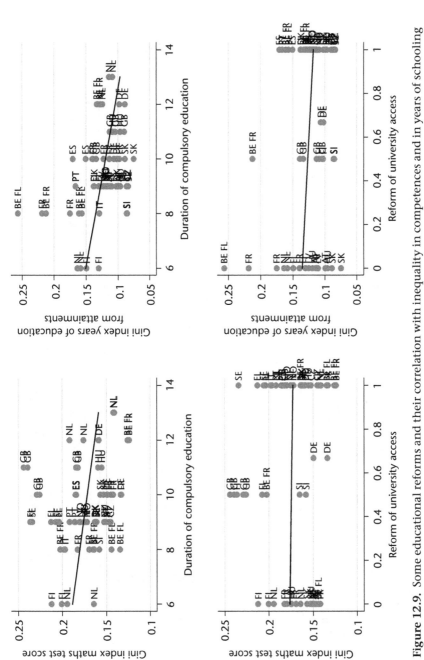

**Figure 12.9.** Some educational reforms and their correlation with inequality in competences and in years of schooling

*Source:* Checchi and Van de Werfhorst, 2013.

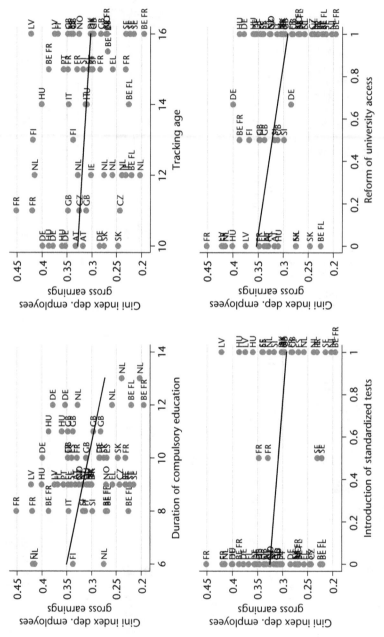

**Figure 12.10.** Some educational reforms and their correlation with inequality in earnings

*Source:* Checchi and Van de Werfhorst, 2013.

against the social consequences of inequalities, which have been surveyed in previous chapters of this volume.

Yet, an orientation towards educational policies in order to address income inequalities offers an important complement to other policies addressed in the previous two chapters of this volume. The dispersion in attained level of education has been decreasing in many societies, a matter that can be explained by rising educational attainments in educational structures that are rather fixed. Yet, the contemporary political debates in Europe imply that we should focus more on improving excellence in the distribution of skills in secondary schools too. If a focus on improved performances in mathematics and languages improves the performance of all, it may be possible to enlarge the stock of skills in society without affecting the income distribution. However, if excellence is generated at the top, while the middle and bottom parts of the skill distribution do not benefit from education policy, it may be the case that rising income inequalities are to be expected.

# 13

# Conclusions: Inequality, Impacts, and Policies

*Wiemer Salverda, Brian Nolan, Daniele Checchi, Ive Marx, Abigail McKnight, István György Tóth, and Herman van de Werfhorst*

This volume and the collaborative research project on which it is based come at a time of ever more pervasive worries about growing inequalities in rich and not-so-rich countries, their consequences for society, and the potential for collective action to counteract these trends and effects. The worsening of the income distribution in most of the advanced economies in the last thirty years has been a main reason behind the resurgence of the debate on inequality.

As early as the 1980s, influential writings were already predicting a growing divide between 'winners' and 'losers' in post-industrial advanced economies. De-industrialization, economic globalization, and technological progress played a central role in such claims. Standardized mass production, it was argued, was giving way to specialist production in rich countries, with profound implications for the relative fortunes of more-skilled versus less-skilled workers in those countries. The winners, estimated at roughly a third of the population, would be those with the talents and education to compete and thrive in the global economy, with the costs being borne by the less skilled.

Looking back over the past twenty to thirty years from where we stand now, the biggest 'winners' have turned out to be even more of an elite group than the top third of highly educated and talented workers, or so it appears. The fiercest debate today is about the disproportionate income gains made by the top 1%, and the even more extreme gains by a tiny group at the peak of that elite segment. The Great Recession, meanwhile, may have made the rich temporarily somewhat less rich, but it is deeply affecting the daily lives of the unemployed and the poor and the prospects for the future of many of the employed.

Against the backdrop of such debates and concerns, this volume first re-examines claims that inequality is inexorably on the rise, and that this is part of a general trend across developed economies. We systematically map income inequality trends at various levels, and elaborate on earnings and wealth, in thirty countries over the past three decades, complementing existing analyses. Jointly with this mapping we endeavour to shed additional light on the drivers of inequality, the forces underpinning observed trends, with a special focus on education and its tremendous expansion in recent times.

The GINI project and this volume have devoted much of their attention to investigating the impacts of increasing inequality across core domains of social and political life. Wilkinson and Pickett have prompted much interest in this issue with their book *The Spirit Level*, which argues that income inequality is harmful to society in a range of ways. Societies with higher income inequality are judged to have lower levels of social cohesion, higher crime rates, higher mortality rates, worse health, more educational inequalities, lower social trust, and lower political involvement. While their claims have been the subject of much academic debate and at times strong criticism on methodological and empirical grounds, they have resonated remarkably in the wider societal debate. Thus the question of what impacts there are from income inequality on other spheres, if any, has been a major concern of the book and the underlying research.

A third major component has been policy. What has policy done to restrict—or perhaps endorse—the growth in market income inequalities? What, if anything, can policy do to counteract that growth? What can policy do to make sure that those at the lower end of the income redistribution obtain a share of economic resources that allows for a decent life in a rich society? Here the book looks in particular into employment, social protection, social investment, and education, which are core elements of European Union policy objectives and strategies at national and supranational level. In addition to the headline targets of an employment rate of 75% and tertiary educational attainment by 40% of the younger generation, the Europe 2020 agenda contains clear poverty and social-inclusion targets. Together with the European's recent Social Investment Package (European Commission, 2013) aimed at human-capital investment, these are a cornerstone of an effective policy to combat poverty and social exclusion in Europe, complementing the effects of growth and employment.

In the remainder of this concluding chapter we concisely sum up the key findings in the different fields and the broader messages coming out of this book. We will also mention remaining research questions and possible avenues for further research and end with reflections on what this means for policy.

## 13.1 Income, Earnings, and Wealth Inequalities

As a point of departure for the present volume the Introduction summarizes evidence from the companion volume of thirty country studies (Nolan et al., 2014) that income inequality has increased in most of the developed world from the 1980s, albeit with some variation in timing and magnitude. In Chapter 2, when looking at the sources of variation in this respect, we find that the thirty-year period can be split into two main sub-periods: in the first one, earnings are the main driver of increasing inequality in income; in the second one, reduced redistribution by the state and the shift from labour to capital become the main drivers. Sometimes, regional inequality growth lies hidden behind a stable national outcome (Belgium); also, increasing inequality at the top and bottom tails of the income distribution may not show up in the standard Gini coefficient (Spain, Greece, Ireland), or a stable outcome at the beginning and end of the period may be the product of decline followed by increase (France). An assessment of causal explanations found in the literature shows that the focus on long-run 'equilibrium' stories such as international trade and technical change presents some significant empirical puzzles. A more convincing story that takes into account a broader set of stylized facts, suggests a role for structural imbalances related to international relations and the global distribution of capital, and also for ideological changes that shape policy orientations. The same factors seem to be closely intertwined with the increase of instability of the global economy that paved the way for the financial crisis. The linkage between an unequal world and an unstable world is a strong argument in favour of reducing the sources of inequality. Finally, there may also be a causal channel running from the financial crisis to inequality. As a response to the crisis strong fiscal consolidation is put in place, through increasing indirect taxation, cuts in public spending, and other measures that tend to increase inequality. As long as the national or international *fault lines* that created inequality and financial instability persist, the timing and the way in which fiscal consolidation has been implemented will result in a higher level of inequality, without addressing its main underlying causes.

Chapters 3 and 4 dwell on two important issues that are not captured in the above focus on income inequality (and are examined here in addition to the GINI country studies): the effects of earnings from labour on the income distribution on the one hand, and the distribution of wealth, a dimension of riches significantly different from income, on the other hand. Annual earnings in the labour market are by far the most important contributor to household market incomes. In a cross-country perspective of twenty-five European countries based on the EU-SILC survey data, the inequality of these earnings also drives the distribution of household incomes to a large extent and at all levels—not only for market incomes but also after transfers, taxation, and equivalization in relation to household size and composition. This labour effect concerns the inequality over the distribution as a whole, as measured by the Gini coefficient, but particularly also the top shares in the income distribution.

We consider how income generated by individuals in the labour market links to the household earnings distribution, how household earnings inequality compares to labour market inequality, and how joint labour supply is organized across households. The main conclusion is this: households do in fact enhance labour-market inequality, slightly more than doubling it, primarily by working more hours as a result of household joint labour supply higher up the distribution. Interestingly, this enhancing effect is rather similar across the twenty-five countries with only a few exceptions. So, households do make an important contribution to the level of inequality in earnings within all countries but they add relatively little to cross-country variation. As a result, between countries the initial individual wage inequality is decisive, its cross-country differences are substantial, and these are amplified by the household contributions. Investigating the organization of joint labour supply across households distinguished by the number of earners (single, dual, and multiple) we find multiple earning—and their hours worked—strongly concentrated at the top of the earnings distribution. The incidence of dual earners and multiple earners differs significantly between countries, but the two are largely complementary to each other, which helps to mitigate the inequality effect. Thus the composition of the household population may differ between countries while at the same time the aggregate contribution of household earner demographics to inequality is much the same across the countries.

Wealth is an important dimension of inequality receiving far less attention than income or earnings, partly because of data availability and quality but also because it has been regarded as less important than income when looking at the wellbeing of households. While income and expenditure are typically analysed separately from each other, wealth cannot be fully understood without accounting for the opposite side of the balance sheet, debt, if only in terms of assessing current liabilities and financial wellbeing. In addition, studying wealth is complicated by its varied nature— housing, capital, business ownership—and the lack of information about

331

often highly important elements such as pension entitlements; studying wealth inequality can be complicated also by the presence of negative values. Even if the comparison of cross-country indicators of wealth inequality is cumbersome, there are two straightforward facts to be noted. First, wealth inequality is high relative to income inequality. Second, it increased over the last decades in some countries and over the few years from the Great Recession in others. The reasons for this increase can be found in the growing importance of financial assets, of debt in some countries, and of billionaires, and in the developments of taxation. Our examination also highlights that an insightful analysis of wealth inequality needs to take into account the income position of households. The distribution of wealth over income is less dispersed than wealth itself, with the exception of the USA. This can be explained by the role played by debt, which is clearly linked to income.

As the stock of wealth reflects the accumulation of historical inequalities between households and gives an indication of how current inequalities will project into the future, it can convey more information about the financial wellbeing of households than an exclusive emphasis on the financial flows of incomes. There is also evidence that wealth is a driver of socioeconomic inequalities, over and above income and education, through a 'wealth effect'. As higher-quality comparable wealth data become available it is likely that this topic will attain more prominence in the future.

## 13.2 Educational Inequalities

Educational inequality is a well-known key driver of income and other socioeconomic inequalities and is further discussed in Chapter 5. Educational inequality can be identified according to three main indicators of individual education: the number of years of schooling completed, the levels and types of qualification achieved, and the test scores that capture actual competences. The first and the last are the more comparable across countries, while the second is more reliant on the institutional design of the education system, which is country specific. While all three indicators define inequality within each generation, inequality of opportunities can be assessed by looking at the distribution of educational attainment in one generation relative to the same distribution in the generation of its parents. Over the last century, most rich and not-so-rich countries have achieved almost universal attendance at secondary schooling (saturation). Therefore a core issue facing educational policies in advanced economies is the further expansion of schooling at tertiary level, where social origins are still strong determinants of educational opportunities.

At tertiary education level, countries are still very different, and cross-country convergence is far from being realized. Up to the oldest generations the Nordic, Eastern European, and Anglo-Saxon countries have higher participation rates while, in spite of growth, Continental European countries remain behind and do not catch up. The difference mainly relates to dual systems, as found in Germany and elsewhere, that for a long time have constrained access to tertiary education while promoting higher secondary vocational training. The persistence of cross-country differences and the absence of convergence to a 'common European model' are also witnessed by the lack of a common pattern of development. While some still claim that there is an inverted U-shaped relationship between income inequality and economic development, no such relationship is found in the data on educational inequality in Europe. If anything, inequality in schooling (measured by the Gini index computed over the years of schooling) is rising among the youngest cohorts in many European regions.

Despite a declining trend in educational inequality, we do not observe an analogous trend in earnings inequality, even though the two measures are positively correlated (though at a varying degree of explanatory power). Among the possible explanations of these diverging trends, one main factor concerns the distribution of competences in the adult population. Unfortunately, for the vast majority of European countries we do not have repeated observations on the level of competences of the same individuals, and scholars are forced to make heroic assumptions about the stability of the distributions over different age cohorts. However, existing datasets (such as IALS, ALL, or the forthcoming PIACC) provide snapshots of the distribution in representative samples of the population, which allow decomposition of the relative contribution of social origin, schooling, and labour-market experience in the formation of competences.

## 13.3 Social Impacts

Increasing inequalities in income, wealth, and education may be regarded by many as objectionable in themselves, but another core concern to which they give rise is the potential negative impact they may have on a very wide and diverse range of social problems. We have examined the relationship between income, education, or wealth inequality and a range of outcomes, including poverty, family formation, trust, crime, health, housing, and intergenerational mobility. There are indeed sometimes striking correlations at the country level between income inequality levels and aggregate indicators of social outcomes in the domains just listed. There is considerable debate about whether such correlations reflect a causal relationship, the joint determination of these outcomes and inequality by other underlying factors, or a purely spurious relationship. While there has been interesting debate and speculation about potential channels of influence, strong channels of causal transmission from increasing inequality to these social outcomes have not been convincingly demonstrated in the literature.

The first main focus of attention here (in Chapter 6) is on a range of outcomes brought together under the broad banner of 'social cohesion', such as poverty and deprivation, the family, crime, trust, and social capital. In addition to looking at overall outcomes, we have looked at social gradients and other measures of inequality.

The empirical relationship between income inequality and poverty depends in the first place on how poverty is defined and measured. When poverty is measured vis-à-vis relative income thresholds, poverty and income inequality are seen to be strongly associated with each other, but one still cannot simply 'read off' trends in poverty in a particular country, or rankings compared with other countries, from conventional summary inequality measures. When the focus is instead on poverty vis-à-vis thresholds fixed in purchasing-power terms, or on material deprivation, the major factor accounting for differences across countries and change over time is average income levels. Income inequality contributes little extra to explaining cross-country differences in deprivation once this is taken into account, though changes in inequality over time may have some impact on trends in deprivation. Average income levels and deprivation both influence subjectively assessed levels of economic stress, but deprivation seems to have the greatest impact where national income levels are high and inequality is low.

As far as family-related features such as fertility, marriage and divorce, lone parenthood, etc. are concerned, many of these are not characterized by a distinct and consistent social gradient across countries. Even where they are, income inequality per se does not seem to play a major role in accounting for differences across countries, and trends in income inequality explain little of the dramatic changes in family life seen in many countries in recent decades. The relationship between income inequality and crime is particularly difficult to assess empirically, partly due to the variability in crime statistics across countries and over time. There is some evidence for a relationship between income inequality and levels of violent crime, but crime rates in many counties have fallen when income inequality was increasing, notably in the USA, and income inequality is clearly only one of a complex set of factors at work. Patterns of punishment, however, bear a much clearer relationship to income inequality and welfare regimes.

Some social-psychological features such as levels of social solidarity and trust are associated with inequality levels in a bivariate context, but when appropriate control variables are introduced and multi-level and longitudinal forms of statistical analysis applied the relationship is weak or non-existent. While there is some evidence of a negative association between income inequality and self-reported happiness, it is limited and not clear-cut. Overall, the findings with respect to inequality and various aspects of social cohesion highlight the importance of seeing income inequality as only one facet of social stratification more broadly conceived.

In Chapter 7, the focus then turns to the relationship between income inequality and health, the topic of some of the most active debates and research on the social impacts of inequality. Research in this field in the course of the GINI project looked *inter alia* at the relationship between self-assessed health, income, and material deprivation, using longitudinal data for Spain. The results show at the general level that individuals' relative position in the income distribution, in terms of the gap between their income and others, has a negative effect on health, while absolute income level does not (controlling for this gap). However, with the more detailed focus on poverty it is actual material deprivation that has a negative effect on health rather than one's deprivation level relative to others'. Where individuals suffer financial difficulties, lack basic necessities, live in poor housing, and go without key durables this is bad for their self-assessed health, but relative income also matters. This provides an important perspective on the 'absolute versus relative income' debate.

Another study, of the relationship between mortality rates and poverty rates across rich countries, used pooled cross-sectional time-series models to identify a significant relationship between child poverty and infant/child mortality. Interesting differences were found between welfare regime types, with Nordic regimes outperforming other regime types in terms of limiting infant and, to a lesser extent, child mortality; however, a number of other regime types outperformed Nordic regimes when it comes to adult mortality.

The fracturing of jobs into 'good jobs' and 'bad jobs' has accompanied the general upward trend in inequality in many countries. The link between job quality (working conditions and employment relations) and health has received far less attention than that between income or social gradients despite the fact that employment relations and conditions form the conceptual basis of many social classifications. There is accumulating evidence that adverse working conditions are related to poorer health, particularly the mental health of workers, and that low pay is related to poorer physical health. This is an important area of research not just for understanding the social determinants of health inequalities but also the social impacts of and behind recent inequality trends.

Poor housing conditions are detrimental for health but the overall relationship between inequality and housing is complex and could run in both directions. The literature in this area explores relationships between inequality and house prices, housing quality, access to different tenure types, and status competition encouraging households to make riskier investment decisions. Home-ownership rates have tended to rise across much of Europe in recent decades (except in Germany). Governments have tended to encourage home ownership, even among low-income households—a subject of much recent debate in the USA—and ownership rates have been affected by property value developments, demographic change, mortgage-market deregulation, and building activity. Increases in income inequality can drive up house prices as higher-income households can afford to pay more. Increasing house prices can benefit existing owners but can also prevent low-income households entering the housing market, or mean a fall in the quality of the houses they can afford to buy. There is some evidence from the USA that increasing income inequality results in low income households experiencing more crowding and leads to increases in house prices. Research reported in this volume has focused specifically on the relation between income inequality and access to housing for low-income households. The effect of income inequality in countries at a similar level of economic affluence is found to operate through the absolute level of resources, while in countries at different stages of economic development, differences in affluence determine access to housing. Higher inequality was found to be positively related to the likelihood of experiencing crowded housing conditions for low-income owners.

The growth in income inequality across many countries over the last thirty years and the variation in inequality across countries at a point in time have led analysts to question whether higher inequality is associated with lower rates of intergenerational mobility. The evidence on cross-country variation in intergenerational income mobility suggests it is negatively correlated with income inequality. The evidence from within-country studies analysing the effects of changes in inequality on intergenerational mobility are less clear-cut. For the UK, for example, economists find falling intergenerational income mobility as inequality increased, but sociologists dispute this, pointing to estimates of stable social class fluidity over the same period. Evidence for the USA suggests that intergenerational mobility remained fairly stable as income inequality increased.

Recent contributions to the intergenerational-mobility literature present new evidence on intergenerational mobility in the top of the income and earnings distributions. Using a large dataset of matched father–son pairs in Sweden, intergenerational transmission is found to be very strong in the top of the two distributions, more so for income than for earnings. Sons' IQ, non-cognitive skills, and education are all found to be unlikely channels in explaining this strong transmission. The greater persistence in income than earnings suggests that it is the capital income component that drives this finding. Results suggest that Sweden, known for having relatively high intergenerational mobility in general, is a society where transmission remains strong in the very top of the distribution, and that wealth is the most likely channel. These findings are important particularly as a number of countries have experienced increases in concentration of income, earnings, or wealth at the very top of the distributions over recent years. In a similar vein, GINI project studies have looked at the effects of parental wealth holdings, financial assets, and housing equity, on children's outcomes in early adulthood, including educational attainment, labour-force participation, earnings, and home ownership. For all these outcomes positive associations were found with parental wealth, which operate over and above the influence of parental education and income. These results suggest that wealth plays an important part in the way parents' financial position can influence their children's future lives.

## 13.4 Political and Cultural Impacts

Important societal consequences of inequalities may be found in the political and attitudinal spheres. If political attitudes and behaviours become more strongly stratified between status groups in unequal societies, inequality may have far-reaching effects on what people believe is fair, how they participate in politics and associations, and how they vote. And, perhaps even more important, if such strongly stratified political behaviours and opinions are reinforced by the distribution of incomes, there may be severe consequences for the legitimacy of the political system of Western societies.

Several economic and sociological theories formulate a link between income inequality and redistributive preferences, which is examined in Chapter 8. When inequality increases, people with falling incomes will obviously express increased needs for social redistribution. However, some theories also highlight that under circumstances of rising economic uncertainty (of which inequality is only one aspect) it is not only the social groups with falling incomes but also the less well-off facing uncertainties who may opt for higher levels of social spending. People's expectations, their social context or values, and their views on the reasons for poverty (whether it is due to lack of individual effort or to luck in life) may have a significant impact on the individual preferences for social policy.

When the evidence about macro and contextual determinants of redistributive preference is analysed, it turns out that higher inequality is associated with stronger preferences for redistribution. In addition, it is found that the structure of inequality (i.e. the relative distances between the various income groups) matters for the determination of the demand for more social spending. The deeper the poverty is, the larger the demand for redistribution. However, while higher inequality induces a larger strain on the state, the existing (pre-crisis) size of the state may constrain its further growth and the extension of redistribution, not only in terms of the public budget but also in terms of the attitudes of the public. Also, support for policies depends on the form of the proposed redistributive programmes (cash or in kind, assistance or insurance type), and the potential targets (which segments and social groups are considered as the needy), as well as on the institutional setting (whether education, unemployment benefits, or health spending, to name a few).

If people have preferences concerning the level of inequality, then their desired level of redistribution will depend also on the difference between the level of inequality perceived and the level of inequality desired. Consequently, the information people have about the level of existing income inequality and the values they hold about the acceptable level of inequality are important inputs into the formation of redistributive preferences. Cross-sectional studies show that perceived levels of inequality is to some extent higher in countries with higher income inequality, and accepted levels of inequality also tend to be higher. Results exploiting inter-temporal variation in inequality and attitudes show that attitudes towards inequality seem to respond to changes in actual inequality: discontent with inequalities increases when inequality is rising. Discontent with the level of inequality, however, increases only moderately with the rise of inequality, which might result from the increase in individuals' accepted levels of inequality when actual inequality is on the rise.

Political participation is one of the most important factors that can have a large effect on the level of redistribution. More highly educated people are more likely to vote, and, if voter turnout decreases—and it has been decreasing dramatically in most European countries—it is likely that the turnout for less educated, lower-income people will decrease relatively more, as observed, for example, in the UK. Lower-income people are more likely to support greater redistribution, and therefore a diminishing turnout might influence politics to reduce the level of redistribution aspired to, which in turn might affect the resulting level of inequality. This has an impact on political choices (regarding redistribution), but can also affect legitimacy and approval of democratic procedures.

As has been said, rising inequality may have important repercussions on the legitimacy of democracies in European and other Western societies. Inequality, according to the research carried out in the GINI project and reported in Chapter 9, systematically affects both public opinion and the orientations of political parties.

It appears that positive attitudes towards democracy are negatively related to the level of inequality in a society. Individual-level income is positively related to support for democracy, a relationship that holds regardless of the level of income inequality in the country. Importantly, in established democracies, the gap between rich and poor in terms of their support for democracy increases as inequality rises. This increasing polarization occurs not so much because the poor are less supportive of democracy than the rich in unequal societies, but mainly because the rich are much more supportive of democracy in egalitarian societies. This finding also has implications for electoral politics. If governments hope to increase democratic values, they must convince the wealthier part of society that an egalitarian society may be in their own interest.

In addition, as inequality rises, people tend to be less concerned with societal responsibilities such as politics and civic participation. However, there is also evidence that higher inequality is associated with a stronger work ethic. In unequal societies people tend to think that wellbeing is the responsibility of individuals themselves rather than of government or society as a whole. These findings are consistent with the idea that the level of income inequality found in a particular society largely reflects public opinion. That is, high levels of income inequality are largely a function of limited policies of redistribution, which in turn reflects the idea of individuals' own responsibility. Such a pattern of increased reliance on one's own efforts, and less on others, may be detrimental to the 'social contract' underlying collective social policies. In that sense, high levels of trust and solidaristic sentiments can serve as a protective factor, with policies to combat increasing inequality more likely to be supported, and their erosion can heighten the risk of further increases.

Importantly, the *salience* of the redistribution issue mentioned above is of paramount importance. Inequality appears to influence public opinion on redistribution only when inequality is a significant political issue. Salience is not guaranteed, however, because those who benefit most from redistribution—i.e. those on low incomes—often feel they have little say in politics and thus tend to be less engaged. Of particular concern to the salience issue is the legitimacy of political decisions. The gap in participation between the rich and poor, or between the well-educated and the poorly educated, is larger in unequal societies than in egalitarian societies. This would mean that, in more unequal societies, there is a larger gap between public opinion on redistribution and actual political decision-making on this issue, simply because redistribution is a less important issue. A misrepresentation of public opinion (especially of people belonging to the lower parts of the income distribution) could invoke further gaps in political participation between the advantaged and the disadvantaged. As income inequality rises, politics could become more strongly the domain of the well-educated and the better-off.

Finally, we also explored how transnational forms of governance may be affected by inequality. In this regard, it is clear that inequality has direct repercussions both for how political parties position their public platforms and commitments, and for public opinion on European integration. Political parties tend to be more concerned with the protection of workers against globalization when inequality is high. Globalization has winners and losers, and the 'losers' (i.e. low-skilled workers) need protection. Not surprisingly, there is evidence that the losers have become increasingly critical of European integration. It is particularly interesting that parties on the far right of the political spectrum have become especially affected by inequality. Centre-left and centre-right parties, however, have become less protectionist or nationalistic, illustrated by more modest anti-globalization positioning irrespective of the level of inequality. The general effect of increasing inequality, however, has been to dampen enthusiasm of parties and publics to embrace supranational integration.

Together with a range of other findings, the bottom line of our research is that inequality poses substantial dangers to democracy and openness in national political life, highlighting the importance of policies and measures that may redress inequality.

## 13.5 Redistributive and Educational Policies

Observing the debate on how to reduce income inequality and what is arguably its most problematic manifestation, poverty, one is struck by how widely opinions vary about the relative merits of alternative courses of action. On some key issues views are in effect diametrically opposed. This is perhaps nowhere more true than when it comes to the role of work, particularly paid employment. An important section of opinion basically holds that more people in work equals fewer people in poverty and, by implication, that an elaborate welfare state with large-scale redistributive efforts is not a prerequisite for a low level of poverty, provided that enough people have jobs. The idea that, ultimately, the best and most sustainable egalitarian strategy is an employment-based strategy has long been advocated and is scrutinized in Chapter 10. The basic argument has common-sense appeal. People who are not in work tend to occupy the lower strata of the income distribution. If more jobs become available and low-income people take up these jobs, improving their income position, the result is a selective rise of incomes at the lower end and thus a reduction in income inequality and the share of the population in poverty relative to the median. An alternative view holds that we are increasingly confronted with a trade-off between employment (that is, non-government employment) and income equality. The idea here is that high levels of non-subsidized employment can in present-day economic circumstances only be achieved at the cost of a large low-paid (service) sector and more 'poverty in work'. Such arguments are in line with an important stream in the academic and popular literature on the effects of economic globalization and skill-biased technological change on the labour-market position of less qualified workers in rich countries. Research does suggest that this picture of a uniform shift away from low-skilled work needs nuance. Technological change, real as it is, has not simply entailed a demand shift away from lower-skilled labour and towards more highly educated workers. There has been job growth in both the highest-skilled (professional and managerial) and lowest-skilled occupations (personal services), with declining employment in the middle of the distribution (manufacturing and routine office jobs) as a result. While the dynamics in the different segments of the labour market are complex, the overall picture does add up to one of increasing inequality.

What is also clear is that past employment growth in Europe and elsewhere—and we should not forget that there were very strong net employment gains prior to the crisis—did not deliver the hoped-for declines in poverty and inequality. In fact, the contrary was true for the most part. Employment growth, where it occurred, did not primarily benefit poor people, and this happened in a context of eroding income support as provided through social insurance and social assistance. The overall redistributive impact of the tax/benefits systems also declined. The reasons why job growth did not benefit the poor are complex. Policy options exist to make sure that the poor partake more when new job opportunities arise. Active labour-market policies can play an important role here. But we should be under no illusion. When it comes to improving the plight of persons with the weakest profiles in terms of skills, experience, and aptitudes, active labour-market policies appear to have their limits. There are simply no examples of countries that achieve low poverty just by having well-functioning labour markets without extensive direct income redistribution mechanisms. The Nordic countries stand out in having high employment rates in combination with low poverty rates and overall inequality levels. It should not be forgotten that precisely the same countries also spend heavily on direct income transfers, including towards those already in work. The combination of work and welfare-state income is more pervasive there than anywhere else. In addition, income support provisions for those with no work attachment are among the most generous and adequate from the point of view of poverty relief. The European Commission recently stated that social protection is an additional cornerstone of an effective policy to combat poverty and social exclusion in Europe, complementing the effects of growth and employment. It is important that this does not remain a vague intention. Minimum-income protection levels have declined.

Policymakers can, if they have the political support, bring about a (partial) reversal by bringing social safety nets to a higher level.

Important voices argue, however, that policy should shift from fighting symptoms to tackling in more comprehensive and radical ways the root causes of exclusion, low earnings, and limited upward mobility. Within the social-investment strategy public services are a key instrument. These are the subject of Chapter 11. Some actually advocate a drastic reallocation of social expenditures towards such services, and then especially those services that support families in coping with the work–family life balance, and those that enhance human capital. The social-investment strategy intends to sustain a skilled and flexible labour force, which can easily adapt to the constantly changing needs of the economy and thrive in it. Optimally, it brings both an increase in economic efficiency and also a reduction in inequality and poverty, or so it is claimed. In-kind provisions of all types matter if societies are to be made more egalitarian. The mounting empirical evidence on childcare services and early childhood education brings out very diverse results, with some cautionary notes. In most countries the actual use of childcare services remains socially stratified. This is even the case in some countries where the consumer cost of such services is close to zero for those on the lowest incomes. Other parameters matter, such as access, availability, and quality of the services. Moreover, if quality of childcare is not similar within a country and low-income families typically mainly use lower-quality care, then this may hamper egalitarian outcomes in the longer run. As a result, investment in equal quality is also important, as are connections with other policy domains, such as complementary parental-leave systems and the quality of the regular school system.

As already mentioned, educational policies are effective in reducing educational inequalities, even if some reforms are more effective than others, irrespective of whether inequality is measured within generations or across generations. Policies that broaden the access to secondary and tertiary education are the most effective in reducing inequality in schooling. By matching age cohorts from different datasets we have established that competences acquired when in school are as important as years of schooling in shaping earnings inequality later on in the labour market. This throws up the question of which policies are capable of reducing educational inequalities along either the quantity dimension (years of schooling) or the quality dimension (competences acquired in school). When considering the first dimension (schooling), we claim that some policies (such as expansion of compulsory education or financial support in college) have a clear impact of inequality reduction, mostly through raising the bottom tail of the distribution of intended attainments. However, other policies (especially those aiming to expand the autonomy of educational institutions) may have more uncertain effects on inequality, since they foster differentiation among schools and universities, thus boosting the attainment of financially better endowed students at the risk of leaving behind students from more disadvantaged backgrounds. Conversely, when looking at the other dimension (competences) there is consensus in the literature that postponing the age of tracking in the educational system contributes to reducing the dispersion of competences. This contrasts with policies aimed at raising the degree of standardization of inputs (i.e. reducing the degree of school autonomy) and/or introducing central examinations, which seem less effective in reducing educational inequality in competences. In addition, a vocationally oriented secondary school system, which stimulates retaining in school the least motivated students (who often are also students with poorer cultural backgrounds), reduces the dispersion in competences in the adult population.

We have also highlighted the possibility that policies increase inequality because they raise the selectivity in admissions to education. In addition, we have investigated what drives the adoption of different educational policies within countries, and found support for the notion that progressive parties favour the expansion of access to education as a means to reduce income inequality, while conservative parties disregard the necessary homogeneity of public education, supporting policies that lead to school differentiation and competition.

## 13.6 Further Research

The *evolution of income inequality* throws up the interesting question of whether the groupings of countries that we established at the face value of their trends in income inequality can be linked to shared underlying factors and thus stand up to further scrutiny. Similarly, it is important to see how the examples found of episodic instead of gradual changes in inequality, which bring inequality to a seemingly structurally different level over a short period, relate to possible factors driving such rapid changes, and to tease out the implications for a broader understanding of inequality trends and explanations.

The findings on the *contribution of earnings inequality* raise some important questions for further research. First, they underline the role of household-earner demographics as a contributor to earnings and income inequality, in conjunction with the distribution of employment in relation to household joint labour supply. Beyond the effects of part-time employment in relation to dual earning, multiple earning in itself deserves more attention, including in relation to the role of single-person households, which seem to abound where multiple-earner households are few. There is also a case for examining the effects of pay correlation between household members in a comparative framework. In addition, it seems commendable to analyse the relationship in the opposite direction and look at the effect that the household dimension of labour supply and earnings may have on labour-market inequalities, going beyond the perspective of the individual that is so central to the common analysis of these inequalities. For example, as a result of household joint labour supply a specific part-time segment of employment may be growing where a full-time worker 'can no longer go' and where the motives of labour supply and the rules of labour-market competition may differ. Finally, the rise in individual educational attainment may affect household labour supply and shift the boundary of household joblessness upwards along the educational distribution if educational homogamy concentrates labour market success among a smaller fraction of households.

With regard to *the role of wealth and wealth inequalities* there is still a long way to go for the systematic collection of internationally comparable and more comprehensive data. This can provide a more complete description of levels and trends with an improved country coverage, but should allow also a deeper analysis of the contributions of individual and household characteristics.

With respect to the generation of inequality in individual earnings as a *result of educational attainment*, there are at least two lines of research that are in their infancy: one concerns the formation of competences and their connection to the labour market; the other deals with modelling the institutional design of educational systems. Social scientists still know little about the role of cognitive and non-cognitive abilities, except for the fact that when they are partially observed these measures appear to be strongly correlated with labour-market outcomes (employability, earnings, prospect of career). It is not yet clear how these abilities are formed and whether (and when) they start decaying over the life-cycle. We do not even know whether there is some assortative mating based on these traits. Most of our ignorance derives from lack of appropriate data, despite their collection in other research fields, and a priority for the future is that research should progress in this direction. The other major knowledge gap relates to cross-country differences. The vast literature on the varieties of capitalism has proposed various classifications of national economies according to scope and size of welfare systems. The equivalent effort with respect to educational systems is less developed. The existence of tracking versus comprehensive systems of secondary education is well-recognized, but it is more complex to combine various dimensions and cover the whole range from pre-primary to tertiary education. The underlying issue here is whether there is a spontaneous convergence towards a unified model for educational systems in advanced countries, or whether this can be encouraged by means of imitating best practices. Here the literature seems not to have achieved a unanimous consensus.

In seeking to capture and understand the ways in which increasing inequality may *impact on social outcomes* that are central to individual and societal wellbeing, further research might usefully take as its point of departure the message emphasized here, that at a focus on income inequality per se, especially as captured by single summary indicators such as the Gini coefficient, is unduly narrow. Adopting a broader stratification perspective incorporating (at least) social class and education, while much more complex to implement, is likely to be productive in moving forward a contentious set of interlinked debates that risk being trapped down a succession of blind alleys. To make significant progress, it will be important to develop and use longitudinal and multi-level data that allow causal processes to be properly explored. It will also be helpful to focus even more on mechanisms and on specifying testable hypotheses. This is a challenging task because of the data requirements and necessary modelling sophistication. Indicators of some social outcomes also need to be elaborated and combined into validated reliable indices where possible, since at present undue reliance has to be placed on specific individual items. In certain key domains, notably the study of deprivation and of the intergenerational transmission of advantage and disadvantage, the scope for comparative analysis is increasing but will continue to be constrained by the pace of improvement in the availability of harmonized data.

The research reviewed in this volume suggests a number of areas where future research could improve our understanding of the relative importance of *various drivers* and the *dynamic relationship between inequality and social outcomes*. For health, it was shown that relative income and absolute material deprivation are associated with poorer health outcomes in one country. It would be interesting to see if this finding can be replicated across countries and whether changes in relative income and absolute material deprivation over time are associated with a deterioration in health outcomes. A better understanding of the link between adverse working conditions and health and how recent trends in income inequality have been accompanied by changes in job quality is also important for developing policy recommendations to limit avoidable poor health.

The relationship between inequality and intergenerational mobility describes how inequality in one generation is imprinted onto the fortunes of the next generation. Recent research that seeks to establish the *transmission processes* and identify *policies that increase mobility* needs to be fostered. The increase in concentration at the top of income and wealth distributions observed in a number of countries appears to be a greater cause for concern if the results for Sweden are indicative of a broader trend towards rich dynasties. To explore this social phenomenon further requires high-quality longitudinal data.

Concerning the *impact of inequality on political outcomes*, this volume has mostly looked at citizen's attitudes and behaviours, and the legitimacy problem that arises from a stratification in politics among the population. It is, however, possible that the political consequences of increasing inequalities extend beyond individual outcomes, implying that there may be other channels through which inequality threatens the legitimacy of the political system. Some of these alternative routes could be studied in future research. One line of research that could be fruitful is to study how money can 'buy' political influence in different systems, and to study whether inequality enhances the opportunities for the top-income groups to mobilize their political power in this way. In the United States, the exceptionally high costs involved in running for elections is likely to induce a power difference between the rich and the poor that cannot be observed by simply looking at attitudes or political participation in population surveys. It will also be important to study the extent to which, among European countries, differences in how political parties are funded and in how elites are able to mobilize their political interest through financial contributions run in parallel with inequality levels in societies.

Another possible future line of research on political outcomes of inequality concerns the process of public opinion formation, and how different organizations are able to influence the population's viewpoints on poverty, meritocracy, and the redistribution of resources. It is interesting to see that opinions on inequality largely reflect factual inequality levels. It is possible that think tanks, public intellectuals, and non-governmental organizations play a key role in how the attitudes are formed, and it would be relevant to study whether inequality is related to the level of influence that these parties are able to exert.

Several *key challenges in the area of policy research* remain. Boosting employment rates continues to be a prime policy objective in many countries, in part driven by the idea that 'the best protection against poverty is a job'. We know that employment growth has so far not delivered better outcomes in terms of reduced poverty and inequality. We know in part why this is, but the many and complex underlying causal dynamics have not been fully charted. One important question is why joblessness at the household level tends to be so persistent even in a context of high labour demand. The relative role of economic mechanisms, for example financial incentives of tax and benefit systems as these operate at the household level, versus more sociological mechanisms, for example the effects of educational homogamy, social capital, or neighbourhood effects, needs to be explored more systematically. Another crucial question is how we can improve minimum-income provisions for those unable to make a decent living through the labour market. The adequacy of minimum-income protection leaves much to be desired almost everywhere, but at least a number of countries manage to combine relatively high minimum-income protection levels with well-functioning labour markets. What are the key conditions for generous income protection to be compatible with low chronic dependence? Particularly, what is the role of activation, empowerment, monitoring, and sanctioning policies? Income-support provisions that supplement low earnings appear to work relatively well in some settings, although relatively little is known about their longer-term effects, for example on wages, mobility, and skill formation. There continues to be a lively debate on whether targeting low incomes actually enhances or reduces the redistributive impact of policies. New evidence suggests that targeting may not be so bad, but the optimal level for various policies and in various settings still remains to be determined. Attaching requirements to benefits is also increasingly in vogue. There is a growing literature on conditional cash transfers (CCTs) in developing economies, but the short- and longer-term effects of various conditions still require further exploration, especially in the context of advanced economies.

Human and social investment is now high on the policy agenda. It seems entirely sensible that policy should focus on tackling in more comprehensive and radical ways the root causes of economic disadvantage. The range of policies that are discussed under the heading of social investment is very broad, and it is impossible to discuss here the many research questions that remain open. One clear research priority concerns the social stratification in the take-up and longer-term effects of many of such social-investment policies. Childcare services, for example, tend to have more beneficiaries towards the top of the income distribution. Even where childcare is not scarce, of good quality, and provided almost free of private costs for people on low incomes, the effective take-up remains skewed towards the higher-income groups. This may have less to do with the design of the policy itself than with the context in which the policy is embedded. In addition to the social stratification in take-up, there is evidence of social gradients in the longer-term effects. This may have to do with quality differences in the services to which people of various means have access, but many other factors appear to be at play as well.

## 13.7 Summing Up

Summing up, richer countries appear to face an uphill battle to keep economic inequality in check. The evidence that income inequality, at the level of earnings, market income, or disposable household income, has been trending upwards over the past decades in a majority of these countries is relatively robust, albeit that sometimes important discrepancies exist across data sources that create uncertainty about the magnitudes of those increases. In addition, the trend towards rising inequality has not been universal. It has not happened in all countries, or to the same extent. Trends have rarely been linear. Increases in inequality, where these have happened, often occur in relatively short spells. This observation raises the issue of whether rather uniform and long-run structural trends such as globalization or skill-biased technological and organizational change, which are often proposed as the main drivers, are mediated, moderated, accelerated, or perhaps up to a point even replaced by other changes such as in demography, institutions, or even outright policymaking, which in turn could relate to a shifting politico-cultural basis.

The major question addressed in the book, and the research project underpinning it, was then the following: even if one did not regard rising inequality as problematic in itself, should it be a cause of great concern because of its impact on other outcomes of general importance, such as health outcomes and educational attainment (at the same time potential drivers of inequality), social cohesion and inclusion, intergenerational mobility, crime, democracy, and political participation and values? The evidence that higher income inequality in and of itself is harmful to a range of such outcomes, in terms of national averages or within-country gradients, varies across domains, and much of that evidence relates to cross-country variation in inequality and outcomes, which may reflect deeper factors. Increases in inequality over time have not been robustly linked to worsening social outcomes, though these may emerge in time as higher-quality longitudinal data become available and techniques that allow us to test causal relations are applied: the challenge of identifying, quantifying, and explaining a robust causal link between rising inequality and worsening outcomes remains. The fundamental role of social stratification more broadly conceived is manifest across most of the social domains studied, but income inequality on its own may be too narrow and specific a focus to fully capture this very complex set of phenomena. If the concern is not with income inequality itself but with its potential negative social impacts, redistribution of income may not in any case be the most obvious way of addressing such unwanted outcomes. Even if lower levels of income inequality create a setting conducive to better (distributional) outcomes in terms of health, education, social connectedness, etc., a strategy of income redistribution is unlikely to be very cost-effective. Public money is probably much more efficiently used on direct interventions to improve health, education, or social-cohesion outcomes, and to reduce social gradients in those outcomes.

That said, people at the very bottom of the income distribution do face very real consequences from having insufficient financial resources. Financial poverty does affect health, material living conditions, social ties, etc., although the effects are not just a result of financial constraints. Financial poverty also affects child development and later chances in life. In other words, from the viewpoint of the empirical evidence there does exist a clear imperative to redistribute income so as to alleviate poverty and promote equality of opportunities. Designing policies aimed at preventing situations of economic disadvantage arising in the first place does not mean relegating direct redistribution to the background. Focusing on the other tail of the income distribution, though, the findings with respect to political behaviour presented here also underpin deep concerns about the way in which increasing income inequality can lead to greater political influence for the better-off, and especially the rich, feeding in turn into policies that further increase inequality. Such a dynamic may be among the many factors contributing to the economic crisis, which poses such risks for the life chances of the young and disadvantaged in many of the countries studied here.

This brings the state, and its redistributive role, back to centre stage. A substantial role for the state is compatible with a well-functioning and dynamic economy, where high and rising levels of inequality are not an inescapable fact of life. Higher employment, productivity, and social cohesion are achievable, but this requires collective action, with an associated price in terms of the share of income that individuals retain for their personal consumption. The best performers among the rich countries in terms of employment and economic and social cohesion have one thing in common: a large welfare state that invests in people, stimulating and supporting them to be active and adequately protecting them when everything else fails. This continues to offer the best prospect for rich countries pursuing growth with equality.

# References

Aaberge, R., M. Bhuller, A. Langørgen, and M. Mogstad (2010a). 'The Distributional Impact of Public Services When Needs Differ'. *Journal of Public Economics*, 94: 549–62.

Aaberge R. and A. Langørgen (2006). 'Measuring the Benefits from Public Services: The Effects of Local Government Spending on the Distribution of Income in Norway'. *Review of Income and Wealth*, 52(1): 61–83.

Aaberge, R., A. Langørgen, and P. Lindgren (2010b). 'The Impact of Basic Public Services on the Distribution of Income in European Countries'. Paper presented at Net-SILC conference, Warsaw, March 2010.

Acemoglu, D. (2002). 'Technology and the Labor Market'. *Journal of Economic Literature*, 40: 7–72.

Acemoglu, D. (2007). 'Equilibrium Bias of Technology'. *Econometrica*, 175: 1371–1410.

Acemoglu, D. (2011). 'Thoughts on Inequality and the Financial Crisis'. Available at <http://econ-www.mit.edu/files/6348>

Acemoglu, D. and D. Autor (2011). 'Skills, Tasks and Technologies: Implications for Employment and Earnings'. In O. Ashenfelter and D. Card (eds), *Handbook of Labor Economics, Vol. 4B*. Amsterdam: North Holland, 1043–1171.

Adema, W., P. Fron, and M. Ladaique (2011). 'Is the European Welfare State Really More Expensive?: Indicators on Social Spending, 1980–2012; and a Manual to the OECD Social Expenditure Database (SOCX)'. Paris: OECD.

Aebi, M. and A. Linde (2010). 'Is There a Crime Drop in Western Europe?' *European Journal on Criminal Policy and Research*, 16(4): 251–77.

Aghion, P. (2002). 'Schumpeterian Growth Theory and the Dynamics of Income Inequality'. *Econometrica*, 70: 855–82.

Aghion, P., E. Caroli, and C. García-Peñalosa (1999). 'Inequality and Economic Growth: The Perspective of the New Growth Theories'. *Journal of Economic Literature*, 37: 1615–60.

Alesina, A., R. Di Tella, and R. MacCulloch (2004). 'Inequality and Happiness: Are Europeans and Americans Different?' *Journal of Public Economics*, 88: 2009–42.

Alesina, A. and P. Giuliano (2010). 'Preferences for Redistribution'. In A. Bisin and J. Benhabib (eds), *Handbook of Social Economics, Vol. 1A*. Amsterdam: North Holland, 93–132.

Alesina, A., E. Glaeser, and B. Sacerdote (2001). 'Why Doesn't the United States Have a European-Style Welfare State?'. Brookings Papers on Economic Activity 2. Washington, DC: The Brookings Institution.

Alesina, A. and E. La Ferrara (2000a). 'Participation in Heterogeneous Communities'. *The Quarterly Journal of Economics*, 115(3): 847–58.

Alesina, A. and E. La Ferrara (2000b). 'The Determinants of Trust'. National Bureau of Economic Research Working Paper WB7621.

Alessie, R., V. Angelini, and G. Pasini (2011). 'Is It True Love? Altruism versus Exchange in Time and Money Transfers'. Ca' Foscari University of Venice Working Paper 7.

Allègre, G. and K. Jaehrling (2011). 'Making Work Pay for Whom? Tax and Benefits Impacts on In-Work Poverty'. In: N. Fraser, R. Gutiérrez, and R. Peña-Casas (eds), *Working Poverty in Europe: A Comparative Approach*. Basingstoke: Palgrave Macmillan, 278–303.

Allmendinger, J. (1989). 'Educational Systems and Labor Market Outcomes'. *European Sociological Review*, 5: 231–50.

Amiel, Y., F. Cowell, and A. Polovin (1996). 'Inequality amongst the Kibbutzim'. *Economica*, 63: 63–85.

Ammermüller, A. (2005). 'Educational Opportunities and the Role of Institutions'. ZEW Discussion Paper, 05-44.

Andersen, R. (2012). 'Support for Democracy in Cross-National Perspective: The Detrimental Effect of Economic Inequality'. *Research in Social Stratification and Mobility*, 30: 389–402.

Andersen, R. and T. Fetner (2008). 'Economic Inequality and Intolerance: Attitudes toward Homosexuality in 35 Democracies'. *American Journal of Political Science*, 52: 942–58.

Andersen, R. and S. Milligan (2011). 'Immigration, Ethnicity and Voluntary Association Membership in Canada: Individual and Contextual Effects', *Research in Social Stratification and Mobility*, 29(2): 139–54.

Andersen, R. and M. Yaish (2012). 'Public Opinion on Income Inequality in 20 Democracies: The Enduring Impact of Social Class and Economic Inequality'. GINI Discussion Paper 48.

Anderson, C. and M. Singer (2008). 'The Sensitive Left and the Impervious Right: Multilevel Models and the Politics of Inequality, Ideology, and Legitimacy in Europe'. *Comparative Political Studies*, 41(4–5): 564–99.

Andress, H.-J. and H. Lohmann (2008). *The Working Poor in Europe*. Cheltenham and Northampton, MA: Edward Elgar.

Andrews, D., A. Caldera Sanchez, and A. Johansson (2011). 'Housing Markets and Structural Policies in OECD Countries'. OECD Economics Department Working Paper 836.

Andrews, D. and A. Leigh (2009). 'More Inequality, Less Social Mobility'. *Applied Economics Letters*, 16: 1489–92. Extended version available as ANU CEPR Discussion Paper 566.

Antoninis, M. and P. Tsakloglou (2001). 'Who Benefits from Public Education in Greece? Evidence and Policy Implications'. *Education Economics*, 9(2): 197–222.

Arrighi, G. (2008). *Adam Smith in Beijing* (2nd edition). Verso.

Atkinson, A. (2009). 'Factor Shares: The Principal Problem of Political Economy?' *Oxford Review of Economic Policy*, 25(1): 3–16.

Atkinson, A. and A. Brandolini (2006). 'From Earnings Dispersion to Income Inequality'. In F. Farina and E. Savaglio (eds), *Inequality and Economic Integration*. London: Routledge, 35–62.

Atkinson, A., B. Cantillon, E. Marlier, and B. Nolan (2002). *Social Indicators: The EU and Social Inclusion*. Oxford: Oxford University Press.

Atkinson, A. and S. Morelli (2010). 'Inequality and Banking Crises: A First Look'. Available at <http://isites.harvard.edu/fs/docs/icb.topic457678.files/ATKINSON%20 paper.pdf>

Atkinson, A. and T. Piketty (2007). *Top Incomes Over the Twentieth Century: A Contrast Between Continental European and English-Speaking Countries*. Oxford: Oxford University Press.

Atkinson, A., T. Piketty, and E. Saez (2011). 'Top Incomes in the Long Run of History'. *Journal of Economic Literature*, 49(1): 3–71.

Atkinson, A. and J. Stiglitz (1976). 'The Design of Tax Structure: Direct Versus Indirect Taxation'. *Journal of Public Economics*, 6(1–2): 55–75.

Austen, S. (2002). 'An International Comparison of Attitudes to Inequality'. *International Journal of Social Economics*, 29: 218–37.

Autor, D. et al. (2003). 'The Skill Content of Recent Technological Change: An Empirical Exploration'. *The Quarterly Journal of Economics*, 118(4): 1279–1333.

Backlund, E., P. Sorlie, and N. Johnson (1996). 'The Shape of the Relationship Between Income and Mortality in the United States: Evidence from the National Longitudinal Mortality Study'. *Annals of Epidemiology*, 6: 12–20.

Ball, M., M. Harloe, and M. Martens (1988). *Housing and Social Change in Europe and the USA*. London: Routledge.

Ballarino, G. (2011). 'Germany: Change through Continuity'. In M. Regini, (ed.), *European Universities and the Challenge of the Market*. Cheltenham: Edward Elgar, 132–52.

Ballarino, G., F. Bernardi, H. Schadee, and M. Requena (2009). 'Persistent Inequalities? Expansion of Education and Class Inequality in Italy and Spain'. *European Sociological Review*, 25: 123–38.

Ballarino, G., E. Meschi, and F. Scervini (2013). 'Expansion of Schooling in Europe—A Long-Run Perspective'. GINI Discussion Paper 83. Available at <http://gini-research. org/articles/papers>

Ballarino, G., H. Schadee (2010). 'Allocation and Distribution. A Discussion of the Educational Transition Model, with Reference to the Italian Case'. *Research in Social Stratification and Mobility*, 28: 45–58.

Banca d'Italia (2000). *Supplements to the Statistical Bulletin—Methodological Notes and Statistical Information*.

Banca d'Italia (2012). 'Household Income and Wealth in 2010'. *Supplement to the Statistical Bulletin* 6.

Banerjee, A. and E. Duflo (2011). *Poor Economics: A Radical Rethinking of the Way to Fight Global Poverty*. New York: Public Affairs.

Barbier, J.-C. and W. Ludwig-Mayerhofer (2004). 'Introduction: The Many Worlds of Activation'. *European Societies*, 6(4): 423–36.

Bargain, O., H. Immervoll, A. Peichl, and S. Siegloch (2010). 'Distributional Consequences of Labor Demand Adjustment to a Downturn'. GINI Discussion Paper 1.

Bargain, O. and K. Orsini (2007). 'Beans for Breakfast? How Exportable Is the British Workfare Model?'. In O. Bargain (ed.), *Microsimulation in Action. Policy Analysis in Europe using EUROMOD*. Research in Labour Economics, 25. Oxford: Elsevier, 165–98.

Baron, R. and D. Kenny (1986). 'The Moderator-Mediator Variable Distinction in Social Psychological Research'. *Journal of Personality and Social Psychology*, 51(6): 1173–82.

Barro, R. and J.-W. Lee (1996). 'International Measures of Schooling Years and Schooling Quality'. *American Economic Review*, 86(2): 218–23.

Barro, R. and J.-W. Lee (2001). 'International Data on Educational Attainment. Updates and Implications'. *Oxford Economic Papers*, 3: 541–63.

Barro, R. and J.-W. Lee (2010). 'A New Data Set of Educational Attainment in the World, 1950–2010'. NBER Working Papers 15902, National Bureau of Economic Research, Inc. Available at <http://www.nber.org/papers/w15902.pdf>

Barth, E. and K. Moene (2009). 'The Equality Multiplier'. NBER Working Paper 15076. Cambridge MA: National Bureau of Economic Research.

Bassanini, A. and R. Duval (2006). 'Employment Patterns in OECD Countries— Reassessing the Role of Policies and Institutions'. OECD Social, Employment, and Migration Working Papers 35. Paris: OECD Publishing.

Bassanini, A. and T. Manfredi (2012). 'Capital's Grabbing Hand?' OECD Social, Employment, and Migration Working Papers. Paris: OECD Publishing.

Bastagli, F. (2011). 'Conditional Cash Transfers as a Tool of Social Policy'. *Economic & Political Weekly*, 46: 61–6.

Bauer, P. and R. Riphahn (2006). 'Timing of School Tracking as a Determinant of Intergenerational Transmission of Education'. *Economics Letters*, 91: 90–7.

Bedard, K. and C. Ferrall (2003). Wage and Test Score Dispersion: Some International Evidence. *Economics of Education Review*, 22: 31–43.

Beer, A., D. Faulkner, C. Paris, and T. Clower (2011). *Housing Transitions Through the Life Course*. Bristol: The Policy Press.

Bell, L. and R. Freeman (1994). 'Why Do Americans and Germans Work Different Hours?'. No. w4808. National Bureau of Economic Research.

Bell, L. and R. Freeman (2001). 'The Incentive for Working Hard: Explaining Hours Worked Differences in the US and Germany'. *Labour Economics*, 8: 181–202.

Benabou, R. and E. Ok (2001). 'Social Mobility and the Demand for Redistribution: The POUM Hypothesis'. *Quarterly Journal of Economics*, 116: 447–87.

Benach, J., F. Benavides, S. Platt, et al. (2000). 'The Health-Damaging Potential of New Types of Flexible Employment. A Challenge for Public Health Researchers'. *American Journal of Public Health*, 90: 1316–17.

Benach, J., C. Muntaner, O. Solar, V. Santana, M. Quinlan, and the Emconet Network (2009). *Employment, Work, and Health Inequalities: A Global Perspective*. Geneva: WHO.

Bentolila, S. and G. Saint-Paul (2003). 'Explaining Movements in the Labor Share'. *Contributions to Macroeconomics*, 3(1): 1–33.

Beramendi Alvarez, P. (2001). 'The Politics of Income Inequality in the OECD. The Role of Second Order Effects'. Luxembourg Income Study Working Paper 284.

Beramendi, P. and C. Anderson (eds) (2008). *Democracy, Inequality, and Representation. A Comparative Perspective*. New York: Russell Sage Foundation.

Beramendi, P. and C. Anderson (2008). 'Income Inequality and Democratic Representation'. In P. Beramendi and C. Anderson (eds), *Democracy, Inequality, and Representation. A Comparative Perspective*. New York: Russell Sage Foundation, 3–24.

# References

Berger-Schmitt, R. and H. Noll (2000). 'Conceptual Framework and Structure of a European System of Social Indicators'. EU Reporting Working Paper no. 14. Mannheim: Centre for Survey Research and Methodology (ZUMA).

Berggren, N. and H. Jordahl (2006). 'Free to Trust? Economic Freedom and Social Capital'. *Kyklos*, 59: 141–69.

Bergh, A. (2005). 'On the Counterfactual Problem of Welfare State Research: How Can We Measure Redistribution?'. *European Sociological Review*, 21(4): 345–57.

Bergh, A. and G. Fink (2008). 'Higher Education Policy, Enrollment, and Income Inequality'. *Social Science Quarterly*, 89(1): 217–35.

Berman, E., J. Bound, and S. Machin (1998). 'Implications of Skill-Biased Technological Change: International Evidence'. *Quarterly Journal of Economics*, 113(4): 1245–79.

Bernanke, B., C. Bertaut, L. DeMarco, and S. Kamin (2011). 'International Capital Flows and the Returns to Safe Assets in the United States, 2003–2007'. *Banque de France Financial Stability Review*, 15: 13–26.

Beugelsdijk, S., L. de Groot, and A. van Schaik (2004). 'Trust and Economic Growth: A Robustness Analysis'. *Oxford Economic Papers* New Series, 56(1): 118–34.

Biffl, G. (2007). 'Development of the Distribution of Household Income in Austria'. Österreichisches Institut für Wirtschaftsforschung (WIFO), Working Paper 293.

Bishop, J. (1997). 'The Effect of National Standards and Curriculum-Based Exams on Achievement'. *American Economic Review*, 87: 260–4.

Bishop, J. (2006). 'Drinking from the Fountain of Knowledge: Student Incentive to Study and Learn'. In E. Hanushek and F. Welch (eds), *Handbook of the Economics of Education, Vol 2*. Amsterdam: North-Holland, 909–44.

Björklund, A. (2005). 'Does Family Policy Affect Fertility?'. *Journal of Population Economics*, 19(1): 3–24.

Björklund, A. and M. Jäntti (2009). 'Intergenerational Income Mobility and the Role of Family Background'. In *Oxford Handbook of Economic Inequality*. Oxford: Oxford University Press.

Björklund, A., J. Roine, and D. Waldenström (2008). 'Intergenerational Top Income Mobility in Sweden: A Combination of Equal Opportunity and Capitalist Dynasties'. IZA Discussion Paper 3801.

Bjørnskov, C. (2007). 'Determinants of Generalized Trust: A Cross-Country Comparison'. *Public Choice*, 130: 1–21.

Blanden, J. (2013). 'Cross-Country Rankings in Intergenerational Mobility: A Comparison of Approaches from Economics and Sociology'. *Journal of Economic Surveys*, 27(1): 38–73.

Blanden, J., A. Goodman, P. Gregg, and S. Machin (2004). 'Changes in Intergenerational Mobility in Britain'. In M. Corak (ed.), *Generational Income Mobility in North America and Europe*. Cambridge: Cambridge University Press, 122–46.

Blau, D. and J. Currie (2006). 'Who's Minding the Kids? Preschool, Day Care and After School Care'. In F. Welch and E. Hanushek (eds), *Handbook of Education Economics*. New York: North Holland, 1163–1278.

Blau, F. and L. Kahn (2005). 'Do Cognitive Test Scores Explain Higher US Wage Inequality?'. *Review of Economics and Statistics*, 87(1): 184–93.

Blau, F. and L. Kahn (2009). 'Inequality and Earnings Distribution'. In W. Salverda, B. Nolan, and T. Smeeding (eds), *Oxford Handbook of Economic Inequality*. Oxford: Oxford University Press, 177–203.

Blau, P. (1977). *Inequality and Heterogeneity. A Primitive Theory of Social Structure*. New York: The Free Press.

Blázquez, M., E. Cottini, and A. Herrarte (2012). 'Socioeconomic Gradient in Health: How Important Is Material Deprivation?' GINI Discussion Paper 39. Available at <http://gini-research.org/articles/papers> (also in *Journal of Economic Inequality*, 2013).

Bloom, D., D. Canning, G. Fink, and J. Fimlay (2011). 'Microeconomic Foundations of the Demographic Dividend'. Working Paper 93, Programme on the Global Demography of Aging (PGDA). Harvard.

Blumstein, A. and J. Wallman (eds) (2000). *The Crime Drop in America*. Cambridge: Cambridge University Press.

Bogliacino, F. and M. Lucchese (2011). 'Endogenous Skill Biased Technological Change: Testing for Demand Pull Effect'. GINI Discussion Paper 26.

Bogliacino, F. and V. Maestri (2012a). 'Increasing Income Inequality'. In G. Ballarino, F. Bogliacino, M. Braga, M. Bratti, D. Checchi, A. Filippin, V. Maestri, E. Meschi, and F. Scervini, *Drivers of Growing Inequality*. WP3 Report. GINI Project.

Bogliacino, F. and V. Maestri (2012b). 'Wealth Inequality'. In G. Ballarino, F. Bogliacino, M. Braga, M. Bratti, D. Checchi, A. Filippin, V. Maestri, E. Meschi, and F. Scervini, *Drivers of Growing Inequality*. WP3 Report. GINI Project.

Bol, T. and H. van de Werfhorst (2013a). 'Measuring Educational Institutional Diversity: External Differentiation, Vocational Orientation and Standardization'. GINI Discussion Paper 81.

Bol, T. and H. van de Werfhorst (2013b). 'Educational Systems and the Trade-off Between Labor Market Allocation and Equality of Educational Opportunity'. *Comparative Education Review*, 57(2): 285–308.

Bonoli, G. (2007). 'Time Matters: Postindustrialization, New Social Risks and Welfare State Adaptation in Advanced Industrial Democracies'. *Comparative Political Studies*, 40(5): 495–520.

Borck, R. (2007). 'Voting, Inequality and Redistribution'. *Journal of Economic Surveys*, 21(1): 90–109.

Bover, O. (2008). 'The Dynamics of Household Income and Wealth: Results from the Panel of the Spanish Survey of Household Finances (EFF) 2002–2005'. Banco de España, Documentos Ocasionales, 0810.

Bowles, S. and Y. Park (2005). 'Emulation, Inequality, and Work Hours: Was Thorsten Veblen Right?'. *The Economic Journal*, 115(507): F397–F412.

Brady, H. (2003). 'An Analytical Perspective on Participatory Inequality and Income Inequality'. Paper for the Russell Sage Foundation Project on the 'Social Dimensions of Inequality'.

Braga, M., D. Checchi, and E. Meschi (2013). 'Institutional Reforms and Educational Attainment in Europe: A Long Run Perspective'. *Economic Policy*, 73: 45–100.

Brandolini, A. and G. Alessio (2001). 'Household Structure and Income Inequality'. CHILD Working Paper 6. (Also published in D. del Boca and R. G. Repetto (eds), 2003. *Women's Work, Family and Social Policies in Italy*. Peter Lang.)

Brandolini, A., L. Cannari, G. Alessio, and I. Faiella (2004). 'Household Wealth Distribution in Italy in the 1990s'. Banca d'Italia Working Paper 530.

Bratt, R. (2008). 'Homeownership as Social Policy in the US: Risk and Responsibility after the Subprime Crisis'. Paper presented at the ENHR Working Group 'Building on Home Ownership: Housing Policies and Social Strategies', 13–14 November 2008, Delft University of Technology, the Netherlands.

Breen, R. (ed.) (2004). *Social Mobility in Europe*. Oxford: Oxford University Press.

Breen, R. and J. Jonsson (2005). 'Inequality of Opportunity in Comparative Perspective: Recent Research on Educational Attainment and Social Mobility'. *Annual Review of Sociology*, 31: 223–43.

Breen, R. and R. Luijkx (2004). 'Social Mobility in Europe between 1970 and 2000'. In R. Breen (ed.), *Social Mobility in Europe*. Oxford: Oxford University Press, 37–75.

Breen, R., R. Luijkx, W. Müller, and R. Pollak (2009). 'Non-Persistent Inequality in Educational Attainment: Evidence from Eight European Countries'. *American Journal of Sociology*, 114: 1475–1521.

Brint, S. (2006). *Schools and Societies*. Palo Alto: Stanford University Press.

Brown, G., J. Micklewright, S. Schnepf, and R. Waldmann (2007). 'International Surveys of Educational Achievement: How Robust Are the Findings?'. *Journal of the Royal Statistical Society: Series A (Statistics in Society)*, 170(3): 623–46.

Brunello, G. and D. Checchi (2007). 'Does School Tracking Affect Equality of Opportunity? New International Evidence'. *Economic Policy*, 22: 781–861.

Brunello, G., M. Fort, and G. Weber (2009). 'Changes in Compulsory Schooling, Education and the Distribution of Wages in Europe'. *Economic Journal*, 119(536): 516–39.

Brzozowski, M., M. Gervais, P. Klein, and M. Suzuki (2010). 'Consumption, Income, and Wealth Inequality in Canada'. *Review of Economic Dynamics*, 13: 52–75.

Burgoon, B. (2013). 'Inequality and Anti-globalisation Backlash by Political Parties'. *European Union Politics*, 14(3). (Also published as GINI Discussion Paper 14, 2011.)

Burtless, G. (2011). 'Demographic Transformation and Economic Inequality'. In S. Wiemer, B. Nolan, and T. Smeeding (eds), *Oxford Handbook of Economic Inequality*. New York: Oxford University Press, 435–54.

Burtless, G. and C. Jencks (2003). 'American Inequality and Its Consequences'. In H. Aaron, J. Lindsay, and P. Nivola (eds), *Agenda for the Nation*. Washington, DC: Brookings.

Busemeyer, M. (2012). 'Inequality and the Political Economy of Education: An Analysis of Individual Preferences in OECD Countries'. *Journal of European Social Policy*, 22(3): 219–40.

Callan, T., C. Leventi, H. Levy, M. Matsaganis, A. Paulus, and H. Sutherlands (2011). 'The Distributional Effects of Austerity Measures: A Comparison of Six EU Countries'. Euromod Working Paper EM6/11.

Callan, T., T. Smeeding, and P. Tsakloglou (2008). 'Short-Run Distributional Effects of Public Education Transfers to Tertiary Education Students in Seven European Countries'. *Education Economics*, 16(3): 275–88.

Calvert, E. and T. Fahey (2013). 'Income Inequality and the Family'. GINI Discussion Paper. Available at <http://gini-research.org/articles/papers>

Calvert, E. and B. Nolan (2012). 'Deprivation, Income and Inequality in the EU'. GINI Discussion Paper 75. Available at <http://gini-research.org/articles/papers>

Caminada, K., K. Goudswaard, and O. Van Vliet (2010). 'Patterns of Welfare State Indicators in the EU: Is There Convergence?'. *Journal of Common Market Studies*, 48: 529–56.

Caminada, K., K. Goudswaard, and C. Wang (2012). 'Disentangling Income Inequality and the Redistributive Effect of Taxes and Transfers in 20 LIS Countries Over Time'. LIS Working Paper, 581/2012.

Campbell, J. (2011). 'The US Financial Crisis: Lessons for Theories of Institutional Complementarity'. *Socio-Economic Review*, 9: 211–34.

Canberra Group (2011). *Handbook on Household Income Statistics* (2nd edition). Geneva: United Nations.

Cantillon, B. (2011). 'The Paradox of the Social Investment State: Growth, Employment and Poverty in the Lisbon Era'. *Journal of European Social Policy*, 21(5): 432–49.

Cantillon, B. (2013). 'Beyond Social Investment. Which Concepts and Values for Social Policy-Making in Europe?'. In B. Cantillon and F. Vandenbroucke, *Reconciling Work and Poverty Reduction. How Successful are European Welfare States?* Oxford: Oxford University Press.

Card, D. (1999). 'The Causal Effect of Education on Earnings'. In O. Ashenfelter and D. Card (eds), *Handbook of Labor Economics, Vol. 3*. Amsterdam: Elsevier North Holland, 1801–63.

Card, D. and J. DiNardo (2002). 'Skill-Biased Technological Change and Rising Wage Inequality: Some Problems and Puzzles'. *Journal of Labor Economics*, 20: 733–83.

Card, D., J. Kluve, and A. Weber (2010). 'Active Labor Market Policy Evaluations: A Meta-Analysis'. *The Economic Journal*, 120: F452–F477.

Caselli, F. (1999). 'Technological Revolutions'. *American Economic Review*, 89: 78–102.

Castelló, A. and R. Doménech (2002). 'Human Capital Inequality and Economic Growth: Some New Evidence'. *Economic Journal*, 112(478): C187–C200.

Castles, F. (2009). 'What Welfare States Do: A Disaggregated Expenditure Approach'. *Journal of Social Policy*, 38: 45–62.

Caussat L., S. Le Minez, and D. Raynaud (2005). 'L'assurance-maladie contribue-t-elle à redistribuer les revenus?'. *In DREES, Dossiers solidarité et santé—Études sur les dépenses de santé*. Paris: La Documentation Française.

Cavadino, M. and J. Dignan (2006). *Penal Systems: A Comparative Approach*. London: Sage.

Chamley, C. (1986). 'Optimal Taxation of Capital Income in General Equilibrium with Infinite Lives'. *Econometrica*, 54(3): 607–22.

Champernowne, D. and F. Cowell (1998). *Economic Inequality and Income Distribution*. Cambridge University Press.

Chan, T.-W. and J. Goldthorpe (2007). 'Class and Status: The Conceptual Distinction and its Empirical Relevance'. *American Sociological Review*, 72: 512–32.

Chang, H.-J. (2010). *23 Things They Don't Tell You About Capitalism*. New York: Bloomsbury Press.

Checchi, D. (2001). 'Education, Inequality and Income Inequality', LSE STICERD Research paper DARP 52.

Checchi, D., V. Peragine, and L. Serlenga (2008). 'Income Inequality and Opportunity Inequality in Europe'. *Rivista di Politica Economica*, 98(5): 263–92.

Checchi, D. and H. van de Werfhorst (2013). 'Does Inequality in Education Affect Inequality in Incomes?'. Mimeo.

Chennells, L. and J. Van Reenen (2002). 'The Effects of Technical Change on Skills, Wages and Employment: A Survey of the Micro-Econometric Evidence'. In N. Greenan, Y. L'Horty, and J. Mairesse (eds), *Productivity, Inequality and the Digital Economy*. Cambridge: MIT Press, 175–225.

Chetty, R., J. Friedman, and E. Saez (2013). 'Using Differences in Knowledge across Neighborhoods to Uncover the Impacts of the EITC on Earnings'. NBER Working Paper 18232.

Chiesi, A. (2002). 'Social Cohesion and Related Concepts'. In N. Genov (ed.), *Advances in Sociological Knowledge*. Paris: International Social Science Council, 235–53.

Cohen, D. and M. Soto (2007). 'Growth and Human Capital: Good Data, Good Results'. *Journal of Economic Growth*, 12(1): 51–76.

Collins, R. (2000). 'Comparative and Historical Patterns of Education'. In M. Hallinan (ed.), *Handbook of the Sociology of Education*. New York: Kluwer, 213–39.

Corak, M. (2013). 'Inequality from Generation to Generation: The United States in Comparison'. In R. Rycroft (ed.), *The Economics of Inequality, Poverty, and Discrimination in the 21st Century*. Santa Barbara, CA: ABC-CLIO Praeger, 107–26.

Corak, M., C. Lietz, et al. (2005). 'The Impact of Tax and Transfer Systems on Children in the European Union'. IZA Discussion Paper 1589. Bonn: Institute for the Study of Labour.

Corluy, V. and F. Vandenbroucke (forthcoming). 'Household Joblessness'. In B. Cantillon and F. Vandenbroucke (eds), *Reconciling Work and Poverty Reduction. How Successful Are European Welfare States?* Oxford: Oxford University Press.

Corneo, G. (2011). 'Income Inequality, Value Systems, and Macroeconomic Performance'. GINI Discussion Paper 17.

Corneo, G. and H. P. Grüner (2002). 'Individual Preferences for Political Redistribution'. *Journal of Public Economics*, 83: 83–107.

Cornia, G. A. (2012). 'Inequality Trends and Their Determinants. Latin America over 1990–2010'. UNU/WIDER Working Paper 2012/09.

Coronado, J., D. Fullerton, and T. Glass (2000). 'The Progressivity of Social Security'. NBER Working Paper, 7520.

Cottini E. (2012). 'Is Your Job Bad for Your Health? Explaining Differences in Health at Work across Gender'. *International Journal of Manpower*, 33(3): 301–21.

Cottini, E. and C. Lucifora (2010). 'Mental Health and Working Conditions in European Countries'. IZA Discussion Paper 4717, IZA, Bonn.

Cottini, E. and C. Lucifora (2013). 'Inequalities at Work. Job Quality, Health and Low Pay in European Workplaces'. GINI Discussion Paper 86. Available at <http://www.gini-research.org/articles/papers>

Cowell, F. (2008). 'Gini, Deprivation and Complaints'. In G. Betti and A. Lemmi (eds), *Advances on Income Inequality and Concentration Measures*. London, Routledge, 25–43.

Cowell, F., E. Karagiannaki, and A. McKnight (2012). 'Mapping and Measuring the Distribution of Household Wealth: A Cross-Country Analysis'. GINI Discussion Paper 71.

Cowell, F., E. Karagiannaki, and A. McKnight (2013). 'Accounting for Cross-Country Differences in Wealth Inequality'. GINI Discussion Paper 85.

Crettaz, E. (2011). *Fighting Working Poverty in Post-Industrial Economies. Causes, Trade-Offs and Policy Solutions.* Cheltenham and Northampton, MA: Edward Elgar.

Cunha, F. and J. Heckman (2007). 'The Technology of Skill Formation'. *American Economic Review*, 97(2): 31–47.

Cunha, F. and J. Heckman (2008). 'Formulating, Identifying and Estimating the Technology of Cognitive and Noncognitive Skill Formation'. *Journal of Human Resources*, 43(4).

Cunha, F. and J. Heckman (2009). 'The Economics and Psychology of Inequality and Human Development'. *Journal of the European Economic Association*, 7(2–3): 320–64, 04–05.

Cunha, F., J. Heckman, L. Lochner, and D. Masterov (2006). 'Interpreting the Evidence on Life Cycle Skill Formation'. In E. Hanushek and F. Welch (eds), *Handbook of the Economics of Education*. Amsterdam: North-Holland, 697–812.

Currie, J. (2001). 'Early Childhood Education Programs'. *Journal of Economic Perspectives*, 15(2): 213–38.

Currie J. and F. Gahvari (2008). 'Transfers in Cash and In-Kind: Theory Meets the Data'. *Journal of Economic Literature*, 46(2): 333–83.

D'Addio, A. (2007). 'Intergenerational Transmission of Disadvantage: Mobility or Immobility across Generations? A Review of Evidence for OECD Countries'. OECD Social, Employment, and Migration Working Paper 52.

Daly, M., M. Wilson, and S. Vasdev (2001). 'Income Inequality and Homicide Rates in Canada and the United States'. *Canadian Journal of Criminology*, 43(2): 219–36.

Davey Smith, G. and M. Egger (1996). 'Commentary: Understanding It All—Health, Meta-Theories and Mortality Trends'. *British Medical Journal*, 313(7072): 1584– 5.

Davies, J. (2009). 'Wealth and Economic Inequality'. In *The Oxford Handbook of Economic Inequality*. Oxford: Oxford University Press, 127–50.

Davies, J., S. Sandström, A. Shorrocks, and E. Wolff (2011). 'The Level and Distribution of Global Household Wealth'. *Economic Journal*, 121(551): 223–54.

Davies, J. and A. Shorrocks (2000). 'The Distribution of Wealth'. In A. Atkinson and F. Bourguignon (eds), *Handbook of Income Distribution, Vol. 1*. Amsterdam: Elsevier, 605–75.

DeBacker, J., B. Heim, V. Panousi, S. Ramnath, and I. Vidangos (2013). 'Rising Inequality: Transitory or Permanent? New Evidence from a Panel of U.S. Tax Returns'. Conference paper presented at the Spring 2013 Brookings Panel on Economic Activity, 21–22 March 2013.

De Deken, J. and B. Kittel (2007). 'Social Expenditure Under Scrutiny: The Problems of Using Aggregate Spending Data for Assessing Welfare State Dynamics'. In J. Clasen and N. Siegel (eds), *Investigating Welfare State Change. The 'Dependent Variable Problem' in Comparative Analysis*. Cheltenham and Northampton, MA: Edward Elgar, 72–104.

De Graaf Zijl, M. and B. Nolan (2012). 'Household Joblessness and Its Impact on Poverty and Deprivation in Europe'. *Journal of European Social Policy*, 21(5): 413–31.

De Gregorio, J. and J.-W. Lee (2002). 'Education and Income Inequality: New Evidence from Cross-Country Data'. *Review of Income and Wealth*, 48(3): 395–416.

De La Croix, D. and M. Doepke (2003). 'Inequality and Growth: Why Differential Fertility Matters'. *American Economic Review*, 93(4): 1091–1113.

De la Fuente, A. and A. Ciccone (2002). 'Human Capital in a Global and Knowledge-Based Economy'. Mimeo.

Del Boca, D. and S. Pasqua (2003). 'Employment Patterns of Husbands and Wives and Family Income Distribution in Italy (1977–98)'. *Review of Income and Wealth*, 49(3): 221–45.

Delhey, J. and K. Newton (2005). 'Predicting Cross-National Levels of Social Trust: Global Pattern or Nordic Exceptionalism?'. *European Sociological Review*, 21(4): 311–27.

Dell, F., T. Piketty, and E. Saez (2007). 'Income and Wealth Concentration in Switzerland over the 20th Century'. In A. Atkinson and T. Piketty (eds), *Top Incomes over the Twentieth Century*. Oxford: Oxford University Press, 472–500.

De Long, J., A. Shleifer, L. Summers, and R. Waldmann (1990). 'Noise Trader Risk in Financial Markets'. *Journal of Political Economy*, 98: 703–38.

Dewilde, C. (2011). 'The Interplay between Economic Inequality Trends and Housing Regime Changes in Advanced Welfare Democracies'. GINI Discussion Paper. Available at <http://www.gini-research.org/articles/papers>

Dewilde, C. and B. Lancee (2012). 'Income Inequality and Access to Housing in Europe'. GINI Discussion Paper 32. Available at <http://www.gini-research.org/articles/papers> (also in *European Sociological Review*, first published online 23 April 2013).

Diaz-Alejandro, C. (1985). 'Good-Bye Financial Repression, Hello Financial Crash'. *Journal of Development Economics*, 19: 1–24.

Dickens, R. and A. McKnight (2008). 'Changes in Earnings Inequality and Mobility in Great Britain 1978/9–2005/6'. CASE paper 132. London: Centre for Analysis of Social Exclusion.

DiNardo, J., N. Fortin, and T. Lemieux (1996). 'Labor Market Institutions, and the Distribution of Wages, 1973–1992: A Semiparametric Approach'. *Econometrica*, 64: 1001–44.

Di Paolo, A., J. Raymond, and J. Calero (2010). 'Exploring Educational Mobility in Europe'. Working Papers 2010/10, Institut d'Economia de Barcelona (IEB).

Doerrenberg, P. and A. Peichl (2012). 'The Impact of Redistributive Policies on Inequality in OECD Countries'. IZA Discussion Paper 6505.

Dolado, J., F. Felgueroso, and J. Jimeno (2000). 'The Role of the Minimum Wage in the Welfare State: An Appraisal'. IZA Discussion Paper 152.

Dolado, J., F. Kramarz, S. Machin, A. Manning, D. Margolis, and C. Teulings (1996). 'The Economic Impact of Minimum Wages in Europe'. *Economic Policy*, 23: 317–72.

Dolls, M., C. Fuest, and A. Peichl (2011). 'Automatic Stabilizers, Economic Crisis and Income Distribution in Europe'. In H. Immervoll, A. Peichl, and K. Tatsiramos (eds), *Who Loses in the Downturn? Economic Crisis, Employment and Income Distribution*

(Research in Labor Economics, Volume 32). Bingley: Emerald Group Publishing, 227–55. (Also GINI Discussion Paper 23.)

Dolls, M., C. Fuest, and A. Peichl (2012). 'Automatic Stabilizers and Economic Crisis: US vs. Europe'. *Journal of Public Economics*, 96: 279–94.

Dolton, P. and O. Marcenaro-Gutierrez (2011). 'If You Pay Peanuts Do You Get Monkeys? A Cross-Country Analysis of Teacher Pay and Pupil Performance'. *Economic Policy*, 26(65): 5–55.

Domeij, D. and M. Floden (2010). 'Inequality Trends in Sweden 1978–2004'. *Review of Economic Dynamics*, 13: 179–208.

Döring, H. and P. Manow (2010). 'Parliament and Government Composition Database (ParlGov): An Infrastructure for Empirical Information on Political Institutions'. Version 10/02. Available at <http://www.parlgov.org>

Douglas, T. (1995). *Scapegoats: Transferring Blame*. London: Routledge.

Downs, A. (1957). *An Economic Theory of Voting*. New York: Harper and Row.

Drandakis, E. and E. Phelps (1965). 'A Model of Induced Invention, Growth and Distribution'. *Economic Journal*, 76: 823–40.

Dumenil, G. and D. Levy (2011). 'The Crisis of the Early 21st Century: General Interpretation, Recent Developments, and Perspectives'. Available at <http://www.jourdan.ens.fr/levy/dle2011h.htm>

Durlauf, S. and M. Fafchamps (2004). 'Social Capital'. In S. Durlauf and P. Aghion (eds), *Handbook of Economic Growth*. Amsterdam: North-Holland, 1639–99.

Duru-Bellat, M. and B. Suchaut (2005). 'L'approche sociologique des effets du contexte scolaire: Méthodes et difficultés'. *Revue Internationale de Psychologie Sociale*, 18: 5–42.

Dustmann, C. (2004). 'Parental Background, Secondary School Track Choice and Wages'. *Oxford Economic Papers*, 56: 209–30.

Dwyer, R. (2009). 'The McMansionization of America? Income Stratification and the Standard of Living in Housing, 1960–2000'. *Research in Social Stratification and Mobility*, 27: 285–300.

Eggers, A., G. Gaddy, and C. Graham (2006). 'Well-Being and Unemployment in Russia in the 1990s: Can Society's Suffering Be Individuals' Solace?' *Journal of Socio-Economics*, 35: 209–42.

Eichhorst, W., M. Gienberger-Zingerle, and R. Konle-Seidl (2008). 'Activation Policies in Germany: From Status Protection to Basic Income Support'. In O. Eichhorst, O. Kaufmann, and R. Konle-Seidl (eds), *Bringing the Jobless into Work? Experiences with Activation Schemes in Europe and the US*. Berlin: Springer.

Eissa, N. and H. Hoynes (2004). 'Taxes and the Labor Market Participation of Married Couples: The Earned Income Tax Credit'. *Journal of Public Economics*, 88: 1931–58.

Elgar, F. (2010). 'Income Inequality, Trust, and Population Health in 33 Countries'. *American Journal of Public Health*, 100(11): 2311–15.

Elgar, F. and N. Aitken (2011). 'Income Inequality, Trust and Homicide in 33 Countries'. *European Journal of Public Health*, 21(2): 241–6.

Elgar, F., W. Craig, W. Boyce, A. Morgan, and R. Vella-Zarb (2009). 'Income Inequality and School Bullying: Multilevel Study of Adolescents in 37 Countries'. *Journal of Adolescent Health*, 45: 351–9.

Elias, P. and A. McKnight (2003). 'Earnings, Unemployment and NS-SEC'. In D. Rose and D. Pevalin (eds), *A Researcher's Guide to the National Statistics Socio-economic Classification*. London: SAGE Publications, 151–72.

Enzmann, D. et al. (2010). 'Self-Reported Youth Delinquency in Europe and Beyond: First Results of the Second International Self-Report Delinquency Study in the Context of Police and Victimisation Data'. *European Journal of Criminology*, 7(2): 159–83.

Epple, D. and R. Romano (1996). 'Ends Against the Middle: Determining Public Service Provision When There Are Private Alternatives'. *Journal of Public Economics*, 62: 297–325.

Erikson, R. and J. Goldthorpe (1992). *The Constant Flux*. Oxford: Clarendon Press.

Erikson, R. and J. Goldthorpe (2010). 'Has Social Mobility in Britain Decreased? Reconciling Divergent Findings on Income and Class Mobility'. *The British Journal of Sociology*, 61(2): 211–30.

Erikson, R. and J. Torsander (2008). 'Social Class and Causes of Death'. *European Journal of Public Health*, 18(5): 473–8.

Esping-Andersen, G. (1990). *The Three Worlds of Welfare Capitalism*. Cambridge and Princeton, NJ: Polity Press/Princeton University Press.

Esping-Andersen, G. (2004). 'Unequal Opportunities and the Mechanisms of Social Inheritance'. In M. Corak (ed.), *Generational Income Mobility in North America and Europe*. Cambridge: Cambridge University Press, 289–314.

Esping-Andersen, G. (2008). 'Childhood Investment and Skill Formation'. *International Tax and Public Finance*, 15(1): 19–44.

Esping-Andersen, G., D. Gallie, A. Hemerijck, and J. Myles (2002). 'Why We Need a New Welfare State'. Oxford: Oxford University Press.

Esping-Andersen, G., I. Garfinkel, W. Han, K. Magnuson, S. Wagner, and J. Waldfogel (2012). 'Child Care and School Performance in Denmark and the United States'. *Children and Youth Services Review*, 34: 576–89.

Esping-Andersen, G. and J. Myles (2009). 'Economic Inequality and the Welfare State'. In W. Salverda, B. Nolan, and T. Smeeding (eds), *Oxford Handbook of Economic Inequality*. Oxford: Oxford University Press, 639–64.

Estevez-Abe, M., T. Iversen, and D. Soskice (2001). 'Social Protection and the Formation of Skills: A Reinterpretation of the Welfare State'. In P. Hall and D. Soskice (eds), *Varieties of Capitalism*. New York: Oxford University Press, 145–84.

Eurofound (2010). *Working Poor in Europe*. Dublin: European Foundation.

Eurofound (2012). *Trends in Job Quality in Europe*. Luxembourg: Publications Office of the European Union.

European Central Bank (2013). 'The Eurosystem Household Finance and Consumption Survey Results from the First Wave'. Statistics Paper Series, 2.

European Commission (2008). *Employment in Europe*. Luxembourg: Publications Office of the European Communities.

European Commission (2009). *The Provision of Childcare Services—A Comparative Review of 30 European Countries*. Luxembourg: Publications Office of the European Union.

European Commission (2011). *Employment and Social Developments in Europe 2011*. Brussels: DG Employment, Social Affairs, and Equal Opportunities.

European Commission (2012a). 'Communication on Action for Stability, Growth and Jobs'. COM(2012) 299 final.

European Commission (2012b). *Employment and Social Developments in Europe 2012*. Luxembourg: Publications Office of the European Union.

European Commission (2013). 'Communication from the Commission to the European Parliament, the Council, the European Economic and Social Committee and the Committee of the Regions. Towards Social Investment for Growth and Cohesion—Including Implementing the European Social Fund 2014–2020'. COM(2013) 83 final.

European Council (2011). *SPC Assessment of the Social Dimension of the Europe 2020 Strategy*. Brussels: European Council.

Eurostat (2012). *Taxation Trends in the European Union*. Luxembourg: Publications Office of the European Union.

Evandrou, M., J. Falkingham, J. Hills, and J. Le Grand (1993). 'Welfare Benefits in Kind and Income Distribution'. *Fiscal Studies*, 14(1): 57–76.

Fahey, T. and M. Norris (2010). 'Housing'. In F. Castles, S. Leibfried, J. Lewis, H. Obinger, and C. Pierson (eds), *Oxford Handbook of the Welfare State*. Oxford: Oxford University Press, 479–93.

Fajnzylber, P., D. Lederman, and N. Loayza (2002). 'Inequality and Violent Crime'. *Journal of Law and Economics*, 45(1): 1–40.

Ferrer-i-Carbonell, A. and X. Ramos (2010). 'Inequality, Aversion and Risk Attitudes'. IZA Discussion Paper 4703. Bonn: IZA.

Ferrer-i-Carbonell, A. and X. Ramos (2012). 'Inequality and Happiness: A Survey'. GINI Discussion Paper. Available at <http://www.gini-research.org/articles/papers>

Figari, F. (2011). 'Can In-Work Benefits Improve Social Inclusion in the Southern European Countries?'. *Journal of European Social Policy*, 20: 301–15.

Figari, F. (2012). 'The Impact of Indirect Taxes and Imputed Rent on Inequality: A Comparison with Cash Transfers and Direct Taxes in Five EU Countries'. GINI Discussion Paper 28.

Figari, F., A. Salvatori, and H. Sutherland (2011). 'Economic Downturn and Stress Testing European Welfare Systems'. In H. Immervoll, A. Peichl, and K. Tatsiramos (eds), *Who Loses in the Downturn? Economic Crisis, Employment and Income Distribution* (Research in Labor Economics, Volume 32). Bingley: Emerald Group Publishing, 257–86.

Finseraas, H. (2009). 'Income Inequality and Demand for Redistribution: A Multilevel Analysis of European Public Opinion'. *Scandinavian Political Studies*, 32(1): 94–119.

Fisher, J. and B. Torgler (2013). 'Do Positional Concerns Destroy Social Capital: Evidence from 26 Countries'. *Economic Inquiry*, 51(2): 1542–65.

Fisher, L. and A. Jaffe (2003). 'Determinants of International Home Ownership Rates'. *Housing Finance International*, 2003 (September): 34–42.

Fitoussi, J. and F. Saraceno (2010). 'Inequality and Macroeconomic Performance'. OFCE/POLHIA 2010/3.

Flora, P., F. Kraus, and W. Pfenning (1987). *State, Economy and Society in Western Europe 1815–1975*. London: McMillan.

Forbes, K. (2000). 'A Reassessment of the Relationship between Inequality and Growth'. *American Economic Review*, 90: 869–87.

Forma, P. (1997). 'The Rational Legitimacy of the Welfare State: Popular Support for Ten Income Transfer Schemes in Finland'. *Policy & Politics*, 25(3): 235–49.

Förster, M. and G. Verbist (2012). 'Money or Kindergarten—What Is the Optimal Mix? A Comparative Analysis of the Distributive Effects of Family Cash Transfers and Childcare Services'. OECD Social, Employment, and Migration Working Papers, 135. Paris: OECD Publishing.

Franklin, M. (2004). *Voter Turnout and the Dynamics of Electoral Competition in Established Democracies since 1994*. Cambridge: Cambridge University Press.

Fraser, N., R. Gutiérrez, and R. Peña-Casas (2011). *Working Poverty in Europe: A Comparative Approach*. Basingstoke: Palgrave Macmillan.

Frattini, T. (2012). 'Immigration and Inequality in the EU'. GINI Discussion Paper 44.

Freeman, R. (1996). 'The Minimum Wage as a Redistributive Tool'. *Economic Journal*, 106: 639–49.

Freeman, R. (2007). 'Labor Market Institutions around the World'. Working Paper 13242. Cambridge: National Bureau of Economic Research.

Frémeaux, N. and T. Piketty (2012). 'Country Report on Growing Inequality and its Impacts in France'. GINI Project.

Frenkel, R. and M. Rapetti (2009). 'A Developing Country View of the Current Global Crisis: What Should Not Be Forgotten and What Should Be Done'. *Cambridge Journal of Economics*, 33(4): 685–702.

Frick, J., M. Grabka, T. Smeeding, and P. Tsakoglou (2010). 'Distributional Effect of Imputed Rents in Five European Countries'. *Journal of Housing Economics*, 19: 167–79.

Friedkin, N. (2004). 'Social Cohesion'. *Annual Review of Sociology*, 30: 409–25.

Fritzell, J., O. Kangas, J. Hertzman, J. Blomgren, and H. Hiilamo (2012). 'Cross-Temporal and Cross-National Poverty and Mortality Rates among Developed Countries'. GINI Discussion Paper 64. Available at <http://gini-research.org/articles/papers>

Fuchs-Schündeln, N., D. Krueger, and M. Sommer (2010). 'Inequality Trends for Germany in the Last Two Decades: A Tale of Two Countries'. *Review of Economic Dynamics*, 13: 103–32.

Galbraith, J. K. (2007). 'Global Inequality and Global Macroeconomics'. *Journal of Policy Modeling*, 29: 587–607.

Galbraith, J. K. (2012). *Inequality and Instability: A Study of the World Economy Just Before the Great Crisis*. Oxford: Oxford University Press.

Galindo-Rueda, F. and A. Vignoles (2004). 'The Heterogeneous Effect of Selection in Secondary Schools: Understanding the Changing Role of Ability'. IZA Discussion Papers 1245, Institute for the Study of Labour (IZA).

Gallo W. et al. (2004). 'Involuntary Job Loss as a Risk Factor for Subsequent Myocardial Infarction and Stroke: Findings from the Health and Retirement Study'. *American Journal of Industrial Medicine*, 45: 408–16.

Galor, O. (2011). 'Inequality, Human Capital Formation and the Process of Development'. In E. Hanushek, S. Machin, and L. Wössmann (eds), *Handbook of the Economics of Education*. Amsterdam: Elsevier, 441–93.

Galor, O. and D. Tsiddon (1997). 'Technological Progress, Mobility and Economic Growth'. *American Economic Review*, 87(3): 363–82.

García-Peñalosa, C. and O. Orgiazzi (2011). 'Factor Components of Inequality'. GINI Discussion Paper 12.

Garfinkel, I., L. Rainwater, and T. Smeeding (2006). 'A Re-Examination of Welfare State and Inequality in Rich Nations: How In-Kind Transfers and Indirect Taxes Change the Story'. *Journal of Policy Analysis and Management*, 25: 855–919.

Gelbach J. (2002). 'Public Schooling for Young Children and Maternal Labour Supply'. *American Economic Review*, 92(1): 307–22.

Gerber, T. and M. Hout (1998). 'More Shock than Therapy: Market Transition, Employment, and Income in Russia, 1991–1995'. *American Journal of Sociology*, 104: 1–50.

Geys, B. (2006). 'Explaining Voter Turnout: A Review of Aggregate-Level Research'. *Electoral Studies*, 25(4): 637–63.

Gijsberts, M. (2002). 'The Legitimation of Income Inequality in State-Socialist and Market Societies'. *Acta Sociologica*, 45: 269–85.

GINI Country Reports (2013). Available at <http://gini-research.org/.org/CR-[country name]>.

Glyn, A. (2009). 'Functional Distribution and Inequality'. In W. Salverda, B. Nolan, and T. Smeeding (eds), *Oxford Handbook of Economic Inequality*. Oxford: Oxford University Press, 101–26.

Goldthorpe, J. (2000). 'Social Class and the Differentiation of Employment Contracts'. In J. Goldthorpe, *On Sociology: Numbers, Narratives, and the Integration of Research and Theory*. Oxford: Oxford University Press, 206–29.

Goldthorpe, J. (2001). 'Causation, Statistics and Sociology', *European Sociological Review*, 17(1): 1–20.

Goldthorpe, J. (2007a). *On Sociology. Volume 1: Critique and Program*. Stanford: Stanford University Press.

Goldthorpe, J. (2007b). *On Sociology. Volume 2: Illustration*. Stanford: Stanford University Press.

Goldthorpe, J. (2010). 'Analysing Social Inequality: A Critique of Two Recent Contributions from Economics and Epidemiology'. *European Sociological Review*, 26(6): 731–44.

Goldthorpe, J. and A. McKnight (2006). 'The Economic Basis of Social Class'. In S. Morgan, D. Grusky, and G. Fields (eds), *Mobility and Inequality: Frontiers of Research in Sociology and Economics*. Palo Alto: Stanford University Press, 109–36.

Goldthorpe, J. and C. Mills (2004). 'Trends in Intergenerational Class Mobility in Britain in the Late Twentieth Century'. In R. Breen (ed.), *Social Mobility in Europe*. Oxford: Oxford University Press, 195–224.

Goos, M., A. Manning, and A. Salomons (2009). 'The Polarization of the European Labor Market'. *American Economic Review*, 99(2): 59–63.

Gornick, J. and M. Jäntti (2012). 'Child Poverty in Cross-National Perspective: Lessons from the Luxembourg Income Study'. *Children and Youth Services Review*, 34: 558–68.

Gornick, J. and M. Meyers (2003). 'Families That Work: Policies for Reconciling Parenthood and Employment'. New York: Russell Sage Foundation.

Gottschalk, P. and S. Danziger (2005). 'Inequality of Wage Rates, Earnings and Family Income in the United States, 1975–2002'. *Review of Income and Wealth*, 51(2): 231–54.

Gottschalk, P. and T. Smeeding (1997). 'Cross-National Comparisons of Earnings and Income Inequality. *Journal of Economic Literature*, 35(2): 633–87.

Green, A., J. Preston, and J. G. Janmaat (2006). *Education, Equality and Social Cohesion: A Comparative Analysis*. Basingstoke: Palgrave Macmillan.

Green, D. and W. Riddell (2003). 'Literacy and Earnings: An Investigation of the Interaction of Cognitive and Unobserved Skills in Earnings Generation'. *Labour Economics*, 100(2): 165–84.

Gregg, P., R. Scutella, and J. Wadsworth (2010). 'Reconciling Workless Measures at the Individual and Household Level. Theory and Evidence from the United States, Britain, Germany, Spain and Australia'. *Journal of Population Economics*, 23(1): 139–67.

Gregg, P. and J. Wadsworth (1996). 'More Work in Fewer Households?'. In: J. Hills (ed.), *New Inequalities*. Cambridge University Press, 181–207.

Gregg, P. and J. Wadsworth (2008). 'Two Sides to Every Story: Measuring Polarization and Inequality in the Distribution of Work'. *Journal of the Royal Statistical Society: Series A (Statistics in Society)*, 171: 857–75.

Grogger, J. (2003) 'The Effects of Time Limits, the EITC, and Other Policy Changes on Welfare Use, Work, and Income among Female-Headed Families'. *Review of Economics and Statistics*, 85(2): 394–408.

Grosfeld, I. and C. Senik (2010). 'The Emerging Aversion to Inequality: Evidence from Subjective Data'. *Economics of Transition*, 18: 1–26.

Guillaud, E. (2013). 'Preferences for Redistribution: An Empirical Analysis over 33 Countries'. *The Journal of Economic Inequality*, 11(1): 57–78.

Guio, A.-M., A. Fusco, and E. Marlier (2009). 'A European Union Approach to Material Deprivation Using EU-SILC and Eurobarometer Data'. IRISS Working Paper, CEPS/INSTEAD, Luxembourg.

Guscina, A. (2006). 'Effects of Globalization on Labor's Share in National Income'. IMF Working Papers, WP/06/294.

Gustavsson, M. and H. Jordahl (2008). 'Inequality and Trust in Sweden: Some Inequalities Are More Harmful than Others'. *Journal of Public Economics*, 92: 348–65.

Haas, C. (2013). 'Income Inequality and Support for Development Aid'. GINI Discussion Paper 73.

Hadler, M. (2005). 'Why Do People Accept Different Income Ratios?'. *Acta Sociologica*, 48(2): 131–54.

Haider, S. and K. McGarry (2006). 'Recent Trends in Resource Sharing among the Poor'. In R. Blank, S. Danziger, and R. Schoeni (eds), *Working and Poor*. New York: Russell Sage Foundation, 205–32.

Haider, S. and G. Solon (2006). 'Life-Cycle Variation in the Association Between Current and Lifetime Earnings'. *American Economic Review*, 96: 1308–20.

Hakhverdian, A. and T. van der Meer (2011). 'Does Economic Inequality Structure Political Competition?'. Paper presented at the Gini Year-One Conference, Milan, 4–5 February 2011.

Hakhverdian, A., E. van Elsas, W. van de Brug, and T. Kuhn (2012). 'Euroscepticism and Education: A Longitudinal Study of Twelve EU Member States, 1973–2010'. Published online, June 2012. (Also GINI Discussion Paper 92.)

Hall, P. and D. Soskice (eds) (2001). *Varieties of Capitalism. The Institutional Foundations of Comparative Advantage.* Oxford: Oxford University Press.

Halpern, D. (2001). 'Moral Values, Social Trust and Inequality'. *British Journal of Criminology,* 41(2): 236–51.

Hanushek, E. and D. Kimko (2000). 'Schooling, Labor-Force Quality, and the Growth of Nations'. *American Economic Review,* 90(5): 1184–1208.

Hanushek, E., S. Link, and L. Wössmann (2013). 'Does School Autonomy Make Sense Everywhere? Panel Estimates from PISA'. *Journal of Development Economics,* 104: 212–32.

Hanushek, E. and M. Raymond (2004). 'The Effect of School Accountability Systems on the Level and Distribution of Student Achievement'. *Journal of the European Economic Association,* 2(2–3): 406–15.

Hanushek, E. and S. Rivkin (2006). 'Teacher Quality'. In E. Hanushek and F. Welch (eds), *Handbook of the Economics of Education, Vol. 1.* Amsterdam: North Holland, 1050–78.

Hanushek, E. and L. Wössmann (2005). 'Does Educational Tracking Affect Performance and Inequality? Differences-in-Differences Evidence Across Countries'. *Economic Journal,* 116: C63–C76.

Hanushek, E. and L. Wössmann (2010). 'The Economics of International Differences in Educational Achievement'. NBER Working Paper 15949, National Bureau of Economic Research, Inc. Available at <http://www.nber.org/papers/w15949.pdf>

Hanushek, E., L. Wössmann, and L. Zhang (2011). 'General Education, Vocational Education, and Labor-Market Outcomes over the Life-Cycle'. NBER Working Paper 17504.

Harding, A. (2002). *Trends in Income and Wealth Inequality in Australia.* Melbourne: Institute of Applied Economic and Social Research.

Harding, A., N. Warren, and R. Lloyd (2006). 'Moving Beyond Traditional Cash Measures of Economic Well-Being: Including Indirect Benefits and Indirect Taxes'. NATSEM Discussion Paper 61.

Harloe, M. (1985). *Private Rented Housing in the United States and Europe.* London: Croom Helm.

Harloe, M. (1995). *The People's Home? Social Rented Housing in Europe and America.* Oxford: Blackwell.

Hauser, R. and H. Stein (2003). 'Inequality of the Distribution of Personal Wealth in Germany, 1973–1998'. Paper presented at the Levy Institute Conference 'International Perspectives on Household Wealth', 17–18 October 2003.

Healy, D., A. Mulcahy, and I. O'Donnell (2013). 'Crime, Punishment and Inequality in Ireland'. GINI Discussion Paper. Available at <http://www.gini-research.org/articles/papers>

Heathcote, J., F. Perri, and G. Violante (2010). 'Unequal We Stand: An Empirical Analysis of Economic Inequality in the United States, 1967–2006'. *Review of Economic Dynamics,* 13: 15–51.

Heckman, J., L. Lochner, and P. Todd (2006). 'Earnings Functions, Rates of Return and Treatment Effects: The Mincer Equation and Beyond'. In E. Hanushek and F. Welch (eds), *Handbook of the Economics of Education, Vol. 4a*. Amsterdam: Elsevier North Holland, 307–458.

Henry, J. (2012). 'The Price of Offshore Revisited'. Tax Justice Network Report. Available at <http://www.taxjustice.net/cms/upload/pdf/Price_of_Offshore_ Revisited_120722.pdf>

Hertz, T. (2007). 'Trends in the Intergenerational Elasticity of Family Income in the United States'. *Industrial Relations*, 46(1): 22–50.

Hirschman, A. (1973). 'Changing Tolerance for Income Inequality in the Course of Economic Development'. *Quarterly Journal of Economics*, 87: 544–66.

Hoare, J. (2009). 'Extent and Trends'. In A. Walker, J. Flatley, C. Kershaw, and D. Moon (eds), *Crime in England and Wales 2008/09, Volume 1: Findings from the British Crime Survey and Police Recorded Crime*. Home Office Statistical Bulletin 11/09. London: Home Office.

Hooghe, L. and G. Marks (2005). 'Calculation, Community, and Cues: Public Opinion on European Integration'. *European Union Politics*, 6(4): 419–43.

Horn D. (2009). 'Age of Selection Counts: A Cross-Country Analysis of Educational Institutions'. *Educational Research and Evaluation*, 15: 343–66.

Horn, D. (2011). 'Income Inequality and Voter Turnout'. GINI Discussion Paper 16.

Horn, D. (2012). 'Educational Selectivity and Opinions on Educational Spending'. GINI Discussion Paper 43.

Hotz, V. and J. Scholz (2003). 'The Earned Income Tax Credit'. In R. Moffit (ed.), *Means-Tested Transfer Programs in the U.S.* Chicago: University of Chicago Press.

Hox, J. (2010). *Multilevel Analysis: Techniques and Applications* (2nd edition). New York and Hove: Routledge.

Hoxby, C. (2009). 'The Changing Selectivity of American Colleges'. *Journal of Economic Perspectives*, 23(4): 95–118.

Hsieh, C. and M. Pugh (1993). 'Poverty, Income Inequality and Violent Crime: A Meta-Analysis of Recent Aggregate Data Studies'. *Criminal Justice Review*, 18(2): 182–202.

Huang, M.-H. (2009). 'Classroom Homogeneity and the Distribution of Student Math Performance: A Country-Level Fixed-Effects Analysis'. *Social Science Research*, 38: 781–91.

Immervoll, H. (2012). 'Minimum-Income Benefits in OECD Countries: Policy Design, Effectiveness and Challenges'. In D. Besharov and K. Couch (eds), *Measuring Poverty, Income Inequality, and Social Exclusion. Lessons from Europe*. Oxford: Oxford University Press, 171–209.

Immervoll, H. and D. Barber (2006). 'Can Parents Afford to Work? Childcare Costs, Tax-Benefit Policies and Work Incentives'. IZA Discussion Paper 1932.

Immervoll, H. and M. Pearson (2009). 'A Good Time for Making Work Pay? Taking Stock of In-Work Benefits and Related Measures Across the OECD'. OECD Social, Employment, and Migration Working Paper 81. Paris: OECD.

Immervoll, H. and L. Richardson (2011). 'Redistribution Policy and Inequality Reduction in OECD Countries: What Has Changed in Two Decades?' IZA Discussion Paper 6030. Bonn: Institute for the Study of Labour.

Inglehart, R. and W. Baker (2000). 'Modernisation, Cultural Change, and the Persistence of Traditional Values'. *American Sociological Review*, 65(1): 19–51.

Inglehart, R. et al. (2001). 'World Values Surveys and European Values Surveys, 1981–1984, 1990–1993, 1995–1997 and 1999–2000'. Ann Arbor, MI: Inter-University Consortium for Political and Social Research.

Iversen, T. and D. Soskice (2001). 'An Asset Theory of Social Policy Preferences'. *American Political Science Review*, 95: 875–93.

Iversen, T. and D. Soskice (2006). 'Electoral Institutions and the Politics of Coalition'. *American Political Science Review*, 100: 165–81.

Iversen, T. and D. Soskice (2009). 'Distribution and Redistribution: The Shadow of the Nineteenth Century'. *World Politics*, 61(3): 438–86.

Iversen, T. and J. Stephens (2008). 'Partisan Politics, the Welfare State, and Three Worlds of Human Capital Formation'. *Comparative Political Studies*, 41: 600–37.

Iversen T. and A. Wren (1998). 'Equality, Employment, and Budgetary Restraint: The Trilemma of the Service Economy'. *World Politics*, 50(4): 507–46.

Jacobs, B. and F. Van der Ploeg (2006). 'Guide to Reform of Higher Education: A European Perspective'. *Economic Policy*, 21(47): 535–92.

Jaeger, M. M. and A. Holm (2011). 'Socioeconomic Change and Social Policy Preferences'. Manuscript.

Janmaat, J. G. (2011). 'Ability Grouping, Segregation and Civic Competences among Adolescents'. *International Sociology*, 26(4): 455–82.

Jäntti, M. (2006). 'Trends in the Distribution of Income and Wealth—Finland 1987–1998'. In E. Wolff, *International Perspectives on Household Wealth*. Cheltenham and Northampton, MA: Edward Elgar, 295–328.

Jäntti, M., B. Bratsberg, K. Røed, O. Raaum, R. Naylor, E., Österbacka, A. Björklund, and T. Eriksson (2006). 'American Exceptionalism in a New Light: A Comparison of Intergenerational Earnings Mobility in the Nordic Countries, the United Kingdom and the United States'. IZA Discussion Papers 1938. Bonn: Institute for the Study of Labour.

Jäntti, M. and E. Sierminska (2007). 'Survey Estimates of Wealth Holdings in OECD Countries: Evidence on the Level and Distribution across Selected Countries'. WIDER Research Paper 2007/17.

Jäntti, M., E. Sierminska, and T. Smeeding (2008). 'The Joint Distribution of Household Income and Wealth: Evidence from the Luxembourg Wealth Study'. OECD Social, Employment, and Migration Working Papers 65.

Jäntti, M., E. Sierminska, and P. Van Kerm (2013). 'The Joint Distribution of Income and Wealth'. In J. Gornick and M. Jäntti (eds), *Income Inequality. Economic Disparities and the Middle Class in Affluent Countries*. Palo Alto: Stanford University Press, 312–34.

Jappelli, T., M. Padula, and G. Pica (2012). 'Transfer Taxes and Inequality'. GINI Discussion Paper 21.

Jappelli, T. and L. Pistaferri (2010). 'Does Consumption Inequality Track Income Inequality in Italy?'. *Review of Economic Dynamics*, 13: 133–53.

Jasso, G. (1999). 'How Much Injustice Is There in the World? Two New Justice Indices'. *American Sociological Review*, 64: 133–68.

Jayadev, A. (2007). 'Capital Account Openness and the Labour Share of Income'. *Cambridge Journal of Economics*, 31(3): 423–44.

Jencks, C. and L. Tach (2006). 'Would Equal Opportunity Mean More Mobility?'. In S. Morgan, D. Grusky, and G. Fields (eds), *Mobility and Inequality: Frontiers of Research from Sociology and Economics*. Stanford: Stanford University Press, 23–58.

Jenkins, S., A. Brandolini, J. Micklewright, and B. Nolan (eds) (2012). *The Great Recession and the Distribution of Household Income*. Oxford: Oxford University Press.

Jesuit, D. and V. Mahler (2010). 'Comparing Government Redistribution Across Countries: The Problem of Second-Order Effects'. *Social Science Quarterly*, 91(5): 1390–1404.

Jones, F. (2008). 'The Effect of Taxes and Benefits on Household Income, 2006–2007'. Office of National Statistics.

Jordahl, H. (2009). 'Economic Inequality'. In G. T. Svendsen and, G. L. H. Svendsen (eds), *Handbook of Social Capital*. Cheltenham and Northampton, MA: Edward Elgar, 323–36.

Judd, K. (1999). 'Optimal Taxation and Spending in General Competitive Growth Models'. *Journal of Public Economics*, 71: 1–26.

Jürges, H., K. Schneider, and F. Büchel (2005). 'The Effect of Central Exit Examinations on Student Achievement: Quasi-Experimental Evidence from TIMSS Germany'. *Journal of the European Economic Association*, 3(5): 1134–55.

Kakwani, N. (1977). 'Measurement of Tax Progressivity: An International Comparison'. *Economic Journal*, 87: 71–80.

Kangas, O. (1995). 'Attitudes on Means-Tested Social Benefits in Finland'. *Acta Sociologica*, 38(4): 299–310.

Kaplan, G., E. Pamuk, J. Lynch, R. Cohen, and J. Balfour (1996). 'Inequality in Income and Mortality in the United States: Analysis of Mortality and Potential Pathways'. *British Medical Journal*, 312: 999–1003.

Karagiannaki, E. (2011). 'The Impact of Inheritance on the Distribution of Wealth: Evidence from the UK'. LSE STICERD Research Paper CASE148.

Karagiannaki, E. (2012). 'The Effects of Parental Wealth on Children's Outcomes in Early Adulthood'. GINI Discussion Paper 58. Available at <http://www.gini-research.org/articles/papers>

Karasek, R. and T. Theorell (1990). *Healthy Work*. New York: Basic Books.

Karoly, L., P. Greenwood, S. Everingham, J. Hoube, M. Kilburn, C. Rydell, M. Sanders, and J. Chiesa (1998). *Investing in Our Children: What We Know and Don't Know about the Costs and Benefits of Early Childhood Interventions*. Santa Monica: RAND Corporation.

Kasl, S. and B. Jones (2000). 'The Impact of Job Loss and Retirement on Health'. In L. Berkman and I. Kawachi (eds), *Social Epidemiology*. Oxford: Oxford University Press, 118–36.

Katz, L. and D. Autor (1999). 'Changes in the Wage Structure and Earnings Inequality'. In O. Ashenfelter and D. Card (eds), *Handbook of Labor Economics, Vol. 3*. Elsevier, 1463–1555.

Kauto, M. (2002). 'Investing in Services in West European Welfare States'. *Journal of European Social Policy*, 12(1): 53–65.

Kawachi, I. (2000). 'Income Inequality and Health'. In L. Berkman and I. Kawachi (eds), *Social Epidemiology*. Oxford: Oxford University Press, 76–94.

Kawachi, I. and B. Kennedy (1999). 'Income Inequality and Health: Pathways and Mechanisms'. *Health Services Research*, 34: 215–27.

Kawachi, I., B. Kennedy, K. Lochner, and D. Prothrow-Stith (1997). 'Social Capital, Income Inequality and Mortality'. *American Journal of Public Health*, 87(9): 1491–8.

Keely, L. and C. M. Tan (2008). 'Understanding Preferences for Income Redistribution'. *Journal of Public Economics*, 92(5–6): 944–61.

Keister, L. and S. Moller (2000). 'Wealth Inequality in the United States'. *Annual Review of Sociology*, 26: 63–81.

Kelley, J. and K. Zagorski (2005). 'Economic Change and the Legitimation of Inequality: The Transition from Socialism to the Free Market in Central-East Europe'. In D. Bills (ed.), *Research in Social Stratification and Mobility, Vol. 22*. Oxford: Elsevier.

Kelly, S. (2001), 'Trends in Australian Wealth: New Estimates for the 1990s'. Paper presented at the 30th Annual Conference of Economists, University of Western Australia, 26 September.

Kemeny, J. (1981). *The Myth of Home Ownership*. London: Routledge and Keegan Paul.

Kemeny, J. (1995). *From Public Housing to the Social Market: Rental Policy Strategies in Comparative Perspective*. London: Routledge.

Kemeny, J. (2006). 'Corporatism and Housing Regimes'. *Housing, Theory and Society*, 32(1): 1–18.

Kemeny, J., J. Kersloot, and P. Thalmann (2005). 'Non-Profit Housing Influencing, Leading, and Dominating the Unitary Rental Market: Three Case Studies'. *Housing Studies*, 20(6): 855–72.

Kennickell, A. (2009). 'Ponds and Streams: Wealth and Income in the U.S., 1989 to 2007'. Finance and Economics Discussion Series 2009–13. Washington, DC: Federal Reserve Board.

Kenworthy, L. (2004). *Egalitarian Capitalism? Jobs, Incomes and Inequality in Affluent Countries*. New York: Russell Sage Foundation.

Kenworthy, L. (2008a). *Jobs with Equality*. Oxford: Oxford University Press.

Kenworthy, L. (2008b). 'Sources of Equality and Inequality: Wages, Jobs, Households, and Redistribution'. LIS Working Paper 471. (Also published as Chapter 3 of L. Kenworthy, *Jobs with Equality*. Oxford: Oxford University Press.)

Kenworthy, L. (2010). 'Labor Market Activation'. In F. Castles, S. Leibfried, J. Lewis, H. Obinger, and C. Pierson (eds), *Oxford Handbook of the Welfare State*. Oxford: Oxford University Press.

Kenworthy, L. (2011a). *Economic Growth, Social Policy and Poverty*. Oxford: Oxford University Press.

Kenworthy, L. (2011b). *Progress for the Poor*. Oxford: Oxford University Press.

Kenworthy, L. and L. McCall (2008). 'Inequality, Public Opinion and Redistribution'. *Socio-Economic Review*, 6(1): 35–68.

Kenworthy, L. and J. Pontusson (2005). 'Rising Inequality and the Politics of Redistribution in Affluent Countries'. *Perspectives on Politics*, 3: 449–71.

Kenworthy, L. and T. Smeeding (2013). 'The USA: High and Rising Inequality'. In B. Nolan, W. Salverda, D. Checchi, I. Marx, A. McKnight, I. Tóth, and H. van de

Werfhorst (eds), *Changing Inequalities and Societal Impacts in Rich Countries: Thirty Countries' Experiences*. Oxford: Oxford University Press.

Kerckhoff, A. (2001). 'Education and Social Stratification Processes in Comparative Perspective'. *Sociology of Education*, 74: 3–18.

Kerr, W. (2011). 'Income Inequality and Social Preferences for Redistribution and Compensation Differentials'. NBER Working Paper 17701.

Kilcommins, S., I. O'Donnell, E. O'Sullivan, and B. Vaughan (2004). *Crime, Punishment and the Search for Order in Ireland*. Dublin: IPA.

Kitschelt, H. (1992). 'The Formation of Party Systems in East Central Europe'. *Politics and Society*, 20: 7–50.

Klevmarken, N. (2004). 'On the Wealth Dynamics of Swedish Families, 1984–98'. *Review of Income and Wealth*, 50(4): 469–91.

Klevmarken, N., J. Lupton, and F. Stafford (2003). 'Wealth Dynamics in the 1980s and 1990s: Sweden and the United States'. *Journal of Human Resources*, 38(2): 322–53.

Knack, S. and P. Keefer (1997). 'Does Social Capital Have an Economic Pay-Off? A Cross-Country Investigation'. *Quarterly Journal of Economics*, 112: 1251–88.

Koçer, R. and H. van de Werfhorst (2012). 'Does Education Affect Opinions on Economic Inequality? A Joint Mean and Dispersion Analysis'. *Acta Sociologica*, 55(3): 251–72.

Kopczuk, W. and E. Saez (2004). 'Top Wealth Shares in the United States 1916–2000: Evidence from Estate Tax Returns'. NBER Working Papers 10399.

Korpi, W. and J. Palme (1998). 'The Paradox of Redistribution and Strategies of Equality: Welfare State Institutions, Inequality, and Poverty in the Western Countries'. *American Sociological Review*, 63(5): 661–87.

Korpi, W. and J. Palme (2003). 'New Politics and Class Politics in the Context of Austerity and Globalization: Welfare State Regress in 18 Countries, 1975–1995'. *American Political Science Review*, 97(3): 425–46.

Kriesi, H., E. Grande, R. Lachat, M. Dolezal, S. Bornschier, and T. Frey (2008). *West European Politics in the Age of Globalisation*. Cambridge: Cambridge University Press.

Krippner, G. (2005). 'The Financialization of the American Economy'. *Socio-Economic Review*, 3(2): 173–208.

Krueger, A. and M. Lindahl (2001). 'Education for Growth: Why and for Whom?'. *Journal of Economic Literature*, 39: 1101–36.

Krueger, A. and M. Lindahl (2009). 'An Evaluation of Selected Reforms to Education and Labor Market Policy in Sweden'. *Studier i Finanspolitik*, 4: 5–40.

Krueger, D., F. Perri, L. Pistaferri, and G. Violante (2010). 'Cross Sectional Facts for Macroeconomists'. *Review of Economic Dynamics*, 13(1): 1–14.

Krugman, P. (1991). 'Increasing Returns and Economic Geography'. *Journal of Political Economy*, 99(3): 483–99.

Krugman, P. (2012a). *End This Depression Now*. W. W. Norton & Co.

Krugman, P. (2012b). 'Robots and Robber Barons'. *The New York Times*, 9 December 2012. Available at <http://www.nytimes.com/2012/12/10/opinion/krugman-robots-and-robber-barons.html?_r=0>

Krusell, P., L. Ohanian, J. Rios-Rull, and G. Violante (2000). 'Capital-Skill Complementarity and Inequality: A Macroeconomic Analysis'. *Econometrica*, 68: 1029–54.

Kuhn, A. (2011). 'In the Eye of the Beholder: Subjective Inequality Measures and the Demand for Redistribution'. *European Journal of Political Economy*, 27(4): 625–41.

Kuhn, T., E. van Elsas, A. Hakhverdian, and W. van der Brug (2013). 'An Ever Wider Gap in an Ever Closer Union. Rising Inequalities and Euroscepticism in 12 West European Democracies, 1976–2008'. GINI Discussion Paper 91.

Kumlin, S. and S. Svallfors (2008). 'Social Stratification and Political Articulation: Why Attitudinal Class Differences Vary across Countries'. Luxembourg Income Study (LIS), Working Paper 484.

Lacey, N. (2008). *The Prisoners' Dilemma: Political Economy and Punishment in Contemporary Democracies*. Cambridge: Cambridge University Press.

Lakin C. (2004). 'The Effects of Taxes and Benefits on Household Income, 2002–2003'. *Economic Trends*, 607.

Lalonde, R. (1995). 'The Promise of Public Sector-Sponsored Training Programs'. *Journal of Economic Perspectives*, 9(2): 149–68.

Lambert, P. (2001). *The Distribution and Redistribution of Income* (3rd edition). Manchester: Manchester University Press.

Lancee, B. and H. van de Werfhorst (2012). 'Income Inequality and Participation: A Comparison of 24 European Countries'. *Social Science Research* (41): 1166–78. (Also appeared as GINI Discussion Paper 6, 2011.)

Landais, C., T. Picketty, and E. Saez (2011). *Pour une revolution fiscal*. Paris: Seuil La République des Idées.

Lansley, S. (2012). *The Cost of Inequality*. London: Gibson Square.

Lappi-Seppala, T. (2001). 'Sentencing and Punishment in Finland: The Decline of a Repressive Ideal'. In M. Tonry and R. Frase (eds), *Punishment and Penal Systems in Western Countries*. New York: Oxford University Press, 92–150.

Larrimore, J. (2013). 'Accounting for United States Household Income Inequality Trends: The Changing Importance of Household Structure and Male and Female Labor Earnings Inequality'. *Review of Income and Wealth*, doi: 10.1111/roiw.12043.

Layte, R. (2012). 'Association between Income Inequality and Mental Health: Testing Status Anxiety, Social Capital and Neo-Materialist Explanations'. *European Sociological Review*, doi.org.10.1093/esr.jce012.

Layte, R. and C. Whelan (2009). 'Explaining Social Class Inequalities in Smoking: The Role of Education, Self-Efficacy, and Deprivation'. *European Sociological Review*, 25(4): 399–410.

Layte, R. and C. Whelan (2013). 'Who Feels Inferior: A Test of the Status Anxiety Hypothesis of Social Inequalities in Health'. GINI Discussion Paper 78. Available at <http://gini-research.org/articles/papers>

Lee, C. and G. Solon (2009). 'Trends in Intergenerational Income Mobility'. *Review of Economics and Statistics*, 91(4): 766–72.

Le Grand, J. (1982). *The Strategy for Equality: Redistribution and the Social Services*. London: Allen & Unwin.

Leigh, A. (2006). 'Does Equality Lead to Fraternity?'. *Economics Letters*, 93(1): 121–5.

Leigh, A. (2009). 'Top Incomes'. In W. Salverda, B. Nolan, and T. Smeeding (eds), *Oxford Handbook of Economic Inequality*. Oxford University Press, 150–74.

Leigh, A. (2010). 'Who Benefits from the Earned Income Tax Credit? Incidence among Recipients, Coworkers and Firms'. *The B.E. Journal of Economic Analysis & Policy*, 10(1): 1–43.

Lejeune, G., V. Maestri, and J. Peschner (2012). 'Taxation in the Context of the Europe 2020 Strategy on Employment and Poverty'. In *Employment and Social Developments in Europe 2012*. Brussels: European Commission.

Lemieux, T. (2006). 'Increased Residual Wage Inequality: Composition Effects, Noisy Data, or Rising Demand for Skill?'. *American Economic Review*, 96: 461–98.

Lemieux, T. (2008). 'The Changing Nature of Wage Inequality'. *Journal of Population Economics*, 21(1): 21–48.

Leschke, J., A. Watt, and M. Finn (2012). 'Job Quality in the Crisis—an Update of the Job Quality Index (JQI)'. Brussels: European Trade Union Institute.

Letki, N. and I. Mierina (2012). 'The Power of Networks. Individual and Contextual Determinants of Mobilising Social Networks for Help'. GINI Discussion Paper 45.

Liebman, J. (2002). 'Redistribution in the Current U.S. Social Security System'. In M. Feldstein and J. Liebman (eds), *The Distributional Aspects of Social Security and Social Security Reform*. Chicago: University of Chicago Press, 11–48.

Lipset, S. (1959). 'Some Social Requisites of Democracy: Economic Development and Political Development'. *American Political Science Review*, 53: 69–105.

Lister, M. (2007). 'Institutions, Inequality and Social Norms: Explaining Variations in Participation'. *The British Journal of Politics & International Relations*, 9(1): 20–35.

Lochner, L. and A. Monge-Naranjo (2011). 'Credit Constraints in Education'. NBER Working Paper 17435.

Lohmann, H. (2008). 'The Working Poor in European Welfare States: Empirical Evidence from a Multilevel Perspective'. In H.-J. Andress and H. Lohmann (eds), *The Working Poor in Europe: Employment, Poverty and Globalisation*. Cheltenham and Northampton, MA: Edward Elgar, 47–74.

Lohmann, H. (2009). 'Welfare States, Labour Market Institutions and the Working Poor: A Comparative Analysis of 20 European Countries'. *European Sociological Review*, 25(4): 489–504.

Lohmann, H. and H.-J. Andress (2008). 'Explaining In-Work Poverty Within and Across Countries'. In H.-J. Andress and H. Lohmann (eds), *The Working Poor in Europe: Employment, Poverty and Globalisation*. Cheltenham and Northampton, MA: Edward Elgar, 293–313.

Lohmann, H. and I. Marx (2008). 'The Different Faces of In-Work Poverty across Welfare State Regimes'. In H.-J. Andress and H. Lohmann (eds), *The Working Poor in Europe: Employment, Poverty and Globalisation*. Cheltenham and Northampton, MA: Edward Elgar, 17–46.

Loughnan, S., P. Kuppens, J. Allok, K. Balazs, S. de Lemus, K. Dumont, R. Grgurevich, I. Hideguti, B. Leidener, L. Matos, J. Park, A. Realo, J. Shi, V. Sojo, Y. Tong, J. Vaes, P. Verduyn, V. Yeung, and N. Haslam (2011). 'Economic Inequality Is Linked to Biased Self-Perception'. *Psychological Science*, 22(10): 1254–8.

Lubbers, M. and E. Jaspers (2011). 'A Longitudinal Study of Euroscepticism in the Netherlands: 2008 versus 1990'. *European Union Politics*, 12(1): 21–40.

Lübker, M. (2004). 'Globalization and Perceptions of Social Inequality'. *International Labour Review*, 143(1–2): 91–128.

Lübker, M. (2007). 'Inequality and the Demand for Redistribution: Are the Assumptions of the New Growth Theory Valid?' *Socio-Economic Review*, 5: 117–48.

Lucifora, C. and W. Salverda (2008). 'Low Pay'. In W. Salverda, B. Nolan, and T. Smeeding (eds), *Oxford Handbook of Economic Inequality*. Oxford: Oxford University Press, 257–83.

Lupu, N. and J. Pontusson (2011). 'The Structure of Inequality and the Politics of Redistribution'. *American Political Science Review*, 105(2): 316–36.

Lynch, J., G. Kaplan, E. Pamuk, R. Cohen, K. Heck, and J. Balfour (1998). 'Income Inequality and Mortality in Metropolitan Areas of the United States'. *American Journal of Public Health*, 88: 1074–80.

Lynch, J., G. Smith, S. Harper, M. Hillemeier, N. Ross, G. Kaplan, and M. Wolfson (2004). 'Is Income Inequality a Determinant of Population Health? (Parts 1 and 2)'. *Milbank Quarterly*, 82: 5–99 and 355–400.

McCall, L. and L. Kenworthy (2009). 'Americans' Social Policy Preferences in the Era of Rising Inequality'. *Perspective on Politics*, 7: 459–84.

McCarty, N. and J. Pontusson (2009). 'The Political Economy of Inequality and Redistribution'. In W. Salverda, B. Nolan, and T. Smeeding (eds), *Oxford Handbook of Economic Inequality*. Oxford: Oxford University Press, 665–92.

McCarty, N., K. Poole, and H. Rosenthal (2003). 'Political Polarization and Income Inequality'. Unpublished manuscript, Department of Politics, Princeton University.

McKnight, A. (2000). Trends in Earnings Inequality and Earnings Mobility, 1977–1997: The Impact of Mobility on Long Term Inequality'. Department of Trade and Industry, Employment Relations Research Report Series 8.

Maestri, V. (2012a). 'Imputed Rent and Income Re-Ranking: Evidence from EU-SILC Data'. GINI Discussion Paper 29.

Maestri, V. (2012b). 'Economic Well-Being and Distributional Effects of Housing-Related Policies in 3 European Countries'. GINI Discussion Paper 31.

Maestri, V. and A. Roventini (2012). 'Business Cycles and Inequality'. GINI Discussion Paper 30.

Mahler, V. (2008). 'Electoral Turnout and Income Redistribution by the State: A Cross-National Analysis of the Developed Democracies'. *European Journal of Political Research*, 47(2): 161–83.

Mahler, V. (2010). 'Government Inequality Reduction in Comparative Perspective: A Cross-National Study of the Developed World'. *Polity*, 42(4): 511–41.

Maître, B., B. Nolan, and C. Whelan (2012). 'Low Pay, In-Work Poverty and Economic Vulnerability: A Comparative Analysis using EU-SILC'. *Manchester School*, 80(1): 99–116.

Marchal, S., I. Marx, and N. Van Mechelen (2011). 'Do Europe's Minimum Income Schemes Provide Adequate Shelter Against the Economic Crisis and How, If At All, Have Governments Responded?'. IZA Discussion Paper 6264. Bonn: Institute for the Study of Labour.

Marchal, S. and N. Van Mechelen (2013). 'Activation Regimes of European Minimum Income Schemes'. GINI Discussion Paper 87. Available at <http://gini-research.org/articles/papers>

Marical, F., M. Mira d'Ercole, M. Vaalavuo, and G. Verbist (2008). 'Publicly-Provided Services and the Distribution of Households' Economics Resources'. *OECD Economic Studies*, 44(1): 9–47.

Marks, G. (2005). 'Cross-National Differences and Accounting for Social Class Inequalities in Education'. *International Sociology*, 20(4): 483–505.

Marlier, E., D. Natali, and R. Van Dam (2010). *Europe 2020: Towards a More Social EU?* Brussels: Peter Lang.

Marmot, M. (2002). 'The Influence of Income on Health: Views of an Epidemiologist: Does Money Really Matter? Or Is It a Marker for Something Else?'. *Health Affairs*, 21(2): 31–46.

Marmot, M. (2005). 'Social Determinants of Heath Inequalities'. *Lancet*, 365: 1099–1104.

Marmot, M., G., Rose, G., Shipley, M., and Hamilton, P. J. (1978). 'Employment Grade and Coronary Heart Disease in British Civil Servants'. *Journal of Epidemiology and Community Health*, 32(4): 244–9.

Marmot, M. and R. Wilkinson (2006). *Social Determinants of Health*. Oxford: Oxford University Press.

Martikainen, P. and T. Valkonen (1996). 'Excess Mortality of Unemployed Men and Women during a Period of Rapidly Increasing Unemployment'. *Lancet*, 348: 909–12.

Martin, J. and H. Immervoll (2007). 'The Minimum Wage: Making It Pay'. *OECD Observer*, 261.

Marx, I., S. Marchal, and B. Nolan (2013). 'Mind the Gap: Net Incomes of Minimum Wage Workers in the EU and the US'. In I. Marx and K. Nelson (eds), *Minimum Income Protection in Flux*. Basingstoke and New York: Palgrave Macmillan. (Also GINI Discussion Paper 56.)

Marx, I. and K. Nelson (2013). 'A New Dawn for Minimum Income Protection?'. In I. Marx and K. Nelson (eds), *Minimum Income Protection in Flux*. Basingstoke and New York: Palgrave Macmillan.

Marx, I. and B. Nolan (2012). 'In-Work Poverty'. GINI Discussion Paper 51. Available at <http://gini-research.org/articles/papers>

Marx, I. and B. Nolan (2013). 'In-Work Poverty'. In B. Cantillon and F. Vandenbroucke (eds), *Reconciling Work and Poverty Reduction. How Successful Are European Welfare States?* Oxford: Oxford University Press.

Marx, I., L. Salanauskaite, and G. Verbist (2013). 'The Paradox of Redistribution Revisited, and That It May Rest in Peace?' GINI Discussion Paper 82. Available at <http://gini-research.org/articles/papers>

Marx, I., P. Vandenbroucke, and G. Verbist (2012). 'Will Rising Employment Levels Bring Lower Poverty?: Regression Based Simulations of the Europe 2020 Target'. *Journal of European Social Policy*, 22(5): 472–86.

Marx, I., J. Vanhille, and G. Verbist (2012). 'Combating In-Work Poverty in Continental Europe: An Investigation Using the Belgian Case'. *Journal of Social Policy*, 41(1): 19–41.

Marx, I. and G. Verbist (2008). 'Combating In-Work Poverty in Europe: The Policy Options Assessed'. In, H.-J. Andress and H. Lohmann (eds), *The Working Poor in Europe: Employment, Poverty and Globalisation*. Cheltenham and Northampton, MA: Edward Elgar, 273–92.

Masso, J., K. Espenberg, A. Masso, I. Mierina, and K. Philips (2013). 'Between Economic Growth and Social Justice: Different Inequality Dynamics in the Baltic States'. In B. Nolan, W. Salverda, D. Checchi, I. Marx, A. McKnight, I. Tóth, and H. van de Werfhorst (eds), *Changing Inequalities and Societal Impacts in Rich Countries: Thirty Countries' Experiences*. Oxford: Oxford University Press.

Matlack, J. and J. Vigdor (2008). 'Do Rising Tides Lift All Prices? Income Inequality and Housing Affordability'. *Journal of Housing Economics*, 17(3): 212–24.

Matsaganis, M. and M. Flevotomou (2007). 'The Impact of Mortgage Interest Tax Relief in the Netherlands, Sweden, Finland, Italy and Greece'. EUROMOD Working Paper EM2/07.

Matsaganis, M. and G. Verbist (2009). 'Distributional Effects of Publicly Funded Childcare'. In T. Ward, O. Lelkes, H. Sutherland, and I. Tóth (eds), *European Inequalities. Social Inclusion and Income Distribution in the European Union*. Budapest: Tarki, 177–85.

Matthews, S. (2011). 'Trends in Top Incomes and their Tax Policy Implications'. OECD Taxation Working Papers, 4. doi: 10.1787/5kg3h0v004jf-en.

Medgyesi, M. (2012). 'Egyenlőtlenségek Iránti Attitűdök Magyarországon (Attitude towards Income Inequality in Hungary)'. In T. Kolosi and I. Tóth (eds), *Társadalmi Riport 2012*. Budapest: Tárki. English version available at <http://www.tarki.hu/en/news/2013/items/20130305_medgyesi.pdf>

Medgyesi, M. (2013). 'Increasing Income Inequality and Attitudes to Inequality: A Cohort Perspective'. GINI Discussion Paper 5.1.6.

Medgyesi, M. and Z. Temesváry (2013). 'Conditional Cash Transfers in OECD Countries and Their Effects on Human Capital Accumulation'. GINI Discussion Paper 84. Available at <http://gini-research.org/articles/papers>

Meeusen, L. and A. Nys (2012). 'Are New Social Risk Expenditures Crowding Out the Old?'. CSB Working Paper 12/08. Herman Deleeck Centre for Social Policy, University of Antwerp.

Meghir, C. and M. Palme (2005). 'Educational Reform, Ability, and Family Background'. *American Economic Review*, 95(1): 414–24.

Meltzer, A. and S. Richard (1981). 'A Rational Theory of the Size of Government'. *The Journal of Political Economy*, 89(5): 914–27.

Meschi, E. and F. Scervini (2011). 'Educational Inequality'. In W. Salverda (ed.), *Inequalities' Impacts. GINI State of the Art Review 1*. Amsterdam: Amsterdam Institute for Advanced Labour Studies.

Meschi, E. and F. Scervini (2012). 'Expansion of Schooling and Educational Inequality in Europe: Educational Kuznets Curve Revisited'. GINI Discussion Paper 61. Amsterdam: Amsterdam Institute for Advanced Labour Studies.

Meschi, E. and F. Scervini (2013). 'A New Dataset on Educational Inequality'. *Empirical Economics* (forthcoming). (Also GINI Discussion Paper 3.)

Meyer, J., F. Ramirez, R. Rubinson, and J. Boli-Bennett (1977). 'The World Educational Revolution, 1950–1970'. *Sociology of Education*, 50: 242–58.

Meyer, J., F. Ramirez, and Y. Soysal (1992). 'World Expansion of Mass Education, 1870–1980'. *Sociology of Education*, 65: 128–49.

Micklewright, J. and S. Schnepf (2007). 'Inequality of Learning in Industrialized Countries'. In S. Jenkins and J. Micklewright (eds), *Inequality and Poverty Re-Examined*. Oxford: Oxford University Press, 129–45.

Milanovic, B. (2000). 'The Median-Voter Hypothesis, Income Inequality and Income Redistribution'. *European Journal of Political Economy*, 16(2–3): 367–410.

Minsky, H. (1975). *John Maynard Keynes*. New York: Columbia University Press.

Moene, K. and M. Wallerstein (2001). 'Inequality, Social Insurance, and Redistribution'. *American Political Science Review*, 95(4): 859–74.

Moene K. and M. Wallerstein (2003). 'Earnings Inequality and Welfare Spending: A Disaggregated Analysis'. *World Politics*, 55(4): 485–516.

Monden, C. (2005). 'Current and Lifetime Exposure to Working Conditions: Do They Explain Educational Differences in Subjective Health?'. *Social Science and Medicine*, 60: 2465–76.

Morel, N., B. Palier, and J. Palme (2012). *Towards a Social Investment Welfare State? Ideas Policies and Challenges*. Bristol: The Policy Press.

Morris, J., D. Cook, and A. Shaper (1994). 'Loss of Employment and Mortality'. *British Medical Journal*, 308: 1135–9.

Morissette, R. and X. Zhang (2006). 'Revisiting Wealth Inequality'. *Perspectives* (December): 5–16.

Mueller, D. and T. Stratmann (2003). 'The Economic Effects of Democratic Participation'. *Journal of Public Economics*, 87: 2129–55.

Munchau, W. (2010). *The Meltdown Years*. New York: McGraw Hill.

Murthi, M. and E. Tiongson (2008). 'Attitudes to Equality: The Socialist Legacy Revisited'. World Bank Policy Research Working Paper 4529.

Murtin, F. and M. Viarengo (2011). 'The Expansion and Convergence of Compulsory Schooling in Western Europe, 1950–2000'. *Economica*, 78(311): 501–22.

Neckerman. K. and F. Torche (2007). 'Inequality: Causes and Consequences'. *Annual Review of Sociology*, 33: 335–57.

Nelson, K. (2004). 'Mechanisms of Poverty Alleviation: Anti-Poverty Effects of Non-Means Tested and Means-Tested Benefits in Five Welfare States'. *Journal of European Social Policy*, 14(1): 371–90.

Nelson, K. (2007). 'Universalism versus Targeting: The Vulnerability of Social Insurance and Means-Tested Minimum Income Protection in 18 Countries, 1990–2002'. *International Social Security Review*, 60: 33–58.

Newton, K. and S. Zmerli (2011). 'Three Forms of Trust and Their Association'. *European Political Science Review*, 3: 169–200.

Nicoletti, C. and J. Ermish (2007). 'Intergenerational Earnings Mobility: Changes across Cohorts in Britain'. *The B.E. Journal of Economic Analysis and Policy*, 7: 1–36.

Noël, A. and J.-P. Thérien (2002). 'Public Opinion and Global Justice'. *Comparative Political Studies*, 35(6): 631–56.

Nolan, B. (forthcoming). 'What Use Is Social Investment?'. *Journal of European Social Policy*.

Nolan, B., B. Maître, S. Voitchovsky, and C. Whelan (2012). 'Inequality and Poverty in Boom and Bust: Ireland as a Case Study'. GINI Discussion Paper 70. Available at <http://gini-research.org/articles/papers>

Nolan, B. and I. Marx (2000). 'Low Pay and Household Poverty'. In M. Gregory, W. Salverda, and S. Bazen (eds), *Labour Market Inequalities: Problems and Policies of Low-Wage Employment in International Perspective*. Oxford: Oxford University Press, 100–99.

Nolan, B. and I. Marx (2009). 'Inequality, Poverty and Social Exclusion'. In W. Salverda, B. Nolan, and T. Smeeding (eds), *Oxford Handbook of Economic Inequality*. Oxford: Oxford University Press, 315–41.

Nolan, B., W. Salverda, D. Checchi, I. Marx, A. McKnight, I. Tóth, and H. van de Werfhorst (eds) (2014). *Changing Inequalities and Societal Impacts in Rich Countries: Thirty Countries' Experiences*. Oxford: Oxford University Press.

Nolan, B. and C. Whelan (2007). 'On the Multidimensionality of Poverty and Social Exclusion'. In J. Micklewright and S. Jenkins (eds), *Poverty and Inequality: New Directions*. Oxford: Oxford University Press.

Nolan, B. and C. Whelan (2010). 'Using Non-Monetary Deprivation Indicators to Analyse Poverty and Social Exclusion in Rich Countries: Lessons from Europe?'. *Journal of Policy Analysis and Management*, 29: 305–23.

Nolan, B. and C. Whelan (2011a). *Poverty and Deprivation in Europe*. Oxford: Oxford University Press.

Nolan, B. and C. Whelan (2011b). 'The EU 2020 Poverty Target'. GINI Discussion Paper 19. Available at <http://www.gini-research.org/articles/papers>

Norris, M. and N. Winston (2012). 'Home-Ownership, Housing Regimes and Income Inequalities in Western Europe'. GINI Discussion Paper 42. Available at <http://www.gini-research.org/articles/papers>

Notten, N., B. Lancee, and H. van de Werfhorst (2012). 'Cognitive Competency and Signalling Status. A Study of Cultural Participation in Comparative Perspective'. Manuscript.

O'Higgins M. and P. Ruggles (1981). 'The Distribution of Public Expenditures and Taxes among Households in the United Kingdom'. *Review of Income and Wealth*, 27(3): 298–326.

OECD (1994). *Jobs Study: Evidence and Explanations*. Paris: OECD.

OECD (1998). *Employment Outlook 1998*. Paris: OECD.

OECD (2004). *Employment Outlook 2004*. Paris: OECD.

OECD (2007a). *Employment Outlook 2007*. Paris: OECD.

OECD (2007b). *No More Failures: Ten Steps to Equity in Education*. Paris: OECD.

OECD (2008). *Growing Unequal: Income Distribution and Poverty in OECD Countries*. Paris: OECD.

OECD (2009). *Employment Outlook 2009*. Paris: OECD.

OECD (2010). *Education at a Glance 2010*. Paris: OECD.

OECD (2011). *Divided We Stand: Why Inequality Keeps Rising*. Paris: OECD.

OECD (2012a). *Employment Outlook 2012*. Paris: OECD.

OECD (2012b). *Going for Growth*. Paris: OECD.

Oliveira Martins, J., R. Boarini, H. Strauss, C. de la Maisonneuve, and C. Saadi (2007). 'The Policy Determinants of Investment in Tertiary Education'. OECD Economics Department Working Papers 576.

Olivera, J. (2012). 'Preferences for Redistribution in Europe'. GINI Discussion Paper 67.

Oreopoulos, P. and K. Salvanes (2009). 'How Large Are Returns to Schooling? Hint: Money Isn't Everything'. NBER Working Paper 15339.

Osberg, L. and T. Smeeding (2006). '"Fair" Inequality? Attitudes toward Pay Differentials: The United States in Comparative Perspective'. *American Sociological Review*, 71: 450–73.

Park, K. (1996). 'Educational Expansion and Educational Inequality on Income Distribution'. *Economics of Education Review*, 15(1): 51–8.

Paskov, M. and C. Dewilde (2012). 'Income Inequality and Solidarity in Europe'. *Research in Social Stratification and Mobility*, 30: 415–32. (Also GINI Discussion Paper 33.)

Paskov, M., K. Gërxhani, and H. van de Werfhorst (2013). 'The Relationship between Income Inequality and Social Status Anxiety'. GINI Discussion Paper 90. Available at <http://gini-research.org/articles/papers>

Patomäki, H. (2001). *Democratising Globalisation: The Leverage of the Tobin Tax*. Zed Books.

Patterson, S. (2010). *The Quants*. New York: Crown Business.

Paulus, A., H. Sutherland, and P. Tsakloglou (2010). 'The Distributional Impact of In-Kind Public Benefits in European Countries'. *Journal of Policy Analysis and Management*, 29(2): 243–66.

Peichl, A., N. Pestel, and H. Schneider (2010). 'Does Size Matter? The Impact of Changes in Household Structure on Income Distribution in Germany'. CESifo Working Paper 3219.

Pekkarinen, T., R. Uusitalo, and S. Pekkala (2006). 'Education Policy and Intergenerational Income Mobility: Evidence from the Finnish Comprehensive School Reform'. IZA Discussion Paper 2204.

Peracchi, F. (2006). 'Educational Wage Premia and the Distribution of Earnings: An International Perspective'. In E. Hanushek and F. Welch (eds), *Handbook of the Economics of Education, Vol. 4a*. Amsterdam: Elsevier North Holland, 189–254.

Pichler, F. and C. Wallace (2007). 'Patterns of Formal and Informal Social Capital in Europe'. *European Sociological Review*, 23(4): 423–35.

Pichler, F. and C. Wallace (2009). 'Social Capital and Social Class in Europe: The Role of Social Networks in Stratification'. *European Sociological Review*, 25: 319–22.

Piketty, T. (2000). 'Theories of Persistent Inequality and Intergenerational Mobility'. In A. Atkinson and F. Bourguignon (eds), *Handbook of Income Distribution, Vol. 1*.

Piketty, T. (2011). 'On the Long-Run Evolution of Inheritance—France 1820–2050'. *Quarterly Journal of Economics*, 61(3): 1071–1131.

Piketty, T. and E. Saez (forthcoming). 'A Theory of Optimal Inheritance Taxation'. *Econometrica*.

Pontusson, J. and D. Rueda (2008). 'Inequality as a Source of Political Polarisation'. In P. Beramendi and C. Anderson (eds), *Democracy, Inequality, and Representation. A Comparative Perspective*. New York: Russell Sage Foundation, 312–53.

Pontusson, J. and D. Rueda (2010). 'The Politics of Inequality: Voter Mobilization and Left Parties in Advanced Industrial States'. *Comparative Political Studies*, 43(6): 675–705.

Pratt, T. and T. Godsey (2003). 'Social Support, Inequality and Homicide: A Cross-National Test of an Integrated Theoretical Model'. *Criminology*, 41(3): 611–43.

Pridemore, W. and C. Trent (2010). 'Do the Invariant Findings of Land, McCall and Cohen Generalize to Cross-National Studies of Social Structure and Homicide?'. *Homicide Studies*, 14(3): 296–335.

Putnam, R. (1993). *Making Democracy Work*. Princeton: Princeton University Press.

Putnam, R. (2000). *Bowling Alone: The Collapse and Revival of American Community*. New York: Simon & Schuster.

Radner, D. (1997). 'Non-Cash Income, Equivalence Scales and the Measurement of Economic Well-Being'. *Review of Income and Wealth*, 43(1): 71–88.

Rainer, H. and T. Siedler (2008). 'Subjective Income and Employment Expectations and Preferences for Redistribution'. *Economics Letters*, 99(3): 449–53. doi: 10.1016/j.econlet.2007.09.011.

Rajam, R. (2010). *Fault Lines*. Princeton University Press.

Ram, R. (1990). 'Educational Expansion and Schooling Inequality: International Evidence and Some Implications'. *Review of Economics and Statistics*, 72(2): 266–74.

Ravallion, M. (2012). 'Fighting Poverty One Experiment at a Time: A Review Essay on Abhijit Banerjee and Esther Duflo, *Poor Economics'. Journal of Economic Literature*.

Ravallion, M. and M. Loskhin (2000). 'Who Wants to Redistribute? The Tunnel Effect in 1990s Russia'. *Journal of Public Economics*, 76: 87–104.

Rawlings, L. and G. Rubio (2005). 'Evaluating the Impact of Conditional Cash Transfer Programs'. *World Bank Research Observer*, 20(1): 29–55. doi:10.1093/wbro/lki001.

Reich, R. (2007). *Supercapitalism*. New York: Vintage Books.

Rivkin, S., E. Hanushek, and J. Kain (2005). 'Teachers, Schools and Academic Achievement'. *Econometrica*, 73(2): 417–58.

Roemer, J. (2000). *Equality of Opportunity*. Harvard University Press.

Roemer, J. (2011). 'The Ideological and Political Roots of American Inequality'. GINI Discussion Paper 8.

Rohrschneider, R. (2002). 'The Democracy Deficit and Mass Support for an EU-Wide Government'. *American Journal of Political Science*, 46(2): 463–75.

Roine, J., D. Waldenström, and J. Chesters (2012). 'The World's Billionaires 1987–2011: Lessons from the Global Distribution of Extreme Wealth'. Mimeo.

Romer, T. (1975). 'Individual Welfare, Majority Voting and the Properties of a Linear Income Tax'. *Journal of Public Economics*, 14: 163–85.

Ronald, R. (2008). *The Ideology of Home Ownership. Homeowner Societies and the Role of Housing*. Houndmills: Palgrave Macmillan.

Rose, D. and D. Pevalin (2003). *A Researcher's Guide to the National Statistics Socio-Economic Classification*. London: SAGE Publications.

Rosen, S. (1981). 'The Economics of Superstars'. *American Economic Review*, 71(5): 845–58.

Rosen, S. (1986). 'The Theory of Equalizing Differences'. In O. Ashenfelter and R. Layard (eds), *Handbook of Labor Economics*, Vol 1. Amsterdam: Elsevier, 641–92.

Rothstein, B. and E. Uslaner (2005). 'All for All: Equality, Corruption, and Social Trust'. *World Politics*, 58(1): 41–72.

Rothstein, J. (2010). 'Is the EITC as Good as an NIT? Conditional Cash Transfers and Tax Incidence'. *American Economic Journal: Economic Policy*, 2(1): 177–208.

Saez, E. and F. Alvaredo (2009). 'Income and Wealth Concentration in Spain from a Historical and Fiscal Perspective'. *Journal of the European Economic Association*, 7(5): 1140–67.

Sanfey, P. and U. Teksoz (2007). 'Does Transition Make You Happy?' *The Economics of Transition*, 15: 707–31.

Saunders, P. (1990). *A Nation of Home Owners*. London: Unwin Hyman.

Saunders, P. (2010). *Beware False Prophets: Equality, the Good Society and the Spirit Level*. London: Policy Exchange. Available at <http://www.policyexchange. org.uk/publications/category/item/beware-false-prophets-equality-the-g ood-society-and-the-spirit-level>

Sawhill, I., S. Winship, and K. Grannis (2012). 'Pathways to the Middle Class: Balancing Personal and Public Responsibilities'. Brookings Center on Families and Children, 20 September. Available at <http://www.brookings.edu/research/papers/2012/09 /20-pathways-middle-class-sawhill-winship>

Scervini, F. and P. Segatti (2012). 'Education, Inequality and Electoral Participation'. *Research in Social Stratification and Mobility*, 30(4): 403–13.

Schäfer, A. (2010). 'Die Folgen Sozialer Ungleichheit für die Demokratie in Westeuropa'. *Zeitschrift für Vergleichende Politikwissenschaft*, 4: 131–56.

Schattschneider, E. (1960). *The Semisovereign People: A Realist's View of Democracy in America*. New York: Holt, Rinehart, and Winston.

Schmitt, C. and P. Starke (2011). 'Explaining Convergence of OECD Welfare States: A Conditional Approach'. *Journal of European Social Policy*, 21: 120–35.

Schofer, E. and J. Meyer (2005). 'The Worldwide Expansion of Higher Education in the Twentieth Century'. *American Sociological Review*, 70: 898–920.

Schütz, G., H. Ursprung, and L. Wössmann (2008). 'Education Policy and Equality of Opportunity'. *Kyklos*, 61(2): 279–308.

Schwarze, J. and M. Harpfer (2007). 'Are People Inequality Averse, and Do They Prefer Redistribution by the State? Evidence from German Longitudinal Data on Life Satisfaction'. *Journal of Socio-Economics*, 36: 233–49.

Sefton, T. (2002). 'Recent Changes in the Distribution of the Social Wage'. CASE paper 62. London: London School of Economics.

Sen, A. (1985). *Commodities and Capabilities*. Oxford: Elsevier Science Publishers.

Senik, C. (2009). 'Income Distribution and Subjective Happiness: A Survey'. OECD Social, Employment, and Migration Working Papers 96.

Servén, L. and H. Nguyen (2013). 'Global Imbalances. Origins and Prospects'. *World Bank Research Observer*. Online first.

Shavit, Y. and H. Blossfeld (eds) (1993). *Persistent Inequalities: A Comparative Study of Educational Attainment in Thirteen Countries*. Boulder: Westview Press.

Shavit, Y. and W. Müller (1998). *From School to Work: A Comparative Study of Educational Qualifications and Occupational Destinations*. Oxford: Clarendon Press.

Shaxson, N., J. Christensen, and N. Mathianson (2012). 'Inequality: You Don't Know the Half of It'. Tax Justice Network Report.

Shorrocks, A., J. Davies, and R. Lluberas (2010). *Global Wealth Databook 2010*. Zürich: Credit Suisse Research Institute.

Shorrocks, A., J. Davies, and R. Lluberas (2011). *Global Wealth Databook 2011*. Zürich: Credit Suisse Research Institute.

Shorrocks, A. and G. Wan (2009). 'Ungrouping Income Distributions: Synthesising Samples for Inequality and Poverty Analysis'. In K. Basu and R. Kanbur (eds), *Arguments for a Better World: Essays in Honor of Amartya Sen. Volume I: Ethics, Welfare and Measurement*. Oxford: Oxford University Press, 414–34.

Siegrist, J., J. Benach, A. McKnight, and P. Goldblatt (2009). 'Employment Arrangements, Work Conditions and Health Inequalities'. Report on new evidence on health inequality reduction, for the strategic review of health inequalities post 2010.

Skidelsky, R. (2009). *Keynes: Return of the Master*. New York: Public Affairs.

Smeeding, T. (1977). 'The Antipoverty Effectiveness of In-Kind Transfers'. *Journal of Human Resources*, 12: 360–78.

Smeeding T. (1982). 'Alternative Methods for Valuing Selected In-Kind Transfer Benefits and Measuring Their Effect on Poverty'. US Bureau of Census Technical Paper 50. Washington DC: US Government Printing Office.

Smeeding, T. (2013). 'On the Relationship between Income Inequality and Intergenerational Mobility'. GINI Discussion Paper 89. Available at <http://www.gini-research.org/articles/papers>

Smeeding T., P. Saunders, J. Coder, S. Jenkins, J. Fritzell, A. Hagenaars, R. Hauser, and M. Wolfson (1993). 'Poverty, Inequality, and Family Living Standards Impact across Seven Nations: The Effect of Noncash Subsidies for Health, Education and Housing'. *Review of Income and Wealth*, 39(3): 229–56.

Smith, S., B. Searle, and N. Cook (2008). 'Rethinking the Risks of Home Ownership'. *Journal of Social Policy*, 38: 83–102.

Snijders, T. and R. Bosker (1999). *Multilevel Analysis: An Introduction to Basic and Advanced Multilevel Modeling*. Thousand Oaks, CA: Sage.

Snowdon, C. (2010). *The Spirit Level Delusion: Fact-Checking the Left's New Theory of Everything*. Democracy Institute/Little Dice.

Social Protection Committee (2011). *SPC Assessment of the Social Dimension of the Europe 2020 Strategy*. Brussels: Social Protection Committee.

Solon, G. (1992). 'Intergenerational Income Mobility in the United States'. *American Economic Review*, 82: 383–408.

Solon, G. (2004). 'A Model of Intergenerational Mobility Variation over Time and Place'. In M. Corak (ed.), *Generational Income Mobility in North America and Europe*. Cambridge, MA: Cambridge University Press.

Solt, F. (2008). 'Economic Inequality and Democratic Political Engagement'. *American Journal of Political Science*, 52(1): 48–60.

Solt, F. (2009). 'Standardizing the World Income Inequality Database'. *Social Science Quarterly*, 90(2): 231–42. SWIID Version 3.0, July 2010.

Solt, F. (2010). 'Does Economic Inequality Depress Electoral Participation? Testing the Schattschneider Hypothesis'. *Political Behavior*, 32(2): 285–301.

Spadaro, A., L. Mangiavacchi, I. Moral-Arce, M. Adiego-Estella, A. Blanco-Moreno (2012). 'Evaluating the Redistributive Impact of Public Health Expenditure Using an Insurance Value Approach'. *European Journal of Health Economics*. Online first.

Steijn, S. and B. Lancee (2011). 'Does Income Inequality Negatively Affect Trust?'. GINI Discussion Paper 20. Available at <http://gini-research.org/articles/papers>

Stein, H. and R. Hauser (2004). 'Inequality of the Distribution of Personal Wealth in Germany 1973–1998'. Levy Economics Institute Working Paper 398.

Stiglitz, J. (2010). *Freefall*. New York: Norton.

Stiglitz, J. (2012). *The Price of Inequality*. New York: Norton.

Subramanian, S. and I. Kawachi (2006). 'Being Well and Doing Well: On the Importance of Income for Health'. *International Journal of Social Welfare*, 15(1): 13–22.

Suhrcke, M. (2001). 'Preferences for Inequality. East vs. West'. UNICEF Innocenti Working Paper 89.

Svallfors, S. (1997). 'Worlds of Welfare and Attitudes to Redistribution: A Comparison of Eight Western Nations'. *European Sociological Review*, 13(3): 283–304.

Sylwester, K. (2002). 'Can Education Expenditures Reduce Income Inequality?'. *Economics of Education Review*, 21: 43–52.

Takayama, N. (1994). 'Household Asset- and Wealthholdings in Japan'. In Y. Noguchi and D. Wise (eds), *Ageing in the United States and Japan: Economic Trends*. Chicago: University of Chicago Press, 85–108.

Tett, G. (2009). *Fool's Gold*. New York: Little Brown.

Thomas, V., Y. Wang, and X. Fan (2001). 'Measuring Education Inequality: Gini Coefficients of Education'. World Bank Policy Research Working Paper 2525.

Thompson, J. and T. Smeeding (2012). 'Country Case Study—USA'. In S. Jenkins, A. Brandolini, J. Micklewright, and B. Nolan (eds), *The Great Recession and the Distribution of Household Income*. Oxford: Oxford University Press, 203–33.

Torsander, J. and R. Erikson (2010). 'Stratification and Mortality—A Comparison of Education, Class, Status and Income'. *European Sociological Review*, 26(4): 465–74.

Tóth, I. (2013). 'Revisiting Grand Narratives of Growing Inequalities: Lessons from 30 Country Studies'. In B. Nolan, W. Salverda, D. Checchi, I. Marx, A. McKnight, I. Tóth, and H. van de Werfhorst (eds), *Changing Inequalities and Societal Impacts in Rich Countries: Thirty Countries' Experiences*. Oxford: Oxford University Press.

Tóth, I. and T. Keller (2011). 'Income Distribution, Inequality Perceptions and Redistributive Claims in European Societies'. GINI Discussion Paper 7.

Tóth, I. G. and T. Keller (2013). 'Income Distribution, Inequality Perceptions, and Redistributive Preferences in European Countries'. In J. C. Gornick and M. Jäntti (eds.), *Income Inequality*. Stanford: Stanford University Press, 173–203.

Tridico, P. (2012). 'Financial Crisis and Global Imbalances: Its Labour Market Origins and the Aftermath'. *Cambridge Journal of Economics*, 36: 17–42.

Tsanov, V., P. Ivanova, S. Panteleeva, and B. Bogdanov (2013). 'Bulgaria: Rising Inequality in the Period of Transition and Restrictive Incomes Policy'. In B. Nolan, W. Salverda, D. Checchi, I. Marx, A. McKnight, I. Tóth, and H. van de Werfhorst (eds), *Changing Inequalities and Societal Impacts in Rich Countries: Thirty Countries' Experiences*. Oxford: Oxford University Press.

Tseloni, A., J. Mailley, G. Farrell, and N. Tilley (2010). 'Exploring the International Decline in Crime Rates'. *European Journal of Criminology*, 7(5): 375–94.

Ultee, W. (1986). 'Hoge Werkloosheid en Sociale Differentiëring'. In *Sociaal en Cultureel Rapport 1986*. Den Haag: Sociaal en Cultureel Planbureau/Staatsuitgeverij, 285–326.

Usher, A. and A. Cervenan (2005). *Global Higher Education Rankings 2005*. Toronto: Educational Policy Institute.

Uslaner, E. (2002). *The Moral Foundations of Trust*. Cambridge: Cambridge University Press.

Uslaner, E. and M. Brown (2005). 'Inequality, Trust, and Civic Engagement'. *American Politics Research*, 33(6): 868–94.

Vaalavuo, M. (2011). 'Towards an Improved Measure of Income Inequality. The Impact of Public Services in Income Distribution. An International Comparison'. PhD Thesis. European University Institute, Florence, Italy.

Vandelannoote D., P. Vanleenhove, A. Decoster, J. Ghysels, and G. Verbist (2013). 'Maternal Employment: The Impact of Triple Rationing in Childcare in Flanders'. Flemosi Discussion Paper 18.

Vandenbroucke, F., B. Cantillon, N. Van Mechelen, T. Goedemé, and A. Van Lancker (2013). 'The EU and Minimum Income Protection: Clarifying the Policy Conundrum'. In I. Marx and K. Nelson (eds), *Minimum Income Protection in Flux*. Basingstoke: Palgrave Macmillan, 318–35.

Vandenbroucke, F., A. Hemerijck, and B. Palier (2011). 'The EU Needs a Social Investment Pact'. OSE Working Paper.

Vandenbroucke, F. and K. Vleminckx (2011). 'Disappointing Poverty Trends: Is the Social Investment State to Blame?'. *Journal of European Social Policy*, 21: 432–49.

Vandevyvere, W. and A. Zenthofer (2012). 'The Housing Market in the Netherlands'. European Commission Economic Paper 457.

Van de Werfhorst, H. (2007a). 'Vocational Education and Active Citizenship Behavior in Comparative Perspective'. AIAS Working Paper 07/62.

Van de Werfhorst, H. (2007b). 'Scarcity and Abundance: Reconciling Trends in the Effects of Education on Social Class and Earnings in Great Britain 1972–2003'. *European Sociological Review*, 23(2): 239–61.

Van de Werfhorst, H. and B. Lancee (2011). 'How Inequality Relates to Outcomes: Two Perspectives'. Note.

Van de Werfhorst, H. and J. Mijs (2010). 'Achievement Inequality and the Institutional Structure of Educational Systems: A Comparative Perspective'. *Annual Review of Sociology*, 36: 407–28.

Van de Werfhorst, H. and W. Salverda (2012). 'Consequences of Economic Inequality: Introduction to a Special Issue'. *Research in Social Stratification and Mobility*, 30: 377–87.

Van Lancker, W. (2013). 'Putting the Child-Centred Investment Strategy to the Test: Evidence for the EU27'. CSB Working Paper 13/01.

Van Lancker, W. and J. Ghysels (2012). 'Who Benefits? The Social Distribution of Subsidized Childcare in Sweden and Flanders'. *Acta Sociologica*, 55: 125–42.

Van Mechelen, N. and J. Bradshaw (2013). 'Child Poverty as a Government Priority: Child Benefit Packages for Working Families, 1992–2009'. In I. Marx and K. Nelson (eds), *Minimum Income Protection in Flux*. Basingstoke: Palgrave Macmillan. (Also GINI Discussion Paper 50.)

Van Mechelen, N. and S. Marshal (2013). 'Struggle for Life: Social Assistance Benefits, 1992–2009'. In I. Marx and K. Nelson (eds), *Minimum Income Protection in Flux*. Basingstoke: Palgrave Macmillan. (Also GINI Discussion Paper 55.)

Van Mechelen, N., S. Marchal, T. Goedemé, I. Marx, and B. Cantillon (2011). *The CSB-Minimum Income Protection Indicators Dataset (CSB-MIPI)*. Antwerp: Herman Deleeck Centre for Social Policy, University of Antwerp.

Van Mechelen, N., I. Marx, S. Marchal, T. Goedemé, and B. Cantillon (2010). 'The Evolution of Social Assistance and Minimum Wages in 25 EU Countries, 2001–2009'. Antwerp: Report to the European Commission.

Van Oorschot, W. (2002). 'Targeting Welfare: On the Functions and Dysfunctions of Means-Testing in Social Policy'. In P. Townsend and D. Gordon (eds), *World Poverty: New Policies to Defeat an Old Enemy*. Bristol: The Policy Press, 171–93.

Van Rie, T. and I. Marx (2012). 'The European Union at Work? The European Employment Strategy from Crisis to Crisis'. *Journal of Common Market Studies*, 50(2): 335–56.

Van Rie, T. and I. Marx (2013). 'Belgium: When Growing Background Inequalities Meet Resilient Institutions'. In B. Nolan, W. Salverda, D. Checchi, I. Marx, A. McKnight, I. Tóth, and H. van de Werfhorst (eds), *Changing Inequalities and Societal Impacts in Rich Countries: Thirty Countries' Experiences*. Oxford: Oxford University Press.

Večerník, J. (2010). 'Earnings Disparities and Income Inequality in CEE countries: An Analysis of Development and Relationships'. LIS Working Paper 540.

Verbist, G., M. Förster, and M. Vaalavuo (2012). 'The Impact of Publicly Provided Services on the Distribution of Resources: A Review of New Results and Methods'. OECD Social, Employment, and Migration Working Paper 130.

Verbist, G. and M. Matsaganis (2013). 'The Redistributive Capacity of Services in the EU'. In B. Cantillon and F. Vandenbroucke (eds), *Reconciling Work and Poverty Reduction. How Successful are European Welfare States?* Oxford: Oxford University Press.

Verme, P. (2011). 'Life Satisfaction and Income Inequality'. *Review of Income and Wealth*, 57: 111–38.

Wade, R. (2008). 'Financial Regime Change?'. *New Left Review*, 53: 5–21.

Wade, R. (2009). 'The Global Slump: Deeper Causes and Harder Lessons'. *Challenge*, 52(5): 5–24.

Waldvogel, J. (2002). 'Child Care, Women's Employment, and Child Outcomes'. *Journal of Population Economics*, 15(3): 527–48.

Weber, M. (1922/1968). *Economy and Society*. Berkeley and Los Angeles: University of California Press.

Weisbrod, B. and W. Hansen (1968). 'An Income Net Worth Approach to Measuring Economic Welfare'. *American Economic Review*, 58(5): 1315–29.

Weishaupt, J. T. (2013). 'Origin and Genesis of Activation Policies in "Old" Europe: Toward a Balanced Approach?'. In I. Marx and K. Nelson (eds), *Minimum Income Protection in Flux*. Basingstoke: Palgrave Macmillan, 190–216.

Whelan, C. and B. Maître (2009a). 'The Europeanization of Reference Groups: A Reconsideration Using EU-SILC'. *European Societies*, 11: 283–309.

Whelan, C. and B. Maître (2009b). 'Europeanization of Inequality and European Reference Groups'. *Journal of European Social Policy*, 19: 117–30.

Whelan, C. and B. Maître (2010). 'Comparing Poverty Indicators in an Enlarged EU'. *European Sociological Review*, 26: 713–30.

Whelan, C. and B. Maître (2012). 'Understanding Material Deprivation in Europe: A Multilevel Analysis'. *Research in Social Stratification and Mobility*, 30: 489–503.

Whelan, C. and B. Maître (2013). 'Material Deprivation, Economic Stress and Reference Groups in Europe: An Analysis of EU-SILC 2009'. *European Sociological Review*, doi: 10.1093/esr/jct006.

Whelan, C., B. Nolan, and B. Maître (2013). 'Analysing Intergenerational Influences on Income Poverty and Economic Vulnerability with EU-SILC'. *European Societies*, 15(1): 82–105.

Whiteford, P. (2007). 'Targeting, Redistribution, and Poverty Reduction in OECD Countries'. Unpublished manuscript.

Whiteford, P. (2013). 'Australia: Inequality and Prosperity and their Impacts in a Radical Welfare State'. In B. Nolan, W. Salverda, D. Checchi, I. Marx, A. McKnight, I. Tóth, and H. van de Werfhorst (eds), *Changing Inequalities and Societal Impacts in Rich Countries: Thirty Countries' Experiences*. Oxford: Oxford University Press.

Wilensky, H. (1975). *The Welfare State and Equality: Structural and Ideological Roots of Public Expenditures*. Berkeley: University of California Press.

Wilensky, H. (2002). *Rich Democracies. Political Economy, Public Policy, and Performance*. London: University of California Press.

Wilkinson, R. (1996). *Unhealthy Societies: The Afflictions of Inequality*. London: Routledge.

Wilkinson, R. and K. Pickett (2006). 'Income Inequality and Population Health: A Review and Explanation of the Evidence'. *Social Science and Medicine*, 62: 1768–84.

Wilkinson R. and K. Pickett (2008). 'Income Inequality and Socioeconomic Gradients in Mortality'. *American Journal of Public Health*, 98: 699–704.

Wilkinson, R. and K. Pickett (2009a). *The Spirit Level: Why More Equal Societies Almost Always Do Better*. London: Allen Lane.

Wilkinson, R. and K. Pickett (2009b). 'Income Inequality and Social Dysfunction'. *The Annual Review of Sociology*, 33: 493–511.

Wilkinson, R. and K. Pickett (2010). 'Reply to the Critics'. Equality Trust. Available at <http://gemensamvalfard.se/wp-content/uploads/2012/10/Responses-to-all-critics-Wilkinson.pdf>

Wolff, E. (2005). 'Is the Equalizing Effect of Retirement Wealth Wearing Off?'. Levy Economics Institute Working Paper 420.

Wolff, E. (2006). 'Changes in Household Wealth in the 1980s and 1990s in the United States'. In E. Wolff (ed.), *International Perspectives on Household Wealth*. Cheltenham and Northampton, MA: Edward Elgar, 107–50.

Wolff, E. (2013). 'The Asset Price Meltdown and the Wealth of the Middle Class'. Report to the US2010 Project. Available at <http://www.russellsage.org/research/reports/asset-price-meltdown>

Wössmann, L. (2005). 'The Effect Heterogeneity of Central Examinations: Evidence from TIMSS, TIMSS-Repeat and PISA'. *Education Economics*, 13(2): 143–69.

Wössmann, L. (2008). 'Efficiency and Equity of European Education and Training Policies'. *International Tax and Public Finance*, 15(2): 199–230.

Wössmann, L., E. Lüdemann, G. Schütz, and M. West (2009). *School Accountability, Autonomy, and Choice around the World*. Cheltenham and Northampton, MA: Edward Elgar.

Wrohlich, K. (2011). 'Labor Supply and Child Care Choices in a Rationed Child Care Market'. Discussion Papers of DIW Berlin 1169. Berlin: German Institute for Economic Research.

WVS (2009). 'World Value Survey 1981–2008 Official Aggregate'. v.20090901. World Values Survey Association. Madrid: ASEP/JDS. <http://www.worldvaluessurvey.org>

Zagorski, K. and K. Piotrowska (2012). 'Income Inequality, Happiness and Etatist Attitudes' Manuscript.

Zak, P. and S. Knack (2001). 'Trust and Growth'. *Economic Journal*, 111(470): 291–321.

Zimring, F. (2007). *The Great American Crime Decline*. New York: Oxford University Press.

Zucman, G. (2013). 'The Missing Wealth of Nations: Are Europe and the U.S. Net Debtors or Net Creditors?' *Quarterly Journal of Economics*, 128(3): 1321–64.

# Index

Note: 'n.' after a page number indicates the number of a note on that page

# Index

# Index